FOR DUMMIES™

COMPUTER
BOOK SERIES
ROM IDG

WordPerfect For Windows F...

Y0-BDD-422

Cheat Sheet

General Information

To start WordPerfect, double-click on the WPWin icon in the Windows Program Manager (the little picture of a fountain-pen nib). It may be in the WPWin program group — double click-on the program group to open it.

To leave WordPerfect, choose File from the menu bar and then choose Exit. (Or press Alt+F and then X.)

When we say "press Alt+*some key*" or "press Ctrl+*some key*," it means to hold down the Alt or Ctrl key (like a Shift key) while you type another key and then release it.

While you are typing	Press this key
For help	Press F1
To erase the character you just typed	Press the Backspace key
To erase the character to the right of your cursor (insertion point)	Press Delete
To start a new paragraph	Press Enter
To start a new page	Press Ctrl+Enter
To indent the first line of a paragraph	Press Tab
To indent all the lines in a paragraph	Move your cursor to the beginning of the paragraph and press F7
To center a title	Move your cursor to the beginning of the title and then press Shift+F7

Mouse Droppings

To do this	Do this on your mouse
Select (highlight) text	Click in the text or left margin, hold down the button, and drag
Select a word	Double-click on the word
Select a sentence	Click once in the left margin
Select a paragraph	Double-click in the left margin
Move text or graphics	Select it and then click on it and drag
See a QuickMenu	Click the right button in the text or left margin
Change font	Double-click on font area of status bar
Go somewhere	Double-click on position area of status bar
Close a file	Double-click on minus sign on menu bar
Exit from WordPerfect	Double-click on minus sign on title bar

. . . For Dummies: #1 Computer Book Series for Beginners

WordPerfect For Windows For Dummies

Cheat Sheet

Getting Around Your Document

The following keys move the cursor around your screen:

Up	Up one line
Down	Down one line
Left	Left one character
Right	Right one character
Ctrl+Left	Left one word
Ctrl+Right	Right one word
Home	Beginning of the line
End	End of the line
PgUp	Top of the screen or up one screenful
PgDn	Bottom of the screen or down one screenful
Ctrl+Home	Beginning of the document
Ctrl+End	End of the document

Helpful Tips

✔ Tell WordPerfect what you have in mind. Never type page numbers yourself, use lots of tabs to create a table, or type multiple columns of text yourself. Instead, use WordPerfect's multitude of features, such as page numbering, tables, or columns.

✔ Save your documents often by pressing Ctrl+S. To save all your open documents, press Ctrl+Shift+S.

Kommon Kwick Key Kombinations

These quick key combinations help you manage your files and text:

Ctrl+C	Copy to Clipboard
Ctrl+X	Cut to Clipboard
Ctrl+V	Paste from Clipboard
Ctrl+S or Shift+F3	Save document
F3	Save with new name
Ctrl+Shift+S	Save all open documents
Ctrl+P or F5	Print document
F4 or Ctrl+O	Open document
Shift+F4 or Ctrl+N	New document
Ctrl+F4	Close document
Alt+F4	Exit from WordPerfect
Ctrl+B	Boldface
Ctrl+I	Italics
Ctrl+U	Underline
Ctrl+F1	Spell-check
Alt+F3	Reveal Codes
Ctrl+F or F9	Font dialog box
Ctrl+G	Go To
Ctrl+K	Change capitalization

Recovering from Errors

If you don't like what's going on	Press Esc a few times
If you have just deleted something and you want it back	Press Ctrl+Shift+Z or Alt+Backspace
If you have just given a command and you want to undo it	Press Ctrl+Z

. . . For Dummies: #1 Computer Book Series for Beginners

™

References for the Rest of Us

COMPUTER BOOK SERIES FROM IDG

Are you intimidated and confused by computers? Do you find that traditional manuals are overloaded with technical details you'll never use? Do your friends and family always call you to fix simple problems on their PCs? Then the . . . *For Dummies*™ computer book series from IDG is for you.

. . . *For Dummies* books are written for those frustrated computer users who know they aren't really dumb but find that PC hardware, software, and indeed the unique vocabulary of computing make them feel helpless. . . . For Dummies books use a lighthearted approach, a down-to-earth style, and even cartoons and humorous icons to diffuse computer novices' fears and build their confidence. Lighthearted but not lightweight, these books are a perfect survival guide to anyone forced to use a computer.

> *"I like my copy so much I told friends; now they bought copies."*
>
> **Irene C., Orwell, Ohio**

> *"Quick, concise, nontechnical, and humorous."*
>
> **Jay A., Elburn, IL**

> *"Thanks, I needed this book. Now I can sleep at night."*
>
> **Robin F., British Columbia, Canada**

Already, hundreds of thousands of satisfied readers agree. They have made . . . *For Dummies* books the #1 introductory-level computer book series and have written asking for more. So if you're looking for the most fun and easy way to learn about computers, look to . . . *For Dummies* books to give you a helping hand.

IDG BOOKS

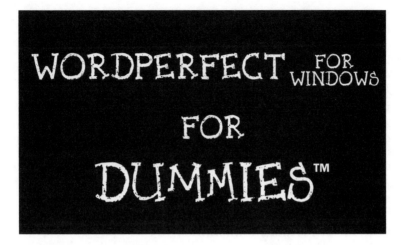

WORDPERFECT FOR WINDOWS FOR DUMMIES™

by **Margaret Levine Young**
and David C. Kay

IDG Books Worldwide, Inc.
An International Data Group Company

San Mateo, California ♦ Indianapolis, Indiana ♦ Boston, Massachusetts

WordPerfect For Windows For Dummies

Published by
IDG Books Worldwide, Inc.
An International Data Group Company
155 Bovet Road, Suite 310
San Mateo, CA 94402

Library of Congress Catalog Card No.: 93-80355

ISBN: 1-56884-032-2

Printed in the United States of America

10 9 8 7 6 5 4 3 2 1

Distributed in the United States by IDG Books Worldwide, Inc.

Distributed in Canada by Macmillan of Canada, a Division of Canada Publishing Corporation; by Computer and Technical Books in Miami, Florida, for South America and the Caribbean; by Longman Singapore in Singapore, Malaysia, Thailand, and Korea; by Toppan Co. Ltd. in Japan; by Asia Computerworld in Hong Kong; by Woodslane Pty. Ltd. in Australia and New Zealand; and by Transword Publishers Ltd. in the U.K. and Europe.

For information on where to purchase IDG Books outside the U.S., contact Christina Turner at 415-312-0633.

For information on translations, contact Marc Jeffrey Mikulich, Foreign Rights Manager, at IDG Books Worldwide; FAX NUMBER 415-358-1260.

For sales inquiries and special prices for bulk quantities, write to the address above or call IDG Books Worldwide at 415-312-0650.

COMPUTER
BOOK SERIES
FROM IDG

About the Authors

Margaret Levine Young

Unlike most of her peers in that mid-30-something bracket, Margaret Levine Young was exposed to computers at an early age. In high school, she got into a computer club known as the Resistors. "We were a group of kids who spent all day Saturday together in a barn fooling around on three computers that ran on vacuum tubes." Their goal, she admits was to do language processing "so that the computers could make smart-aleck remarks back to us."

Although Levine got into computers "for fun" and because "my brother did," she stayed in the field through college, graduating from Yale with a degree in computer science. She was one of the first microcomputer managers in the early 80s and was placed in charge of the MIS division for Columbia Pictures.

Since then, Levine has written four other computer books, but this is her first book written with coauthor, Dave Kay. "We've known each other for a long time, but Dave is funnier than I am," she says. "Each of us did a chapter and then we'd pass them back and forth on the modem. I love writing Dummies books because I can write the way I think. It's fun being able to say: this is important, but you can forget about it."

Oh, by the way, Levine also met her future husband in the Resistors, and her other passion is her child, Meg. She loves gardening, "anything to do with eating," and wandering the Amazon, which she periodically revisits.

David C. Kay

After graduating from Worcester Polytechic Institute, Dave Kay began his career as an engineer for General Electric and Peradyne. That all changed at the age of 34 when Kay decided he was too comfortable and needed to start his own business. He began his new career in marketing communications and now calls himself an independent communications consultant (otherwise known as a writer).

This is Kay's second book, but he's keeping his coauthoring status "in the family." He coathored his first book with Margaret Levine Young's brother, John Levine. "It's a lot faster to coauthor," he says. "Because I have another business, it gives me a lot of flexibility. Writing can be a lonely business and it's hard to write well in a vacuum." Kay says that he's enjoyed writing the *Dummies* book because "it gave me an opportunity to write more freely and to editorialize on life."

As far as WordPerfect goes, Kay says that he's impressed with how far the company has taken the new version of the program. "It really is a major boost in capability," he says.

In his spare time, Kay likes to paint, sketch, and sing. He's also an inventor. One of his goals is to write about nature awareness and the wilderness. "I've been studying this stuff for a couple of years and have just started teaching classes on it," he says, but he admits that "I don't get into a survival situation too often."

About IDG Books Worldwide

Welcome to the world of IDG Books Worldwide.

IDG Books Worldwide, Inc., is a division of International Data Group, the world's largest publisher of computer-related information and the leading global provider of information services on information technology. IDG publishes over 194 computer publications in 62 countries. Forty million people read one or more IDG publications each month.

If you use personal computers, IDG Books is committed to publishing quality books that meet your needs. We rely on our extensive network of publications, including such leading periodicals as *Macworld*, *InfoWorld*, *PC World*, *Computerworld*, *Publish*, *Network World*, and *SunWorld*, to help us make informed and timely decisions in creating useful computer books that meet your needs.

Every IDG book strives to bring extra value and skill-building instruction to the reader. Our books are written by experts, with the backing of IDG periodicals, and with careful thought devoted to issues such as audience, interior design, use of icons, and illustrations. Our editorial staff is a careful mix of high-tech journalists and experienced book people. Our close contact with the makers of computer products helps ensure accuracy and thorough coverage. Our heavy use of personal computers at every step in production means we can deliver books in the most timely manner.

We are delivering books of high quality at competitive prices on topics customers want. At IDG, we believe in quality, and we have been delivering quality for over 25 years. You'll find no better book on a subject than an IDG book.

John Kilcullen
President and C.E.O.
IDG Books Worldwide, Inc.

IDG Books Worldwide, Inc. is a division of International Data Group. The officers are Patrick J. McGovern, Founder and Board Chairman; Walter Boyd, President. International Data Group's publications include: **ARGENTINA's** Computerworld Argentina, InfoWorld Argentina; **ASIA's** Computerworld Hong Kong, PC World Hong Kong, Computerworld Southeast Asia, PC World Singapore, Computerworld Malaysia, PC World Malaysia; **AUSTRALIA's** Computerworld Australia, Australian PC World, Australian Macworld, Network World, Reseller, IDG Sources; **AUSTRIA's** Computerwelt Oesterreich, PC Test; **BRAZIL's** Computerworld, Mundo IBM, Mundo Unix, PC World, Publish; **BULGARIA's** Computerworld Bulgaria, Ediworld, PC & Mac World Bulgaria; **CANADA's** Direct Access, Graduate Computerworld, InfoCanada, Network World Canada; **CHILE's** Computerworld, Informatica; **COLOMBIA's** Computerworld Colombia; **CZECH REPUBLIC's** Computerworld, Elektronika, PC World; **DENMARK's** CAD/CAM WORLD, Communications World, Computerworld Danmark, LOTUS World, Macintosh Produktkatalog, Macworld Danmark, PC World Danmark, PC World Produktguide, Windows World; **EQUADOR's** PC World; **EGYPT's** Computerworld (CW) Middle East, PC World Middle East; **FINLAND's** MikroPC, Tietoviikko, Tietoverkko; **FRANCE's** Distributique, GOLDEN MAC, InfoPC, Languages & Systems, Le Guide du Monde Informatique, Le Monde Informatique, Telecoms & Reseaux; **GERMANY's** Computerwoche, Computerwoche Focus, Computerwoche Extra, Computerwoche Karriere, Information Management, Macwelt, Netzwelt, PC Welt, PC Woche, Publish, Unit; **HUNGARY's** Alaplap, Computerworld SZT, PC World, ; **INDIA's** Computers & Communications; **ISRAEL's** Computerworld Israel, PC World Israel; **ITALY's** Computerworld Italia, Lotus Magazine, Macworld Italia, Networking Italia, PC World Italia; **JAPAN's** Computerworld Japan, Macworld Japan, SunWorld Japan, Windows World; **KENYA's** East African Computer News; **KOREA's** Computerworld Korea, Macworld Korea, PC World Korea; **MEXICO's** Compu Edicion, Compu Manufactura, Computacion/Punto de Venta, Computerworld Mexico, MacWorld, Mundo Unix, PC World, Windows; **THE NETHERLAND'S** Computer! Totaal, LAN Magazine, MacWorld; **NEW ZEALAND's** Computer Listings, Computerworld New Zealand, New Zealand PC World; **NIGERIA's** PC World Africa; **NORWAY's** Computerworld Norge, C/World, Lotusworld Norge, Macworld Norge, Networld, PC World Ekspress, PC World Norge, PC World's Product Guide, Publish World, Student Data, Unix World, Windowsworld, IDG Direct Response; **PANAMA's** PC World; **PERU's** Computerworld Peru, PC World; **PEOPLES REPUBLIC OF CHINA's** China Computerworld, PC World China, Electronics International, China Network World; **IDG HIGH TECH BEIJING's** New Product World; **IDG SHENZHEN's** Computer News Digest; **PHILLIPPINES'** Computerworld, PC World; **POLAND's** Computerworld Poland, PC World/Komputer; **PORTUGAL's** Cerebro/PC World, Correio Informatico/Computerworld, MacIn; **ROMANIA's** PC World; **RUSSIA's** Computerworld-Moscow, Mir-PC, Sety; **SLOVENIA's** Monitor Magazine; **SOUTH AFRICA's** Computing S.A.; **SPAIN's** Amiga World, Computerworld Espana, Communicaciones World, Macworld Espana, NeXTWORLD, PC World Espana, Publish, Sunworld; **SWEDEN's** Attack, ComputerSweden, Corporate Computing, Lokala Natverk/LAN, Lotus World, MAC&PC, Macworld, Mikrodatorn, PC World, Publishing & Design (CAP), Datalngenjoren, Maxi Data, Windows World; **SWITZERLAND's** Computerworld Schweiz, Macworld Schweiz, PC & Workstation; **TAIWAN's** Computerworld Taiwan, Global Computer Express, PC World Taiwan; **THAILAND's** Thai Computerworld; **TURKEY's** Computerworld Monitor, Macworld Turkiye, PC World Turkiye; **UNITED KINGDOM's** Lotus Magazine, Macworld, Sunworld; **UNITED STATES'** AmigaWorld, Cable in the Classroom, CD Review, CIO, Computerworld, Desktop Video World, DOS Resource Guide, Electronic News, Federal Computer Week, Federal Integrator, GamePro, IDG Books, InfoWorld, InfoWorld Direct, Laser Event, Macworld, Multimedia World, Network World, NeXTWORLD, PC Games, PC Letter, PC World Publish, Sumeria, SunWorld, SWATPro, Video Event; **VENEZUELA's** Computerworld Venezuela, MicroComputerworld Venezuela; **VIETNAM's** PC World Vietnam

 The text in this book is printed on recycled paper.

Dedication

We would like to dedicate this book to our parents: to Ginny and Bob Levine, who were always both knowledgeable and funny, and to Hester and Harold Kay, who always taught that "if you can read, you can do anything!" (They didn't say anything about writing.)

Who knows? Maybe someday we'll surprise our parents and get real jobs.

Acknowledgments

We would like to thank Jordan Young, Katy Weeks, Matt Wagner, Bill Gladstone, Steve Emmerich, the folks at IDG Books, and our ever patient friends and families.

We are also indebted to Dan Gookin, the originator of the . . . *For Dummies* series. His irreverent style and deep knowledge of software combine to create winning books. We are honored to follow in the footsteps of this original dummy.

The publisher would like to give special thanks to Patrick J. McGovern, without whom this book would not have been possible.

Credits

Publisher
David Solomon

Managing Editor
Mary Bednarek

Acquisitions Editor
Janna Custer

Production Manager
Beth Jenkins

Senior Editors
Sandra Blackthorn
Diane Graves Steele

Production Coordinator
Cindy Phipps

Acquisitions Assistant
Megg Bonar

Editorial Assistant
Patricia R. Reynolds

Project Editor
Rebecca Whitney

Technical Reviewer
Michael Partington

Production Staff
Tony Augsburger
Valery Bourke
Mary Breidenbach
Sherry Gomoll
Drew R. Moore
Gina Scott

Proofreader
Kathleen Prata

Indexer
Sherry Massey

Book Design
University Graphics

Say What You Think!

Listen up, all you readers of IDG's international bestsellers: the one — the only — absolutely world famous ...*For Dummies* books! It's time for you to take advantage of a new, direct pipeline to the authors and editors of IDG Books Worldwide. In between putting the finishing touches on the next round of ...*For Dummies* books, the authors and editors of IDG Books Worldwide like to sit around and mull over what their readers have to say. And we know that you readers always say what you think. So here's your chance. We'd really like your input for future printings and editions of this book — and ideas for future ...*For Dummies* titles as well. Tell us what you liked (and didn't like) about this book. How about the chapters you found most useful — or most funny? And since we know you're not a bit shy, what about the chapters you think can be improved? Just to show you how much we appreciate your input, we'll add you to our Dummies Database/Fan Club and keep you up to date on the latest ...*For Dummies* books, news, cartoons, calendars, and more! Please send your name, address, and phone number, as well as your comments, questions, and suggestions, to our very own ...*For Dummies* coordinator at the following address:

...*For Dummies* Coordinator
IDG Books Worldwide
3250 North Post Road, Suite 140
Indianapolis, IN 46226

(Yes, Virginia, there really is a . . . *For Dummies* coordinator: We are not making this up.)

Please mention the name of this book in your comments.

Thanks for your input!

Don't forget to fill out the Reader Response Card in the back of this book and send it in!

Contents at a Glance

Cartoons at a Glance

By Rich Tennant

page 50

page 88

page 378

page 103

page xx

page 197

page 313

page 9

page 228

page 363

Table of Contents

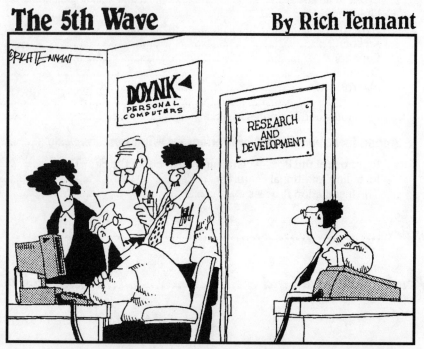

Introduction

1 If you thought that the idea of word processing was to write, not to do amazing things on a computer . . . .

If you ever have secretly wondered who the heck uses all those features advertised on the box your software came in . . . .

If you ever have had to humiliate yourself in front of some computer wizard just to get words on paper . . . .

Congratulations — you're a "dummy!" Dummies are an underground group of people smart enough to say, "Call me what you will — I just want to get some work done, please!" If you're that sort of person, this book is for you.

This book is a reference book, so the idea is to thumb through it whenever you have a question. It's also a book that can be read any old way you want. So sit back, prop your feet up on your wastebasket, and let the vibrant, yellow cover of *WordPerfect For Windows For Dummies* proudly proclaim your dummyhood to all who pass by.

What Goes On in This Book

In this book, we do the following:

- ✔ Start from the beginning, in case you're a beginner. We use genuine English words, not cryptic technobabble.
- ✔ Separate the basics from the fancy stuff so that you can get real work done.
- ✔ Lead you through the maze of buttons, commands, icons, menus, mice, and windows that make up WordPerfect for Windows.
- ✔ Give you just enough of the fancy stuff to look good — or to convince your boss or spouse that WordPerfect was worth the big bucks you paid for it.

True to the *Dummies* philosophy, this book refuses to take software too seriously. Software is, as one enlightened friend says, "not the Salk vaccine." Software does, however, sometimes provide a localized pain not dissimilar to that engendered by certain inoculations.

What we do take seriously is helping you get your work done. So this book addresses the following topics:

- ✔ Using the keyboard and the mouse
- ✔ Learning what's with all those buttons on the screen
- ✔ Cutting and pasting
- ✔ Saving your work
- ✔ Using different typefaces
- ✔ Finding a file when you have forgotten its name
- ✔ Dealing with printing problems
- ✔ Printing envelopes
- ✔ Popular documents and how to make them

When there's something to watch out for, this book tells you about it. When something really isn't important, it tells you that too.

Probably just as important as what's in this book is what isn't in it. It has no long, technical explanations of underlying principles; no huge tables of the 47 things that feature X can do; and no eyecharts of commands and keystrokes organized in some useless manner, such as alphabetically.

How to Use This Book

No one, absolutely no one, wants to sit down and read a book before he begins using his software. So don't. If you know how to do anything at all in WordPerfect, go to it!

Because this book is a reference book, when some feature in WordPerfect has you tying knots in your mouse cord, you can just look up what you want in the table of contents or the index.

If your brow is already furrowing while you're just looking at the pictures of WordPerfect on the box, check out the earlier chapters first. These chapters speak of mice and menus and similar basics, so they're written for beginners. If you're new to Windows or even to computers, you probably should start there. These chapters help you get used to the what, why, and how of giving commands to WordPerfect. After you understand the basics, though, you don't have to read the chapters in any sequence.

This book stands by itself. (No one else will get near it!) It does not, for example, require you to read the WordPerfect for Windows manual. It may occasionally refer you to a companion book in this series — *Windows For Dummies* by Andy Rathbone (IDG Books Worldwide), available wherever books are sold, read, or generally left lying around.

Most of what you find in this book are full, robust sentences, not cryptic abbreviations or shortcut terminology. Unfortunately, one person's full, robust sentence is another's long-winded description. This statement is true particularly when it comes to describing how to do things in the world of Windows.

If we always used such sentences as, "Move the mouse so that the mouse pointer covers the word *Edit* on the menu and then press the left mouse button; a menu appears and contains the word *Cut;* move the mouse so that the mouse pointer covers the word *Cut,*" you would be comatose by Chapter 2 and this book would take on encyclopedic dimensions. So we generally restrict this sort of thing to chapters on the basics. When we get around to less basic stuff, we say such things as "Choose the Edit Cut command" and hope that you forgive us.

When we want you to type something, it appears in **bold type**. On-screen messages look `like this`. When we suggest pressing two keys at the same time, such as the Ctrl key and the C key, we use a plus sign like this: Ctrl+C. In Chapter 2, we tell you all about choosing commands from menus and using all those interesting keys on your keyboard.

Who Am Us, Anyway?

This section explains what we assume about you, our esteemed (and thanks to the joy of software, occasionally steamed) reader:

- ✔ You use a PC that has DOS and Windows installed.

- ✔ You want to write stuff and make it look nice.

- ✔ You don't really give a bat's eyelash about Windows or DOS except what you absolutely need for your daily work.

- ✔ You have a "guru" available — an expert, like one of those infuriatingly clever ten-year-olds born with a computer cable for an umbilical cord whom you can call for the really tough stuff and whom you can probably pay off in cookies.

- ✔ You don't have fabulous fenestration skills (Windows expertise), but you have a mouse and probably would know a window if it were pointed out to you.

- ✔ You don't intend to make WordPerfect for Windows run like something it's not, such as an earlier version of WordPerfect, by changing the way the keyboard works.

- ✔ You or the person who installed WordPerfect installed it in the standard way. WordPerfect is accommodating almost to a fault and lets itself be twisted and restructured like a ball of Silly Putty. If buttons and things on your screen don't look like the buttons in our pictures or if your keyboard doesn't work as this book describes, be suspicious that someone got clever and changed things.

Although we assume that you have a computer guru at your disposal, we also know that gurus can be hard to coax from their rock on top of the mountain. So we teach you a few of the important guru-type tricks where it's practical and suggest appropriate guru bribes where it's not.

What You're Not Supposed to Read

Don't read anything with a picture of that nerdy-looking "Mr. Science" guy next to it (the Technical Stuff icons) unless you really feel a need to know why something is true rather than how to do something useful. (You know the Mr. Science type — full of brain-glazing explanations of how, for example, "User Preferences set under the XYZ dialog box are actually edits to the .INI file" when what you really need to know is "Press this key now.") The only good part about reading this stuff is that it can help you sound sufficiently informed to your computer wizard to induce her to do technical things for you.

How This Book Is Organized

Unlike computer manuals, which often seem to be organized alphabetically by height, this book is organized by what you might be trying to do. It doesn't explain, for example, all the commands on the Edit menu in one chapter. Our reasoning is that the Edit commands don't necessarily have anything to do with editing and that Edit is a foolish category because isn't almost everything you do in a word processor a sort of edit anyway?

No, what this book does is break things down into the following five useful categories.

Part I: Introducing WordPerfect for Windows

Part I discusses the basics: your keyboard, your mouse, and the WordPerfect screen, and how they all work together to let you write stuff and make it come out of your printer. Part I is the place to go for some of the basics of using WordPerfect menus, keystrokes, and buttons. It also has information about some of the fancier basics, such as searching and replacing, working with blocks of text, and spell-checking. Part I can even help you if you have never worked in Windows or maybe even never used a computer.

Part II: Prettying Up Your Text

If you didn't care how your text looked, you wouldn't be using a word processor, would you? What? You say that all you want to do is put something in boldface type or italics? And perhaps also center a heading? And set the margins too? *And* put in page numbers? It's all here.

Part III: Things You Can Do with Documents

You thought that you were just *word* processing, didn't you? Hah! You are really *creating entire documents*. And now you have to live with your creation, Dr. Frankenstein. Maybe you want to print your document, for example. Or kill it off altogether by deleting it. Or move it somewhere where it can do no harm. Maybe you even want to dress it up with borders and columns and send it out into the world as junk mail! Part III talks all about this kind of stuff.

Part IV: Help Me, Rhonda!

WordPerfect for Windows is big-time software that consumes vast portions of your computer's disk and memory space with lots of incredibly complex, sophisticated, and really clever software. Unfortunately, sometimes it's a tad too complex, sophisticated, and clever for its own good — or yours.

Go to Part IV when things don't work quite right — or at least, when they don't work the way you think that they ought to. Part IV is the place to go when things have to be done in Windows, not just in WordPerfect.

Part V: The Part of Tens

In honor of the decimal system, the ten commandments, and the perfectly silly accident of fate that humans have ten fingers, Part V is where we stick other useful stuff. We would have made this part an appendix, but appendixes have no fingers and — look — just check it out. Part V is full of stuff that everyone who uses WordPerfect for Windows should know.

The appendix explains how to install WordPerfect and its companion utilities, fonts, pictures, templates, and the like. If possible, talk someone into doing the installation for you — it's boring!

Icons Used in This Book

The 1990s will be considered The Age of Icons by future historians, who probably will analyze how humanity lost its ability to read actual words. But — because we're not inclined to buck the trend and to get you accustomed to all the icons you have to deal with in WordPerfect — we have put them in this book too.

What are icons? They're pictures that are far more interesting than the actual words they represent. They also take up less space than do the words, which is why they're used on computer screens in such blinding profusion.

This icon alerts you to the sort of stuff that appeals to people who secretly like software. It's not required reading unless you're trying to date a person like that (or are already married to one).

This icon flags useful tips or shortcuts.

This icon suggests that we are presenting something useful to remember so that you don't wear out your book by looking it up all the time.

This icon cheerfully denotes things that can cause trouble. (Why doesn't life come with these icons?)

Where to Go from Here

If WordPerfect is already installed on your computer, you probably have already tried to do something in WordPerfect. You are probably annoyed, perplexed, or intrigued by the promise of something you have seen. So look it up in the table of contents or the index and see what this book has to say about it. Or peruse the table of contents and see what appeals to you. You might learn something, and it beats the heck out of working.

If WordPerfect isn't already installed on your computer and you have to do it yourself, go first to the appendix at the end of this book. (If Windows is not already installed on your computer and you have to do it yourself, get yourself to a bookstore and pick up a copy of *Windows For Dummies*! It was written by Andy Rathbone and was published by IDG Books Worldwide.)

Part I

Introducing WordPerfect for Windows

The 5th Wave

GREAT MOMENTS IN SOFTWARE

In 1987, the index in NoWord documentation reached a new record- NOT ONE CORRECT PAGE NUMBER!!

In this part...

Y ou are ready to employ the very latest in Windows
      word-processing technology. You have the power to
   create tables, graphics, columns, fonts, borders, tables of
contents, illustrations, sidebars, envelopes, junk mail — you
name it! In short, *you are ready to launch yourself into the
blazing, glorious future of word processing* — except for one
teensy, little problem. You were wondering, perhaps, just
wondering: how do you start the silly thing? And, um, how
do you print something? Or delete a sentence? Or save your
work? Good questions, pilgrim — questions that deserve
answers. And here's where to find them: Part I of
WordPerfect For Windows For Dummies. Read on.

Chapter 1
WordPerfect Basics

● ●

In This Chapter

▶ Starting WordPerfect

▶ Minimizing the program

▶ Looking at the WordPerfect window

▶ Typing your text

▶ Naming files

▶ Getting help

▶ Editing another file

▶ Printing your document

▶ Leaving WordPerfect

● ●

*T*his chapter gets you started using WordPerfect by showing you how to perform the Big Five word-processing operations: get the program (WordPerfect) running, type some text, save the text in a file on disk, open the file again later, and print the file. By the end of this chapter, you will know how to coax WordPerfect into doing them! In later chapters, we get into some refinements, such as editing the text after you have typed it or making it look a little spiffier.

But first, the basics.

Starting WordPerfect

To begin using WordPerfect, you have to see it on the screen; follow these steps:

1. **Get psyched.**

   Repeat to yourself three times, "I love using the computer! This is going to be great!" whether you believe it or not.

2. **Turn on the computer, the screen, the printer, and whatever else looks important.**

3. Wait for Windows to start running.

Windows may run automatically, so you might see the Program Manager (or something like it) on the screen. By this, we mean that lots of little doohickeys, or *icons* (pictures), are on the screen, one for each program you might want to run. If Windows doesn't seem to be running already, type **win** and press Enter. That might do the trick.

4. Look for the WPWin 6.0 icon, with the little picture of a fountain-pen nib.

5. Double-click on the icon.

That is, point to it with the *mouse pointer* (the little arrow symbol that moves when you move the mouse) and click on it twice in less than a second. (If the term "click on" is unfamiliar to you, see the following Tip.) If your mouse has more than one button, press the left one. This action tells Windows that you want to run WordPerfect; in Windows, double-clicking means, "Hey, you! You with the teeth! *Do* something!" You may need to try this procedure a few times to get the double-click at just the right speed.

WordPerfect should begin to run. After a minute or so, you see the WordPerfect screen, described later in this chapter. Suffice it to say that it's a little more complicated than a nice, blank piece of paper.

If you're new to the wonderful world of mice, two terms might need some definition. When we tell you to *click on something,* you should point to it with the pointer on the screen that moves when the mouse does and then briskly press and release the button (usually the left one) on the mouse. When we tell you to *double-click on something,* we mean that you should press and release the button twice in close succession. For more information about mice and mouse acrobatics, see Chapter 2.

This list shows some things that might go wrong:

✔ Someone may have told Windows to run WordPerfect for you automatically. If so, it may already be visible on the screen. Go thank this person.

✔ WordPerfect may run automatically but be "minimized" — the next section describes what to do if you see an extra WPWin icon lying around on your screen.

✔ If you cannot find the WordPerfect icon, it may be hiding in a program group. See the section "Group therapy" in Chapter 21 for information about how to get WordPerfect out of its program group.

✔ If your computer, Windows, or (heaven forbid!) WordPerfect "crashed" the last time you were running WordPerfect, you may see a message that a timed backup document exists. If this message appears, refer to Chapter 23.

✔ If you have trouble either getting WordPerfect to run or wrestling with the Program Manager, you may want to refer to Chapter 21. If that doesn't work, check out *Windows For Dummies,* by Andy Rathbone (IDG Books Worldwide), a great book that tries to clarify this stuff.

Where's the program?

Don't read the information in this sidebar (and the rest of the Technical Stuff sidebars in this book) unless you are curious about what's going on, you are ready for some technical jargon to fly by, and you are prepared to forget the whole thing if it turns out to be uninteresting or incomprehensible.

Anyway, if you used WordPerfect for DOS or other DOS programs before converting your computer to Windows, you may be wondering where the WordPerfect program is. Like all Windows programs, WordPerfect for Windows is actually a group of large, strangely named programs.

They are usually stored in two directories named C:\WPWIN60 and C:\WPC20, one for WordPerfect itself and one for its tagalong programs (the spell-checker and thesaurus, for example). When you double-click on the WordPerfect icon, you run a program named WPWIN.EXE.

When WordPerfect was installed, its installation program created in Program Manager a program group named WordPerfect, with icons for WordPerfect and for its friends QuickFinder, Speller, Thesaurus, Kickoff, and its installation program. We talk about some of these other programs later in this book.

Running Windows automagically

If you always use Windows and you want it to run automatically on your computer when you turn it on, go find a computer wizard and say, "Excuse me, could you put Windows in my AUTOEXEC file?" A true wizard knows what this request means. You may want to arrive armed with a few chocolate-chip cookies for motivational purposes.

Likewise, if you use WordPerfect every day, you might want it to run automatically too. Ask the same wizard, "While you're at it, could you put WordPerfect in my Startup program group?" You can do this yourself — see Chapter 21, which discusses Windows, icons, and program groups.

Honey, I Shrunk the Program!

While WordPerfect is running, it can be *iconized,* or *minimized,* which means that it shrinks into a little icon (the same little WPWin icon with the pen nib) near the bottom of the screen. You may want to minimize a program to get it out of the way temporarily while you do something else. It's still running, ready to do your work, but it's just tiny. It's similar to freeze-drying your program: You can add water later to bring it back to life.

If you want to minimize WordPerfect (and who wouldn't?), click on the little downward-pointing triangle in the upper right corner of the WordPerfect window (described below). Poof! It disappears in a puff of bytes, to be replaced by an icon somewhere in the vicinity of the lower left corner of the screen. Now you see *two* WPWin icons on the screen: the usual one in Program Manager that you click to start the program and the one you just created.

To get WordPerfect back, *don't* click on the WPWin icon in the Program Manager; that runs a *second* copy of WordPerfect (one is bad enough)! Instead, double-click on the icon you made. WordPerfect not only jumps back into existence on your screen but also, if you were working on a document, is just the way you left it.

The WordPerfect Window

After WordPerfect is running, you see the WordPerfect window, as shown in Figure 1-1. The wide expanse of white screen corresponds to the white paper sticking out of your old-fashioned typewriter and is probably no more inspirational.

The following list describes lots of stuff around the edges, however, that you may not be familiar with:

- ✔ **The title bar:** The top edge of the window, with the words `WordPerfect - [Document1 - unmodified]`. This line tells you the name of the document you are editing and reminds you that you are, in fact, running WordPerfect. (More on documents anon.) The "unmodified" part tells you that you haven't typed anything yet.

- ✔ **The Minimize button:** You click on this button to turn WordPerfect into an icon.

- ✔ **The menu bar:** The row of words just below the title bar is WordPerfect's main menu bar. Each word is a *command* you can choose. Later in this chapter, we tell you how to use a command to exit from WordPerfect, and we talk more about commands in Chapter 3.

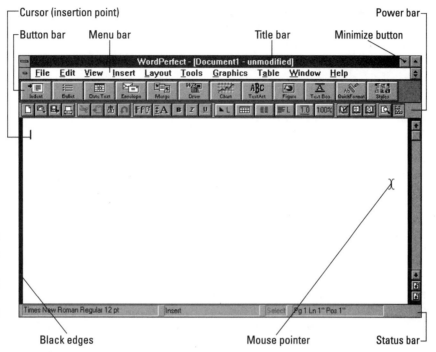

Cursor (insertion point)   Power bar

Button bar   Menu bar   Title bar   Minimize button

Figure 1-1:
The
WordPerfect
screen.

Black edges   Mouse pointer   Status bar

✔ **The button bar:** Below the menu bar is a row of gray boxes called *buttons* that make up the button bar. The buttons usually have little pictures and tiny words on them. (Other Windows programs call this bar the icon bar or tool bar — same thing.) If you don't see the button bar, someone probably has turned it off. Don't worry about it; you don't need any of those buttons yet anyway. (See Chapter 2 to learn how to turn it on.)

✔ **The power bar:** Another row of buttons, and rather small ones. Later in this chapter, you use some of these buttons to save and print a document. If you don't see the power bar on your screen, use the following powerful incantation to make it appear: Press Alt+V (hold down the Alt key while you press the V key) and then press O (the letter, not zero). We explain more about using commands in Chapter 2 and about determining what you want to see on the screen in Chapter 19.

✔ **The status bar:** The bottom line of the WordPerfect window shows information about what is going on right now. Each of the four indented boxes on the status bar contains a different type of information, explained in the following section.

✔ **The scroll bar:** (Why are there so many bars in WordPerfect? Maybe it's because there aren't many bars in Utah, where WordPerfect was written.) Along the right side of the Window is a gray strip that helps you move around the document — you learn to use it in Chapter 2. If your document is too wide to fit across the screen, WordPerfect displays a scroll bar along the bottom of the window too, right above the status bar.

 ✔ **The mouse pointer and the cursor:** The mouse pointer is usually a little arrow, and it shows where your mouse is pointing. It changes to other shapes depending on what you are doing (see Chapter 2). The *cursor* (or *insertion point*) is a blinking vertical line that indicates where you are typing.

 ✔ **Black edges:** On either side of the document you may see black areas that represent your desktop underneath the paper on which you are typing. WordPerfect Corporation seems to have gone overboard in the realism department here, although it might have gone a step farther and displayed simulated wood grain with coffee-mug rings.

Wow! There sure are lots of gizmos to look at while you are trying to type. Chapter 19 contains hints for controlling the things WordPerfect clutters up its window with. Otherwise, you get used to all these little buttons and messages eventually, probably at about the same time a new version of WordPerfect will come along with a whole new concept in screen clutter.

When WordPerfect is busy, the mouse pointer, which is usually a little arrow, turns into an hourglass. The sands of time fall while WordPerfect does something it considers more important than listening to your commands. It means, "Wait around until I'm finished. Consider warming up your coffee in the nuke." Sooner or later (usually within a few seconds), the mouse pointer turns back into its normal pointy self and you can get back to work.

What's on the Status Bar?

The status bar contains squarish boxes (actually, rectangular boxes, for those of you who remember fourth-grade geometry), each containing vital information about your document. You can control the kind of information WordPerfect displays, but you are probably not interested in this rather arcane subject at the moment (see Chapter 20 if we're wrong about your insatiable curiosity). Starting from the left, here's what this gibberish means:

 ✔ The first box tells you the kind of characters you are typing (the font and size). For example, ours says `Times New Roman Regular 12pt`. See Chapter 8 to learn how to change the font and size of your text.

 ✔ The second box says `Insert`, which means that when you type, the letters are inserted wherever the cursor is positioned. The alternative is `Typeover,` which means that the letters you type *replace,* or type over, the characters to the right of the cursor. You switch between Insert and Typeover modes by pressing the Insert (or Ins) key. See Chapter 2 for more details.

✔ The third box indicates whether you have selected some text to move, copy, delete, and so on. See Chapter 6 for information about how to select text and what to do with it.

✔ The fourth box tells you where you are in your document, including the page number (Pg), how far down the page you are (Ln), and where you are across the page (Pos). For the most part, of course, who cares, unless you get paid to write by the inch? Every once in a while, however, you may want to know exactly where on the page your text will appear, and these measurements tell you.

Typing Something

There are certainly many ways in which WordPerfect is completely different from a typewriter, but in one way it is the same: To enter some text, just start typing!

If you make a mistake or change your mind about the wording, move the cursor (the slowly blinking vertical line that shows where you are typing) to the spot you want to change and then change it. You can use either the mouse or the keyboard to get that cursor moving (in fact, Chapter 2 explains endless numbers of ways to move the cursor around).

All the regular keys on the keyboard — the letters, numbers, and punctuation keys — enter characters on the screen when you press them. The rest of the keys — the function keys (F1 and its friends), Enter, Insert, Delete, and all the keys with arrows on them — do not enter characters. Instead, they do something else, and this book tells you exactly what each key does as we get to it.

Normally you are in *Insert mode,* which means that whatever you type is inserted into the text. If your cursor is between two letters and you type a new letter, the new one is inserted between the two letters that were there.

To type a capital letter, first hold down one of the two Shift keys.

To type a bunch of capital letters, press (but do not hold down) the Caps Lock key. Now whatever letters you type are capitalized. To turn off Caps Lock, press the Caps Lock key again. You will notice (with a little experimentation) that Caps Lock doesn't have the slightest effect on numbers or punctuation — only on letters.

Your keyboard may have a light that indicates when Caps Lock is on. The light may even be right on the key. You can tell WordPerfect to display a little Caps Lock indicator on the screen too, as part of the status bar (see Chapter 20).

If you want to type numbers, you can press the number keys just above the QWERTYUIOP row, or you can use the *numeric keypad,* which is the group of number keys on the right side of the keyboard. But watch out: the numeric keypad can also be used for moving the cursor. See Chapter 2 to learn how to determine when these keys do what.

If you want to delete just a letter or two, you can move the cursor just after the letters and press the Backspace key to wipe them out. Or you can move the cursor right *before* them and press the Delete key. Same difference: the letter disappears. See Chapter 4 to learn how to delete larger amounts of text.

Chapters 2 and 3 have lots of information about using the keyboard and the mouse to do things in WordPerfect.

Waxing Eloquent

After you begin typing, you can go ahead and say what you have to say. But what happens when you get to the end of the line? Unlike typewriters, WordPerfect doesn't go "Ding!" to tell you that you are about to type off the edge of the paper and get ink on the platen. Instead, WordPerfect (like all word-processing programs) does something called word wrap: it figures out that you are almost at the right margin and moves down to the next line *all by itself.* What will they think of next?

Because of the miracle of word wrap (not to be confused with plastic wrap), you don't have to keep track of where you are on the line. You can just type away and know that WordPerfect will move you along to the next line as needed.

It is important *not* to press the Enter (or Return) key at the end of each line. WordPerfect, like all word processors, assumes that when you press Enter you are at the end of a paragraph, not just at the end of a line within the paragraph.

If you change the margins later or use a larger font (character style), WordPerfect even moves the words around (and keeps them in order, of course) so that your paragraphs fit within the new margins! This nice side effect of word wrap is called *reformatting.*

Press Enter only when you want to begin a new paragraph. Otherwise, let WordPerfect handle the line endings. Pressing Enter at the end of every line is a sure sign of a word-processing novice, and it makes computer nerds sigh and shake their heads sadly. Worse, it eventually causes you a great deal of work and headaches to keep things looking right.

If you want to split one paragraph into two, you can insert a paragraph mark by pressing Enter. Move your cursor just before the letter where you want the new paragraph to begin and press Enter. Voilà! WordPerfect moves the rest of the line down to a new line and reformats the rest of the paragraph to fit.

What's in a Name?

When you type text in WordPerfect, you are making a document. A *document* is WordPerfect's fancy name for anything typed — it can be a letter, a memo, a laundry list, or the next great American novel. They all are documents to WordPerfect.

To save your document so that you can look at it, edit it, or print it later, you save it in a *file* on the disk. Each document is in one file.

Right now, the prose you have typed is in a document that WordPerfect named Document1. The text is on the screen, but it's not on disk (yet). Documents on-screen are ephemeral and disappear when you exit from WordPerfect or turn off your computer. Here today, gone tomorrow or later this afternoon. It's important to save your documents on disk so that they are saved for good.

Document1 isn't a good name for a document because it doesn't give you a clue about what it's about, but it's the best that WordPerfect could do. You should give the document a more descriptive name, which you can do when you save it.

Saving your document

There are at least three ways to save a document on disk and give it a name. We're sure that your insatiable curiosity will drive you to find out all three, but here's our favorite:

1. **Click the Save button on the power bar.**

   The power bar is the row of little buttons just below the title bar. (Refer to the section "The WordPerfect Window" and Figure 1-1 again if you can't find the power bar.) The Save button is the one with a tiny picture of a floppy disk. (You are probably really saving your document on a hard disk, but hard disks aren't as cute as floppy disks.) This button is probably the third from the left.

When your mouse pointer points to a button on the power bar, a description of the button appears on the title bar just above it. Thank goodness it does, because many of those little, teeny buttons look alike to us (and don't tell us that it's time to break down and get reading glasses)! When your mouse pointer is on the Save button, for example, you see this helpful reminder: `Save - Save the current document - Ctrl+S`. This message tells you that the name of the button is "Save," what the button does (as though you couldn't guess from the name), and the key or keys you can press to do the same thing (Chapter 3 has more about this subject).

As soon as you click on the Save button with the mouse, a window appears on your screen, right on top of the WordPerfect window. The window is a *dialog box,* a window that WordPerfect displays when it wants to ask you some questions. (Chapter 3 tells you more than you ever want to know about dialog boxes.)

This particular dialog box is titled (not surprisingly) Save As (see Figure 1-2). It lets you tell WordPerfect where to store the document on the disk and what to call it. We talk more about where you can store documents in Chapter 15. For now, WordPerfect suggests that you store your document in the "default document directory," the directory to put files in unless someone says otherwise.

2. **In the little box entitled Filename, enter a name for the document.**

   Filenames are extremely limited in length; the complete rules are listed in the following section. Type a name with as many as eight letters followed by a period and then the letters **wpd** (which means that this file contains a WordPerfect document rather than, for example, a program that plays Pigs in Space). If this is just a test document, how about naming it TEST.WPD?

3. **Press Enter or click the OK button with the mouse.**

   WordPerfect saves the document in the file you named. You can tell that this procedure worked because the title bar displays the following line:

   ```
   WordPerfect - [c:\wpwin\test.wpd - unmodified].
   ```

When you save a document in a file, you can choose which directory the file should be in. See Chapter 15 to learn how to tell WordPerfect where to store it.

Save early and often. Save whenever you think of it and whenever you wonder when was the last time you saved. A save in time saves the loss of your document. You get the idea. If you kick the computer's cord out of the plug, or if your two-year-old presses the Reset button, or if you have a brain spasm that causes you to delete several paragraphs of perfectly good text, you will be happy if you know that the document is safe and sound on your disk. See Chapter 20 to learn how to get your document back if these or other catastrophes occur.

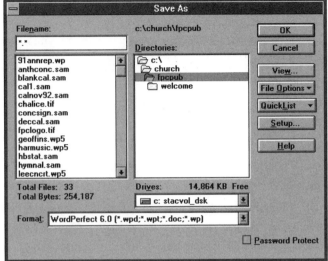

Figure 1-2:
Telling
WordPerfect
the name of
your
document.

You can tell WordPerfect to save your document automatically every five or ten minutes or at any interval you choose (see Chapter 20).

What if a file named TEST.WPD *already* exists? WordPerfect, which always watches out for your interests, lets you know when this happens. A dialog box is displayed which tells you that the file already exists and asks whether you really want to replace it (irrevocably deleting the existing file in the process). WordPerfect provides these three buttons to click to indicate what you want to do:

✔ **Yes:** To replace the existing file

✔ **No:** To enter a different name for your new file

✔ **Cancel:** To forget about using that name to save the document

If you are looking at the Save As dialog box and change your mind about saving the document, press the Escape (or Esc) key. This action makes the dialog box disappear.

Chapter 15 describes everything you want to know about files, including how to delete, move, copy, and rename them.

Filename rules

When you enter a name for a new WordPerfect document, you must follow the rules for naming files. WordPerfect didn't make up these rules; DOS, a program you may not even know you were running, is in charge of files on the disk and makes the rules about their names.

So here are the rules, boring and annoying as they may be:

- Filenames have three parts: the name, a period, and the extension, like this: SURFS.UP.

- The *name* can be as long as eight characters, and the *extension* can be as long as three.

- You can omit the extension if you want, but you cannot omit the name.

- You can use letters, numbers, and some punctuation in the name and extension, but you cannot use any spaces, and some punctuation is verboten. Rather than memorize which symbols are OK and which are no good, it is simpler to stick with letters and numbers in your filenames.

- You can use either capital or small letters: neither DOS nor WordPerfect cares. In fact, they don't even distinguish between them. READ.ME, read.me, and rEaD.mE all are the same filename as far as DOS is concerned.

These three filenames, for example, are OK:

LETTER.WPD

SMITH.94B

read.ME

But these filenames aren't:

MEMO 2.WPD (you cannot use a space)

$/&@\(-! (you cannot use all these funny characters)

LETTERTOMY.MOM (too long)

Save it again, Sam

After you have saved your document and given it a name, you don't have to tell WordPerfect the name again. If you enter some more text and want to save it, you can just click the Save button again. WordPerfect updates the file on the disk with the new version of your document, which replaces the old one.

TECHNICAL STUFF

Of BATS and DOCS

The extension part of the filename usually indicates which kind of information the file contains. If a file contains a program, for example, its extension is EXE (for "executable") or COM (for "command"). Most people use the extension WPD for WordPerfect documents. You may run into these file extensions also:

BAT   A DOS batch file (another type of program)

COM   A command (that is, also an executable program)

DOC   A Microsoft Word document (or a document created by another word-processing program)

EXE   An executable program

INI   An initialization file for a Windows program (for example, WordPerfect's file is called WPWP.INI)

SAM   An AmiPro document (don't ask who Sam is — he must be a friend of Doc's)

SYS   A system file — *stay away from these!*

TXT   Text created by a text editor

WKS   A Lotus 1-2-3 worksheet
(or WK1
or WK3)

XLS   A Microsoft Excel worksheet

Even though these files are not created by WordPerfect or saved in WordPerfect's own format, WordPerfect can read some of them. See Chapter 14 for information about how to turn files from other word-processing programs into WordPerfect documents.

Getting Some Help

Clearly, you have a great deal to remember here. And you probably have better things to do than to memorize all this computer trivia. Luckily, WordPerfect can provide help when you need it — at least, it can provide a description in computerese that may be of limited help.

Like almost all Windows programs, WordPerfect has a *Help key:* the F1 function key. Pressing F1 runs the WordPerfect Help system, which contains most of the text in the WordPerfect reference manual, and it's usually easier to find information in the on-line Help than to riffle through printed pages. Chapter 2 describes on-line Help.

Editing Another File

So far, you have made a document from scratch. But frequently you will want to edit a document that is already stored on disk. It might be a document you made earlier and saved, a document created by someone else, or a love note left on your disk by a secret admirer (secret admirers are getting more high-tech these days). Whatever the document is, you can look at it in WordPerfect; this process is called *loading*, or *opening*, the document.

These steps show the easiest way to open a document that has been stored on the disk:

1. Click the Open button on the power bar.

This button is the one with a tiny folder on it. It is usually the second button from the left.

WordPerfect displays the Open File dialog box on the screen (see Figure 1-3). Displaying this screen is the program's subtle way of saying that it wants to know which file you want to open.

2. Choose a file from the list that is displayed.

To choose one, click on a name in the Filename list. WordPerfect highlights the name by displaying it in another color, to show that it knows the one you want.

3. Choose the OK button.

That is, click on it with your mouse button. WordPerfect opens the file, reads the document, and displays it on-screen.

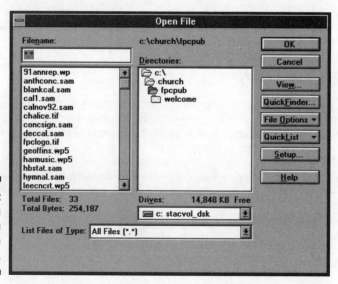

Figure 1-3:
Opening a file you made earlier.

Now you can make changes to it, save it again, print it, or whatever!

If the document is long, it doesn't all fit on-screen. Don't panic — it is still there. See Chapter 2 for information about how to move around in the document, including the parts that aren't currently visible.

You may want to open a file in a different directory from the one displayed in the Open File dialog box. See Chapter 15 to learn how to use directories.

If the document was created using a word processor other than WordPerfect, see Chapter 14 to learn how to open it.

After you have opened a document in WordPerfect, you can see it on-screen, make changes to it, save the new version, and print it. We talk about how to print a document in the following section.

A brief diversion for conversion

When you open a document, you may see a little box with the message that a conversion is in progress. This message usually means that the document you are opening was created in a different version of WordPerfect, such as WordPerfect for Windows 5.2 or WordPerfect for DOS. (Don'tcha love all these long names?) Each version of WordPerfect stores documents in its own way.

Not to worry — our WordPerfect (WordPerfect for Windows 6.0) reads these files just fine.

When you save the file, WordPerfect asks which flavor of WordPerfect document you want to save it as. If you plan to give the document back to someone who uses one of these older, less technologically advanced WordPerfects, save the file in the same format it was in when you opened it (WordPerfect tells you what that version was). If you plan to keep the document, save it in WordPerfect's 6.0 format so that you don't have to see that `Conversion in progress` message every time you open the document.

Printing Your Document

After you have typed a document or edited it until it looks the way you want it, you probably will want to print it. After all, the goal of most word processing is to produce on paper a letter, memo, report, or what-have-you. If you work in the Paperless Office of the Future (reputed to be just down the hall from the Paperless Bathroom of the Future), you may be able to send your memo or letter electronically with the touch of a button; for the rest of us, though, paper works well — typing paper, that is.

These steps show a fast way to print your document:

1. **Save it first, just it case something goes wrong while you are trying to print it.**

   That is, click the Save button on the power bar. (See the section "Saving your document," earlier in this chapter, if you don't know what we're talking about.)

2. **Turn on your printer.**

   Good luck finding the switch!

3. **Make sure that some paper is in the printer.**

4. **Click the Print button on the power bar.**

   It's the one with a little printer with a piece of paper sticking out the top, usually the fourth button from the left.

   WordPerfect displays the Print dialog box, shown in Figure 1-4. As you can see, WordPerfect provides billions of options when it comes to printing. Stay calm.

5. **All you have to do is click the Print button.**

   WordPerfect then prints the document in all its glory.

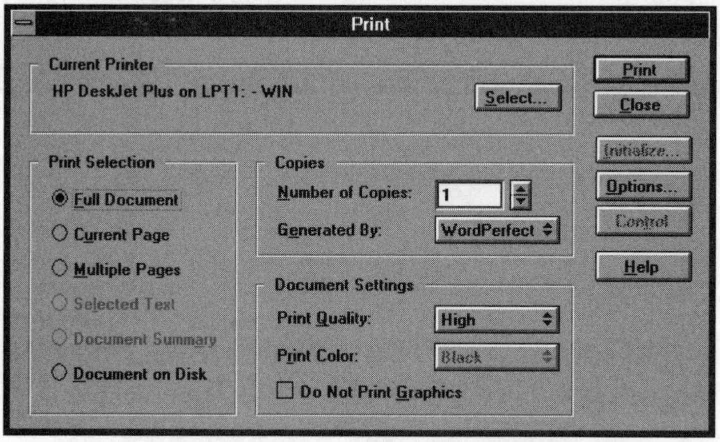

Figure 1-4:
Printing
your
document.

Chapter 13 contains lots more information about printing, including the care and feeding of your printer.

If you don't like the way your polished prose looks on the page, look in Chapter 8 to learn how to choose which typeface (or typefaces) to use for the text. Chapter 9 tells you how to center and justify text, and Chapter 10 shows you how to number pages and print page headers and footers.

Leaving WordPerfect

We know that you're having fun, but sooner or later you may need to stop running WordPerfect. Because you use Windows, you can run other programs at the same time you run WordPerfect and not have to leave WordPerfect every time you want to change the budget figures in your Excel spreadsheet, receive a fax with your fax board, or play a little game of Minesweeper. In fact, you may want to leave WordPerfect running all day so that you can switch back to it in a jiffy, but you must exit from WordPerfect (and from Windows) before you turn off your computer.

To leave WordPerfect, you use the File Exit command. (Why choose File when you want to exit? This strange trait is shared by almost all Windows programs.) We talk more about how to use commands in Chapter 3, but these steps show what you have to do:

1. **Click on the word *File* on the menu bar.**

   The File menu appears, by dropping down from the word File. (Wonder why they call it a pull-down menu when you don't have to pull on any-thing?)

2. **Click on the word *Exit* near the bottom of the File menu.**

   If you have created or changed a document but you haven't saved the document in a file, WordPerfect asks whether you want to save it now. You see a little dialog box like the one in Figure 1-5. Click on Yes to save the document, No to skip saving it, or Cancel to return to WordPerfect. Choose No only if you are sure that the document doesn't contain anything you ever want to see again.

   WordPerfect packs up and goes home, and you are probably thinking about doing the same.

 Never turn off the computer without exiting from WordPerfect and from Windows. Otherwise, you may catch these programs unawares (with their digital pants down, as it were), and they may not have saved everything on disk. When you start up the computer again, you may get some complaints (see Chapter 20 for information about what to do if you see them).

Figure 1-5:
Don't forget
to save your
work!

If you want to exit from Windows and turn off the computer, you can also switch to the Windows Program Manager (the window with the little icons for all your programs) and choose the File Exit command. Before the Program Manager exits, it politely asks all running programs to vamoose. WordPerfect takes the hint and exits, just as though you had given it the File Exit command yourself. If unsaved documents are open, you get the usual messages.

Chapter 2
Using the Mouse and Keyboard

• •

In This Chapter

▶ To mouse or not to mouse

▶ Choosing commands from menus

▶ Using dialog boxes

▶ Using QuickMenus for even more ways to choose commands

▶ Using the button bar, the power bar, and the ruler bar

▶ Identifying keys on the keyboard

▶ Pressing and releasing keys

▶ Knowing when to press Enter

▶ Using Tab and the spacebar

▶ Using the Undo button

▶ Using Help

• •

*U*sing WordPerfect for Windows is a little like dining at a fine restaurant in another country, or maybe on another planet. And as anyone who has ever ordered in a foreign restaurant knows, you can tell the waiter what you want in three ways:

 ✔ The difficult, old-fashioned (but highly impressive) way — speak the language.

 ✔ Order by the numbers (works mainly in Chinese-American restaurants).

 ✔ Point at the menu and grunt.

Until recently, telling a computer what you wanted was also a matter of speaking the language: typing a command or "ordering by the numbers" by pressing a special key, such as F3. Now, however, with the advent of Windows, PC software is smart enough that you can just "point and grunt."

It's just in time too because the "menu" of things that today's software can do is huge — so huge that to use the old-fashioned keyboard method, you have to hold down as many as three keys at a time and develop a keyboard method that would prostrate Paderewski.

That's why you have a rodent-like object, called a mouse, next to your keyboard. (If you don't, don't panic; see the section "Mouse Anatomy and Behavior Basics," later in this chapter). Move your mouse around and you can point with the correspondingly moving arrow on the screen. Click a button on the mouse and you can "grunt" electronically. (Ain't science grand?) But to avoid disgruntling the folks who have already put a great deal of effort into refining their keyboard style (such as old WordPerfect for DOS users), WordPerfect for Windows also lets you order it around the old-fashioned way — by using the keyboard.

The result of all this highly obliging, verging on sycophantic user-friendliness is that you now have three more or less alternative ways to order WordPerfect for Windows around:

- ✔ The "regular" keyboard, with letters and numbers and stuff

- ✔ The "function" keys, labeled F1 through F12 (some keyboards don't have F11 and F12)

- ✔ The mouse, which you can use by itself in about three different ways to command WordPerfect — try not to think about this for now

Another result of all this is that your keyboard and screen begin to resemble the cockpit of a jet fighter. As always when you face jet fighters, the important thing is not to let it intimidate you. It's a friendly jet fighter (oxymoronically speaking), and you can't crash and burn. Nor can you hurt any hardware, software, or data on your PC. About the worst you can do is lose whatever work you have done since the last time you used WordPerfect, and even that's pretty hard to do.

If you're already fully fenestrated (Windows-familiar) and keyboard-qualified, you can just skim over the next two sections of this chapter to pick up the WordPerfect peculiarities.

To Mouse or Not to Mouse

Because of the popularity of the "point and grunt" method (hereafter called "point and click," to be nice), mice are taking over the world. Accept this fact and learn to love your mouse. WordPerfect for Windows is designed for it, even though you can also do almost everything by using the keyboard.

Most people eventually find a particular combination of mousifying and keyboardification that suits them. Because, under Windows, mice are the cat's pajamas, this book generally emphasizes the mouse method and also gives the alternatives.

Let's begin with your mouse.

Mouse Anatomy and Behavior Basics

On PCs with mice, the mouse generally wears two buttons; really snazzy dressers may sometimes sport three. Typically, however, only one button really matters: usually the left one. If you have a third, middle button, consider it a vestigial remnant of the days when giant, Jurassic-era mice roamed the countryside and intimidated each other with their vast array of buttons. If you're left-handed and really sensitive, you can ask your system guru to change it to the right button. (Be sure to motivate your computer expert as needed: This task is a one-cookie task, at current guru rates.)

What about the right button? Try not to think about it — or use it — for now. Well, OK, if you must know: The hard-working folks at WordPerfect felt that it should carry its weight for once and put it to use. It displays something called a *QuickMenu,* whose contents change depending on where the mouse pointer is pointing! This shortcut method, designed by WordPerfect's Department of Redundancy Department, does the same things you can do in about two other ways with your mouse. We talk about this subject later.

Nonmouse mice

If you cannot find your mouse, you're probably beginning to get nervous at this point. This feeling may or may not be appropriate. You might have, especially if you're using a laptop PC, an alternative "pointing device" called a *trackball* that attaches to the keyboard. This device is essentially a mouse turned upside down which you trick into thinking that it's moving by stroking the ball normally found on a mouse's underside. (Stop giggling. It's true.) It has a button or buttons somewhere, which are analogous to the mouse buttons we have been discussing. If you're still worried, check with the guru who bought or set up your computer.

Configuring your mouse

Other useful things your guru can do (if you have a "can do" guru) are shown in this list:

- Adjust how fast the *pointer* moves on your screen when you move the mouse. (Slower makes it easier to point accurately at tiny buttons but takes more room on your desk). The *pointer* is whatever moves when the mouse moves. It can be one of several arrow shapes, a line, a hand, or an hourglass, depending on where it is and what's going on.

- Adjust how fast you have to click the button to make a *double-click.* (We talk more about double-clicking in a minute.)

For more information about how you can save cookies by doing these things yourself, see *Windows For Dummies,* by Andy Rathbone (IDG Books Worldwide).

Mice have their differences, but only The Truly Technical care about them. You can see the most important difference by turning your mouse over to examine its intimate anatomy. If you don't find a hole with a loose ball in it, you have an "optical" mouse that sees with its feet and needs a special pad on which to run.

Mouse skills

The first mouse skill you need in order to control WordPerfect is the ability to point and click, so let's define exactly what this and related terms mean:

- ✔ **To point:** Move the pointer so that the arrow tip is on top of a word or button. Sometimes it only has to be nearby.

- ✔ **To click on something:** Point to it and then press and release the button (usually the left one) on the mouse.

- ✔ **To double-click:** Press and release the button twice in rapid succession. You may need some practice to learn just how fast you need to click.

- ✔ **To click and drag:** Press the mouse button down and hold it down. Then move the mouse while holding down the button; this action "drags" something around on the screen, such as a highlight bar on a menu. Finally, release the button.

Now let's look at how to use the mouse to order WordPerfect around.

Choosing Commands from Menus

Taking their cue from fine dining establishments everywhere, Windows programs such as WordPerfect have more than one menu of commands. They have the computer equivalent of an appetizer menu, an apertif menu, a bread menu, a soup menu, a wine menu, an entree menu, a choice-of-vegetable menu, a *sorbet* menu, and a dessert menu.

To help you sort out these menus, the next-to-topmost line (the one with all the words) in your WordPerfect window lists all the available menus. It's called the *menu bar* (see Figure 2-1).

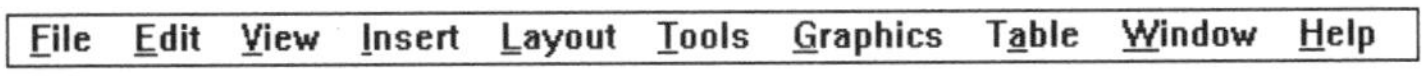

Figure 2-1:
Not an
oyster bar;
not a sushi
bar; it's a
menu bar.

| File | Edit | View | Insert | Layout | Tools | Graphics | Table | Window | Help |

Clicking on the menu bar

To see what's in a menu, click on a word in the menu bar. That word then gets highlighted and a menu of commands drops down from it. Quite unreasonably (because you didn't pull anything), this menu is called a *pull-down menu*. The top selection in the menu is highlighted, but ignore this selection if you're using a mouse. It's just WordPerfect suggesting the selection, similar to a waiter saying, "Perhaps Monsieur would enjoy this tasty first object, no?"

To try out this theory, start up WordPerfect (see Chapter 1) and then click on the word File. The WordPerfect waiter suggests the delightfully savory New command, and the title bar above it cheerfully displays a glowing description of New. Admire this screen, leave things as they are, and read on.

If you don't find anything you like, close the menu by clicking on the menu name again or anywhere else in the WordPerfect window. If you click on another button or menu selection, however, you get whatever you clicked on.

Let go of that button!

Some folks, for fear that the menu they have selected will disappear, continue to hold down the mouse button (particularly if they have learned to use a Macintosh computer). If their hand drifts by accident while holding down the button, they end up selecting something when they finally release the button. If you are one of these people, read the section, "Using Dialog Boxes," later in this chapter.

This alternative menu technique, called *click and drag,* is useful for former Macintosh users but confusing for the rest of us. In Windows, most menus are displayed until you put them away. The exception is the power bar, which we discuss later in this chapter. Otherwise, let go of the button before you move the mouse.

Choosing a command

To choose a command from this menu, point and click on the command. Related commands are clumped together and separated from other command clumps by a line.

In addition to the commands, you may find other suggestive symbols, sort of like the little, red dot next to the hot stuff on a Chinese menu. This list shows what a few of those symbols mean:

- **A little right-pointing triangle after the command:** If you click on these commands, you see a little submenu (similar to choosing chicken and being asked if you want fried, roasted, or Szechuan.)

- **A check mark next to the command:** Means that "It's already on," whatever it is. You can turn it off by clicking on the command.

- **An ellipsis (. . .) after the command:** (As though it has more to say if you ask.) It does, and if you click on it, it gift-wraps its thoughts in attractive, little *dialog boxes,* which are discussed in the following section.

- **An *F* with a number, such as F3:** A reminder that you can perform this command and not ever open a menu. All you have to do is press the key labeled F3 on your keyboard. These F keys are function keys, whose jobs change with every program you run. They are the second way of ordering WordPerfect around that we mentioned earlier. You may want to remember some of these commands to make life easier. Pressing F3, for example, always invokes the Save As dialog box in WordPerfect for Windows.

How we talk about menus and commands in this book

Because darn near every command in WordPerfect appears on a menu, a submenu, or a sub-submenu, it gets really tedious for us to say, "Click on Edit, and then on Select in that menu, and then on Page in the next menu," or whatever. We say it this way in the early chapters of this book, until you get used to the idea. After that, though, we just say "Click on (or select, or choose) Edit Select Page." It's a little terse, but if we don't do it that way, you would be comatose with boredom by the end of a paragraph. Plus, think of all the trees we save by making the book shorter.

U̲nderlined characters
What's w̲ith a̲ll t̲hese u̲nderlined cha̲racters
i̲n menu̲s?

For those of you who are already comfortable with computer keyboards, underlined characters designate the Alt-key combinations that select the command. To save a file, f'rinstance,

you can press Alt+F and then press S. If the preceding information is gibberish to you, read the sections "Know your keys" and "Pressing and releasing keys," later in this chapter.

Using Dialog Boxes

If you click on a menu selection that has an ellipsis (. . .) after it, you get either another menu or a *dialog box*. The dialog box shown in Figure 2-2 looks like a cross between a tax form and a VCR remote control, but it is less painful to use than either one.

To see an example dialog box, with the F̲ile menu open, click on the Save A̲s command.

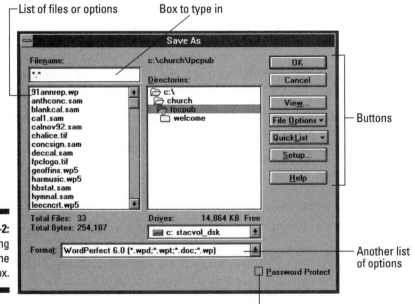

Figure 2-2: Conversing with the dialog box.

List of files or options

Box to type in

Buttons

Another list of options

Stuff to check off

Those wacky dialog thingies

This section shows some of the things (called "dialog thingies" herein) you may find in a dialog box:

Stuff to check off: These items have a little box or circle to their left. This type of item can be turned on (selected) or off (not selected). Click on the little box or circle to select or unselect. The Save As dialog box, for example, has a Password Protect thingy.

Lists of files or options from which to choose: You can tell which item is selected because it has a little box around it or it is shown in a different color. Click on the file or option you want. In the Save As dialog box, for example, a list of the files in your directory appears underneath the Filename box.

Lists of options, but you see only one option: For some lists of options, WordPerfect shows only the option that is selected. To see all the options, click on the little downward-pointing arrow just to its right. In the Save As dialog box, for example, the Format option shows WordPerfect 6.0 as the selected option, but it has others.

Boxes in which you type: Click on these boxes to highlight them and then type stuff. For example, you can type a name in the Filename box (refer to Figure 2-2). *Warning:* Don't press Enter when you finish typing or else the dialog box goes away and WordPerfect begins executing your command immediately, even if you aren't finished!

Boxes with numbers you can change: Some dialog boxes contain number settings, such as the width of a margin. To type a number, click on the number and then type the new number. To increase or decrease the number a little at a time, click on the up or down arrows next to the box.

Buttons you can "press" by clicking on them: If these buttons have ellipses, guess what? You see another dialog box! And if they have little triangles on them, they display a menu. For example, the Save As dialog box has a bunch of buttons down its right side.

Icons that run little WordPerfect subprograms: These icons are sort of specialized junior waiters — one for forks, one for spoons.) Double-click on these items to see them scurry.

Don't try to remember all this stuff. We talk about various instances of these dialog thingies as we go along, but you can refer back here if you ever run into an unfamiliar one.

Our favorite buttons

Two very common and very important buttons are the OK and Cancel buttons. Pressing OK means "Do it — and do it the way this box says to do it!" Pressing Cancel means "Forget it — I didn't really want to do this! Get me outta here and ignore everything I said in this box."

"Forget it!" is apparently a popular choice here because Windows lets you say the same thing in four other, different ways:

- ✓ Press the Esc key on the keyboard.
- ✓ Double-click on the minus sign in the upper left corner of the dialog box.
- ✓ Click once on that minus sign and choose <u>C</u>lose.
- ✓ Press Alt+F4.

We're talking overkill here. We just remember to click the Cancel button or press Esc — enough is enough.

You may also see the Close button, which means basically the same thing as OK. Pressing Close just puts away the box without changing anything that hasn't already been changed.

Using QuickMenus for Even More Ways to Choose Commands

If you're beginning to get a headache just thinking about the regular, plain-vanilla menu bar, give this subject a miss.

As usual, in its quest to give you more options than you would have thought possible, WordPerfect provides another way to choose commands. It involves the use of the right mouse button. Until now, whenever we tell you to click the mouse button, we always mean the left one.

Pinky finger alert!

When you use dialog boxes, you should beware of two keyboard keys: Enter and Esc, which mean the same as the OK and Cancel buttons, respectively. This caution applies even if you're typing something in a dialog thingy. Keep a watchful eye on your pinky fingers, lest they unwittingly lead you astray by pressing Enter or Esc before you are really finished with the dialog box.

The people who write Windows programs, however, decided that because most PC mice have two or three buttons, ignoring the additional one or two buttons would be missing an opportunity for more menus, options, and (probably) confusion.

In many Windows programs, clicking on something with the right mouse button pops up a little menu called a QuickMenu, so those wacky WordPerfect people decided to have QuickMenus too. Throughout this book, whenever clicking on something with the right mouse button displays a QuickMenu, we tell you about it. The status bar (the bar at the bottom of the screen), for example, has a QuickMenu that lets you hide it if you get tired of looking at it.

These steps show you how to see a QuickMenu:

1. **Point to the status bar with the mouse pointer.**

2. **Click once using the right mouse button.**

   A little box pops up, right where your mouse pointer is.

Voilà! Now that you can see a QuickMenu — specifically, the one for the scroll bar — what good does it do? This QuickMenu has two options: Hide Status Bar and Preferences.

Most QuickMenus have a Preferences option that lets you customize the way WordPerfect works. We talk about customizing WordPerfect much later in this book, in Chapter 20, when you might be calmer about the idea of fooling around with the things that appear on the screen and how they work.

Each QuickMenu contains choices that have something to do with the thing you were pointing at (the status bar, in this case). This particular QuickMenu contains the command Hide Status Bar.

To choose a command, such as Hide Status Bar, from a QuickMenu, you have (as usual) a choice of methods:

✔ Point to the command with the mouse pointer and click on it with the button — either the left *or* the right mouse button will do.

✔ Press the underlined letter from the command (H, in this case)

Either way, WordPerfect leaps into action and performs the command. In this case, the status bar vanishes like M&Ms at a birthday party. (To get the command back, by the way, you can use the View Status Bar command.)

Unbuttoning the Secrets of the Button Bar

As accustomed to bars as writers traditionally are, the number of bars in WordPerfect for Windows is inspiring even to us. We are about to discuss two of these word-processing watering holes: the button bar and the power bar. As in real life (restaurants, that is), you can think of going to these bars as a way to get quick service without a menu.

The *button bar* is a line of rectangles with pictures and words on them under the menu bar, as shown in Figure 2-3. The button bar is one of those cool icon things that make Windows programs such as WordPerfect look really impressive — like your VCR or CD player's remote control. Unlike your remote control, though, the button bar is also very useful and simple after you get to know it.

Figure 2-3:
Belly up to
the button
bar.

The first thing to know about the button bar is that it's not always displayed. This knowledge should be reassuring to those who are now frantically looking for rectangular buttons with pictures and words on them. The second thing to know is that it's not the same as the power bar, which has even smaller buttons with pictures but no words (thankfully, for those of us whose eyes have trouble with the small print). If you're not sure which bar you're looking at on your screen, check Figure 1-1 in Chapter 1.

If you don't see the button bar, you can display it by opening the View menu and clicking on Button Bar. Notice that you may not have the same buttons in your bar that we have in ours. If that's the case, it's because the person who set up your software decided to change them. If he went to all that trouble, there's probably a good reason, and you should ask him to explain what he had in mind.

Button bar buttons are quick ways to do everyday things — things you can do with menus but that take longer. Some are self-explanatory and pretty simple, such as Indent, which indents a paragraph. Thanks again to the Department of Redundancy Department (again), you can also indent by choosing Layout Paragraph Indent from the menus or by pressing the F7 function key. Some buttons, such as Envelope, do things that are a little more complicated. If you want more explanation about a button, just move your pointer to it (don't click). The title bar delivers a brief one-liner about the button and lists the function-key equivalent, if there is one.

Shuffling your buttons

Here's the cool thing about the button bar: you can tell WordPerfect which buttons you want on the bar and even make your own buttons. Then you can make different sets of buttons for different kinds of documents you work on, such as one set of buttons for writing memos and a different set of buttons for writing reports.

Thankfully, we are not going to tell you how to do all this stuff right now. But we want to warn you, in case someone else has set up specialized button bars on your computer, in which case the buttons on your button bar will change mysteriously when you use different documents. If you think that this sounds as cool as we think it does, check out Chapter 17 for details.

The Very Sharp-Sighted among us will notice that if they put the pointer in the gray area around the buttons, the pointer turns into a hand. The More Adventuresome will discover that if they hold down the mouse button and move the mouse, the "hand" drags an outline of the button bar to another location. After releasing the button, the button bar reappears in the new location and in a chunkier form. If you find its original location annoying, you might give this technique a try.

If you decide that you don't like the button-down atmosphere of the button bar, just open the View menu and click on Button Bar again.

We talk more about buttons on the button bar as we go along.

Power Lunch at the Power Bar

The concept of something called a *power bar* is intriguing, although it's vaguely disconcerting to those of us who made it through the 1980s without ever having a power lunch. Perhaps that's why we brown-bag, tuna-sandwich types find its function barely distinguishable from the more humble and homely sounding button bar. Yet there it is.

If the power bar is displayed, it looks something like Figure 2-4. Like the button bar, its buttons can be changed by the Very Knowledgeable. (Indeed, so yours may not look like ours.) If the power bar is not visible, open the View menu and click on Power Bar.

Figure 2-4:
Lots of
teeny-tiny
buttons on
the power
bar.

Like the button bar, the power bar is a quick, convenient way to do something that would take longer using the menus. If you place the pointer over a button, the title bar provides a brief explanation of the button's function. Because there are no words on the buttons and because some symbols seem to mean darn near anything, from "take a U-turn" to "show me a calendar," this explanation is quite useful.

The power bar has one peculiarity. Some buttons have little submenus. And unlike most Windows menus, these submenus stay up only as long as you hold down the mouse button. To select something from the menu, you have to hold down the button and move the mouse, to "drag" the highlight to the option you want. Nothing happens until you release the button.

As with the button bar, if you decide that you really don't like the power bar, click on Power Bar in the View menu again.

Throughout this book, we tell you when a button on the power bar would be useful. In Chapter 1, for example, we used power bar buttons to open, save, and print documents in one fell click.

Using the Ruler

OK, now we're on familiar ground! Everybody knows what a ruler is, right? Ummm, maybe. The WordPerfect ruler is not your ordinary tick-marks-along-the-edge sort of thing (although it has those too). It's a behavior-controlling ruler bar (like your teacher used to have in grade school) except that this ruler bar controls the behavior of your paragraphs. Specifically, it controls the indents and tabs of whatever paragraph you're working in (where the cursor, not your mouse pointer, is). The *cursor,* or *insertion mark,* is a stationary, usually blinking, vertical line on which text appears when you type. The mouse pointer is an I-beam or arrow shape that moves when the mouse moves.)

Like the various bars, the ruler may or may not be displayed. Open the View menu and click on Ruler to make it either appear or disappear (see Figure 2-5).

Figure 2-5:
Pay homage
to your ruler.
He's picking
up your tab.

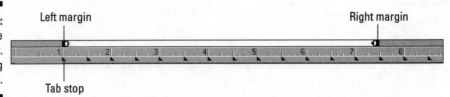

Left margin   Right margin

Tab stop

The light-colored bar across the top of the ruler shows your left and right margins and your paragraph indents. In the bar below the actual ruler, the little triangles show tab settings. They take different shapes according to which kind of tabs they are. When you look at your ruler, you find that some tabs are already set. These settings are not your fault: they are "default" tabs you can change if you want. You can add tabs, remove tabs, or move tabs around.

We discuss all this in fascinating detail in Chapter 9, but the quick tour goes like this:

✔ To move tabs and paragraph margins around, you *drag* them: Point to it, press the mouse button, and *hold it down.* Move the mouse and release the button when the selected item is where you want it.

✔ To change the type of tabs you're putting in, point to the power bar button that has a tab symbol on it, press down the mouse button, and *hold it down.* A menu of possible tab types is displayed; move the mouse to drag the highlight to the type you want and release the button.

Make sure that the blinking cursor (the blinking vertical bar, not the mouse pointer) is in the correct paragraph before you set tab stops or indents with the ruler.

Using the Keyboard

What with all these bars and windows and icons, the keyboard begins to seem rather old and dowdy. Still, it beats the heck out of trying to type with the mouse. And for those of us who are reluctant to change our ways just because some software engineer has decided to give us a mouse, it still provides a pretty fast way to give commands to WordPerfect.

Know your keys

Take a look at your keyboard. With any luck, it looks like Figure 2-6. If it's a laptop, you're on your own 'cause the keys can be anywhere. Notice that there are different areas, each one with its own role to play. This section describes the different groups and what they do.

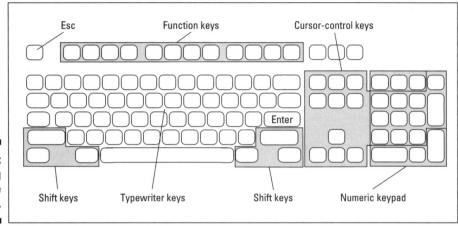

Figure 2-6:
Interesting
keys on the
keyboard.

Function keys: Usually located along the top of the keyboard and labeled F1 through F10 or F12, these keys are assigned to different commands in WordPerfect. They perform many of the same commands you can do from the menu bar, button bar, or power bar. The function keys perform one set of commands when you use them by themselves, and others when you use them with the "shift" keys: Alt, Ctrl, and Shift.

Typewriter keys: These keys have the same familiar characters, numbers, and punctuation that are on your old Royal typewriter, plus a few new, jazzy ones. You use these keys mostly to type stuff, but you can use them with the "shift" keys to issue commands.

Cursor-control keys: These keys are the ones off to the right of the typewriter keys. Four of them have arrows on them and move the cursor when you're typing or move the highlight that appears when you're using Windows menus or scroll bars. The others, marked Insert, Delete, Home, End, PgUp (or Page Up), and PgDn (or Page Down), are pairs of keys that move the cursor in large gulps. The size of the gulp depends on which "shift" keys you're holding down, if any. See Chapter 3 for details about how to use these keys to move around in your document.

Florida Keys: You retire here after learning WordPerfect for Windows. Hang out in an RV along lovely Smathers Beach in Key West, cruise Duvall Street, and watch the college kids throw up during spring break.

Numeric keypad keys: The keys on this keypad basically duplicate the number keys, useful "math" symbols, and the Enter key. They can also be used rather than the cursor keys if you don't have any others. Just press the Num Lock button that is probably nearby and they switch to being cursor keys.

Shift keys: The members of this shifty bunch don't do anything by themselves — only in combination with other keys, sort of like the pedals on a piano. Like the Shift key on your Smith-Corona, when the Shift, Alt, and Ctrl (pronounced Control) keys are held down, they impart new meanings to function keys and cursor-control keys and cause certain typewriter keys to execute commands when you press them.

Enter key: This key is generally marked as such or with a funny L-shaped arrow. Pressing this key ends your paragraphs when you're typing (*not* every line) or finishes up a command when you're in a menu or dialog box. Some people call this key the Return key. Used with the Ctrl key, it inserts a page break (see Chapter 10).

Esc key: Called the "escape" key, this little guy can help you back out of menus you didn't mean to get into.

Pressing and releasing keys

As an example of how computer technology makes your life easier than it was with your Smith-Corona (or not, as the case usually is), you must now be careful about not only which keys you press but also precisely how you press *and* release them — at least with some keys.

The computer is particularly fussy about using the shift keys, which work only in conjunction with other keys. All is well if you use them exactly like the Shift key on your beloved Periwinkle-Marmosette typewriter, as shown in these steps:

1. **Press the shift key (Shift, Alt, or Ctrl, as directed) *first* and *hold it down.***

   Don't crush it — just push it.

2. **Press the other key (F7, for example).**

3. **Finally, release both of them.**

   If your fingers don't work well together, release the shift key last.

These types of combinations are written as Shift+F7, for example, or Ctrl+F7 or Alt+F7.

Sometimes, you must press more than one shift key. This instruction is written as Ctrl+Shift+F3, but it might as well be written Shift+Ctrl+F3 because it doesn't matter in which order you press the shift keys. Just get both of 'em down before you press the last key and release 'em all at once.

Knowing when to press Enter

This section probably should be titled "Knowing when not to press Enter." With WordPerfect and any other word processor, you do *not* press the Enter key at the end of every line — you press Enter at the end of every *paragraph*. Failure to observe this rule causes you regular consternation and grief and marks you as a tyro (a novice) to all who observe your work.

Do not worry about the ends of your lines. WordPerfect takes care of most paragraphs automatically and can usually do it far better than you can (ragged right, justified, whatever you need). The *only* time you should press Enter at the end of a line is when you are entering a list and the line must end before it is full.

Because pressing the Enter key marks the end of a paragraph, it inserts a little paragraph symbol like this: ¶. Trouble is, the symbol is invisible. To make it visible, open the View menu and click on Show ¶.

Whether the symbol is visible or not, it's there. If you delete it — which you can do in the same way as you delete any normal, visible character — your paragraph gets merged with the one below it.

The story of Tab and the spacebar

This story sounds like an entertaining tale of Tab, the swinging Astro Kitty. Alas, although this story is about space, it's not about black holes and watering holes. It's about "white space."

Like pressing Enter at the end of every line, another way to cause yourself no end of unnecessary grief is to overuse the Tab key and the spacebar to get your text where you want it. There are generally better ways to do this than the way you did it on your Stombrowski-Danglowicz steam-powered typing machine, fondly remembered from the old days in the KGB.

The Tab and spacebar keys insert *white space* characters. Like cockroaches in the Keys (Florida, that is), you might not see them, but they're there. A certain WordPerfect command is equivalent to snapping on the light switch to see these critters. It's the same command in the View menu that shows the invisible paragraph mark: choose View from the menu bar and then choose Show (you can also press Ctrl+Shift+F3).

Whoa! Suddenly, all the spaces in your document appear as little black dots, all the tabs appear as arrows, and your little paragraph markers show up at the end of each paragraph. Don't worry — your document doesn't look like this when it's printed. This is just a useful way to see exactly which characters you have.

There are better ways to position your text than to use a bunch of spaces and tabs, and we get into them in Chapter 9. This list tells you how to use these guys properly:

🖝 Use the spacebar only between words or at the beginning of a sentence.

🖝 For the most part, you press the Tab key only to indent the *first line* of a paragraph or put white space in the middle of a sentence. (To indent an entire paragraph, click on the Indent button in the button bar; see Chapter 9.)

If you want to create a table of words and numbers, you might have to use tabs too or you can tell WordPerfect to help you make a table (see Chapter 16).

Choosing commands by using keys

As we intimated above, you can use the keyboard rather than the mouse to choose commands from the menu bar. For touch typists, this method can be more efficient than mousing it, because you don't have to move your fingers from that all-important home row.

To choose a command without touching the mouse, follow these steps:

1. **Look at the menu bar and note which letter of the command is under-lined.**

   It's always a letter or a number.

2. **Hold down the Alt key while you press the key; then release the Alt key.**

   Aha! WordPerfect grasps your meaning and displays the menu associated with that command. For example, if you press Alt+V, WordPerfect rolls down the View menu.

3. **Again, check the command on this menu to see which letter is under-lined.**

   Press it with or without the Alt key. WordPerfect has now guessed that you are giving a command, so you don't have to press the Alt key to tip it off.

   If you choose a command that has a little triangle after it, such as the Layout Line command, WordPerfect displays another little menu. Repeat step 2 to choose the command from this menu.

For commands you use frequently, you may learn the letters that give the command, and you can probably type them faster (even including pressing the Alt key) than you can choose the command with the mouse.

This list shows some other keys you can use while you give commands:

- ✔ To cancel a menu by using the keyboard, press the Esc key. Every time you press it, WordPerfect backs up one step. Keep pressing Esc until the menus go away and no command is highlighted on the menu bar.

- ✔ Computer-literate types might be tempted to think that the Break key cancels commands too, but, in fact, WordPerfect ignores it.

- ✔ You can also use the keyboard to get around in dialog boxes, although this method is rather cumbersome. In every dialog box, every item and every button have an underline letter in their name, and pressing Alt and that letter moves the cursor there.

Undoing Mistakes

Not that you're likely to make a mistake or anything, but for those of us who occasionally give the wrong command, the power bar has a Highly Useful button called Undo. Actually, it's not called anything. It doesn't say Undo on it — it just has an icon of an arrow doing a U-turn.

When you click on this button (or press Ctrl+Z or choose Edit Undo from the menu), WordPerfect usually can undo whatever the last command did, including deleting a bunch of characters, whether you used the Delete key, the Backspace key (see Chapter 3), or both.

For specifically undoing deletions, an even more useful but somewhat trickier command called Undelete is discussed in Chapter 4.

Help, Help-Help, and More Help

Calling for help in a Windows program such as WordPerfect is a little like calling for help at the Arnold Schwarznegger-Leona Helmsley School of Lifeguard Training: prepare to be a little overwhelmed. You don't just get information — you get an entire, muscle-bound information-retrieval and -management system designed to meet your assistance requirements. And a mint on your pillow.

We're not even going to try to explain everything this Dream Team of lifesavers can do — we just give you the simplest way to use Help. For all the fancy stuff, we recommend that you play around in Help to your heart's content. You can't break anything and you might learn a lot.

Help

The simplest part is calling for Help. It's Help on the menu bar (or press Alt+H). At this point, it's a good thing that you're not literally drowning when you call for help in WordPerfect because you must now decide precisely *how* you are going to ask for help. Two of the options, Contents and How Do I, are reasonable and straightforward. Another option, Search, is a little confusing. The Coach option is truly cool (see the upcoming section "More help").

The following options are the quickest and easiest choices from the Help menu:

- ✔ **Search for Help On:** A list of all topics, arranged alphabetically, is displayed. Click on any topic highlighted in green. Click the close button to make the list go away.

- ✔ **How Do I:** Used when you want to know how to do something. As you type, WordPerfect tries to match what you type with topics from its list.

- ✔ **Contents:** Click on this option to look up commands, keystrokes, and buttons. Then just click on any topic highlighted in green.

Whichever method you choose, you get exactly the same window full of information. Often, several areas of text are highlighted in green, each of which is itself a topic. When you click on one of these areas, you get information on that topic. If you get lost in this labyrinthine Hall of Help and want to find your way back, look for a Back button at the top of the Help window and click on it.

To make the Help window go away, the easiest thing to do is double-click on the minus sign in the upper left corner or choose File Exit (press Alt+F and then X).

Help-Help

Thanks to the WordPerfect Department of Redundancy Department's Department of Hierarchical Consistency (consultants to Arnold and Leona), you can also get help about Help. From the Help menu, you just choose Contents and then Using Help. Have fun.

More help

You can also safely play around with the other stuff on the Help menu. It's fun and informative and beats the heck out of actually working. The tutorials are good and Coach is wonderful! It's a fabulous "Dummies" feature because it works right along with you. A Show Me button in Coach even moves the mouse pointer for you and points out what to click on! You can't break anything and it's pretty clear what to do, so go wild.

Context-sensitive Help

If you want the Help feature to pare down the list of topics to things related to whatever you're doing right now, you can choose Context-Sensitive Help. (Imagine Arnold and Leona trying to be sensitive to your personal needs, and you get the picture.) When you're in the middle of using a menu or a dialog box, press F1. Zap! Arnold figures out exactly which topic you ought to be interested in (whether you are or not). If you press F1 with the pointer in the middle of your text, you see the same window that appears when you choose Contents from the Help menu.

Many dialog boxes also have a Help button that works just like the F1 key: click on it to see helpful information about using the dialog box.

Another form of context-sensitive help is available — kind of in the Tinkerbell school of lifesaving (for you Peter Pan fans). It provides information about only commands and buttons. These steps show you how to use this technique:

1. **Press Shift+F1.**

   Your mouse pointer turns into a little cartoon thought-balloon with a question mark on it. (We cannot help but think of this as Tinkerbell. Sorry.)

2. **Point to a menu selection or button and click the left mouse button.**

3. **If you're looking in a menu, continue to hold down the mouse button and drag the highlight (by moving the mouse) to whatever you want help with.**

4. **Release the mouse button.**

Poof! Tinkerbell helps you with whatever you have selected. When you exit from the Help window, she goes away and doesn't come back until you press Shift+F1 again.

The 5th Wave

"I'D LIKE TO THANK EVERYONE FOR AWARDING MY COMPANY THE LEADER IN COPY PROTECTED SOFTWARE PRODUCTS."

Chapter 3
Cruising the Document

....

....

After you have typed some text in your document, you undoubtedly will want to do some editing. After all, that's what word processing is all about. When you use a regular typewriter, making changes involves splashing a viscous white liquid all over your paper, yourself, and the furniture, or slicing and dicing little slips of paper only to reassemble them with glue or tape. But those days are over now that you have entered the Age of Word Processing — you can slice and dice your text right on the screen, with no paper cuts or white-out stains.

To be able to edit, of course, you must move your cursor (the blinking vertical bar) to the text you want to change. Your cursor is your pencil point on the page — its location determines where actions will happen. So that's what this chapter is about — moving the cursor around in your document. In later chapters, we tell you what to do when you get there, such as deleting things (Chapter 4), moving text around (Chapter 6), or making the text look different (Chapter 8).

Two — Count 'Em — Two Ways

You have, of course, two ways of navigating around your document. (Computer people like to talk about navigation rather than just moving — we must be a group of frustrated sailors.) As you use WordPerfect, you find that two is the absolute minimum number of ways to do anything, and in many cases WordPerfect provides four or five ways. (Remember from the last chapter how many ways there are to give a command?) You can move the cursor in two general ways:

✔ Use the mouse to point to where you want to go.

✔ Use keys on the keyboard to move in the direction you indicate.

Two cursor-like things are also on the screen (as they are in most Windows programs):

✔ *The mouse pointer:* Tells you where the mouse is pointing. It can change shapes and does so depending on what WordPerfect thinks it is pointing at. When the mouse pointer is pointing at your text, it looks like a skinny capital I (called an *I-bar*). When it's pointing at anything else, such as menus or buttons, it is usually a little white arrow. If you don't see it, just move the mouse a little and it appears.

✔ *The insertion point:* Also called the plain old *cursor,* it tells you where your typing will appear. We hope that you don't mind that we call this thing the cursor because it's the term we're used to. The cursor is a slowly blinking vertical bar — you can't miss it.

The purpose of this chapter is to get the cursor into firing position so that you can take aim at some text. First we talk about using the mouse and then about using the boring old keyboard; finally, we throw in a few other ways WordPerfect lets you cruise your document.

Mousing Around

Now that WordPerfect runs with Windows, it uses Window's snazzy graphical user interface, including the mouse, for just about everything except typing text. (Gee, maybe the next version will let you use the mouse to point to letters on a little picture of a keyboard. Can you imagine a slower way to type?)

Moving nearby

If the place you want to go is displayed on the screen, just position the mouse pointer there and click the left mouse button. Follow these steps:

1. **Move the mouse pointer to the position where you want to work.**

   When the mouse is pointing to your text, or near it, the mouse pointer changes to a skinny capital I (the I-bar), but it's still called a pointer. If the mouse pointer is a little arrow, you are pointing to something other than your text and you cannot move your cursor there; move the cursor to the beginning of the paragraph.

2. **Click the mouse button without moving the mouse.**

   This action tells WordPerfect to put the cursor right where the mouse pointer is.

3. **You may want to move the mouse pointer out of the way so that it doesn't obscure the text you are going to edit.**

   As soon as you begin typing, the mouse pointer disappears, in an effort to stay out of the way.

Moving to the far reaches of the document

If you cannot see the text you want to edit, don't panic. It is still there but has fallen off the edge of the screen. WordPerfect displays your document as though it were written on a long scroll (imagine medieval monks or Egyptian scribes). The beginning and ending of the document are rolled up and just the middle part is visible. If you want to see a different section of the text, WordPerfect unrolls the scroll for you and displays it on-screen.

You may have noticed a gray bar running vertically along the right side of the screen. This *scroll bar* (mentioned in Chapter 1) is shown in Figure 3-1. You use it to tell WordPerfect to roll and unroll the metaphorical scroll that contains your document.

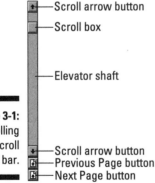

—Scroll arrow button

—Scroll box

—Elevator shaft

Figure 3-1:
Unrolling
the scroll
bar.

—Scroll arrow button
—Previous Page button
—Next Page button

The scroll bar is similar to a little map of your document, with the full length of the scroll bar representing your entire document: The top end is the beginning of the document, and the bottom end is the end of it. The little gray box on the scroll bar (the scroll box, in Windows parlance) represents the part of the document you can see on the screen right now. The scroll box moves up and down the scroll bar like an elevator moves up and down a shaft. By looking at the position of the scroll box in the scroll bar, you can tell where you are in the document — at the beginning, middle, or end.

You can also move around the document by using the scroll bar, as you may have guessed already. This list shows the things you can do to the scroll bar with your mouse:

✔ **Move anywhere in the document in a big hurry:** Use the mouse to drag the scroll box up and down the scroll bar. As you move the scroll box, thus scrolleth the text of the document. To drag the scroll box, point to it with your mouse pointer, press and hold down the mouse button, and move the mouse pointer up or down. The scroll box moves with the mouse pointer as long as you hold down the mouse button. When you release the button, the scroll box stays where you left it, and the document scrolls to match.

✔ **Move to the end of your document:** You can drag the scroll box down to the bottom of its elevator shaft.

✔ **Move to the beginning of the document:** Do the reverse — drag the scroll box up to the tippy top.

✔ **Move forward or backward one screenful of text at a time:** Click on the scroll bar (not on the scroll box). To move to the next screenful of text in the document, click on the scroll bar below the scroll box. To move to the previous screenful, click above the scroll box. The scroll box moves and the document scrolls down one screen.

✔ **Scroll your text one line at a time:** Click on the scroll arrow buttons, the little buttons with arrows on them at either end of the scroll bar. The upward-pointing scroll arrow button at the top of the scroll bar moves you toward the beginning of the document, and the downward-pointing arrow moves toward the end.

✔ **Move through the document page by page:** Click on the Next Page and Previous Page buttons. These buttons are at the bottom of the scroll bar, and have little pages with up and down arrows on them. When you click on the Next Page button, WordPerfect scrolls the document so that the top of the next page is at the top of the screen. The Previous Page button scrolls so that the top of the previous page is at the top of the screen.

Clicking on the scroll box itself doesn't do a blessed thing — not even double-clicking.

If you click on the scroll bar with the *right* mouse button, WordPerfect pops up the scroll bar's QuickMenu. We talk about this menu at the end of this chapter.

If your document is too wide to fit across the WordPerfect window, a scroll bar runs across the bottom of the window too, right above the status bar. It works just like the vertical scroll bar we have been talking about, except that it moves sideways. It has no Next and Previous Page buttons.

Using the Keyboard, Staying Close to Home

If you type like the wind, you probably don't want to have to move your hands from the home row of your keyboard, not even to have lunch. Your speedy fingers know where every key is, and they can hit them faster than a two-year-old can grab an Oreo. Faster, even.

After reading about all this mouse stuff, you are probably thinking, "The mouse is cute, but it slows me down! I don't want to have to lift up my hand, grope around for my mouse, and knock over my coffee cup just to see the next page of my letter!" For you, dear friend, WordPerfect has navigation keys. You can forget about using the mouse — just press keys to get where you want to go.

The main keys you use are the *cursor-control keys,* which are outlined in Figure 3-2. They include these keys:

🖛 The *arrow keys,* for moving the cursor up, down, left, and right

🖛 Keys labeled Home, End, Page Up (or PgUp), and Page Down (or PgDn)

Using the arrow keys

You can use the arrow keys, with the little up-, down-, left-, and right-pointing arrows, to move up or down one line, or left or right one character. These keys are great for positioning the cursor in the exact spot you want.

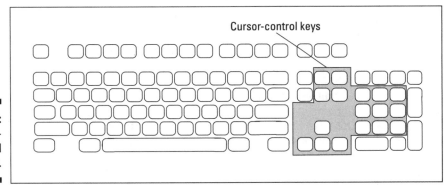

Figure 3-2:
The cursor-
control
keys.

Lock those numbers

Notice that your keyboard probably has two sets of arrow keys. (Sigh.) There are two of everything, as usual. One set is labeled only with arrows, and the keys in this set always work as arrow keys. The keys in the other set, however, have numbers on them too; they are part of the *numeric keypad*. These keys act like arrow keys some of the time, and you can type numbers with them the rest of the time.

To switch between these uses, you press the Num Lock key. (Num Lock stands for *num*eric *lock*, although it sounds like a wrestling grip.) This

key should be in the general vicinity of the numeric keypad (ours is right above the 7 key). When Num Lock is *on*, the numeric keypad types numbers. When it is *off*, it moves the cursor. Your keyboard may have a little light that tells you whether Num Lock is on or off — the light may even be right on the Num Lock key. If not, you can tell WordPerfect to display NUM on the status bar of the screen when Num Lock is on (see Chapter 20). Just press the Num Lock key if you don't like what these keys are doing.

This list shows some of the finer points of using cursor-control keys:

- ✔ If the cursor is on the top line of the screen and you press the up arrow, WordPerfect does your bidding. To move up a line, it must display that line, so it scrolls the document down a tad.

- ✔ Ditto if the cursor is on the bottom line of the screen and you press the down arrow.

- ✔ Don't confuse the left-arrow key with the Backspace key, which usually also has a left-pointing arrow on it (a longer one). The Backspace key *eats* your text as it moves leftward. The left-arrow key just moves the cursor to the left and slides around under the letters like a hot knife through ice cream.

- ✔ As you move the cursor, it moves from letter to letter in your text. When you move rightward off the end of a line, the cursor moves to the left end of the next line. Unlike the mouse pointer, the cursor can go only where there is text. The cursor must have text to walk around on, as it were. You cannot move it off the text into the white void of the blank page.

Using Ctrl with the arrow keys

By pressing the Ctrl key while you press an arrow key, you can make the cursor move farther, as shown by the key combinations in this list:

Ctrl+up arrow	Moves the cursor to the beginning of the current paragraph; if you are already there, it moves up to the beginning of the previous paragraph
Ctrl+down arrow	Moves the cursor down to the beginning of the next paragraph
Ctrl+left arrow	Moves the cursor left one word
Ctrl+right arrow	Moves the cursor right one word

To use the Ctrl key, press it while you press another key, as though it were the Shift key. Don't release it until you have released the other key.

Moving farther and faster

How about those other keys we mentioned earlier — the Home, End, Page Down (or PgDn), and Page Up (or PgUp) keys? You can use them to range farther afield in your documents, which is especially useful as they get larger (the documents, not the keys). As with the arrow keys, your keyboard probably has two sets of these keys, and you can use only the ones on the numeric keypad if Num Lock is turned off.

You can move to the beginning or end of the line by pressing these keys:

| Home | Moves the cursor to the beginning of the current line |
| End | Moves the cursor to the end of the current line |

We use the End key all the time to get back to the end of the line we are typing so that we can type some more.

You can move up and down one screenful of information by pressing these keys:

| Page Up | Moves the cursor to the top of the screen. If you are already there, it moves up one screen's worth of text and scrolls the document as it does so. |
| Page Down | Moves the cursor down to the bottom of the screen. If you are already there, it moves down one screenful of text. |

To move to the beginning or end of the entire document, press these keys:

| Ctrl+Home | Moves the cursor to the beginning of the document |
| Ctrl+End | Moves the cursor to the end of the document |

If you are wondering how long a document is, press Ctrl+End to get to the end of it. Then look on the status bar to see what page you are on (the number after Pg).

Go To Where?

WordPerfect has a Go To dialog box you can use to tell it where to go. Unfortunately, you cannot tell it to go where you probably want to tell it to go, but it's better than nothing. And it's useful for moving around in really large documents.

There are four — count 'em — four ways to display the Go To dialog box:

- ✔ Select the Edit Go To command from the menu.
- ✔ Press Ctrl+G.
- ✔ Use the scroll bar's QuickMenu — that is, point to the scroll bar and click with the *right* mouse button to display the QuickMenu. Then choose the Go To command.
- ✔ Double-click on the location section of the status bar (the part that gives you the page, line, and cursor position).

Actually, there are many more than four ways because you can use the keyboard or the mouse to select commands, but you see our point. And you see the Go To dialog box, shown in Figure 3-3.

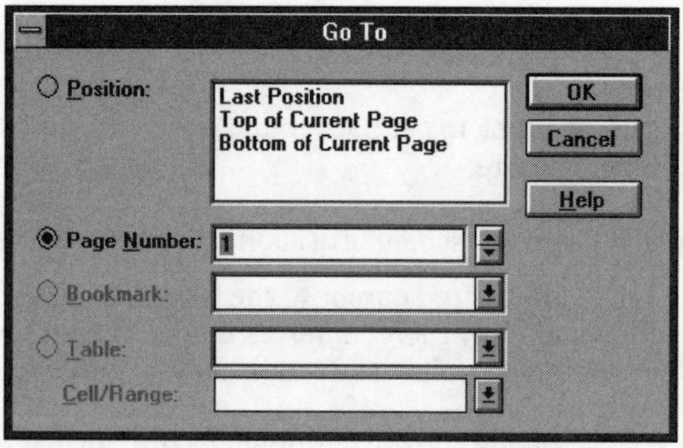

Figure 3-3:
Using the Go To dialog box to tell WordPerfect where to go.

Go To dialog box:
- ○ Position: Last Position / Top of Current Page / Bottom of Current Page
- OK / Cancel / Help
- ◉ Page Number: 1
- ○ Bookmark:
- ○ Table:
- Cell/Range:

There are four other commands you can use to tell WordPerfect where to go: Position, Page Number, Bookmark, and Table. We talk about the last two later in this book, when you know what the heck bookmarks and tables are.

Top of the page to you!

The following list shows how to use the Go To dialog box to get to the top of any page in your document:

- ✔ **To move the cursor to the top of the current page:** Choose Position and then choose Top of Current Page from the list of possible positions (sounds indecent, doesn't it?). Finally, either click on OK or press Enter.

- ✔ **To move the cursor to the bottom of the current page:** Do the same thing you do for moving to the top, but choose Bottom of Current Page as the Position.

- ✔ **To move the cursor to the top of a different page:** Choose Page Number. Enter the number of the page you want and either click on OK or press Enter.

Getting unlost

If you use any of the mouse or keyboard methods described in this book to move your cursor or if you use the search commands described in Chapter 5, you may find that you have made a dreadful error and you want to go back to where you started and try again. Amazingly enough, WordPerfect has a "go back to where I started" command. (It's these nice little surprises that keep up our faith in computers.)

To return the cursor to its previous location, use the Go To dialog box. Choose Position and then Last Position and then either click on OK or press Enter. Your cursor flies back to its earlier location like a well-trained homing pigeon.

Chapter 4
Trashing Your Text

● ●

In This Chapter

▶ Using insert and typeover modes

▶ Dealing with one character at a time: Backspace and Delete

▶ Deleting secret codes

▶ Deleting blocks of text

▶ Undeleting

▶ Undoing versus undeleting

● ●

The greatest boon to writers after the discovery of caffeine has been, arguably, white-out. It is therefore not surprising that the word processor's capability to do white-out one step better by absolutely, indetectably deleting text as though it had never been there — like really, really gone — is quite popular.

Insert and Typeover Modes

If you're replacing existing text, one of the simplest ways to delete the old stuff is to write over it. Normally, WordPerfect doesn't let you do that. When you type, the new text is inserted at the cursor position. This feature is called, not surprisingly, *insert mode.*

If you want to type over your old text, however, all you have to do is press the Insert key (it's probably above the arrow keys), and you enter *typeover mode.* Move the cursor to where you want to begin; anything you type then overwrites the old text as though it had never been there. (Old fogies can now put to rest the ghost of their typing instructors, for whom "strikeovers" were cardinal sins.)

A ghost of the former text does remain, however, in the form of character formatting, such as italics. If the original text was 20 characters in italics, the new text also is 20 characters in italics. Hmm. This situation might not be what you had in mind (see Chapter 8 to learn how to format text in italics or to get rid of this type of formatting).

To return to insert mode, just press the Insert key again.

Typeovers and popovers

Sometimes, in the frenzy of typing, a flying finger mysteriously hits the Insert key and accidentally sends you into typeover mode, which really messes things up. Or you forget to switch back to insert mode.

If it looks like you're overtyping and you didn't want to, following these steps:

1. **Check out the status bar at the bottom of the WordPerfect window.**

   It should tell you which mode you're in by displaying Insert or Typeover. If it doesn't and you use typeover mode frequently, get your guru to add this feature to the status bar or see Chapter 20 to learn how to do it yourself.

2. **Undo your most recent typing by choosing Edit Undo from the menu (or press Alt+E and then U).**

   See the section "Undeleting," later in this chapter.

3. **Switch back to insert mode by pressing the Insert key.**

   Check the status bar to make sure that you're really in the right mode now.

We recommend that you stay in insert mode while you work in WordPerfect so that you don't find yourself deleting stuff by mistake. Also, some keys (such as Tab and Backspace) work a little differently in typeover mode — our descriptions refer to the way things work in insert mode.

 WordPerfect has a way to replace text without changing to typeover mode. Just select the text you want to replace and then begin typing. This step deletes the original text and puts in your new text. For information about selecting text, see the section "Deleting Blocks of Text," later in this chapter, and also Chapter 6.

Dealing with One Character at a Time: Backspace and Delete

You can delete one character at a time in these two ways:

   ✔ The Delete key deletes the character *after* the cursor.

   ✔ The Backspace key deletes the character *before* the cursor.

In either case, the text closes up behind you as you go. Surgery without scars.

Make sure that you don't have any text *selected* if you want to delete just one character at a time. Both the Backspace and Delete keys delete whatever text is selected. Selected text is indicated by highlighting (actually, it's darklighting, but who's counting?).

Deleting Secret Codes

Feeling a tad paranoid? Can it be that everyone around you is, undetected by you, exchanging secret glances and signs? Well, just to add to your paranoia, be aware that WordPerfect is indeed using secret codes. And, like your glory days in the CIA, if you lose the codes by accident, you may be in deep guacamole.

As we discuss in Chapter 11, lots of hidden, secret codes are sprinkled throughout every WordPerfect document. These codes are cryptic notes WordPerfect makes to itself to remember to, for example, "turn on boldface type here" and "turn off boldface type here."

While you are deleting text, you may also delete one or more of these secret codes. If you do, the appearance of a bunch of text then changes. Fortunately, WordPerfect prevents you from accidentally doing this in many cases (like the boldface case).

If you really, really want to, you can tell WordPerfect to show you the secret codes. Seeing them can be helpful if you're trying to recover from an unwanted deletion, but only if you like this kind of spooky stuff.

If the formatting of a block of text changes while you are deleting, you probably deleted a secret code. If you catch your mistake soon enough, you may be able to undelete it with Edit Undelete or Edit Undo (or with their equivalent keyboard commands, Ctrl+Shift+Z or Ctrl+Z, respectively, which we talk about later in this chapter). Otherwise, just reformat it back to the way it was.

Deleting Blocks of Text

The simplest way to delete a block of text is to *select* it (highlight it) with your mouse or keyboard and press the Delete or Backspace key. WordPerfect has other, weird ways you can delete, for example, a single word to the left or right, but we say, "Go with the rodent."

For the full details about selecting text, see Chapter 6. The quick summary is as follows:

1. **Position the mouse pointer.**

   Place it at the beginning or end of the text you want to delete.

2. **Click and drag the mouse pointer to the other end.**

   A block of text will be highlighted.

3. **Press the Delete or Backspace key.**

If you would rather not take your hand off the mouse to delete, just select your text, click the right button on the mouse, and then click on Delete in the QuickMenu that appears.

On the other hand, if you insist that you would rather not take your hands off the keyboard, you can also select blocks as shown in this list and then press Delete:

Shift+left- or right-arrow	Selects from the current insertion point to the left or right, one character at a time
Shift+up- or down-arrow	Selects from the current insertion point to the same location in the line above or below it
Shift+Home	Selects from the current insertion point to the beginning of the line
Shift+End	Selects from the current insertion point to the end of the line
Shift+PgUp or PgDn	Selects from the current insertion point to the top or bottom of the screen
Ctrl+Shift+left- or right-arrow	Selects one word at a time left or right of the current insertion point (by using the mouse, you can do the same thing by double-clicking on a word)

Other nifty key combinations are available for related purposes, but they tend to be hard to remember. (Not that we think that memorizing the little goodies in the preceding list is a snap!)

If you think that you might be able to reuse the text you're deleting, you can cut it out rather than delete it and then paste it later (see Chapter 6).

Undeleting

Undeleting tends to be a popular topic among beginners and old-timers alike. Maybe that's because it sounds like "undulating," which is an even more popular topic. More likely, it's because we all, at some time or another, have deleted that which we ought not to delete (and probably have not deleted that which we ought to have deleted, but that's an editorial problem).

Fortunately, WordPerfect always remembers the last three chunks of stuff you have deleted. Anything beyond that has gone to the big bit-bucket in the sky. The "chunks of stuff" WordPerfect can return from the dead are defined as the following:

✔ A single character, if that's all you deleted

✔ Contiguous characters, deleted by repeatedly pressing the Delete or Backspace key and not doing anything else in between

✔ A block of text deleted all at once

Any of these "last three things deleted" *can be returned to any point in the document,* not just to the place they came from. To get at them, you follow these steps:

1. **Position the cursor at the place where you want the resurrection to occur.**

   Point and click in the document to move the cursor to the right place.

2. **Click on Edit Undelete from the menu bar (or press Ctrl+Shift+Z).**

   You then see the little Undelete dialog box. Also, WordPerfect shows you the most recent deletion and inserts it where your cursor is positioned. WordPerfect highlights it so that it's easy to find.

3. **If you want to keep this text in your document, click on Restore.**

   The text comes back for good, and the dialog box goes away.

4. **If it's not the deletion you want, click on Previous to move back in time.**

   The Next button moves you the other way. Notice that deletions are held like slides in a very small carousel slide projector, so if you change three times, you are back where you began.

5. **When you have the deletion you want, click on Restore. If you don't want any of them, click on Cancel.**

Undoing versus Undeleting

You can also undelete by undoing, which is as simple as selecting Edit Undo from the menu bar. Or you can press Ctrl+Z on the keyboard, or you can click on the button that shows up to suggest a U-turn on the power bar, which explains all the skid marks on it.

Undoing goes back only one deletion and uses pretty much the same definition of a deletion as Undelete does:

- ✔ The character just deleted
- ✔ The block of text just deleted
- ✔ All the consecutive characters just deleted when you repeatedly pressed the Delete or Backspace key

Unlike Undelete, Undo recovers text in only the exact position where it was before. Edit Undo does not recover anything unless the very last thing you did was to delete something. If you do anything to your text after deleting, the deleted stuff is gone, as far as Undo is concerned. It's history. Yesterday's news. Forgetitsville, Daddy-o. You may be able to do stuff that doesn't change your text, though, such as change the view, and Undo still recovers your deletion. If, in a fit of frustration, you press Edit Undo repeatedly, all that happens is that you undo your Undo. This procedure probably will be your undoing, and leave you undo-lating, which, as we said, is more fun anyway.

Chapter 5
Searching for Sanity

• •

In This Chapter

▶ Finding what's lost

▶ Finding and replacing text

• •

*I*f you have lost your marbles, your cool, or your sense of values, you have come to the right place. WordPerfect's Find and Replace commands can not only help you find them again but also replace them with something better: for example, *cottage cheese* for *marbles.* It can even replace your besieged sense of values with a sense of direction.

For finding and replacing words, phrases, and even secret WordPerfect codes, the Edit Find and Edit Replace commands are your buddies.

Finding What's Lost

To start your search for *sanity,* for example, click on the Edit Find command in the menu bar or press F2. The Find Text dialog box, shown in Figure 5-1, springs to your aid.

Figure 5-1:
The Find Text dialog box asks, "What is your quest?"

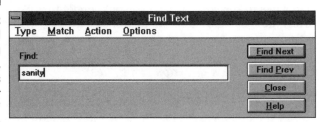

The usual search for "sanity"

In the normal scheme of things, the search for *sanity* requires a journey of only two, or perhaps three, steps in the dialog box:

1. **Type the text you're looking for.**

   It appears in the F_ind window, where you can edit it, if you want, by moving the cursor around, using the Backspace and Delete keys, and so on.

2. **Click on F_ind Next to search toward the end of the document (or press Enter).**

3. **Click on Find P_rev to search toward the beginning of the document.**

If the text you're looking for exists, it appears highlighted in the document window. If the text WordPerfect found is not the precise instance of the text you want, just click on Find Next or Find Prev again until you get it.

If your quest is futile, WordPerfect displays a window saying that it cannot find the text. Reassure it that you're not mad by clicking on the OK button.

This process of choosing in which direction to look may seem a bit nit-picky for your urgent quest, but it makes things faster with long documents (assuming that you have any idea at all where *sanity* lies). Direction, by the bye, is relative to the current cursor position in your document.

Changing the way you search

If you're going to search for one thing after another (such as when you're leaving for work on Monday morning and looking for your keys and your wallet and your umbrella), it might be worthwhile to change the way Find works by using the Options menu. Yes, folks, just when you thought that WordPerfect couldn't have any more menus, here's another one — the Find Text dialog box has its own little menu bar.

If you have no idea in which direction sanity lies:

You can make WordPerfect search the entire document by clicking on Options from the Find Text dialog box's menu and then looking at the choices it presents. Select W_rap at Beg./End of Document. In that way, whether you choose F_ind Next or Find P_rev, WordPerfect ignores the beginning or end of the document and continues the search throughout.

Or choose B_egin Find at Top of Document from the Options menu and then click on F_ind Next in the Find Text dialog box.

If you have a darn good idea where sanity lies but you still cannot find it:

You can make WordPerfect search selected text. With the Find Text dialog box still on-screen, select the area to search. Then choose the Limit Find Within Selection (from the Options menu) before pressing the Find Next or Find Prev buttons in the dialog box.

If you don't know where you are with respect to sanity:

Try choosing the Options command from the Find Text dialog box menu bar and then choosing Begin Find at Top of Document.

To return to your document, click on the Close button. The word that was found remains selected, and your cursor is right there.

After you return to the document, you may want to return to where you were before you began the Find procedure. Select the Edit Go To command (you can also press Ctrl+G) and click on Last Position in the Position list.

If you don't really want to go to the text that was found, press Esc rather than click on Close in the Find Text dialog box.

You can select from your document the text for which you want to look before you use the Edit command. When you do that, it appears automatically as you search for text.

Searching for sanity and finding insanity

Finding the wrong text, like finding the word *insanity* when you're searching for *sanity,* is a common problem, and it is quite treatable. Your therapy is on the Find Text dialog box's menu bar. We prescribe clicking on the Match menu and then on Whole Word. (The Edit Find command otherwise assumes that you are just looking for a set of characters, even within a word.) The phrase "Match Word" appears under the text window to remind you.

Certain things you select in the Find Text dialog box, such as Whole Word mode, are "sticky." They stay "clicked" until you change them. You see a check mark next to them if they are "on."

The capability to find a set of characters, even within words, is a useful feature. If you were searching a document for discussions of *reliability,* for example, you might also want to find *unreliability, reliable,* or *unreliable.* You can find any of these words by entering **reliab** (with Match Word off) as your search text.

Getting picky about what you find

Most of the time you don't much care what kind of *sanity* you find. Any at all will do: Sanity, SANITY, sanity, Sanity, sanIty, or ^SANITY^. Obligingly, the Edit Find command normally ignores the fine points, such as what's uppercase and what's lowercase.

If you are picky about which typeface or size or style or case you want, don't give up: just put a Match to it. That is, you use the Match command on the Find Text dialog box's menu bar: when you choose Match and then Case, Find pays attention to the upper- or lowercase letters you type in the Find box. It finds only versions of your text that are identically typed.

When you choose Match and then Font, a Font dialog box is displayed that lets you look for sanity in Helvetica, **boldly,** if you want. Check off what you want by pointing and clicking. The Font and Style dialog boxes use controls that work the same as they do in the Font dialog box (see Chapter 8). Click on OK when you're finished.

If you are among the WordPerfect secret-code cognoscenti, be aware that you can also Find codes. You can look for specific codes, such as Lft Mar and Bot Mar, by using the Codes command on the Match menu in the Find Text dialog box. If you would rather type a specific code, select Specific Codes from the Type menu in the Find Text dialog box.

Finding Doctor Livingst[*]

In your search for *sanity,* you might seek *Doctor Livingstone.* Or was it Doctor Livingstein? Livingston? Livingstern? Oh, dear! How ever can we find him if we can't spell his name?

Never fear, WordPerfect goes with you into the untamed wilderness of your text, to find the good Doctor What'shisname. You must, however, arm yourself with certain weapons, called *wildcard codes,* to venture into the wild. You can include these special codes in the text you type in the Find box.

Be warned. These codes are not for the timid. But they are very useful, even for novices.

Looking for Mr. Goodchar

The first wildcard code is the [?] (pronounced "[?]"). This code stands for any single character, space, or tab in your Find text. (Don't get carried away yet, though. You cannot create this code by simply typing the three characters. You must use a special dialog box, which we discuss in a minute.)

This section explains how these funky wildcard codes work, as shown in this list of examples:

- ✔ **Livingst[?]n:** Finds Livingston or Livingsten but not Livingstein (it has too many characters between the *t* and the *n*). It finds the better part of Livingstone too — all except the last *e*. If you don't want any part of Livingstone or Livingstonberg, select Match and then Whole Word from the Find Text dialog box menu.

- ✔ **Livingst[?][?]n:** Finds Livingstein and Livingstern but not Livingston. (It has too few characters. You have told WordPerfect to look for exactly two characters between *t* and *n*.)

- ✔ **Livingst[?]n[?]:** Finds Livingstine and Livingston , with a space after it, because [?] can also mean a space unless you have turned on Whole Word. It does not find Livingston, with a comma, however (as in "Doctor Livingston, I presume?"), because the [?] code cannot represent punctuation.

Terrific thing, this [?] code. But if you cannot type it, how the heck do you use it? (This question gets into the mysterious Codes topic, which is best left alone for the most part, at least until Chapter 11.) To use the [?] code, follow these Mysterious Instructions:

1. **Begin typing text in the Find box.**

2. **When you get to the place where you want the [?], click on Match Codes from the Find Text dialog box menu.**

   Up pops the Codes dialog box, with a list of all kinds of weird names, such as BotMar. Also in this list is your friend, the [?]. But it's wearing its formal name, ? [One Char].

3. **Click on the down arrow in the scroll bar to the right of the code list until you find it.**

4. **Double click on ? [One Char] (or click on Insert after clicking on the code) and it is typed in the Find box for you.**

   At this point, you can insert additional [?] codes, if you need them. If you don't need any more of them, click on Close. If you need more but you want to type a few more letters first, click on the Find text box again to continue typing. The Code box remains on-screen. Click on Close when you're finished. Whew!

Notice that [?] is actually [? [One Char]] in your F̲ind box in the Find Text dialog box. We use the short form here because it's hard as heck to see how things work when we print the full name.

Looking for Stars

Back to the original problem. It looks as though the [?] code just isn't powerful enough to let us search for all the variants of Livingstone in one fell swoop. This situation calls for the elephant gun of wildcard codes: the [*] code. This code represents any group of characters, but *only in a word.* It does not represent punctuation, and *it cannot be used to begin a word.* You can find it in the same Codes dialog box in which you found [?]. The formal name for [*] is * [Many Char], and it's at the top of the list in the Codes dialog box.

This list shows some examples:

- **Livingst[*]n:** Finds Livingstein, Livingston, and Livingstern but not Livingstone or "Livingski is quite well; good of you to ask, John."

- **Livingst[*]:** Finds the good doctor no matter how he spells the last syllable.

As with the [?] code, the formal name [* [Many Char]] gets used, not [*]; we just use the abbreviation in this book for simplicity.

Finding and Replacing Text

If your forthcoming best seller *The Search for Sanity* just isn't working out, don't go crazy. Just replace sanity with chocolate, for example, and see how it hangs together.

To accomplish this literary feat, use the E̲dit R̲eplace command, known to its friends as Ctrl+F2 . (Distinguish it from F2, which is the humble E̲dit F̲ind command.) This bold act displays a Find and Replace Text dialog box, as shown in Figure 5-2.

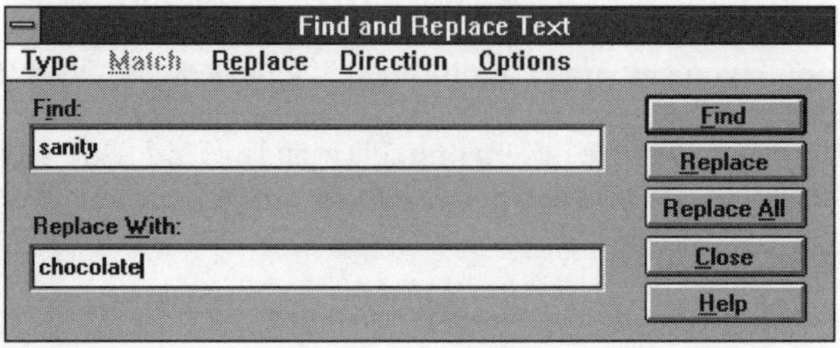

Figure 5-2:
The replace place — yet another dialog box.

Find and Replace Text

T̲ype   Matc̲h   R̲eplace   D̲irection   O̲ptions

Find̲:
sanity

Replace W̲ith:
chocolate

Find
R̲eplace
Replace A̲ll
C̲lose
Help

In the normal scheme of things, replacing *sanity* with *chocolate* is simple. Follow these steps:

1. **Choose Edit Replace from the menu bar (or press Ctrl+F2).**

2. **Type the text you want WordPerfect to find and replace** (sanity, **for example).**

   As with the Edit Find command, if you select *sanity* in your document before issuing the Replace command, the word appears automatically in your Find text box.)

3. **Click on the Replace With box and type the replacement word or phrase** (chocolate, **for example).**

4. **Click on either Find or Replace.**

   WordPerfect goes in search of your search text (*sanity,* for example). If it finds *sanity,* WordPerfect highlights it; if it doesn't find it, it lets you know (as with the Find command).

5. **If your text has been found, you may click on Replace to replace it.**

   The ever-eager Replace goes in search of any additional instances of your search text.

6. **If your text hasn't been found, try changing the direction of your search from the Direction menu on the Find and Replace Text dialog box menu bar.**

   Choose whichever direction is not currently selected (the one without a check mark), either Forward or Backward from the cursor's position. As with the Edit Find command, you can search the entire document by selecting Wrap at Beg./End of Document or Begin Find at Top of Document in the Options menu.

This list shows some general tips for using the Replace command and its dialog box:

✔ The commands in the Type, Match, and Options menus work the same way as they do in the Find Text dialog box.

✔ Replace Case and Replace Font are the commands for getting picky about replacement text — for example, if you want to replace *sanity* with *chocolate* in Helvetica (not to be confused with chocolate in Helvetia, which is also very good).

✔ To replace every instance of the Find text in your document, click on Replace All rather than Replace. Be careful, though: unless you turn on Whole Word mode (from the Match menu), you can end up replacing not only *sanity* with *chocolate* but also *insanity* with *inchocolate,* which is not nearly as nice a situation as it sounds.

✔ To delete every instance of the text in the Find box, first put a space in front of the text in the Find box; then put nothing at all (not even a space) in the Replace text box. This step makes sure that you don't end up with two spaces where the deleted word used to be.

✔ To replace only a limited number of instances of your Find text, choose Options and then Limit Number of Changes.

You can also find and replace text in headers, footers, footnotes, captions, and all those other nooks and crannies in your document. Just move to the Find box and click on Options, Include Headers, Footers, and so on.

Finding and Replacing Codes

If you really, really want to find and replace codes, it's OK, but you don't fit *our* definition of a dummy! Because you're so smart, we just say that you can find the codes you want in the same place you find the wildcard codes — in the Match Codes dialog box. 'Nuff said. For more information, see Chapter 11.

Fun Facts About Finding

The quick way to find text is to press F2 (for Edit Find). To replace text, press Ctrl+F2 (for Edit Replace).

You can leave either the Find Text or the Find and Replace Text dialog box displayed while you work on your document, which can be helpful if you do a great deal of editing.

If you're looking for whole words, turn on the Match Whole Word option, or else you will find *insanity* while searching for *sanity* (and maybe replace it too!).

WordPerfect searches in only one direction from your cursor. To search the entire document, either search both ways manually or turn on either Begin Find at Top of Document or Wrap at Beg./End of Document from the Options menu.

You can limit your Find and Find and Replace work to a selected block of text in your document, but you should make the selection *after* the Find text or the Find and Replace Text dialog box is on-screen. Text selected beforehand is automatically assumed to be the Find text.

Chapter 6
Fooling with Blocks of Text

· ·

In This Chapter

▶ Building basic blocks

▶ Selecting text with the mouse

▶ Selecting text with the keyboard

▶ Selecting text with the Find command

▶ Extending a selection

▶ Doing stuff with selected text

▶ Deleting, moving, and copying text

▶ Using the Windows Clipboard

▶ Copying and pasting with the Clipboard

▶ Cutting and pasting with the Clipboard

· ·

E ver since the first Egyptian hacked his papyrus scroll of *Pyramids For Dummies* into pages, the idea of blocks of text has progressed inexorably. The sentence. The paragraph. The page. The chapter. The volume. The CD. And now WordPerfect "text selection" both embraces and transcends these classic ways of dividing text into blocks and lets you handle any lump of text you want!

Text selection lets you choose precisely what you want to delete, capitalize, italicize, spell-check, or otherwise word-process. Think of the power: You can surgically excise tedious text, rejuvenate a lackluster paragraph with screaming 26-point type, selectively subdue injudicious jargon with grammar- or spell-checking, and eliminate annoying alliteration.

As with most Windows applications, WordPerfect gives you 60-odd quadjillion ways to select text, and about as many things to do with it after it's selected. We stick to the simplest methods, from which you can get the general idea and go on from there.

Basic Blocks

In WordPerfect, a *block* is a chuck of text in your document. Unlike the letter blocks your toddler friends play with, WordPerfect blocks can include a bunch of letters, words, lines, and even pages.

The WordPerfect program understands that humans are fond of blocks — not just arbitrarily defined blocks from "here" to "there," but also certain everyday blocks such as sentences, words, and paragraphs. This list shows the main blocks of text that WordPerfect understands:

- ✔ Arbitrary blocks (as in "Begin with this character over here and end with that character over yonder")
- ✔ Words
- ✔ Sentences
- ✔ Paragraphs
- ✔ Pages

Like an overly fastidious nanny, WordPerfect lets you play with only one block at a time. You cannot select a paragraph here, a paragraph there, and three words over there. Select a block. Have your way with it. Select another block. Do stuff to it. And so on.

Selecting Text with Your Mouse

For most people, the overall best and simplest way to select a block of text is with your buddy, the mouse.

The point-and-shoot approach

To select an arbitrary block of text (from any point to any other point), just follow these steps:

1. **Put the mouse pointer at the beginning of the stuff you want to select.**

2. **Hold down the mouse button and drag the mouse pointer to the end of what you want to select.**

   Text is highlighted as you go, as shown in Figure 6-1.

3. **Release the button.**

   The selected text remains highlighted, and you can do stuff to it (see the section "Doing Stuff with Selected Text," later in this chapter).

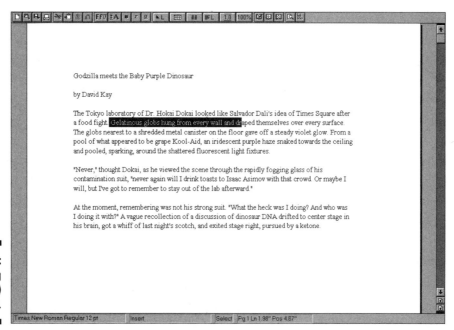

Figure 6-1:
Selecting
(highlighting)
text.

If you're new to this sort of marking procedure, it can look weird. Here are a couple of tips:

- ✔ If the text you want covers several lines, don't bother to drag the mouse pointer to the end of the line and then back to the beginning of the next line, and so on. It wastes effort and looks funny. Like driving in Rome, after you begin, just close your eyes and go. Move boldly and directly toward your final destination.

- ✔ You can go backward as well as forward (up as well as down) — it makes no difference — but you cannot expand in both directions. The place you began must be either a beginning or end point.

That's the simple way to select text. Now here are some faster ways to select words, sentences, and paragraphs.

- ✔ **To select a word:** Double-click on the word (position the mouse pointer anywhere within the word and double-click the left mouse button).

- ✔ **To select a group of words:** Double-click on the first word in the group and *hold down* the mouse button on the second click. Drag the edge of the highlight (in either direction) to the other end of the group you want to select. If you successfully complete this maneuver, you are eligible to receive your advanced mouse driver's license.

✔ **To select a sentence:** Triple-click on the sentence (move the mouse pointer anywhere in the sentence and triple-click the mouse button — it's similar to a double click, but one more time). WordPerfect's idea of a sentence is anything that ends with a period and has a space before the next character. Therefore, this sentence, "i write like e. e. cummings." contains three sentences as far as WordPerfect is concerned.

If you find triple-clicks a bit daunting, you can use another convenient way to select a sentence. Click in the left margin, next to a sentence.

✔ **To select a group of sentences:** This procedure is similar to selecting a group of words. Do the triple-click described in the preceding paragraph (like the samba, but quicker), and hold down the mouse button on the last click. Drag the highlight where you want it.

If you like the click-in-the-margin approach to selecting sentences, as just described, you can select a bunch of sentences by clicking in the margin and dragging the mouse pointer up or down.

✔ **To select a paragraph:** Quadruple-click on the paragraph (move the mouse pointer anywhere within the paragraph and click four times in succession on the mouse button). Yes, the latte consumption in WordPerfect's engineering department must be at record levels if they believe that you can quadruple-click without stuttering, but there it is: four quick clicks of the mouse button nabs you a paragraph.

If you are strictly a decaf drinker (for example, New England hazelnut-acorn blend, our favorite), you might find the Alternative Paragraph Selection Method easier: move your mouse pointer to the left of the paragraph (where the mouse pointer turns into an arrow) and double-click.

✔ **To select a group of paragraphs:** You guessed it. Hold down the mouse button on the fourth click and drag. Or click twice in the left margin and drag.

What about selecting a page? Logically, this procedure should consist of five clicks, but even the highly wired WordPerfect engineers decided that five clicks was beyond their motor skills. Instead, to select a page, try the QuickMenu approach described in the following section.

The QuickMenu approach

You can select sentences, paragraphs, and pages by using the QuickMenu. First, click anywhere within the sentence, paragraph, or page you want to select. Then move your mouse pointer to the left margin (where the mouse pointer turns into an arrow). With a quick click on the right mouse button, you get the QuickMenu shown in Figure 6-2.

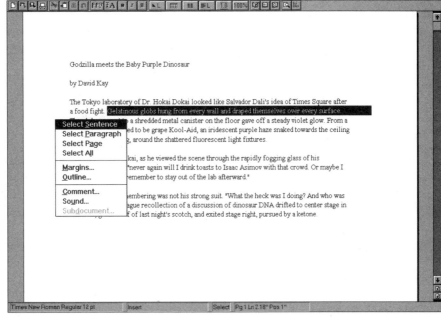

Figure 6-2:
The Left
Margin
QuickMenu
for
selecting
text and
other cool
stuff.

The bottom of this QuickMenu has lots of really cool stuff, such as Sound and Subdocument. Don't play with that stuff now. Show some restraint. This is serious business.

Now you get a chance to Select a Sentence, Paragraph, Page, or the ever-abundant All. Just click (with the left mouse button) on the menu selection you want.

Notice that there's no Word option. You have to point and shoot with the mouse to select a word or group of words.

The menu-bar approach

You can also select a sentence, paragraph, page, or the entire document by using the main menu. Just as you do with the QuickMenu, you begin by clicking anywhere within the text you want. Then choose the Edit Select command from the menu bar, which has the same options as the QuickMenu.

Selecting Text with the Keyboard

Some of us are still a little dubious about this business of taking our hands off the keyboard to use the mouse. We would just as soon use the keyboard, thank you.

Fortunately, there are many alternatives for the rodent-averse among us, whom we prefer to call Speedy Typists. These alternatives all involve the navigation keys.

The navigation keys are the arrow keys and the associated pad full of keys with such useful-looking names as Home and End printed on them. If you use the keyboard for selecting text, first read the section "Using the Keyboard, for Staying Close to Home," in Chapter 3.

Finished reading Chapter 3? OK, now you're briefed and ready for the highly complex secret of selecting text with the navigation keys:

Hold down the Shift key and press the navigation keys.

That's it — really. To be painstakingly specific, these steps show you what to do:

1. **Position the cursor at the beginning or end of the text you want to select.**

   (Click the mouse at that position or press the navigation keys to move the cursor.)

2. **Hold down the Shift key.**

3. **While holding down the Shift key, use the navigation keys to stretch the selection area to the other end of the text you want.**

   The selected text is highlighted and you can do stuff to it. See the section "Doing Stuff with Selected Text, later in this chapter."

The following table shows how to select text from where the cursor is positioned.

To select text up to this position	Press
Next character	Shift+→
Preceding character	Shift+←
Beginning of next word	Shift+Ctrl+→

To select text up to this position	Press
Beginning of current word	Shift+Ctrl←
Same position, down one line	Shift+↓
Same position, up one line	Shift+↑
End of line	Shift+End
Beginning of line	Shift+Home
Beginning of next paragraph	Shift+Ctrl+↓
Beginning of current paragraph	Shift+Ctrl+↑
End of document	Shift+Ctrl+End
Beginning of document	Shift+Ctrl+Home
Bottom of screen	Shift+Page Down
Top of screen	Shift+Page Up
End of the street	Accelerator pedal
Beginning of a tape	Rewind button

Selecting Text with the Find Command

If you know which text you want to select, such as the words *herring fondue,* but you don't want to waste time searching your document for them, use the Find command.

The Find command is under Edit Find on the menu bar; or press the F2 function key. The details of how to use Find are discussed in Chapter 5, but the essence of it is shown in these steps:

1. **Choose Edit Find or press F2.**

   The Find Text dialog box appears.

2. **Type the text you want to find (**herring fondue, **for example).**

   It goes in the box labeled Find.

3. **Press Enter or click on Find Next to search downward through your document.**

   (Click on Find Prev to search upward through your document.) Whatever you are searching for gets selected (if it exists), and you can then do stuff to it.

4. **Press Esc to make the Find Text dialog box go away.**

Or leave it displayed if you find it useful or decorative.

Selecting Text with Your Nose and a Pickle

This approach to selecting text is rather unorthodox and involves thinly sliced pickle spears and breathing through your mouth for a while. It is not recommended for novices and is best reserved for cold and allergy seasons, when its decongestant effect is most welcome.

Extending Selections

Suppose that you have just finished carefully selecting text. With sudden shock, you see that you really should have selected more. You are consumed by regret and self-recrimination. Ah, how much like life itself is word processing. Unlike life, however, WordPerfect gladly lets you select more text — or less, for that matter. You don't even have to do it over again; simply extend your selection.

To extend a selection you made with the mouse (or the Find command), follow these steps:

1. **Hold down the Shift key.**

2. **Press and hold down the left mouse button anywhere in the selected text.**

The endpoint of the selection shrinks back to that point, and you can drag it back and forth with the mouse.

To extend a selection you made by using the keyboard, follow these steps:

1. **Hold down the Shift key.**

2. **Press any of the navigation keys to move the endpoint — just as you did to make the original selection.**

You can also extend any existing selection by using a special feature of the Find command, as shown in these steps:

1. **Choose Edit Find or press F2 to display the Find Text dialog box.**

2. **Type your search text.**

3. **Click on Action in the Find Text dialog box and choose Extend Selection from its menu.**

This feature stays "on" until you turn it off again or close the dialog box.

4. Click on the Find Next or Find Prev buttons in the dialog box.

WordPerfect extends your selection up to and including the text you told it to find.

Notice that WordPerfect doesn't let you change the original starting point of a selection; you can move only the end you moved the first time.

Doing Stuff with Selected Text

This section might as well be called "Doing Stuff with Molecules" for the breadth of discussion it opens up. This list shows a few of the things you can change after you have selected text:

- ✔ Font
- ✔ Type size
- ✔ Type style
- ✔ Capitalization
- ✔ Paragraph layout
- ✔ Position
- ✔ Orientation
- ✔ Color

You can also delete, cut, copy, paste, move, replace, search, spell-check, grammar-check, or typeset the text; turn it into a bulletted or numbered list; or convert it to a subdocument!

Because these topics are covered in most of the other chapters in this book, don't look for them here. Check out those topics in the index or table of contents.

In this section, we cover just a few fundamentals, such as deleting, moving, cutting, copying, and pasting text.

Deleting text

The fastest, easiest, and (depending on how you feel about the document at hand) perhaps most useful thing you can do with selected text is delete it.

After you have selected text, just press the Delete key — or the Backspace key. It goes away, never to return (the selected text — not the key.) The text doesn't utterly, completely go away, however. It passes on to the next dimension, from which you can recall it with the Undo or Undelete command (see Chapter 4).

Moving text

Another simple, useful task is moving text. Just select what you want to move and then click and drag the highlighted text where you want it.

As you perform this procedure, the mouse pointer becomes a shadowed-rectangle icon (or a rectangular blur, if your eyesight isn't so great). The mouse pointer moves to indicate where your text will go (or "wherever your final destination may take you," as they say in the airline business). This pointer movement helps because the icon can go virtually anywhere on the page, although the text can go only where text ought to go.

When you release the mouse button, the move is completed.

Copying text

You can copy text by using almost exactly the same technique as you use to move it. To copy, just hold down the Ctrl key while you drag. A second copy of the selected text is placed in the new location. The original selected text also stays put, just where it was.

The Windows Clipboard

Before we progress to cutting, pasting, and all those other functions that were once well within the capability of kindergartners but that now (thanks to the so-called magic of computers) takes $2,000 worth of hardware and software and a library of books whose titles loudly proclaim your Dummyhood in screaming yellow and black to all who pass your office — whack! Ouch! Thanks, we needed that. Let's see, where were we? Oh, yes, before we go on to cutting and pasting, we should stop and appreciate how Windows has simplified, amplified, and utterly transmogrified our lives by providing a way to cut and paste text and other electronic stuff within and between Windows programs.

A special place within Windows called the *Clipboard* can carry selected text, graphics, spreadsheets, and other useful stuff from any Windows program to any other one. The Clipboard is just as useful within a Windows program as it is between programs. Within WordPerfect, it's used to copy, cut, and paste.

The Clipboard is not really a visible thing in WordPerfect. No cute little Clipboard icon moves around. It's just a sort of hidden storage area. The Windows Program Manager has an adorable, little Clipboard viewer icon, though. You can run it to see what's on the Clipboard: in the Windows Program Manager, double-click on the Clipboard icon in the Main program group.

In this chapter, we talk only about using the Clipboard within WordPerfect. Keep in mind, however, that you can also use it to carry text, charts, graphs, pictures, or even — in these days of multimedia — rude noises into and out of WordPerfect (see Chapter 25).

Copying and pasting with the Clipboard

Suppose that you are writing a contract for the Dingelhausen-Schneitzenbaum Furniture Prefabrication Company, and you are oddly averse to typing Dingelhausen-Schneitzenbaum Furniture Prefabrication Company more than once. Copying and pasting saves your fingers and your sanity by letting you make multiple copies of Dingelhausen-Schneitzenbaum Furniture Prefabrication Company all over your contract. (Guess which feature was useful in writing this paragraph?)

To copy some text, follow these steps:

1. Select the text.

2. Press Ctrl+C or choose Edit Copy from the menu bar.

3. Click where you want the new copy.

4. Press Ctrl+V or choose Edit Paste from the menu bar.

Here's some advice for former DOS users: With Windows, unlike in DOS, Ctrl+C no longer yanks the computer by its toenails to say "knock it off" when it misbehaves.

When you press Ctrl+C, WordPerfect copies your selection to the Windows Clipboard. It stays on the Clipboard so that you can paste as many copies as you want. If you were to switch to a Windows spreadsheet program, you could probably copy "Dingelhausen-Schneitzenbaum Furniture Prefabrication Company" there too.

Maximum Occupancy: 1

The Windows Clipboard can contain only one thing at a time. If you copy or cut out something new, the old contents of the Clipboard are wiped out.

Copying between documents with the Clipboard

The Clipboard is particularly useful for copying between documents. Because WordPerfect lets you have more than one document "open" at a time, you can just copy text in document A and paste it in document B. See Chapter 14 for more information about having more than one document open at a time.

Cutting and pasting with the Clipboard

Cutting and pasting isn't much different from copying and pasting. The only difference is that the original selection gets deleted as soon as you cut it.

To cut and paste some text, follow these steps:

1. **Select the text.**

2. **Press Ctrl+X or choose Edit Cut from the menu bar.**

   The selected text vanishes, but a copy is kept on the Clipboard.

3. **Click at the location where you want to paste the text.**

4. **Press Ctrl+V or choose Edit Paste from the menu bar.**

   Just as you do with copying and pasting, you can paste as many copies as you want. Dingelhausen-Schneitzenbaum Furniture Prefabrication Company. Dingelhausen-Schneitzenbaum Furniture Prefabrication Company.

As with copying, if you cut something new, it replaces the old stuff on the Clipboard.

Keyboard skills to last a lifetime

The keyboard commands (Ctrl+X, Ctrl+C, Ctrl+V) used for cutting, copying, and pasting in WordPerfect are used in many other Windows programs. For this reason, it's slightly to your advantage to learn and use these commands rather than the WordPerfect menu commands.

True, these keyboard names are not particularly mnemonic. We keep track of them by remembering that the X, C, and V keys form a little row on the bottom row of the keyboard in this order: cut, copy, and paste.

The QuickMenu approach to Clipboarding

If you have trouble remembering Ctrl+C, Ctrl+X, and Ctrl+V or where the copy, cut, and paste commands are on the menu bar, the QuickMenu is just your cup of (instant) tea. To order from the QuickMenu, follow these steps:

1. **Select something.**

2. **Click the right mouse button.**

   Your mouse pointer must be somewhere in the text area, not on a menu or in the margins. A QuickMenu appears.

3. **Choose Cut, Copy, or Paste (or Delete) from the QuickMenu.**

If you choose Delete from the QuickMenu, WordPerfect deletes the selected text *without* copying it to the Clipboard first.

A handy list of helpful keystrokes

Double-click to select a word.

Triple-click to select a sentence.

Quadruple-click to select a paragraph.

(Or you can select from a QuickMenu by clicking the right mouse button with the mouse pointer in the left margin.)

Press Ctrl+C to copy selected text.

Press Ctrl+X to cut selected text.

Press Ctrl+V to paste selected text.

(Or you can copy, cut, and paste from a Quick Menu by selecting text and then clicking the right mouse button with the mouse pointer in the text area.)

Copying or cutting new stuff wipes out the old stuff on the Clipboard.

The 5th Wave

"THE PRINTER AND DISK DRIVE ARE CONTAINED IN THE HAT. IT'S GREAT FOR KEEPING AN UNCLUTTERED DESK, BUT IT'S HARD GETTING MORE THAN THREE OF US ON AN ELEVATOR AT THE SAME TIME."

Chapter 7

Spelling, Grammar, and the Mighty Thesaurus

● ●

In This Chapter

▶ Checking your spelling

▶ Dealing with real words that WordPerfect doesn't know

▶ Checking your grammar

▶ Counting words and other amusing statistics

▶ Using, the mighty Thesaurus

● ●

*F*rom a word processor called WordPerfect, you of course expect perfect words: perfectly spelled, perfectly chosen, perfectly used words. Indeed, WordPerfect is chock-full of perfectly good, 100 percent genuine words and the rules for using them grammatically. It's all just waiting for you to mess up by writing something.

Go to it! Then humbly submit your results to the Speller, Grammatik, and the Mighty Thesaurus.

Checking Your Spelling

One of the great joys of today's word processing is that you no longer really have to be able to spell. Don't get too excited, though. WordPerfect doesn't know how to spell either.

What WordPerfect does know how to do is check a word against a list to see whether it's there. This list of words is called a "dictionary," even though it's not really a dictionary (it doesn't have any definitions). You won't, for instance, find the definition of omphaloskepsis anywhere within WordPerfect's dictionary. Come to think of it, you probably won't even find the word listed.

Spell-checking your entire document

To check the spelling of words in your entire document, follow these steps:

1. Bring up the Speller dialog box.

Any of the following actions activates the Speller:

- Click on Tools Speller in the main menu bar.

- Press Ctrl+F1.

- Click on the book-with-a-check-mark-on-it icon in the power bar.

- Click on the right mouse button with your cursor located anywhere in the text area of your document. Click on Speller in the QuickMenu that appears.

The Speller dialog box, shown in Figure 7-1, is then displayed.

2. Click on the Start button.

It doesn't matter where you're working in the document — the Speller checks the whole thing from top to bottom. You can change this setting to check just the page, for example, by using the Check command in the Speller menu bar.

If the Speller finds a word that's not in its dictionary, it assumes that the word is spelled wrong. It highlights the word in your document and lists it after Not found: in the dialog box (refer to Figure 7-1).

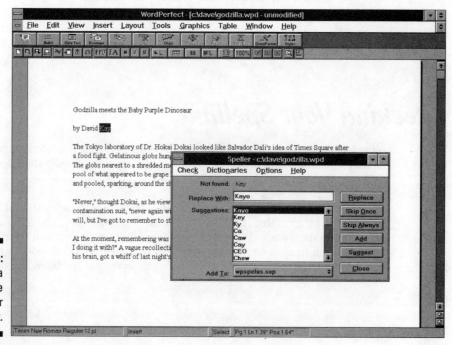

Figure 7-1:
Godzilla
meets the
Speller
dialog box.

In the example, the Speller cannot find the name of this world-famous author in its dictionary. It helpfully lists a variety of suggestions for replacement, ranging from Kayo to Quo, in the Suggestions window. None of these suggestions would satisfy the author's parents.

This sort of thing happens often: you use a person or company name that WordPerfect never heard of, and WordPerfect flags it as misspelled. When it happens, just Skip the word, as described next.

3. Skip or replace the highlighted word in your document.

If the highlighted word is OK, as in the example, you have two options:

- Click on the Skip Once button. This action means "Don't worry about it — get on with the spell checking!"

- Click on Skip Always. This action means the same thing, but it adds "And don't bother me again about this word!" (until the next time you use the Speller).

If you believe that the highlighted word is indeed misspelled, you have three options:

- If you know the correct spelling, just double-click on the Replace With box, type the correct word, and click on the Replace button.

- If the Speller displays the correct spelling in the Replace With box, click on Replace.

- If you're not sure about the correct spelling, scroll through the Suggestions box. If you find the correct spelling, double-click on it. Or guess and type the initial letter; every time you press the key, the Speller places a new suggestion in the Replace With box. Click on Replace to use that suggestion.

4. Repeat the preceding steps for every misspelled word.

WordPerfect continues until every word has been checked. When it is finished, it tells you that the Spell-check is completed and asks you whether you want to close the Speller? Click on Yes, and the Speller goes away. If you choose No, you can leave the Speller box on-screen while you work on your document as usual. If the box is in the way, just click on its top bar and drag it away or click on the downward-pointing triangle in the upper right corner to reduce it to an icon. Double-click on the icon to bring it back when you want it.

Dealing with real words that WordPerfect doesn't know

Perhaps the WordPerfect spell-checker can be forgiven for not knowing names, such as Kay, in our example, or even Godzilla. But it's still annoying to have to repeatedly skip names and other real words unknown to the WordPerfect dictionary.

The solution is to add these words to the Speller's dictionary so that it skips over them every time you use the Speller.

WordPerfect has many dictionaries. It checks at least the following two dictionaries whenever you run the Speller:

 ✔ A "main" dictionary of official, genuine English (or other language) words

 ✔ A "supplementary" dictionary of anything else you consider a word

The speller can also check additional supplementary dictionaries, such as document dictionaries and special-purpose, or topical, dictionaries.

Document dictionaries are specific to each individual document. Our example might have a document dictionary with the name Hokai, for example. Dr. Hokai does not appear in subsequent stories because of a gruesome death by editing. We therefore want WordPerfect to consider the name Hokai to be OK in this document; if it appears in any other document, however, it should be flagged.

Optional special dictionaries also can be created. You create them. You might write about several different topics, for example, each with its own particular jargon. The word *email,* for example, might be intentional when you are writing for programmers, but it would probably be a typo if you were writing for gardeners.

Let's keep it simple and just add words to the basic supplemental dictionary. To add words to the dictionary, start the Speller as you normally do. What? You forgot already? Refer to the first section for details.

When the Speller highlights a word that you consider OK, click on the Add button in the Speller dialog box. This step adds the word to the supplemental dictionary; as far as the Speller is concerned, it's now a real word. The Speller will never bring it up again and sincerely regrets having brought it up in the first place.

Making and unmaking mistakes in your supplemental dictionary

It's easy to go tripping merrily through your document, clicking A<u>d</u>d on every word the Speller flags. Such glibness eventually causes you to add a word such as *klockwurst* to the dictionary. It was supposed to have been *knockwurst,* but you typed it just before quitting time and you were looking at the clock. Now klockwurst is considered a genuine word, so the Speller ignores any subsequent klockwursts.

To correct this situation, you must go deeper into the labyrinthine depths of the Speller than a novice normally goes. Walk this way, please.

1. Click on Dictio<u>n</u>aries in the Speller dialog box's menu bar.

2. Click on <u>S</u>upplementary in the Dictionaries menu.

3. In the Supplementary Dictionaries dialog box that appears, single-click on the word that ends in the letters *sup* (probably WPSPELUS.SUP). Then click on the <u>E</u>dit button in that dialog box.

4. In the Edit dialog box that appears, click on *klockwurst* or whatever your mistake was, in the Key <u>W</u>ords box. Then click on the <u>D</u>elete button. Click on <u>Y</u>es in the confirmation box that appears.

5. Find your way back to the Speller dialog box by clicking on the <u>C</u>lose buttons.

The remainder of this section provides a few other factoids about spell-checking.

To check something less than your entire document, click on Chec<u>k</u> in the Speller's menu bar and then choose <u>W</u>ord, Senten<u>c</u>e, <u>P</u>aragraph, Pa<u>g</u>e, To <u>E</u>nd of Document, or <u>S</u>elected Text. You can also check a specified number of pages from the current insertion point by choosing Number of Pages. Whatever you check remains selected until you put the Speller away again.

Sí usted quería escribir en español or some other language from Afrikaans to Ukrainian, click on <u>D</u>ictionaries in the Speller's menu bar and choose <u>M</u>ain. At the bottom of the Main Dictionaries dialog box that appears, click on <u>L</u>anguage. In the Language dialog box that appears, double-click on the language dictionary of your choice. ¡Que bueno!

The Speller not only checks spelling but also points out common problems, such as duplicated words, words with numbers, and strange capitalization. You can turn these features off if they get in the way. Just click on O<u>p</u>tions in the Speller dialog box to see a checklist of what is turned on or off. Click on a feature to change its on-off status. The Options menu also enables you to turn the document dictionary on or off.

The document dictionary is a useful beast. It can contain all the words that are perfectly fine in the current document but that would be incorrect in other documents. To add words to the document dictionary rather than to the supplemental dictionary, click the arrows at the right edge of the Add To button (in the Speller dialog box) and hold down the mouse button. A dictionary menu appears. While you're still holding down the button, move the cursor to the Document Dictionary selection and release the button. If you don't see the selection listed, click on Options in the menu bar and then on Document Dictionary to turn it on. Now whenever you press the Add button, the high-lighted word goes into the document dictionary.

You can add, delete, or change the way replacement works in your supplementary dictionary. Here's the rush course in how to do it. Choose Dictionaries Supplementary from the Speller dialog box's menu bar. Click on the file ending in .SUP and then on the Edit button. The Edit dialog box is displayed. Click on Add to display the Add Word/Phrase dialog box. Type the word. To give Speller a replacement to suggest, click on Replacement. To add alternatives, click on Alternatives. Type your alternative and then click on Insert to put it in the list. Click on OK and the Close buttons to return to the Speller.

You can also create your own supplemental dictionary for special purposes, clients, or topics. Choose Dictionaries Supplementary and click on Create in the Supplemental Dictionaries dialog box. Invent a name and type it in the next box that appears; press OK when you're finished. You then see the Edit dialog box, discussed in the preceding sidebar, and it works just the same.

Spell-checking is not magic, although the name probably sounds promising if you're a wizard. It does not ensure that the correct word is used. For example, *can't* and *cant* are equally valid to the Speller. For that situation, you need a grammar-checker, which is a perfect segue to the following section.

Checking Your Grammar

First consider which kind of check the dear old gal looks good in — maybe a nice hound's-tooth. Then take her shopping for the day. You both will be glad that you did.

If this plan is impractical for you, you have to settle for the grammar checking that WordPerfect offers, known as Grammatik.

The magic of Grammatik

Unlike the spell-checker, Grammatik *is* magic. Unquestionably. It has digested all the rules that Miss Bower (the English teacher who made everyone sit in alphabetical order and diagram the first sentence of the Gettysburg address) spent her life mastering. Take *that,* Miss Bower! You have been replaced.

As magic as Grammatik is, you probably will want to ignore nine out of ten of its suggestions. Still, it's a fast and thorough proofreader and generally is worth running.

Grammatik is also simple to use. Here's the basic method:

1. **Click on Tools on the main menu bar and then choose Grammatik.**

   Or press Alt+Shift+F1. Or, in the power bar, click on the squinty, little book icon with the letter *G* on it. (It's a fuzzy square with a pink circle, if your eyesight isn't quite up to par.)

   The Grammatik dialog box appears, more or less as shown in Figure 7-2. It reads differently if you alter Grammatik's settings.

   When you first start Grammatik, the advice box contains not advice but information about what Grammatik is going to do. Three lines are displayed, beginning with the words Check, Options, and Style. Here's what these lines mean:

   - The Check: line shown here tells you that Grammatik is about to check the entire document. As with the spell-checker, you can change this setting to have Grammatik check a sentence, paragraph, or whatever by using the Check command on Grammatik's menu bar. Click on Check and select what you want from the menu to change it.

   - The Option line tells you what kinds of optional checking Grammatik is going to do. Later in this chapter, the Technical Stuff sidebar titled "Just what is it that Grammatik does, anyway?" has information about changing these types of checks by using the Options menu selection in the Grammatik dialog box.

   - The Style line tells you the kind of prose Grammatik thinks that you're trying to write. This setting can make the difference in whether Grammatik is useful or annoying to you. The following section provides information about how to change the style of writing Grammatik thinks that you're trying to use.

2. **Click on the Start button.**

   Grammatik now finds fault with your text. Every time. Just like Miss Bower. But now we're grown up and we appreciate the criticism, right?

Errors or suggestions appear in the dialog box window. Grammatik also tells you which "rule class" you have violated or annoyed. It has lots of rules. If you get really peeved, you can turn them off selectively, which is the reason that Grammatik is telling you which one you have triggered. (More about this subject later.)

3. If you disagree with Grammatik or don't care what it thinks, click on Skip.

Grammatik goes on to your next failure.

If you decide that Grammatik is correct and you want to edit your document, just leave the dialog box on-screen. Click anywhere in your document and make your edits. When you finish editing, click on the Resume button that now appears in the dialog box.

4. When you're finished, click on Close.

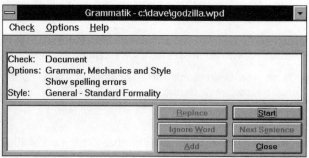

Figure 7-2:
The
Grammatik
dialog box.

Other buttons are used mainly for Grammatik's own spell-checking (not the same as the Speller) and certain word errors. These buttons are explained in this list:

✔ **Replace:** Replaces the highlighted word in your document with the highlighted word in the Grammatik dialog box list

✔ **Ignore Word:** Tells Grammatik to ignore a particular word for the remainder of its proofreading session

✔ **Add:** Enters the word in Grammatik's dictionary

Just what is it that Grammatik does, anyway?

Grammatik can check for three different types of errors: grammar, mechanical, and style.

In the grammar department, Grammatik checks for more than 20 kinds of errors, from proper use of adjectives to incomplete verb forms to subject-verb agreement, subordination, and tense shift. (So *that's* why Miss Bower was always talking about insubordination!)

Grammatik also checks for what it calls *mechanical errors:* capitalization, punctuation, and spelling. Yes, spell-checking is a bit redundant, given the megalithic spell-checker in WordPerfect, but hey — you just can't have too many spell-checkers. (If you disagree, see the following Tip about turning this feature off.)

And then, to frost the gilding on the lily (so to speak), Grammatik also checks for "style" problems. You can turn this feature off by choosing Grammar and Mechanics from Grammatik's Options menu.

It seems inconceivably magic, but the following brief list shows the style problems Grammatik seems to address:

Abbreviation	Overlong shirtsleeves
Archaism	Paragraph problems
Baldness	Passive voice
Clichés	Pejoratives
Colloquialisms	Questionable uses
Commonly confused words	Redundancies
Prepositions at the end of a sentence	Second-person addressing
Foreign words	Sentence variety
Formalisms	Split infinitives
Gender-specificity	Split ends
Improper use of the word *specificity*	Trademarks
Jargon	Vague adverbs
Long sentences	Wordiness
Overstated ideas	

Are you feeling intimidated yet?

Enough spelling, already!

Because WordPerfect already gives you a really nice spell-checker, consider turning off Grammatik's spell-checker. Click on Options in the Grammatik dialog box menu bar and then click on Show spelling errors to turn off the spell-checker. For some reason, Grammatik at this point may warn you that it does not use WordPerfect's supplemental dictionary. If this warning-message window appears, click on its OK button.

The importance of being in style

If you find that Grammatik is a little too severe or even too lax, don't give up on it! It may be just a matter of style. The way Grammatik works "right out of the box" is that it assumes that you want a moderately formal style. (This assumption is the reason that your initial Grammatik dialog box probably says `Style:` `General - Standard Formality`.)

You can select from among ten different predetermined styles, such as Fiction, Journalism, Business Letter, Advertising, or Reports. You can also specify three degrees of formality within each style. You can even create your own style by using rules of your own choosing.

The following steps show you how to select an appropriate style:

1. **Click on Options in the Grammatik dialog box menu bar and then choose** U**nderline**nderline **W**riting Style.

   The Writing Style dialog box appears, as shown in Figure 7-3.

2. **Click on the style most appropriate to what you're writing.**

   Note: Expense reports do not count as Fiction here.

3. **Click on one of the options in the Formality Level box.**

   Don't know what to choose? If you wear a business suit while you write, go for Formal. If you write in your shorts, try Informal. If you wear socks but they don't always match, try Standard.

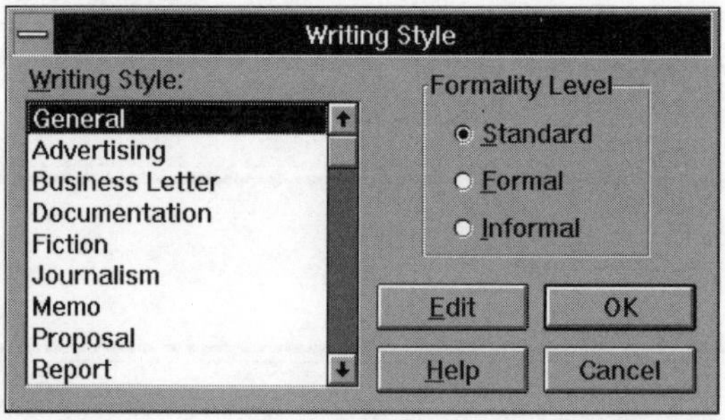

Figure 7-3:
Telling
Grammatik
about your
style.

The Golden Rules

Grammatik performs its magic by applying a variety of preset rules. To see these rules, click on Edit in the Writing Style dialog box. A Writing Style Settings dialog box is displayed, in which you can also change which rules are in effect. Notice that you cannot change an existing style. Your modified style is saved as one of the Custom styles in the style list. You can also edit these styles directly.

The Writing Style Settings dialog box has three separate screens of rules from which you can choose. In the Rule Classes line, pick Style, Grammar, or Mechanical rules. Within each screen, just click on a rule's check box to turn the rule on or off.

Changeable numbers are at the bottom of the dialog box for "how many or how long"-type rules. Click on these numbers and type new numbers, if you want.

Click on Save when you're finished. If you edited one of the named styles, Grammatik can save your new rules only as one of the Custom files. If they have already been defined, a prompt window asks whether it's OK to overwrite the current Custom 1 settings.

Those Checking options

The Options command in the Grammatik menu has these Checking Options (they're not very useful):

✔ **Check for paragraph errors:** This feature looks for too-short paragraphs and bozo typing (where someone—not you, obviously—pressed Enter at the end of every line).

✔ **Ignore periods within words:** You need this feature mostly if you are writing about PC computer stuff, where filenames have periods in the middle.

✔ **Suggest spelling replacements:** Turn this option off if you insist on using the Grammatik speller; it really slows things down. Use the Suggest button instead.

✔ **Start checking immediately:** For those in a hurry.

Word counts and other statistics

Grammatik also provides amusing and occasionally useful statistics about your document. Perhaps the most useful statistic is the word count, particularly if you're a journalist or you frequently write letters to the editor. The other somewhat useful statistic is the Flesch Reading Ease score for readability. A score of 100 indicates "very easy" reading — about grade 4 in the United States; 50-60 is about high-school level, and 0-30 is undergraduate level.

Enable the statistics feature by clicking on Options in the Grammatik menu bar and then on Statistics. Click on the Start button and wait for a report. Notice that Grammatik doesn't do any other grammar checking while it's computing statistics.

To go from statistics checking to regular grammar checking, click on Options in Grammatik's menu bar and then select either Grammar, Mechanics and Style, or Grammar and Mechanics from the bottom of the Options menu.

The Mighty Thesaurus

Although the WordPerfect Thesaurus is not as mighty as the brontosaurus, it is perhaps competitive in intelligence. That is, it does not replace that three-inch-thick thesaurus you have been dragging around since high school. But it's still nice to have around when you're feeling stuck for a word.

The following steps show the quick way to use the Thesaurus:

1. **Highlight in your text the word you want to look up.**

   The easiest way to highlight one word is to double-click on it. The word doesn't have to be completely highlighted — your cursor just has to be inside the word somewhere.

2. **From the main menu bar, choose Tools and then Thesaurus.**

   Or press Alt+F1. Folks with good eyesight may instead use the power bar. Click on the book icon with the blue letter *T* on it. (If your eyes are like ours, look for the fuzzy, bluish square.)

   The Thesaurus dialog box is displayed, as shown in Figure 7-4.

3. **Examine the list of synonyms for your word, shown in the leftmost panel — if the Thesaurus can find your word, that is.**

   Sometimes it substitutes the root word. At other times, you're just out of luck, and the message Word not found appears at the bottom of the window. To try some other word, double-click in the Word area of the dialog box, type a new word, and click on the Look Up button.

   You may also find antonyms listed at the bottom of the synonym list. Scroll down to find out by clicking on the nearby down arrow next to the panel.

4. **Want more synonyms? To see additional related words, double-click on any synonym that has a dot next to it.**

   They appear in the middle panel. You can double-click on any of these words in turn, and more words appear in the rightmost panel. Alternatively, you can click once on a synonym and then on the Look Up button. In this way, the related words appear in the same panel as the selected synonym.

5. **To replace your word with a synonym from the Thesaurus, click on that word and then on the Replace button.**

   The dialog box goes away.

6. **If you don't want to replace your word, click on Close — unless you want to search some other words in your text.**

   If you do, you can leave the Thesaurus dialog box on-screen and double-click on a new word. It appears in the Word box; just click on Look Up to search for synonyms.

Most of the other stuff you can do here is pretty useless.

Figure 7-4:
The word you're looking up appears at the top of a panel of synonyms in the Thesaurus dialog box.

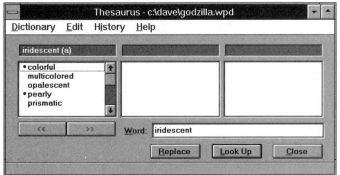

A silly Edit drop-down menu lets you cut and paste and all kinds of weird stuff in the Word box. Ignore it. If you have to edit anything in the Word box, just click your mouse pointer anywhere in it and use the same backspace, delete, and highlighting techniques you would use in your document.

The Dictionary command in the menu bar can also change the Thesaurus file if you happen to have another one kicking around. You probably don't.

A marginally useful Thesaurus command is History, if you're checking several words in one session. Click on this option to go back to looking up words that were used earlier. Just select that word in the History drop-down menu.

The buttons with the chevron-like right arrows and left arrows are supplied in case you exceed the three screenfuls of related words allowed in the Thesaurus dialog box. These buttons let you shift synonym lists into and out of the box. Consider professional psychiatric help if you need this feature.

You can leave the Speller, Grammatik, or Thesaurus dialog box active (on-screen) and return to editing your text. You can grab them by their tops (click on the top bar) and drag out of the way or minimize them to an icon by clicking on the downward-pointing triangle in the upper right corner. Only one of these dialog boxes can be active at a time, though.

Lots of fancy tricks are possible with the Supplemental Dictionary feature of the spell-checker, but it's too easy to get confused. Experiment with these tricks only when you are more familiar with WordPerfect.

If the spell-checker and Grammatik seem too annoying, you probably should customize them a little. In the spell-checker, add some words to the supplemental dictionary. In Grammatik, try a different Style.

You can restrict the activity of any of these tools to a sentence, paragraph, or page if you want, to save time in large documents.

Part II

Prettying Up Your Text

Bob, the laser printer repairman, finds an idle moment that costs him his sideburns.

In this part...

So far, so good. If you are comfortable with the techniques discussed in Part I (or if you skipped over it completely), you can make documents, edit them, save them, spell-check them, and print them. More or less.

But how do they look? Stand back a little and ask yourself, "Am I getting my money's worth from this program? Do these documents look like a million bucks?" (Or at least as much as you paid for your computer and WordPerfect.)

If the answer is No, this part of the book is for you. We talk about how to jazz up, tighten up, and spruce up your documents, including how to use different typefaces, control your margins, set the spacing between paragraphs, and all that good stuff. After all, you don't want your carefully worded documents to come out looking as though you typed them on your old Selectric!

Chapter 8
Charming Characters

. . . .

In This Chapter

▶ Making text boldfaced

▶ Underlining text

▶ Using italics

▶ Making text bigger or smaller

▶ Using different fonts

▶ Getting text back to normal

▶ Copying character formatting

▶ Changing capitalization

. . . .

*W*ordPerfect lets you control the way individual characters look — not where they are on the page, but their size and shape. By "characters," we mean the letters, numbers, and punctuation that make up your text (we are not talking about people like the strange guy next door, who has 47 cats and sings opera while gardening). In addition to using underlining, boldface, and italics to add emphasis to your text, you can choose different typefaces and type sizes. In fact, the range of choices can be overwhelming.

The good news about WordPerfect for Windows is that you can see all these special effects right on the screen. Unlike old-fashioned word processors (the ones that ran under DOS), the new WordPerfect draws each character (with help from Windows) and can draw them in all their formatted splendor.

The bad news is that it is easy to get carried away with character formatting. Nothing is more amateurish or harder to read than a letter or memo that uses five typefaces on one page — readers spend all their **time** *shading* their eyes from the *glare* of all that SNAZZY formatting and don't have time to <u>absorb</u> the import of the text. So watch out when you're formatting text! Use a little restraint, people!

Emphasizing Text with Boldface, Italics, and Underlining

Let's start with the easiest way to add emphasis to your text. **Boldface**, *italics*, and <u>underlining</u> are three methods of making a word or phrase stand out and make itself known. These methods are called *text styles* in WordPerfect-ese.

All you have to do is follow these steps to use boldface, underlining, or italics to your text (not all three at the same time, please!):

1. **Select the text you want to emphasize.**

   Chapter 6 shows you ways to select text.

2. **Click on the Bold Font, Italic Font, or Underline Font button on the power bar.**

   If you haven't guessed, these buttons have the bold **B**, italics *I,* and underlined <u>U</u> on them. Alternatively, press Ctrl+B for bold, Ctrl+I for italics, or Ctrl+U for underlining. Hey, we can even remember *these* key combinations!

   WordPerfect displays the selected text in the font style you chose. Done!

When you use these text styles, WordPerfect inserts secret formatting codes before and after the formatted text. The first code turns the formatting on, and the second code turns it off. The names of these secret codes are Bold, Italc, and Und. (Hey, like we always say, why make these code names readable when you can make them cryptic and hard to spell?). To see, move, and delete these secret formatting codes, see Chapter 11.

Formatting as you type

You can also add text styles to your text as you type it. If you are about to type a word that you want to emphasize, follow these steps:

1. **Click on the Bold Font, Italic Font, or Underline Font button on the power bar or press Ctrl+B, Ctrl+I, or Ctrl+U.**

   This step turns the formatting on so that whatever you type is formatted this way.

2. **Type the text you want emphasized.**

   It appears with the formatting you chose.

3. **Turn off the formatting by clicking the same button or pressing the same key as you used in step 1.**

You can tell when one of these formats is turned on by looking at the status bar. Unless you (or someone else working on your computer) have fooled with the status bar, its leftmost item is the font (typeface) and size of the text you are typing or looking at. The status bar might say `Times New Roman 12 pt`, for example, which indicates that the font in use is called Times New Roman and that the type size is 12 points. (We describe fonts and sizes in more detail later in this chapter.) The font name is shown in boldface, italics, or underlining if one of these formats is turned on.

Yikes! Getting rid of formatting

If you have gone a little overboard with formatting, WordPerfect can turn it off again. Follow these steps:

1. **Select the text you want to unformat.**

2. **Look up at the power bar; you can see that the relevant text style button looks as though it is pressed.**

   If all the text you selected is bold, for example, the Bold Font button looks as though it's pressed in.

3. **Click on the pressed button.**

   This step should "release" the button so that it isn't pressed anymore, and the formatting should disappear. If one click doesn't do the trick, click it again.

   Here's an alternative step 3: Press the equivalent key combination (Ctrl+B,Ctrl+I, or Ctrl+U) to remove the formatting for the selected text.

You can use more than one type of formatting at the same time. You can make text both *bold and italics,* for example. Just click on both the Bold Font and Italic Font buttons (one at a time, please) on the power bar or press Ctrl+B and then Ctrl+I. Ditto to turn the formatting off.

When you format characters, WordPerfect inserts secret codes in your document to tell it where to turn the formatting on and off. If you have trouble removing formatting or getting it to format the right text, see Chapter 11 to learn how to see and delete these secret codes.

Making Text Larger or Smaller

Sometimes you want to make your text big, big, big. For a headline or the title of a report, maybe you want to make a nice, big, centered title. We discuss centering in the next chapter, but, for now, these steps show you how to make the text big:

1. **Select the text whose size you want to change.**

2. Click on the Font Size button on the power bar.

It's the button with the big A on it, with little arrows that indicate its height.

A little menu of font sizes drops down from the button and shows the available sizes. The sizes that are listed depend on which fonts Windows knows about. (We talk about fonts later in this chapter.)

3. Pick a size by clicking on it.

You can also set text back to its original size. Just select it again, press the Font Size button again, and select the same size you used for the surrounding text.

What size is the text you're already using? Take a look at the status line to see — the leftmost information on the status line usually tells you the font name (Courier, for example) and the size (10 pt, for 10 points, for example).

Depending on which font you are using, text looks larger or smaller. For example, 10-point Arial looks much larger than 10 point Times Roman. Luckily, you can see how things look on-screen and make adjustments as necessary. (We talk about fonts next, for those of you who think that Arial is The Little Mermaid.)

It's a rare situation that calls for type less than 7 points high. Have pity on us aging readers and don't make your type too small.

If you plan to fax your document, make the text a little larger than usual, maybe 11 points. Faxes always look grainy, so they are much more readable if the type is large.

When you change the font size of some text, WordPerfect inserts secret codes named — amazingly enough — Font Size.

What are these sizes measured in?

Text sizes are measured in *points,* an old-fashioned term that predates not only word processors and computers but also typewriters. Most normal text is either 10 or 12 points high. There are 72 points to an inch, so 12-point text is ⅙th of an inch high (¹²⁄₇₂nds). If you want to make a title, make it 14 or 18 points.

Don't ask us why they are called points — the Encyclopedia Britannica probably knows.

Fonts of Wisdom

OK, OK — bad pun. We won't let it happen again. Anyway, it's time to talk about the heart of character formatting — the font, which is a fancy word for typeface. (Or is it the other way around?) A *font* is a set of shapes for letters, numbers, and punctuation. The text you are reading at this moment, for example, is printed in a font called Cheltenham. The headlines are printed in the *Cascade* font.

When WordPerfect starts up, it usually displays and prints everything in a fairly nice-looking font called something like Times Roman. This font is based on the typeface that *The Times of London* designed eons ago for its newspaper design.

You can vastly improve the look of your documents by using a nicer-looking font. The following two sections show you how.

Changing the font for some text

To change the font in which some text appears, follow these steps:

1. **Select the text you want to appear in a different font.**

2. **Click on the Font Face button on the power bar (the one with three different *F*s).**

    (Font Face? People say "font" or "typeface," but "Font Face" is a new one on us.) A list of available fonts drops down from the button.

3. **Choose a font from the list.**

Not just another pretty face

You can install lots of fonts for use with Windows and WordPerfect. Some have little doo hickeys (called *serifs*) at the end of the lines that make up the letters — look at the top of the capital letters in the preceding steps. These fonts are called, not surprisingly, *serif fonts.* Other fonts don't have these little lines (check out the *j* and the *a* in the heading of this sidebar) and are called *sans serif fonts* (it makes perfect sense in French). In some fonts all the letters are the same width (*fixed-space fonts*), and in others, such as the one you are reading, some letters are wider than others (they are called *proportionally spaced fonts*).

The most popular fonts for PCs are Times Roman, a serif font that looks like an uglier version of the body text in this book; Helvetica, a modern-looking sans serif font; and Courier, which looks like the type on an old-fashioned typewriter. Because some font names are trademarks, however, your versions of these fonts may have other names: Times Roman may be called Tms Roman or Times New Roman, and Helvetica may be named Arial or Swiss (it makes perfect sense in Latin).

The selected text changes into the new font — poof! The status bar may not show it immediately, but if you move the cursor to the section of text you just formatted, the status bar shows the font and font size in which it is displayed.

When you change the font for some text, WordPerfect inserts two secret formatting codes, one at the beginning and the other at the end of the text you formatted. The first code changes the font, and the second one changes it back. All very logical. Even the name of the code is logical: Font.

Changing the font for the rest of the document

If you want to change fonts part of the way through a document, you can tell WordPerfect that, from this point forward, another font should appear. Follow these steps:

1. **Move your cursor to the location at which you want to use a new font.**

   If you want all the pages starting with page 2 to use a different font, for example, move your cursor to the top of page 2.

2. **Click the Font Face button on the power bar.**

   A list of available fonts drops down from the button.

3. **Choose a font from the list.**

   The font name in the status bar changes to the new font, and the text that comes after the cursor changes to the new font.

Choosing a font from the Font Face list may not change the font for the entire remaining part of the document. It inserts a secret code that tells WordPerfect to change the font at this point, and this change stays in effect until the *next* secret font change code, if another one is in the document. See Chapter 11 to learn how to find and eliminate any secret formatting codes you don't want.

You can use the same method to select a font at the beginning of the document by moving your cursor to the top of the document and using the Font Face button. But a better way exists, which is described in the next section.

TECHNICAL STUFF

Where do fonts live?

If you use Windows version 3.1, and most people do, it includes a built-in font handler called *TrueType.* TrueType keeps track of which fonts are available to you. It is in charge of both *screen fonts,* the characters that Windows and WordPerfect display on the screen, and *printer fonts,* the characters your printer prints. After all, if you want WordPerfect to show you on-screen exactly how your document will look when it's printed, the fonts must match. TrueType also provides *scalable fonts,* which means that you can use its fonts in almost any point size, from teeny-weeny (4 points) to truly gigrondous (72 points).

Before TrueType, other font-handling programs were available, most notably a program named Adobe Type Manager (ATM, for short). If you use Windows 3.1, TrueType usually runs automatically. Your computer may also have ATM and some of its fonts. With luck, a computer guru is available to set this stuff up.

Each font is a collection of information about the size and shape of every single letter, number, and punctuation mark on the keyboard, in addition to some international characters that don't appear on any key. Using TrueType, this information is stored in disk files, at least two for each font, usually stored in your \WINDOWS\SYSTEM directory. The TrueType font files have the extension .TTF, and the files in which Windows stores additional information about the font have the extension .FOT. Many fonts have a font file for the normal font, a file for the font in boldface, one for the font in italics, one for the font underlined, one

for the font bold *and* italicized — you name it. These font files can take up a tremendous amount of space on your disk. We have 28 fonts installed — a lot, admittedly — which take up a whopping 24 MB of disk space.

When you look at the list of available fonts displayed by the Font Face button (or on the Font dialog box, described later in this chapter), you can tell which fonts are which. TrueType fonts are listed with a little double-T logo before the name.

Fonts can live in one other place — in your printer. All printers know how to print at least one font by themselves, usually ugly, old Courier. Some printers come with several built-in fonts, and some have dozens. On WordPerfect's font list, printer fonts appear with a little picture of a printer before the name (it's supposed to be a printer, but it looks more like a tiny TV with static on the screen). But what do you see on-screen when you use a font that lives in your printer? Windows does its best to select a screen font that looks like your printer font, although the match may not be perfect.

What should you do if you need fonts that don't appear on the font list? What if your boss requires reports to be in Letter Gothic, which you have never heard of? You can buy additional fonts, usually in groups with such cutesy names as "fontpaks." You may want to think about bribing a computer guru into helping you buy a package of fonts that are compatible with your system (TrueType or ATM) and installing them on your system.

The Master Control Panel for Character Formats

So far, you have seen three facets of character formatting: text styles (boldface, italics, and underlining), font sizes, and fonts. Wouldn't it be nice to see and change them in one unified display, a place in which you can set all three types of formatting at one time?

Done. We have said the magic word. Such a thing exists: the Font dialog box (shown in Figure 8-1). The easiest way to see it is to press the F9 key.

If you're not in a hurry, you can also choose Layout Font from the menu bar. Another slow way to see this dialog box is to use the text QuickMenu: position the mouse pointer anywhere in your text, press the right mouse button to display the QuickMenu, and choose Font from it.

Using the options in the Font dialog box

This big mother of a dialog box contains all the character formatting you have seen so far and more. This section describes the types of formatting you can do with it.

To select the font (typeface), choose a font from the Font Face list, which is the same list of fonts you get with the Font Face button on the power bar.

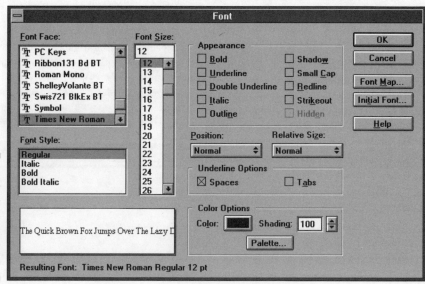

Figure 8-1:
All your character formatting is shown in one easy dialog box.

In the lower left corner of the Font dialog box, a box contains sample text about that quick brown fox that jumps over the lazy dog. (Are these folks original!) As you choose character formats in the dialog box, WordPerfect formats this text accordingly so that you can see how your text will look.

To set the font size (in points), choose a size from the Font Size list, which is the same list of sizes you get with the Font Size button in the power bar.

If you want boldfaced, italicized, or underlined characters, first select the font from the Font Face list. Then look at the Font Style list, which shows you the combinations of bold, italics, and underlining WordPerfect can display and print in a high-quality manner. For these combinations, Windows has stored letter shapes in a font file (see the preceding sidebar, titled "Where do fonts live?", for technical information about this subject). If you see the combination you want, choose it. If not, look over in the Appearance section of the dialog box and click on the Bold, Underline, or Italic options there so that little Xs appear in the boxes for the options you want.

Even though Windows may not know the proper shapes of letters in these font styles, it is willing to try to fake it — it fakes boldface by adding some extra ink, italics by slanting everything forward, and underlining by — what else? — drawing a line. The quality is substandard for typeface aficionados, but it's probably fine for everyone else.

If you want to use additional font styles we haven't talked about yet, check out the other options in the Appearance part of the dialog box. You can choose Double Underline, Outline, Shadow, Small Cap, Redline, Strikeout, and Hidden; see Table 8-1 for samples of all these styles. (Table 8-1 doesn't show hidden text because it's invisible when it's printed.)

Table 8-1	Font Styles and Examples
Character format	*Sample text*
Boldface	This **coffee** tastes like sludge!
Underline	This <u>coffee</u> tastes like sludge!
Double underline	This coffee tastes like sludge!
Italics	This *coffee* tastes like sludge!
Outline	This coffee tastes like sludge!
Shadow	This coffee tastes like sludge!
Small caps	This COFFEE tastes like sludge!
Redline	This coffee tastes like sludge!
Strikeout	This ~~coffee~~ tastes like sludge!

Scientific types who want to create a subscript or superscript should use the Position setting. Click on the setting button, which is usually Normal, and hold down the mouse button. WordPerfect displays a small pop-up list of your choices: Superscript, Normal, and Subscript. While continuing to hold down the mouse button, move the mouse up or down to highlight your choice and then release the mouse button. The Position setting then displays the choice you made. It's a tricky maneuver, but it works.

If you are underlining words and you have strong opinions about underlining spaces and tabs, you can tell WordPerfect about them by using Underline Options in the Font dialog box. You can select Spaces, Tabs, or neither. Normally, only Spaces is selected, but you can change this setting by clicking on the boxes for these options.

When you have selected just the right formatting, click on OK or press Enter to exit from the Font dialog box. In the following section, we tell you what text you just formatted.

If you want to forget the whole thing, click on Cancel or press Esc to escape from the Font dialog box with your text unscathed.

When you use the Font dialog box, WordPerfect sticks the appropriate secret formatting codes into your document. To get rid of them, you may have to refer to Chapter 11.

Knowing when to use the Font dialog box

You can use this colossus of a dialog box to format text. This list shows you the two ways you can use:

- ✔ To format text you have already typed, select the text and then use the Font dialog box. WordPerfect inserts two secret formatting codes, one at the beginning of the selection to turn formatting on and the other at the end of the selection to return formatting to normal.

- ✔ To format the rest of the text in the document, position your cursor at the point where you want the font to change and then use the Font dialog box. WordPerfect inserts just one formatting code, at your cursor location.

Formatting the entire document

What if you want to tell WordPerfect which font to use for the entire document, from soup to nuts? Every document has a *document initial font*, which is the font that WordPerfect uses for all text except where you specifically tell it otherwise. It uses this font not only for the regular text in the document but also for page headers and footers (described in Chapter 10) and for footnotes.

To set the document initial font, you use the Document Initial Font dialog box, as shown in these steps. It doesn't matter where your cursor is when you perform this little operation. Make sure that no text is selected.

1. Choose Layout Document Initial Font from the menu bar.

That is, choose Layout from the menu bar, choose Document from the Layout menu, and then choose Initial Font from the submenu. (Whew!) Alternatively, you can press F9 to see the Font dialog box and then choose the Initial Font button.

WordPerfect displays the Document Initial Font dialog box, as shown in Figure 8-2.

2. Select the Font Face, Font Size, and Font Style.

The settings on this dialog box look and act like the ones in the left half of the Font dialog box.

3. Click on OK or press Enter to exit from the dialog box.

WordPerfect changes the font for all the text in the document, except where you have formatted a section of text by using the Font dialog box or the Font Face and Font Size buttons on the power bar.

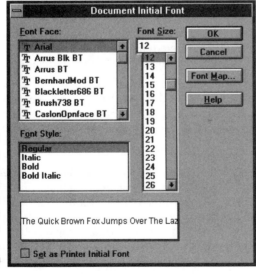

Figure 8-2:
Telling
WordPerfect
the font to
use for the
entire
document.

Copying Character Formatting

After you have formatted some text the way you want it, you can tell WordPerfect to format some other text the same way. Very useful! WordPerfect calls this feature QuickFormat. These steps show you how to use it:

1. **Select some text that is nicely formatted.**

2. **To turn QuickFormat on, choose the Layout QuickFormat command.**

   Alternatively, your button bar may include a button called QuickFormat — if so, click on it. Yet another way to turn QuickFormat on is by using a QuickMenu. (This discussion is getting a little too Quick for us.) With the mouse pointer pointing to your text, click the *right* mouse button to display the QuickMenu and then choose QuickFormat from it.

   The mouse pointer turns into the strangest-looking gizmo we have ever seen — it's a little I-bar insertion point with a little paint roller next to it. We guess that WordPerfect wants to suggest that it will "paint over" any text with the new format.

3. **Select the text to which you want to copy the formatting.**

   As soon as you select the text, it is instantly formatted. Very speedy!

   The mouse pointer still has that strange shape. How the heck do you turn this thing off?

   To turn QuickFormat off, choose Layout QuickFormat from the menu again. Alternatively, just type something. Or use the QuickMenu gambit described in step 2. In any event, the cursor returns to its normal pointy self.

   You can use QuickFormat to get rid of formatting too. Select some unformatted text, choose Layout QuickFormat, and select some text you wish that you hadn't formatted. WordPerfect removes the formatting from the text.

You may ask, "What happens if no text is selected when I turn QuickFormat on? It's just the kind of question an astute, inquiring mind such as yours *would* ask! Here's what happens: WordPerfect assumes that you want to format some other text based on the way the characters around your cursor look. It displays a small dialog box asking whether you want to format some text by using the current fonts and attributes, paragraph styles (described in Chapter 9), or both. When you choose OK, QuickFormat is on — carry on, beginning at step 3 in the preceding set of steps.

Changing Capitalization

dON'T yOU hATE iT wHEN yOU pRESS tHE cAPS lOCK kEY bY mISTAKE? We do. It's easy to type merrily along, hardly looking at the screen, until you see what you have done. Oops. In this situation, WordPerfect is your kind, thoughtful friend; it can fix the capitalization of text you have already typed. Technology to the rescue!

To change some text into all capital letters, all small letters, or even All Small Letters Except For The First Letter Of Each Word, follow these steps:

1. **Select the text you want to fool with.**

2. **Choose the Edit Convert Case command from the menu.**

   WordPerfect gives you three choices: Lowercase, Uppercase, and Initial Capitals. Cool!

3. **Choose one.**

   WordPerfect changes the text as requested. The text remains selected, in case you want to do anything else with it.

You can use these commands only if you have selected some text. Otherwise, they are unavailable and appear in gray on the menu.

The Initial Capitals option isn't smart enough to know exactly which words to capitalize in a title or a name. After you use it, you probably will have to go back and make a few changes, to uncapitalize (smallize?) the first letters of prepositions, articles, and all those other types of words you learned about in third grade.

Chapter 9

Sexy Sentences and Pretty Paragraphs

• •

In This Chapter

▶ Using the ruler bar

▶ Setting margins

▶ Centering text

▶ Pushing text over to the right margin

▶ Hyphenating or not hyphenating

▶ Playing with tabs

▶ Indenting text

▶ Changing the justification

▶ Changing the line spacing and the spacing between paragraphs

• •

*I*n the last chapter, you found out how to use all kinds of spiffy-looking character formatting so that your documents look much more professional. But wait — what about fooling around with margins, centering, indenting, and line spacing? That's what this chapter is all about.

Margins and spacing are extremely important because they can make your documents look much longer or shorter than they really are. Suppose that you are a student with an assignment to write a ten-page paper. With schedules and priorities being what they are, however, not to mention movies and pizza bashes, you have had time to write only seven pages.

Not a problem! Widen those margins! Pad that line spacing! Add a little white space to your prose. You can inflate it like a hot-air balloon. (We are not suggesting any similarity to your prose, of course!)

We can also address the opposite problem — packing it in. What if your boss reads only one-page memos, but you have a great deal of detail to include?

Word processing to the rescue! Shave those margins, tighten that spacing, and maybe even shrink the font size a tad. You can squash it all in. If it still doesn't fit, just remove all the adjectives and adverbs — that's what we do.

Let's look at how to mess around with margins, tabs, and justification, which WordPerfect calls the *line formatting* of your text. Let's also look at controlling the space between lines and paragraphs and indenting the beginning of paragraphs — the *paragraph formatting*.

Using the Ruler Bar

The first thing you do is display the WordPerfect ruler bar, if it is not already on-screen. If you don't see a horizontal strip just below the power bar, marked off in inches (or centimeters, for you jet-setters), choose <u>V</u>iew from the menu bar and then choose <u>R</u>uler Bar from the drop-down menu. The ruler bar appears (see Figure 9-1).

Figure 9-1:
The ruler bar shows all your margins and tabs as little triangles.

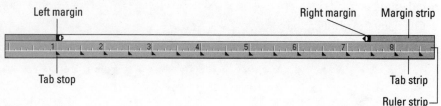

The ruler bar shows you the margins and tabs that are in effect in your document at the point where your cursor is located. When you change settings on the ruler bar, WordPerfect inserts the appropriate codes in your document. No information is really *stored* in, on, or around the ruler bar; it's just a nice graphical display of the state of your document. When you open another document, the stuff on the ruler bar changes to reflect the settings in the new document.

The <u>V</u>iew <u>R</u>uler Bar command makes the ruler bar disappear if it is already on-screen. Another way to display the ruler bar, for those with their hands glued to the keyboard and memories like elephants, is to press Alt+Shift+F3.

What are all those little triangles?

The ruler bar packs a great deal of information about margins and tabs into a small space. It is made up of the following three gray strips:

- **The margin strip:** A thin strip above the ruler that shows you the margins. The rounded ends of the lighter part of this strip show the positions of the left and right margins. The dark gray parts at the left and right ends of this strip are outside the margins. Just within the margins are little triangles that show the position of paragraph format margins, which are separate margins you can set for each paragraph. (You probably won't need them; instead, see the section "Changing margins for a paragraph or two," later in this chapter.)

- **The ruler:** Marked off in eighths of inches. You can also tell WordPerfect to display the ruler bar all the time.

- **The tab strip:** A gray strip below the ruler which contains little triangles that point in various directions. The triangles show the positions of your tab stops. A *tab stop* is the position across the line where the cursor moves when you press the Tab key.

What's the ruler bar for?

The ruler bar shows you the margin and tab settings that are in effect wherever your cursor is right now (not your mouse pointer — the pointy arrow thing — but your cursor, the blinking, black, vertical line). You can set the margins, tabs, and other line formatting at the beginning of your document, and you can change them partway through a document. If you want to include a long quotation in an article you are writing, for example, you can indent just the paragraphs that make up the quotation.

In addition to showing you the current positions of margins and tabs, the ruler bar can change them. That is, you can use the mouse to drag the little gizmos and triangles around on the screen. In the rest of this chapter, we usually tell you (at least) two ways to do each formatting task: one by using a menu or pressing a key and the other by using the ruler bar. You can decide which method you prefer; WordPerfect doesn't care which one you use.

Setting Margins

Margin Change

As you may recall from high school typing class, the left, right, top, and bottom margins control how much blank space to leave along the edges of the paper. Normally, everything you type appears within these margins. The purpose of margins, of course, is to provide white space in which your reader can doodle while staring off into space. WordPerfect usually sets the left, right, top, and bottom margins to one inch, which is quite generous. You may want to make them smaller.

Using the Margins dialog box

These steps show you how to set the margins in your document:

1. **Move your cursor to the tippy-top of the document.**

   The quickest way to do this is to press Ctrl+Home.

2. **Choose Layout from the menu bar and then choose Margins.**

   This step displays the Margins dialog box, as shown in Figure 9-2.

3. **Enter measurements in the Left, Right, Top, and Bottom boxes in the dialog box.**

   You can type numbers or you can click on the little upward- or downward-pointing arrows to the right of each box to increase or decrease the numbers by one-tenth of an inch per click. As you change the measurements, WordPerfect changes the margins on the little page diagram in the dialog box so that you can see the effect you will achieve.

4. **To change the margins to the measurements you entered, press Enter or click on OK.**

   Or to forget the whole thing, press Esc or click on Cancel.

Another way to display the Margins dialog box is to press Ctrl+F8.

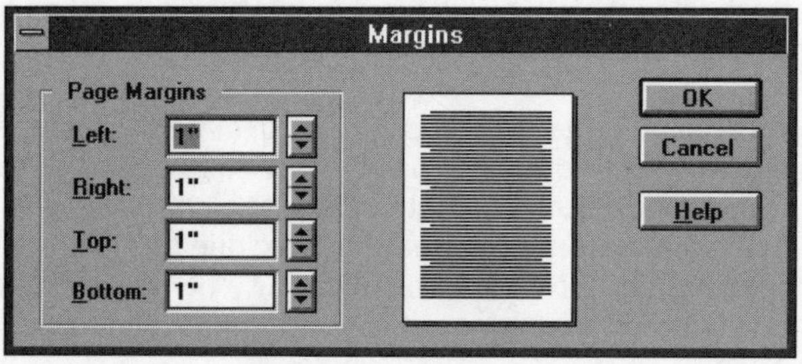

Figure 9-2:
Setting the margins for your document.

	Margins
Page Margins	OK
Left: 1"	Cancel
Right: 1"	Help
Top: 1"	
Bottom: 1"	

Still another way to see the Margins dialog box is to move the mouse pointer to the margin strip or the ruler strip on the ruler bar. Then click the right mouse button to display the ruler bar QuickMenu and choose Margins from it.

Aha! One more way to see the Margins dialog box: double-click on the margin strip on the ruler bar. That's it. No more ways.

When you set the margins, WordPerfect inserts invisible, secret formatting codes that contain the new margin information. The names of the codes are Lft Mar and Rgt Mar. (WordPerfect code names are always cryptic and strange — otherwise, they wouldn't be exciting and secret!) See Chapter 11 to learn how to see these secret codes and delete them, if necessary.

Learning how to use the ruler bar

You can also set the left and right margins by using the ruler bar (not the top and bottom margins, though). Rather than type boring, precise numbers in an intimidating dialog box, you can drag little gizmos around on the margin strip on the ruler bar.

Try these steps to set the left margin:

1. **Move your cursor to the beginning of the document.**

2. **Use the mouse to point to the leftmost speck of light gray on the margin strip of the ruler bar or even a little bit to its left.**

   The idea is to grab the left margin, not those two little triangles that indicate paragraph margins.

3. **Hold down the left mouse button.**

   A vertical dotted line appears along the left edge of the document to show you where the left margin is.

4. **Don't let go of the mouse button! While you're still holding it down, drag the left margin left or right to where you want it.**

   You can refer to the ruler to determine the proper position.

5. **Release the mouse button to drop the margin into position.**

   WordPerfect moves the text of the document to the left to match the new left margin.

Call us old-fashioned, but by the time we're finished with that little maneuver, it's time for lunch. We would rather just use the nice, safe dialog box. But feel free to suit yourself.

Changing the margins for the rest of the document

You can change the margins partway through your document, which is useful if your document contains more than one distinct part (such as an executive summary followed by a detailed proposal). You can use different margins for the different parts of the document. (OK, we're reaching for an example here, but it sounded plausible.)

To change the margins for the rest of the document, follow these steps:

1. **Move the cursor to the position where you want the margins to change.**

   This position is usually at the top of a page, but it doesn't have to be.

2. **Display the Margins dialog box.**

   That is, choose <u>L</u>ayout <u>M</u>argins from the menu or press Ctrl+F8.

3. **Fill in the margin measurements you want.**

4. **Click on OK or press Enter.**

   The dialog box goes away.

These steps show you how to do the same thing with the mouse and the ruler bar:

1. **Move the cursor to the point where you want the margins to change.**

2. **Use the mouse to drag the left or right margin indicator on the ruler bar to the left or right, to the position where you want the new margin.**

   When you release the mouse button, the new margin stays where you put it.

If you changed the left or right margins, WordPerfect changes them beginning with the line your cursor is on. If you changed the top or bottom margins, which you cannot do with the ruler bar, WordPerfect changes them beginning with the following page (not this page). See Chapter 10 for information about page formatting, including top and bottom margins.

Changing margins for a paragraph or two

When you use paragraph formatting, you can specify special margins for one or two paragraphs. If you include long quotations in your text, for example, to impress people with your erudition, you may want the quotations to be indented more than the rest of your prose. WordPerfect provides three separate features for accomplishing this task, but we figure that you probably have more urgent things to do than to learn all of them.

Our favorite way to change the margins for one or more paragraphs is to indent them, as shown in these steps:

1. **Move your cursor to the beginning of the paragraph you want to indent.**

2. **Choose <u>L</u>ayout P<u>a</u>ragraph <u>I</u>ndent from the menu or just press F7.**

   If you see on your button bar a button labeled Indent, you can click on it too.

   WordPerfect inserts an invisible, secret indent code, and the left margin of the paragraph moves to the right by one tab stop (you can read more about tab stops later in this chapter).

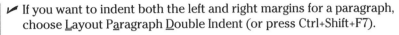

WordPerfect also provides the following useful variations:

- ✔ If you want to indent both the left and right margins for a paragraph, choose Layout Paragraph Double Indent (or press Ctrl+Shift+F7).

- ✔ If you want to create a hanging indent, WordPerfect can do that too. With a *hanging indent,* the first line of the paragraph is not indented, but the rest of the lines are. Choose Layout Paragraph Hanging Indent (or press Ctrl+F7) at the beginning of the paragraph.

- ✔ If you want to indent several paragraphs, you have to indent each one individually. WordPerfect inserts a secret indent code for each one.

- ✔ An indent code indents the paragraph one tab stop. To control how far your paragraph is indented, you can move your tab stops. See the section "Playing with Tab Stops," later in this chapter.

WordPerfect, as usual, inserts a secret format code to record your request to indent the paragraph. The name of the regular code is, believe it or not, Hd Left Ind. The double indent code is Hd Left/Right Ind (which has a certain logic to it). To achieve a hanging indent, WordPerfect inserts two codes: Hd Left Ind and Hd Back Tab. See Chapter 11 to learn how to see and delete these secret codes.

Centering Text

One of the most annoying typing tasks on a regular typewriter is centering text. Do you remember the bad ol' days, in which you had to count the number of letters on the line, press Tab to move over to the middle of the page, and then press Backspace to move backward half that number of times? The memory really makes you appreciate modern technology.

In WordPerfect, centering text is simplicity itself. With your cursor at the beginning of the line you want to center, choose Layout Line Center from the menu. Even simpler, just press Shift+F7. The line leaps to the center of the page.

You can center text that is more than one line long. To center several lines (a title and a subtitle, for example), you can select both lines of text and then press Shift+F7 or choose Layout Line Center.

You can even center a multiple-line paragraph. When you select the entire paragraph and press Shift+F7, all the lines in the paragraph are centered. It looks a little funny, though, except on wedding invitations or graduation diplomas.

WordPerfect's secret formatting code to center a line is Hd Center on Marg. See Chapter 11 for details about formatting codes.

Pushing Text over to the Right Margin

This little operation of pushing text over to the right margin, called *flush right* by typesetters, typing teachers, and small children undergoing potty training, is also a pain to do on a typewriter and extremely easy to do with WordPerfect.

If you want to make an entire line snuggle up to the right margin, follow these steps:

1. **Move your cursor to the beginning of the line.**

2. **Choose Layout Line Flush Right from the menu bar.**

   Or just press Alt+F7.

   The entire line leaps rightward.

You can also move just the rightmost part of a line to the right margin. Your document must include a line, for example, that says Draft over at the left margin and Top Secret at the right margin. Type all the text on one line and then do the following:

1. **Move your cursor to the beginning of the text you want to be flush right.**

   For example, position it just before the T in Top Secret.

2. **Choose Layout Line Flush Right (or press Alt+F7).**

   The text to the left of your cursor stays put and the text to the right moves to the right margin.

When you use this command, WordPerfect inserts another secret code. See Chapter 11 if you want to get rid of it.

WordPerfect's secret formatting code for flush right is Hd Flush Right. See Chapter 11 for details about secret codes.

Printing today's date

Everyone's favorite thing to print flush right is today's date at the beginning of a letter. WordPerfect not only can print the date over at the right margin, but it can also even provide the date! Follow these steps:

1. **Move your cursor to the beginning of the letter in which you want the date to appear.**

   It should be after your letterhead and before the address to which you are sending the letter.

2. **Press Alt+F7 to make the line flush right.**

3. **Press Ctrl+D to insert today's date.**

   Wow! Betcha didn't know that it would be that easy! If your button bar has a Date Text button on it, you can also click it to insert the date.

If WordPerfect inserts the wrong date or if you want to know about other nifty things the program can insert, see Chapter 11.

Changing the Justification

Justification is a serious-sounding word, one that makes us think of moral imperatives, rationales for our actions, and other philosophical stuff. What a disappointment when we learn that it has to do with sticking spaces into lines of text. Such is life.

In word processing and typesetting, as you may already know, justification deals with the moral problem of different lines of text being different lengths. If we could just write so that every line in our document had the same number of characters on it, we wouldn't have this problem. But no, we insist on making sense (with the possible exception of the contents of this book).

Kinds of justification

Most people think that there are four ways to justify text, but WordPerfect has these five:

Left Justification

✔ **Left justification:** Text begins at the left margin and fills up as much space as it takes up. Because different lines contain different text, the right edge of the text is uneven, or *ragged*. That's why this method is also called *ragged right*. Most of the text in this book uses left justification.

Right Justification

Center Justification

Full Justification

✔ **Right justification:** Works the same way as left justification except that the lines are shoved over to the right margin (see the earlier discussion about flush right margins). Now the left edge of the text is ragged and the right edge is straight. (Wonder why nobody calls this *ragged left* or *straight right?*)

✔ **Center justification:** Is usually used only for titles, and centers each line on the page so that both the left and right edges of the text are uneven.

✔ **Full justification:** The trickiest type (both the left and right edges of the text are nice and straight). How do you manage this type if different amounts of text are on each line? The extra space is broken up into little pieces and stuck in among the words on the line so that all the lines are padded out to fill the space between the left and right margins. Magazines, newspapers, and books usually use full justification, which is also called simply *justified text.*

✔ **"All" justification (as WordPerfect calls it):** Similar to full justification, only more so. With full justification, the lines at the end of paragraphs are exempt. If the last line of a paragraph has just a few words in it, for example, it begins at the left margin and stops where it stops. But with "all" justification, WordPerfect justifies *all* the lines, last line or not. No line is safe. If the last line of a paragraph has just a word or two on it, WordPerfect sticks *inches* of white space between each letter if that is what it takes to stretch it out to the right margin. We don't imagine that you will use this type of justification often — it looks downright weird.

TECHNICAL STUFF

Real versus fake justification

Old-fashioned word-processing programs, like the infamous original WordStar, performed a cheesy, fake kind of full justification. They just stuck extra spaces between the words. If a line didn't have much text on it, the gaps between words could become enormous. Modern word-processing programs, such as WordPerfect, do a much suaver, sneakier job of distributing the extra white space along the line of text. WordPerfect breaks it up into many tiny spaces and sticks them between the letters in each word as well as between words. As you edit justified text, you can see WordPerfect shifting the letters slightly to adjust for the widths of the letters you insert or delete.

How to justify your text

To tell WordPerfect how to justify your text, follow these steps:

1. **Move your cursor into position.**

   To select the type of justification to use for the entire document, move your cursor to the beginning of the document. To set justification for the rest of a document, move your cursor to the point at which you want the justification to change. To justify only a paragraph or two, select the text to be justified.

2. **Choose Layout Justification from the menu.**

   WordPerfect comes back at you with another menu of options: the five types of justification.

3. **Choose one.**

Alternatively, you can press one of these key combinations:

✔ Ctrl+L for left-justification

✔ Ctrl+R for right-justification

✔ Ctrl+E for center justification

✔ Ctrl+J for full justification

"All" justification has no key combination, which makes sense because it's hard to imagine that many people use it.

Power bar fans can also click on the Justification button on the power bar. This button usually has an L on it, with a little diagram suggestive of left-justified text. (It's *not* the button with the L and the black triangle on it — that's for tabs, which we discuss in a minute.) To set the justification, click on the button and hold down the mouse button. You see a menu of the five types of justification, with a little diagram for each one. (The folks at WordPerfect just *love* those little diagrams — and we do too! That's why we couldn't resist using them in our margins.) Slide your mouse pointer down to the type of justification you want and then release the mouse button. WordPerfect changes not only the justification in your text but also the way the justification buttons look, with a diagram of the type of justification you chose.

As usual, WordPerfect inserts secret codes to indicate the type of justification to use. If you have selected some text, codes are stuck in at the beginning and end of the selection, one to change the justification and the other to change it back. If no text was selected when you selected the type of justification, WordPerfect adds one code. The code in question looks like Just:Left, Just:Right, Just:Center, Just:Full, or Just:All.

If you really want to fool around with the way WordPerfect spaces the letters across the line, try the <u>L</u>ayout <u>T</u>ypesetting <u>W</u>ord/Letterspacing command, which displays the Word Spacing and Letterspacing dialog box. This technique is overkill if we ever saw it — you can control just how much white space WordPerfect can stick in among the letters to justify your text, suggest that WordPerfect crowd the letters together just a tad, or fiddle with the average amount of space between the words. If this is your cup of tea, go at it. We wouldn't dream of standing in your way.

To Hyphenate or Not to Hyphenate

WordPerfect can hyphenate automatically, by deciding (sometimes rightly, occasionally wrongly) where to hyphenate words that are too long to fit on a line. Hyphenation is usually a good idea when you use full justification; otherwise, it looks dumb.

To tell WordPerfect to hyphenate words as necessary, follow these steps:

1. **Move your cursor to the beginning of the document.**

   Usually, you should use hyphenation on the entire document or not at all. Life is confusing enough as it is.

2. **Choose <u>L</u>ayout <u>L</u>ine Hyph<u>e</u>nation from the menu.**

   WordPerfect displays the Line Hyphenation dialog box. Ignore the cute little diagram and the percentages and everything. No one we have ever met has ever wanted to change the parameters a program uses when it does hyphenation. In fact, you can forget that you ever saw it.

3. **Click in the little Hyphenation On box so that an X appears in it.**

4. **Click on OK or press Enter so that the dialog box vanishes.**

At some point as you work on the document, WordPerfect decides that a word should be hyphenated because it doesn't fit at the end of one line and it's too long to move to the beginning of the next line. Suddenly, with no warning, you see the Position Hyphen dialog box, shown in Figure 9-3.

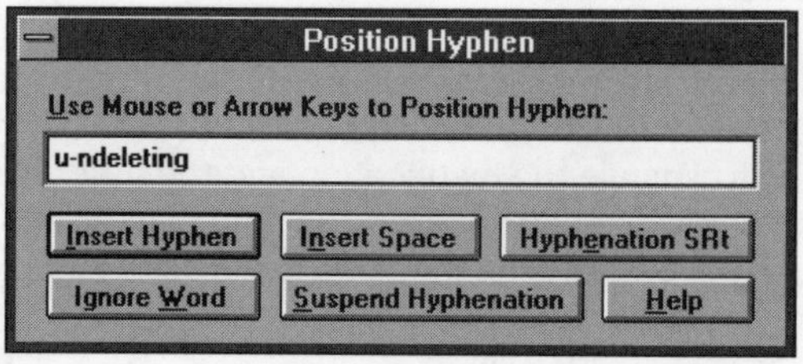

Figure 9-3:
Deciding
where to
split a word.

Position Hyphen
<u>U</u>se Mouse or Arrow Keys to Position Hyphen:
u-ndeleting
Insert Hyphen   **Insert Space**   **Hyphenation SRt**
Ignore Word   **Suspend Hyphenation**   **Help**

You have several options:

- ✔ Click on the Insert Hyphen button to insert the hyphen where WordPerfect suggests.

- ✔ Press the left- and right-arrow keys on the keyboard to move the hyphen to a better place to split the word and then click on Insert Hyphen.

- ✔ Decide that this long word should really be two separate words. Choose this option if you left out a space accidentally (which is our top-rated typo). Click on the Insert Space button.

- ✔ Decide that there is no good way to split the word in two and that the whole thing should be moved to the beginning of the next line. A classic example of this is the word *strength* — it has a bunch of letters but cannot be hyphenated. (Isn't it amazing the trivia we authors can dredge up?) In this case, click on Ignore Word.

When WordPerfect hyphenates a word, it doesn't insert a plain, old, ordinary hyphen. No, indeed. If it did and you edited the paragraph some more so that the word was no longer at the right margin, WordPerfect would glue the word back together but the hyphen would still show up. Every once in a while, you see this situation in a newspaper or magazine: a hyphen in the middle of a word where it doesn't belong. Now when you see it happen, you can sneer, "That word processor should have inserted a *soft hyphen!*"

WordPerfect does insert a soft hyphen, which looks just like a regular hyphen when the word is split in half at the margin but disappears into the World of Secret Codes if the word is glued back together again. Totally cool.

Playing with Tab Stops

In word processing, you use tabs and spaces a little differently than you do when you type with a typewriter. One reason is that WordPerfect is smarter than a typewriter — you can tell it to do such things as center text and flush it to the right without using a bunch of spaces or tabs. Another reason is that because most computer fonts are proportionally spaced (different letters are different widths — see Chapter 8), using spaces to line things up doesn't work very well. If you don't know what we mean, read on. What follows is a discussion of spaces, tabs, and tab stops.

Stop! Tab!

A *tab stop* (did we say this already?) is a position across the line where tabs stop. Logical enough. When you press the Tab key, WordPerfect moves toward the right across the line until it gets to the next tab stop and then it stops. WordPerfect lets you define a more or less unlimited number of them across the line.

Types of tab stops and other boring information

WordPerfect has a bunch of different kinds of tab stops. This subject is the kind of boring, petty stuff you probably haven't thought about since high school, and we urge you to skip this section if you possibly can.

Still with us? OK, here goes. This sidebar discusses the different types of tab stops, along with descriptions of what happens when you press the Tab key to move to each type. (Table 9-1 shows a live demonstration.)

✔ **Left or L:** What you type appears to the right of the tab stop position. On your ruler bar, left tab stops are indicated by little, black triangles that point down and to the left.

✔ **Right or R:** What you type appears to the *left* of the tab stop position. This tab stop doesn't sound too aptly named, does it? It's called a right tab stop because the text is flush right, or *right aligned,* at the stop. On the ruler bar, the triangles for right tab stops point down and to the right.

✔ **Center or C:** What you type appears centered around the tab stop position. On the ruler bar, center tab stops are shown with little upward-pointing triangles.

✔ **Decimal or D:** This type of tab stop is designed for numbers with decimal points, such as columns of dollar amounts. WordPerfect positions the text with the decimal point at the tab stop position — columns of numbers look so much tidier if their decimal points line up vertically. If you type something with no decimal point, WordPerfect right-aligns it. On the ruler bar, a decimal tab stop is indicated by an upward-pointing triangle with a little dot in the middle.

✔ **Dotted versions of the preceding four types:** You can tell WordPerfect to display a line of dots (also called a *dot leader*) that leads up to the entry. You see this kind of thing in the tables of contents in books such as this one. On the ruler bar, dotted tab stops are shown by triangles with dots underneath them.

Table 9-1	Tab Stops at Play			
Left	*Center*	*Right*	*Decimal*	*Dotted right*
Tom	Jones	Blue	$150.00	Page 1
Joe	Bloggswirth	Greenish	75.00	2
Sue	Fish-Frei	Purple	235.50	3
Mary	Green	Red	100.00	4

Setting tab stops

As delivered from the factory, your document probably contains tab stops every half inch. How can you tell? Display the ruler bar, that's how! If you don't see it, choose <u>V</u>iew and then <u>R</u>uler Bar from the menu (or press Alt+Shift+F3).

Just below the inch markings on the ruler, you see little, black triangles that mark the positions of your tab stops. The ones WordPerfect provides are automatically left tab stops (the most commonly used type) and are symbolized by triangles that point down and to the left.

You may not want to have a tab stop every half inch, and you may want to create tab stops of types other than left tab stops. If you are typing a list of names and phone numbers, for example, you might want just one tab stop at the position where you want the phone numbers to appear. Luckily, WordPerfect lets you fool around with the tab stops at will.

When you change or create tab stops, WordPerfect inserts a secret code that contains the positions of *all* the tab stops in effect at that point. The tab stop changes you make take effect at that point and continue for the rest of the document or until they encounter the next secret tab stop code. If you change your tab stops several times with your cursor in different places, you can end up with a document littered with tab stop codes, and your tab stops may change when you don't expect them to. If you think that this situation has occurred, move your cursor to the top of your document and then move down through the document line by line. Keep your eyes glued to the ruler bar. If you see the little triangles flittering around on it, you have lots of tab codes in your document. See Chapter 11 to learn how to see them and get rid of them.

The secret code WordPerfect inserts when you change your tab stops is called Tab Set, followed by the positions of all your tab stops.

You have (as ever) two ways to position your tab stops: use commands and use the ruler bar. The command for setting tab stops, Layout Line Tab Set, displays the Tab Set dialog box. This dialog box is horrific, terrifying, and downright scary-looking, and we refrain from reproducing it here for fear of chasing you away from word processing forever. We prefer that, rather than use it, you stick to the ruler bar method, which is a snap.

Put your tab codes in the right place!

Before setting your tab stops, you *must* move your cursor to the right place. We even tell you where the right place is!

If you want to set the tab stops for the entire document, move your cursor to the beginning of the document by pressing Ctrl+Home.

If you want to change the tab stop positions partway through the document, you can do that too. If your report contains two different tables, for example, you might want to set the tab stops once at the beginning of the first table and again at the beginning of the second. Move your cursor to the place where you want the new tab stop positions to take effect (at the beginning of a table, for example).

See the section "Setting up columnar tables," later in this chapter, to learn where to set the tab stops for a table.

If you double-click on a tab stop triangle on the ruler bar, WordPerfect thinks that it is doing you a favor by displaying the dreaded Tab Set dialog box. Don't panic — just click on the Cancel button or press Esc.

Using the ruler to set tab stops

Fooling with tab stops by using the ruler bar is kind of fun. You also use the Tab Set button on the power bar when you want to create a new one. This section shows you all the moves.

To move an existing tab stop, follow these steps:

1. **Move to the place in your document where you want the modified tab stops to take effect.**

   This spot is usually at the beginning of the document or the beginning of a table.

2. **Click on the little triangle for the tab stop you want to move.**

3. **Hold down the mouse button and drag the triangle along the ruler to its new position.**

   When you release the mouse button, WordPerfect moves the tab stop to the position where you left the triangle.

To get rid of a tab stop, follow these steps:

1. **Move to the place in your document where you want the change to take place.**

2. **Click on the triangle for the tab stop and drag it down off the ruler bar.**

   WordPerfect drops the tab stop in the Bit Bucket, which is the digital equivalent of the trash compactor. You never see the tab stop again.

If you move or delete a tab stop by mistake, choose Edit Undo from the menu or press Ctrl+Z to undo your change.

To get rid of all the existing tab stops, follow these steps:

1. **Click on the Tab Set button on the power bar and hold down the mouse button.**

   This button shows the type of tab stop you have most recently chosen. If you are working with left tab stops, for example, it has an L and a little leftward-leaning triangle in it.

2. **Slide the mouse pointer down to the Clear All Tabs command.**

3. **Release the mouse button.**

   Blammo.

To create a new tab stop, follow these steps:

1. **First, tell WordPerfect which kind of tab stop you want to make.**

   (See the Technical Stuff sidebar titled "Types of tab stops and other boring information," earlier in this chapter, for the types that are available.)

   You can tell which kind WordPerfect thinks that you want by looking at the Tab Set button on the power bar. It displays an L (for Left), R (for Right), C (for Center), or D (for Decimal), along with the appropriate little triangle. If it plans to create dotted tabs (tab stops with dot leaders), it shows a couple of dots beneath the triangle.

2. **If the tab stop type isn't the one you want, change it.**

   Click on the Tab Set button on the power bar and hold it down. A little menu appears that contains all the tab stop types. Slide the mouse pointer down until the one you want is highlighted and then release the mouse button. The button shows the letter and triangle shape for the new tab stop type.

   Now you are ready to create the tab stop. Get ready. This process is complex and painstaking.

3. **On the lower part of the ruler bar (where the triangles appear), point to the position where you want the tab stop and — click.**

   That's all there is to it! WordPerfect creates the tab stop and the little triangle to go with it.

After you have your tab stops where you want them, you are ready to use them.

Using Tabs, Spaces, and Indents

You must be thinking, "What's the big production about using tabs? Can't I just press the Tab key and be done with it?" Yes, you can do that, but your documents work better (that is, they look better and are easier to edit) if you use tabs wisely. Let's look at the ways in which you are likely to want to use tabs.

If you press the Tab key and, rather than insert a tab, your cursor just slides under the existing characters to the next tab stop, you are probably in typeover mode (see Chapter 4). Switch to insert mode by pressing the Insert key.

Indenting the first line of each paragraph

Indenting the first line of each paragraph is one of the all-time favorite uses of tabs. If you want the first line of a paragraph to be indented, you can press the Tab key as you begin typing the paragraph. Or you can insert the tab later, after you type the paragraph. No big news here.

If you want to indent the first lines of a *bunch* of paragraphs, however, you can tell WordPerfect to do it automatically, without your having to stick in a tab at the beginning of each one. These steps show you how:

1. **Select all the paragraphs for which you want to indent just the first line.**

   They all must be together, with no other paragraphs or titles or whatever, mixed in. (You can always select one group of paragraphs at a time and repeat these steps for each one.) If you want to indent the first line of every single paragraph in the document, don't select any text and then move the cursor to the beginning of the document. If you want to indent all the paragraphs starting partway through the document, move your cursor to the point where you want this formatting to begin. Whew!

2. **Choose Layout Paragraph Format from the menu.**

   WordPerfect displays the Paragraph Format dialog box, as shown in Figure 9-4.

3. **In the First Line Indent box, enter the amount by which you want to indent each first line.**

   This amount is usually about half an inch.

4. **Click on OK or press Enter.**

   Voilà! WordPerfect adds that little bit of white space at the beginning of each paragraph, just the way your typing teacher taught you. Look, Ma — no tabs!

Another way to display the Paragraph Format dialog box is to click the right mouse button on the ruler bar and then choose Paragraph Format from the QuickMenu that appears.

Figure 9-4:
Formatting a
bunch of
paragraphs
so that their
first lines
are
indented.

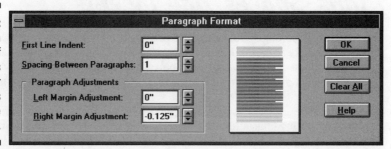

Whether you choose to use tabs or paragraph formatting, don't use spaces to indent paragraphs. This method is considered tacky in word-processing circles. The problem with spaces is that they are different widths depending on which font you use (see Chapter 8 for information about fonts). Tap stops are always exactly the width you see on the ruler bar.

The advantage of using tabs is that if you decide to indent your paragraphs by a different amount, all you have to do is slide that first tab stop over by a hair. All the tabs that depend on that tab stop then move too! When you perform this procedure, be sure that your cursor is in the right place — at the beginning of your document.

Whenever you use a tab to indent a line, you should have pressed Enter to end the preceding line. In other words, the line you are indenting shouldn't begin as a result of WordPerfect's use of word wrap to fill up the lines of a paragraph. Another way to say the same thing is that you should use a tab to indent only the first line of a paragraph. WordPerfect's word-wrap feature (described in Chapter 1) fills up the rest of the lines in your paragraph. To indent *all* the lines in the paragraph or all *except* the first line, see the section "Changing margins for a paragraph or two," earlier in this chapter. Never stick a tab at the beginning of each line of a paragraph! Yuck! Ptooey! If you do, when you edit the paragraph later, the tabs will be all over the place and your paragraph will have unsightly gaps in all the wrong places. *Please,* indent!

When you press the Tab key, WordPerfect inserts different secret codes, depending on the type of tab stop the tab moves to. The codes are called Left Tab, Right Tab, Center Tab, Dec Tab, ...Left Tab, ...Right Tab, and so on.

Setting up columnar tables

The other big reason to use tabs is to make a table (that is, a bunch of columns side by side, such as a phone list). To make a table in WordPerfect, you can use WordPerfect's slick and snazzy tables feature, described in Chapter 16. But if you would rather do it the old-fashioned way, use tabs and follow these steps:

1. **Type your column headings.**

   Most tables have a line or two of column headings at the top of the columns. Type the headings and separate them with tabs — just *one* tab between each column. Because you haven't set your tab stops yet, the spacing probably looks terrible. Stay calm.

2. **Move your cursor to the beginning of the line that contains the column headings (the first line, if there is more than one).**

3. **Set tab stops so that the column headings are spaced the way you want them.**

   You can always move them later if the information doesn't fit in the columns the way you expect. Use only left, center, and right tab stops (don't use decimal or dotted tab stops because they make your column headings look downright odd).

4. **Move to the next line, where the information in the table will begin.**

   Now you are ready to type the information in the body of the table, as they say.

5. Type one line of information and separate the columns with just *one* tab.

Perform this step no matter how lousy it looks — you learn how to fix it in a minute.

6. Move back to the beginning of the line you just typed.

7. Set the tab stops for the table.

Use decimal tabs for numbers with decimal points. Use dotted tab stops as you please. Slide the tab stops around on the ruler bar until everything is just right. But remember — make sure that your cursor is at the beginning of that first line whenever you make a change.

When you get the first line of information the way you like it, you may want to go back and fix the spacing of the column headings. Just make sure to put your cursor at the beginning of the first line of column headings.

8. Type the rest of the table.

Insert just one tab between columns. Everything should line up perfectly.

9. At the end of the table, put the tab stops back to the way they were.

If you want to go back to the WordPerfect default of a left tab stop every half inch, you may want to brave the Tab Set dialog box. Move your cursor to the first line after the table. Display the Tab Set dialog box by choosing Layout Line Tab Set from the menu (or Tab Set from the ruler bar QuickMenu). Click the Default button, which sets the tabs to the WordPerfect defaults. Then click on OK, quickly, before this dialog box does something to your brain.

If you want to see where your tabs are and make sure that no spaces have snuck in, choose View Show ¶ from the menu or press Ctrl+Shift+F3. Suddenly the document fills up with little gizmos: The spaces turn into little dots, the Enters (carriage returns) turn into paragraph symbols, and the tabs — there they are! — appear as right-pointing arrows. If this display gives you a headache (as it does to us), turn it off by choosing the same command again (or by pressing the same keys). If you want to see your tabs and Enters but not all those blasted dots in your spaces, you can use this wacky command to control exactly what WordPerfect shows (see Chapter 20 to learn how to customize which gizmos appear).

Tabbing backward

We know that tabbing backward sounds like a bizarre idea, but it's not the only one in the world of word processing. A *back tab* lets you tab backward to the preceding tab stop. WordPerfect sometimes uses back tabs without telling you: if you use the method described earlier in this chapter for creating a hanging indent, WordPerfect indents the entire paragraph one tab stop and then enters a back tab code to back up to the margin so that the first line isn't indented. Mercifully, it performs this procedure automatically and spares you the gory details.

You can use back tabs yourself, although it escapes us why on earth you would want to. To insert a back tab, you press Shift+Tab. If you want to type some text, such as *aaa,* on top of some other text, such as *bbb,* for example, type **aaa**, press Shift+Tab to back up, and type **bbb**. Looks just peachy, doesn't it?

The only reason we brought the subject up is to warn you in case you press Shift+Tab by mistake. If you see text stomping on other text, a back tab code may be lurking in your document. See Chapter 11 to learn how to find and exterminate it.

If you press Shift+Tab and your cursor — rather than insert a back tab — just slides under the existing characters to the preceding tab stop, you are probably in typeover mode (see Chapter 4). Switch to insert mode by pressing the Insert key.

Changing the Line Spacing

Line Spacing

If the stuff you write is sent to an editor (as ours is — pity the poor woman!), you probably have to double-space your text to leave lots of room for making corrections, expressing confusion, and general doodling. WordPerfect has, as usual, two ways to change line spacing.

If your power bar is displayed, follow these steps:

1. **Move your cursor to the point at which you want the line spacing to change.**

   To change it for the entire document, move to the beginning of the document by pressing Ctrl+Home. To change the line spacing for a paragraph or two (for a long quotation, for example), select the text you want to change.

2. **Click on the Line Spacing button on the power bar and hold down the mouse button.**

   The Line Spacing button, which usually says 1.0", is the one with a number between two horizontal lines. (The 1.0 tells you that the current line spacing is 1.0, or regular ol' single spacing.)

   While you hold down the mouse button, a little menu of line-spacing options appears, including 1.0, 1.5, 2.0, and Other.

3. **Choose your new line spacing.**

   If you want single, single-and-a-half, or double spacing, choose 1.0, 1.5, or 2.0, respectively, by sliding the mouse pointer down to your choice and releasing the mouse button. If you choose Other from this little menu, go directly to step 3 in the following series of steps.

If you don't see the power bar or you don't feel like using it (hey, we all have days like that), follow these steps:

1. **Move your cursor as in step 1 from the preceding series of steps.**

2. **Choose Layout Line Spacing from the menu.**

   Alternatively, you can double-click on the Line Spacing button on the power bar. (Oops! We forgot that you're not using the power bar.)

   WordPerfect displays the Line Spacing dialog box, as shown in Figure 9-5.

3. **Enter a number in the Spacing box.**

   Enter 2 to get double-spaced text, for example. You can also enter fractions. To add just a little space between the lines, for example, you can enter 1.1 or 1.2. Click on the little arrows at the right end of the Spacing box to increase or decrease the number in the box a tad.

4. **Click on OK or press Enter to dismiss the dialog box. (Shoo!)**

   WordPerfect does your bidding and adds the vertical space you requested.

Figure 9-5:
Double-
spacing
your
document to
make it look
longer.

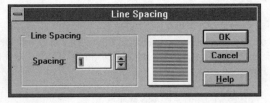

When you change the line spacing, WordPerfect inserts a Ln Spacing secret code.

Changing the Spacing Between Paragraphs

You can tell WordPerfect to leave extra space between each paragraph in your document and not add any between the lines of the paragraph. This capability results in text that looks sort of like this book does, an effect we personally prefer over first-line indenting. Take that, Miss Perpetua! (She was our high school typing teacher. Honest to Pete — we are not making this up.)

This procedure involves paragraph formatting and the use of the Paragraph Format dialog box, which you saw earlier in this chapter (refer to Figure 9-4), as shown in these steps:

1. **Move your cursor to the beginning by pressing Ctrl+Home.**

   Assuming that you probably want to use this kind of thing for the entire document, that is.

2. **Choose Layout Paragraph Format from the menu.**

   WordPerfect displays the Paragraph Format dialog box.

3. **In the Spacing Between Paragraphs box, enter the line spacing you want.**

   Entering 1 means that you want no extra space. We recommend entering 1.5, which adds a blank half-line between each paragraph, enough to separate them visually. (Don't we sound like we know what we're talking about?)

4. **Click on OK or press Enter to leave the dialog box.**

Changing the paragraph spacing inserts a secret Para Spacing code in your document.

Chapter 10
Perfect Pages and Dashing Documents

● ●

In This Chapter

▶ Setting the page size

▶ Adjusting the top and bottom margins

▶ Starting a new page

▶ Keeping text together

▶ Centering a page from top to bottom

▶ Looking at different views of your document

▶ Numbering pages

▶ Adding heads and feet

● ●

*I*n earlier chapters, we talked about making your characters look just right, fooling with margins and indentation, and other heady stuff. Now for the Larger Picture — formatting your document as a whole. This chapter explains how to tell WordPerfect what size of paper you plan to print your masterpiece on, where to begin new pages, and what (if anything) to print at the top and bottom of each page, such as page numbers. This kind of formatting separates the — men from the boys? women from the girls? toads from the water buffaloes? — pros from the amateurs in the world of word processing.

Setting the Page Size

WordPerfect wants to know everything about your document. In particular, it wants to know which kind of paper you plan to print it on: letterhead? envelopes? labels? It doesn't care what your paper looks like — it cannot tell embossed rag stationery with gold leaf edges from cheapo copying paper — it just wants to know its size.

If you don't mention anything about paper, WordPerfect probably assumes the usual: letter-size paper you stick in the printer in the usual way. If you plan to print on the paper sideways (known as landscape orientation), however, or if you plan to use legal-size paper, envelopes, or whatever, you had better tell WordPerfect about it. Otherwise, you may run into trouble with your margins (as described later in this chapter).

To tell WordPerfect about the paper size on which you plan to print your document, follow these steps:

1. **Move your cursor to the beginning of the document by pressing Ctrl+Home.**

   Because paper size is something that usually applies to the entire document, set it right at the beginning.

2. **Choose <u>L</u>ayout <u>P</u>age Paper <u>S</u>ize from the menu.**

   WordPerfect displays the Paper Size dialog box, shown in Figure 10-1. You see a list of paper sizes, titled Paper Definitions. The exact list depends on the kind of printer you use, because different printers can accept different paper sizes. Our list includes the ones shown here:

   A4 (European paper, a tad bigger than American letter size)

   A4 Landscape (same thing as A4 but sideways)

   Envelope #10 Landscape (a regular business envelope, inserted in the printer sideways)

   Legal (legal-size paper, which is longer than letter-size)

   Legal Landscape (same thing as legal but sideways)

   Letter (our favorite)

   Letter Landscape (same thing as letter-size but sideways)

An art lesson: Portraits and landscapes

We interrupt this book for a brief lesson on art, specifically, the shapes of paintings.

As you have noticed from your extensive experience in art galleries, pictures of people tend to be taller than they are wide, to make room to include a complete hat-to-collar *portrait*. Pictures of places tend to be wider than they are tall so that they can include more *landscape* and less sky.

The many art-lovers among the computer scientists of the world decided to use this situation as the basis for naming the way we print on paper. If you hold the paper so that it is taller than it is wide and then print lines of text that run across the short way, it is called *portrait orientation*. This orientation is the normal, everyday way to use paper. If, on the other hand, you turn the paper sideways so that it is wider than it is tall and then print on it accordingly, you have *landscape orientation*. Toddlers usually use paper in this way, in our experience.

3. To use a different paper size, move the highlight up or down to it.

One of the paper sizes is highlighted. That's the one you are currently using for this document. Below the list, you can see the details of what WordPerfect knows about this kind of paper. A little diagram gives you the general idea.

4. Click the Select button.

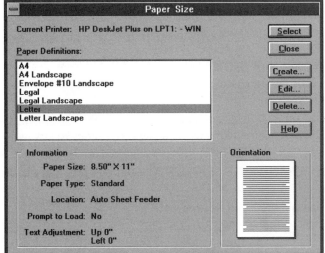

Figure 10-1:
Choosing
the kind of
paper on
which to
print.

For details about how to print on envelopes and mailing labels, see Chapter 19.

If the list of available paper sizes looks odd, make sure that the correct printer is selected (see Chapter 22).

Use landscape printing for documents that are too wide to fit on the paper the regular way, especially for columnar tables that have numerous columns. People always "ooh" and "ahh" when you produce a document printed sideways on the page, so that's another good reason to use it.

When you set the paper size, WordPerfect inserts a secret Paper Sz/Typ code in your document (yes, another inspired code name!). To learn more about these codes, including how to delete them, see Chapter 11.

Adjusting the Top and Bottom Margins

After WordPerfect knows the size of your paper, it has opinions about your margins. Unless you tell it otherwise, it assumes that you want one-inch margins all the way around the page, measuring from the edge of the paper. We generally find this measurement a little too airy and spacious for our tastes, and we usually change them — unless we are getting paid to write by the page, of course.

To change the left or right margin, see Chapter 9, which explains how to use the ruler bar or Margins dialog box for this task.

To change the top or bottom margin, follow these steps:

1. **Move your cursor to the point at which you want the new margins to take effect.**

   To change the top or bottom margin for the entire document, move to the beginning of the document by pressing Ctrl+Home. To change it beginning at a page other than page 1, move to the top of the page.

2. **Display the Margins dialog box by choosing Layout Margins from the menu or by pressing Ctrl+F8.**

   If you get the urge, you can even display it by double-clicking on the part of the ruler bar that shows the margins. If you want to see a picture of this dialog box, flip back to Figure 9-2. But you don't have to — it's just a dialog box with entries for Left, Right, Top, and Bottom margins.

3. **Fill in the measurements for the top and bottom margins.**

   Or you can click on the little arrows next to the measurements to increase or decrease them a little at a time.

   The little page diagram changes to show you how it will look, more or less. If you are using draft view (described later in this chapter), you don't notice a difference, except that the page breaks move.

When you change the top or bottom margin, WordPerfect inserts a secret Top Mar or Bot Mar code in the text, at the top of the current page. See Chapter 11 to learn how to fool with these codes.

Starting a New Page

If you have typed any significant amount of text in WordPerfect, you probably have noticed that every so often it suddenly introduces a huge gap between one line and the next. This gap is WordPerfect's way of telling you that you just filled up one page and are starting at the top of the next page — a sort of digital equivalent to ripping the paper out of the typewriter and sticking a new sheet under the platen.

WordPerfect keeps track of where on the page each line appears. You can see your position on the page by looking at the status bar, where it says Ln (short, we guess, for Line) followed by a measurement in inches (or maybe centimeters). This spot is your position from the top edge of the paper.

But what if you don't want to fill up a page before starting the next one? You can insert a secret code (not another one!) that tells WordPerfect to skip to the top of the next page, regardless of whether this one is full. This feature is called a *page break*. The page breaks WordPerfect sticks in when pages are full are called *soft page breaks*. If you want to put one in, it's called a *hard page break*. (See Chapter 11 to read about the difference between hard and soft codes.)

To insert a hard page break, just press Ctrl+Enter. Poof! Your cursor dashes down to the top of a new page. If you were in the middle of the line, the part of the line after your cursor moves down to the new page with you.

To get rid of a hard page break, move your cursor to the top of the page *after* the page break and press the Backspace key. This step backs you up, and with luck it deletes the page break code in the process. Alternatively, you can move your cursor to the very last character *before* the page break and press the Delete key — same idea. If this step doesn't work, see Chapter 11.

You may be tempted to begin a new page by pressing Enter over and over until your page is full of carriage returns and you arrive at the top of the next page. We hate to be judgmental, but in our humble opinion this action is *wrong, wrong, wrong*. Here's why: if you edit the earlier part of your document so that it gets just a teeny bit shorter, everything shifts up a tad. Now you have too few carriage returns to fill up the page, and the text begins at the bottom of the preceding page rather than on a new page — not the effect you want. Take our advice and insert a hard page break instead. It's so much less work!

The name of the secret hard page break code is HPg, in case you were wondering. The soft page breaks WordPerfect adds are named HRt-SPg or SRt-SPg, depending on whether the page break occurs between paragraphs or in the middle of a paragraph.

Keeping Text Together

You have complete control over where hard page breaks occur, because you put them in yourself. But WordPerfect sticks in soft page breaks whenever it decides that no more lines can fit on a page. Sometimes it chooses singularly bad spots to begin a new page — in fact, sometimes we suspect malice. A technical term was even created for lousy positioning of page breaks: *bad breaks* (and we always thought that this was a skiing term!).

Avoiding broken homes (widows and orphans)

It looks lousy if a paragraph begins on the last line of a page so that only one line of the paragraph appears before the page break. This traditional typesetting no-no has a traditional name: it's called a widow (or is it an orphan?). Our dictionary informs us that this line is called an *orphan*. A *widow* occurs when the last line of a paragraph appears at the top of a page all by itself. (At your next backyard picnic, amaze your friends by conducting a pop quiz to see who knows the difference.)

Luckily, you don't have to know about this stuff or even think about it because WordPerfect does your worrying for you. Follow these steps to avoid the dreaded social disease of bad breaks:

1. **Move your cursor to the beginning of the document by pressing Ctrl+Home.**

   The following command and the resulting secret code apply to the entire document.

2. **Choose Layout Page Keep Text Together from the menu bar.**

   WordPerfect displays the Keep Text Together dialog box, as shown in Figure 10-2. The dialog box contains three different settings that have to do with positioning page breaks, and we discuss all three in this chapter. Our immediate concern, however, is those widows and orphans.

3. **Click on the little box by the instructions** `Prevent the first and last lines of paragraphs from being separated across pages` **so that it contains a little X.**

   It's in the Widow/Orphan section of the dialog box.

4. **Choose OK or press Enter to leave the dialog box.**

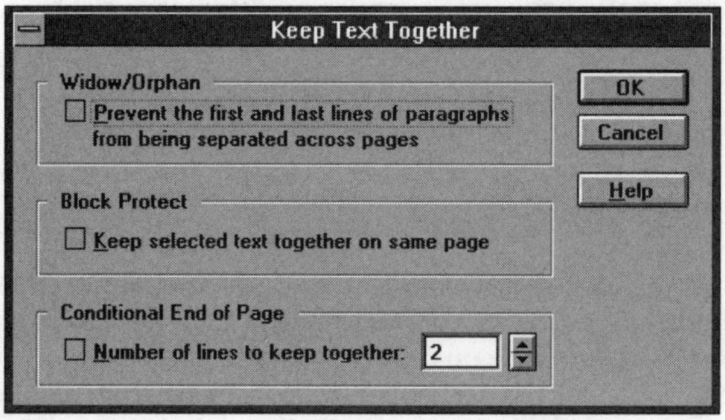

Figure 10-2: Preventing widows and orphans.

Now WordPerfect avoids leaving widows and orphans alone at the top and bottom of pages. Instead, it moves page breaks up or down a line as necessary. The pages won't be completely full, but that's the price you pay for family cohesion.

When you follow the preceding steps, WordPerfect creates a Wid/Orph:On code in your document. Chapter 11 describes how to see and delete it, if necessary.

Keeping your act together

Your document may contain information that should not be split over a page break. A columnar table looks crummy if it is split up, for example, unless it is longer than one page. You can select part of your document and tell WordPerfect, "Let no page break enter here!" Follow these steps:

1. **Select the text you want to keep together.**

   Refer to Chapter 6 to learn how to select text, if you don't already know. For tables, be sure to include any headings or titles.

2. **Choose <u>L</u>ayout <u>P</u>age <u>K</u>eep Text Together from the menu bar.**

   WordPerfect displays the Keep Text Together dialog box (refer to Figure 10-2).

3. **Click on the** `Keep selected text together on the same page` **box so that it contains an X.**

   It's in the Block Protect section of the dialog box.

4. **Choose OK or press Enter.**

Block Protect? It sounds like the maneuver a two-year-old uses when another kid comes to visit. But WordPerfect isn't talking about that kind of block. In earlier versions of WordPerfect, selecting text was always called "marking blocks," and doing anything with a bunch of text was called a "block operation." Now WordPerfect has adopted Windows-speak, which requires that you refer to a bunch of text as a "selection." It's another example of the Great March of Progress.

When you follow these steps, WordPerfect inserts two Block Pro codes in your document, one at the beginning of the selected text and one at the end.

Keeping your head together

Specifically, this heading means keeping your headings with the text that follows them. (You were thinking of the great Carole King hits of yesteryear, weren't you? Unless you're too young to remember them.) Leaving a heading stranded all alone at the bottom of the page while the text that follows the heading begins on the following page is considered tacky and gauche.

Unlike preventing widows and orphans, which you can do by giving one command at the beginning of your document, you must give a separate command for each heading you want to keep with the text that follows it. (The solution to this annoying situation is to use styles to format your headings — jump to Chapter 12 if this subject interests you.)

To prevent WordPerfect from separating a head(ing) from its body, follow these steps:

1. **Move your cursor to the beginning of the line that contains the heading.**

2. **Choose Layout Page Keep Text Together from the menu bar.**

   WordPerfect displays the Keep Text Together dialog box (refer to Figure 10-2). Look at the Conditional End of Page section of the dialog box.

3. **Click on the little box to the left of the title** `Number of lines to keep together` **so that it contains an X.**

4. **Enter a number in the box to the right of the title** `Number of lines to keep together`.

   To keep the heading line and the first two lines of the text that follow it together, enter 3. If you use a blank line to separate the heading from the text, you might want to enter 4.

5. **Choose OK or press Enter to leave the dialog box.**

Now if the heading and the first few lines that follow cannot fit at the bottom of the page, WordPerfect moves the whole kit and caboodle to the top of the next page.

When you follow these steps, WordPerfect inserts a Condl EOP code in your document, which stands for Conditional End Of Page.

Don't use too many Block Protect and Conditional End Of Page codes in your document or else WordPerfect will have a heck of a time finding *anywhere* to put page breaks. Cut it some slack!

Centering a Page, Top to Bottom

When you create a title page for a document, it's nice if the titles appear in the middle of the page, both up and down and left to right. Chapter 9 talked about how to center text between the left and right margins (oh, all right — move to the beginning of the line and press Shift+F7). The following steps show you how to center the titles top to bottom (of course, you can just press Enter a bunch of times above the titles, but why not let WordPerfect put your titles in exactly the right place?):

1. **Move your cursor to the top of the page that contains the text to be centered top to bottom.**

   In most cases, this page is the first page of your document.

2. **Choose Layout Page Center from the menu bar.**

   WordPerfect displays the Center Page(s) dialog box, as shown in Figure 10-3.

3. **To center this page, choose Current Page.**

4. **Choose OK or press Enter.**

   WordPerfect moves the text on the page up or down to its center.

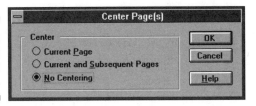

Figure 10-3:
Centering titles on a page.

You can tell the vertical position of the text on the page by looking at the Ln measurement on the status line.

To revoke centering on a page, move your cursor to the top of the page, choose Layout Page Center from the menu bar to display the Center Page dialog box, and choose Turn centering off.

When you center a page, WordPerfect quite sensibly inserts the secret Cntr Cr Pg code. Chapter 11 tells you how to see this magical code for yourself.

Looking at Different Views of Your Document

WordPerfect can show you your document from several angles, depending on how closely you want it to resemble the printed page. This list shows the different views you can choose:

- ✔ **Draft view:** Page breaks appear as horizontal lines across your document, and you cannot see top or bottom margins, headers, footers, or page numbers.

- ✔ **Page view:** WordPerfect shows you how your page will look, including all margins, headers, and footers. Page breaks look like blank gaps between one page and the next.

- ✔ **Two-page view:** You can see two pages side by side, which is a lovely effect but totally illegible because the text is so small. Maybe if your computer screen were three feet across, you could read stuff in this view; except for a quick check of page formatting, however, it's relatively worthless.

To switch between these three views, choose <u>V</u>iew from the menu bar and then choose either <u>D</u>raft, <u>P</u>age, or <u>T</u>wo Page.

The reason we bring up the subject of views is that we are about to talk about page formatting that you can see only in page (and two-page) view: page numbers, headers, and footers.

A faster way to switch to draft view is by pressing Ctrl+F5. A quicker way to jump to page view is by swatting Alt+F5. There is no fast way to see two-page view, and who would want to? For the most part, you can probably just work in page view. Why not see everything, after all?

Numbering Pages

After you have a document with more than one page, you probably will want to number the pages. Few things are more annoying than a sheaf of pages with no page numbers that have gotten (or *may* have gotten) out of order. Don't look like a schnook — number your pages.

For some strange reason — probably some quirk of software history — WordPerfect has not one but *two* ways to number pages. (Why do we say this with surprise? WordPerfect *always* seems to have two ways to do anything!)

The two ways are shown in this list:

- ✔ Use the Layout Page Numbering command to tell WordPerfect to begin numbering the pages. You can tell WordPerfect where the numbers should appear in addition to entering other text, such as today's date or the document title, to include other text with the page number.

- ✔ Use the Layout Header/Footer command to define headers or footers, which can include page numbers.

It's difficult to tell the difference between these two approaches. Anyway, we talk about headers and footers in a minute. These steps show you how to use the first method to number your pages:

1. **Move your cursor to the top of the page on which you want page numbers to begin.**

   If your classy-looking document has a cover page, for example, you can begin numbering on the next page.

2. **Choose Layout Page Numbering from the menu bar.**

   WordPerfect displays another dialog box, the Page Numbering dialog box shown in Figure 10-4.

3. **Tell WordPerfect where to print the page numbers.**

   Click and hold down the mouse button on the little double arrow at the right end of the Position option. It gives you these choices: No Page Numbering, Top Left, Top Center, Top Right, Alternating Top, Bottom Left, Bottom Center, Bottom Right, and Alternating Bottom. The Alternating Top and Bottom options do not mean that you and a friend have gotten your bikinis mixed up — they indicate that the page number appears on the right side of odd-numbered pages and on the left side of even-numbered pages. This setting is just right for documents printed on both sides of the paper (this book, for example).

   As soon as you choose a position (other than No Page Numbering), the little pictures of sample pages show little page numbers! Is this cute, or what?

4. **Choose the font for your page numbers.**

   If you want the page number to appear in a different font, click the Font button and choose the font and font size from the dialog box that looks an awful lot like the Font dialog box described in Chapter 8. Select OK to return to the Page Numbering dialog box.

5. **Choose OK or press Enter to bug out of this dialog box.**

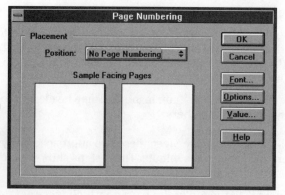

Figure 10-4:
Your pages
are
numbered!

Now WordPerfect prints page numbers on this page and all the following pages in the document, even pages you add later.

When you tell WordPerfect to number your pages, it adds a secret Pg Num Pos code at the top of the page. (See Chapter 11 for info about codes.)

For all you roman numeral fans

You don't have to use boring, pedestrian, Arabic numbers for your page numbers. You can use small roman numerals, for example, to number the pages in the introduction to a report. To tell WordPerfect which type of numbers (roman versus Arabic) to use, follow these steps:

1. **With your cursor at the top of the page in which you want the numbering to begin, choose Layout Page Numbering.**

   WordPerfect displays the Page Numbering dialog box.

2. **Click on the Options button.**

   You see the daunting Page Numbering Options dialog box.

3. **Remain calm and click on the Page setting.**

   It starts out by saying Numbers (Arabic numbers, such as 1, 2, and 3). If you click and hold down the mouse button, you can choose lowercase letters (a, b, c), uppercase letters (A, B, C), lowercase roman (i, ii, iii) or uppercase roman (I, II, III).

4. **Choose OK to leave this scary-looking dialog box and save your selection.**

You can even switch page-number styles part of the way through the document: just move your cursor to the top of the page on which you want the style to change and then follow the preceding steps.

Stop! Don't type that page number!

Untutored word-processing novices have been known to enter page numbers at the bottom of every page. A moment's thought tells you why this is a terrible, awful, yucky idea. If you insert a line at the bottom of each page and type the page number, what are you gonna do when an important update requires you to insert a few additional lines on page 1? Suddenly all the page numbers that used to appear at the bottom of the pages slide down to print a few lines down from the top of the following pages. What a mess!

The moral of the story is "Never type page numbers as text." Always use either page numbering or headers or footers (described later in this chapter) to do it for you.

Starting over again at 1

If you want to change your page numbering part of the way through a document, you can. If your report titled "Ten Thousand Uses for Chocolate" begins with an introduction, for example, you can restart the page numbering at 1 on the first page following the introduction. Follow these steps:

1. **With your cursor at the top of the page on which you want to restart page numbering at 1, choose Layout Page Numbering.**

   You see the Page Numbering dialog box.

2. **Click the Value button.**

   WordPerfect displays the horrifying Numbering Value dialog box. Absolutely, positively ignore all sections of the dialog box except for the Page Settings section in the upper left corner.

3. **For the New Page Number setting, enter 1.**

4. **Choose OK to leave the Numbering Value dialog box and ditto to leave the Page Numbering dialog box.**

Adding Heads and Feets

Now that we have gone through all the gory details of page numbering, we admit that we usually don't use the Page Numbering dialog box to number our pages. We usually have lots of other things we want to include at the top or bottom of each page, such as the title of the document, today's date, and notes that say "Draft" or "Confidential! Destroy Before Reading!" The easiest way to print all this stuff at the top or bottom of each page is by using *headers* and *footers*.

The cool thing about headers and footers is that they can contain almost anything — one line of text, an entire paragraph, or even a picture. Also, your document can contain two different headers (Header A and Header B) and two different footers (Footer A and Footer B, believe it or not), so you can print different headers and footers on the facing pages of documents printed on both sides of the page.

Making a header or footer

These steps show you how to make a header or footer:

1. **Switch to page view so that you can see the headers and footers you create. (They are invisible in draft view.) Choose View Page from the menu bar or press Alt+F5.**

2. **Move to the beginning of your document by pressing Ctrl+Home.**

   If you want headers and footers to begin part of the way through your document, move to the top of the first page on which you want the header or footer to appear.

3. **Choose Layout Header/Footer from the menu.**

   You see the Headers/Footers dialog box, shown in Figure 10-5.

4. **Choose which header or footer you want to create.**

   If you plan to use one header or footer for the entire document, choose Header A or Footer A. If you plan to use two headers or two footers (for numbering facing pages, for example), choose either A or B.

5. **Click the Create button from the Headers/Footers dialog box.**

   This step tells WordPerfect to insert a new secret header or footer code in your document. WordPerfect adds a blank line at the top (for headers) or bottom (for footers) of the page on which you can begin typing your header or footer.

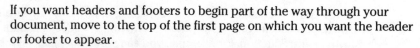

Figure 10-5: Defining heads and feets.

If you want to skip printing the header or footer on the first page of the document (a common technique), move to the beginning of the document anyway. You can tell WordPerfect to suppress printing the header and footer on the first page (this procedure is described later in this chapter).

Some grammar maniacs insist that headers and footers are more properly called *headings* and *footings*. Ignore them.

You can have several different Header As, Header Bs, Footer As, or Footer Bs in your document. If you think that they would be confusing, you are right. Don't do it.

You can create Header or Footer B before you create Header or Footer A. WordPerfect doesn't care. On the other hand, you may get confused. We stick with A if we are using only one.

When you create a header or footer, WordPerfect inserts a secret code named Header A (or whichever header or footer you choose). The code also contains all the text that appears in the header or footer, including formatting. To see or delete this code, see Chapter 11.

Typing the text in a header or footer

Now your job is to type the text to appear in this header or footer. To help you, WordPerfect displays *another* little bar of buttons above your document. The header/footer feature bar is just below the power bar (if you have displayed the power bar) and looks like Figure 10-6.

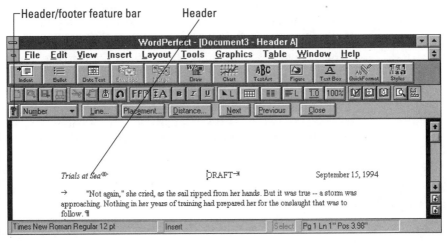

Figure 10-6:
Using the header/footer feature bar.

This new line that WordPerfect adds for your header or footer is no ordinary new line. Until you add a carriage return, this line is in a special zone that contains the text for your header or footer. You cannot use the cursor-control keys to move between the header or footer zone and the rest of the document. You can use the mouse, however, to click where you want to edit, which enables you to switch between editing the regular document and your header or footer.

When you are editing a header or footer, you can use the header/footer feature bar buttons. If you move your cursor to another part of your document, the feature bar stays on the screen but all the buttons are *grayed out,* which means that they go out of focus and do nothing if you click them. If you move your cursor back to your header or footer, the feature bar buttons come back into focus. On the other hand, some of the buttons on the button bar or power bar get fuzzy and unusable when you are editing a header or footer. You cannot use the New, Open, Save, or Print buttons on the power bar, for example, while you are editing a header or footer. C'est la vie.

To enter the text in your header or footer, follow these steps:

1. **Move your cursor to the header or footer zone if it's not already there.**

   You can tell when you are editing a header or footer because the header/footer feature bar buttons come into focus. You can also tell because the title bar of the WordPerfect window displays not only the filename of the document you are editing but also which header or footer you are working on ([ZUKESOUP.WPD - Header A], for example).

2. **Type the text!**

   You can control the font, font size, and text style in the usual ways (refer to Chapter 8). If you want the header or footer to be more than one line long, be our guest — just keep typing. Go ahead and press Enter at the end of the line if you want to include more than one paragraph.

   What about page numbers, you ask? Aha! It's time to use those cute buttons on the feature bar WordPerfect insisted on using to clutter up your screen.

3. **To include the current page number in the header or footer, move your cursor to the place where you want the page number to appear and click the Number button on the feature bar. A little menu drops down. Choose Page Number, as you probably have guessed.**

The standard three-part header

If you want some text at the left margin, some text centered, and some text at the right margin, you can tell WordPerfect to center and right-align parts of your header. You can print the document title at the left margin, for example, the page number in the center of the header, and today's date at the right margin.

To make a header such as this one, type it all on one line with nothing between the left part, the middle part, and the right part. With your cursor just before the part of the line you want centered, choose Layout Line Center (or press Shift+F7). This step centers the rest of the line. Then move your cursor just before the text you want to right-align and choose Layout Line Flush Right (or press Alt+F7). This step moves the rest of the line over to the right margin.

When you type the text of your document, you don't have to leave room for the headers or footers. WordPerfect sticks them in at the top and bottom margins of the page and shoves the other text out of the way.

If you want to print the current date in the header or footer, see Chapter 25 or just press Ctrl+Shift+D.

If you want your header or footer to contain lines, boxes, or even pictures, see Chapter 16.

You can format the text in your headers and footers by using the same commands you can use for text in the rest of your document. Commands you cannot use appear grayed out in the WordPerfect menus, which is WordPerfect's subtle way of telling you that you cannot choose these commands.

If you cannot see your headers or footers, you are probably using draft view, in which they are invisible. Choose View Page (or press Alt+F5) to switch to page view.

Controlling where headers and footers print

After you have created a header or footer and typed its text, you can tell WordPerfect on which pages to print it. Click the Placement button on the header/footer feature bar. WordPerfect displays the dialog box shown in Figure 10-7. Choose Odd Pages, Even Pages, or Every Page and then click the OK button.

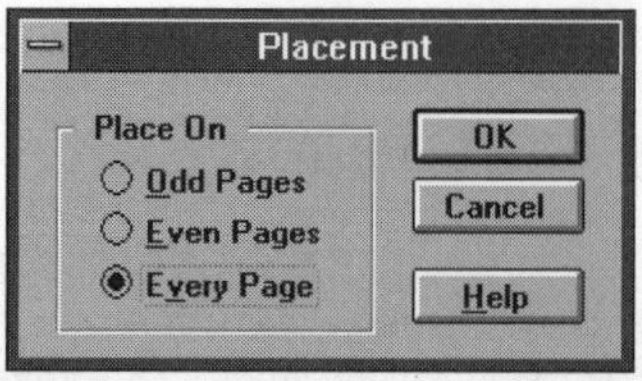

Figure 10-7:
Telling
WordPerfect
where to
print
headers and
footers.

Figure 10-7:
Telling
WordPerfect
where to
print
headers and
footers.

Don't print it here!

You can tell WordPerfect not to print the header or footer you just went to so much trouble to create. Why would you want to? We can think of these two good reasons:

- ✔ You don't want the header to print on the first page of your document. When you write a letter, for example, you might want all the pages except the first one to have a header that says "Joe Jones, Sept. 8, 1994, Page 2" (with the correct page number, naturally). You therefore want to suppress the header or footer for one page.

- ✔ Your document might have two or more sections, and you might want to use a header or footer for only the first section. You can discontinue the header or footer for the rest of the pages in the document.

Suppress that dormouse!

To *suppress* the printing of a header or footer, you tell WordPerfect to skip printing on each page. To suppress a header or footer for one page, follow these steps:

1. **Move your cursor to the page on which you don't want to print the header or footer.**

2. **Choose Layout Page Suppress from the menu bar.**

   WordPerfect displays the Suppress dialog box, shown in Figure 10-8.

3. **Choose the header or footer you don't want to print.**

   If you don't want any headers or footers on this page, check the All box.

4. **Click the OK button.**

   The headers or footers disappear from the page, only to reappear on the next page.

When you suppress the printing of a header or footer on a page, WordPerfect creates at the top of the page a secret code named Suppress.

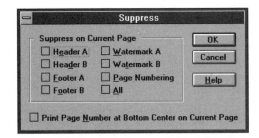

Figure 10-8:
Skipping printing a header or footer on one page.

Discontinuing headers and footers

To *discontinue* printing a header or footer, you tell WordPerfect to stop printing this header or footer for good. Follow these steps:

1. **Move to the first page on which you do *not* want the header or footer to print.**

2. **Choose Layout Header/Footer from the menu bar.**

3. **Choose the header or footer you want to discontinue.**

   If you want to discontinue all of them, you have to repeat these steps for each one. (Sigh.)

4. **Click the Discontinue button.**

   The dialog box disappears in a puff of bytes and so does your header or footer, from this page and all subsequent pages in the document.

When you discontinue a header or footer, WordPerfect inserts a secret code named End Header A (or whichever header or footer you chose). To see or delete this code, see Chapter 11.

After you have discontinued a header or footer, you cannot turn it back on. To cancel discontinuing it (that is, to undo the preceding steps), you must delete the secret end code. If you just want to skip printing the header or footer for a page or three, suppress it on each of the pages rather than discontinue it.

Getting rid of a header or footer

If you change your mind about a header or footer and you want to get rid of it for good, you must delete the secret code that defines it. Chapter 11 tells you how to find and exterminate codes you no longer want.

Making the feature bar go away

When you finish editing your header or footer, you may want to make the header/footer feature bar disappear so that its buttons don't distract you and so that you can see a little more of your document on-screen. To dismiss it from your sight, click the Close button.

If you want to see the feature bar again later so that you can do some more work on your headers or footers, just move your cursor anywhere on any page on which the header or footer prints and then choose Layout Header/Footer from the menu. Choose the header or footer you want to edit. Then click the Edit button.

Chapter 11
The WordPerfect
Secret Decoder Ring

· ·

· ·

*A*fter you have worked on a WordPerfect document awhile, it may develop strange quirks and annoying tics. You may even suspect that your document is haunted and consider calling the local Byte Exorcist. WordPerfect has a simple reason for its mysterious behavior: so far, you haven't been able to see the Whole Picture.

As we have alluded to in preceding chapters, there is more to a WordPerfect document than meets the eye. To perform all its impressive formatting tricks, Word-Perfect scatters hidden and powerful *codes,* or *formatting codes,* in your document. If these codes get discombobulated, your document can go haywire too.

Ideally, you should never have to see these codes. After all, you don't care how WordPerfect does things — you just want them done. This is real life, however, and in real life, things go awry. Horribly awry, at times. At these times, you must know how to roll up your sleeves, face those WordPerfect codes, and fix them. It's not really that bad – you won't even get your hands greasy.

What Are Secret Formatting Codes?

WordPerfect *codes* are special objects that WordPerfect inserts in your document to turn special features on or off. The usual way to insert a code in your document is to choose a formatting command or click on a formatting button. WordPerfect saves the codes with your document.

WordPerfect has three types of codes: character codes, feature codes, and paired codes. (We just made these terms up.) We describe each type of code in gory detail later in this chapter and tell you how to spot them and what they do. The codes are briefly described in this list:

- **Character codes:** Represent special characters, such as Tab. Some codes represent keys on the keyboard and others don't, such as Indent.

  Single codes: Turn on a formatting feature. The Lft Mar and Rgt Mar codes, for example, set the left and right margins, beginning at the position of the code. The meaning of the code remains in effect for the rest of the document or until WordPerfect runs across another of the same code.

  Paired codes: Come in pairs (you guessed that, we know). WordPerfect also calls these codes *revertible codes* – who knows where that little piece of jargon comes from? The first code in the pair turns a feature on, and the second one turns it off. Bold codes come in pairs, for example, one to turn on boldface and the other to turn it off. The text between the two codes is in boldface.

Seeing the Codes

This code business is all very exciting, you say. So where are all these codes that have been running around in my documents like cockroaches in the dark?

It's a good question with a simple answer — you can use the Uliew Reveal Codes command from the menu bar (or press Alt+F3) to see the codes in your document. Figure 11-1 shows the WordPerfect window with the Reveal Codes window at the bottom.

The Reveal Codes window

The Reveal Codes window shows the same text you see in the regular window. Because the Reveal Codes window cannot usually hold as much text as the regular window can, it shows the part right around the cursor position. The cursor appears as a red box. Its location in the Reveal Codes window corresponds to its position in the regular window.

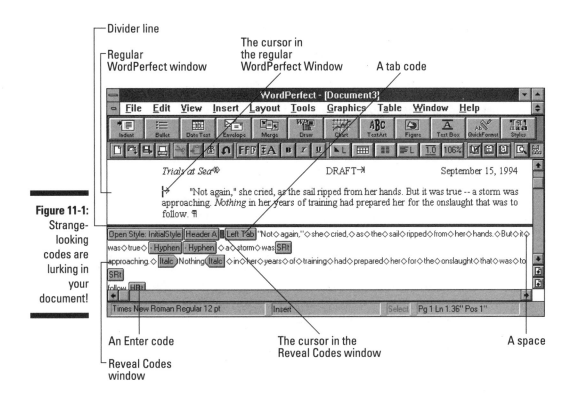

Divider line

Regular
WordPerfect window

The cursor in
the regular
WordPerfect Window

A tab code

Figure 11-1:
Strange-
looking
codes are
lurking in
your
document!

An Enter code

The cursor in the
Reveal Codes window

A space

Reveal Codes
window

TIP

Click into the gap

You can reveal your codes by using the mouse and the scroll bar. You may have noticed (we didn't, until we read the manual) a teeny-tiny gap between the top of the vertical scroll bar and the power bar, and a gap between the bottom of the vertical scroll bar and the status bar. What do you know!

It turns out that if you move your mouse pointer into one of these little gaps, it turns into a double-headed arrow that points up and down. If you then click and drag with the mouse, the dividing line between the regular window and the Reveal Codes window appears, and you can drag it up and down to the position you want.

It's a little hard to scroll up or down in the Reveal Codes window. You cannot use the mouse except by scrolling the regular window and clicking on a new location there. You can, however, press the navigation keys on your keyboard, such as Page Up and Page Down. Or you can move the cursor in the regular window and let the Reveal Codes cursor follow along.

Text in Reveal Codes is completely unformatted. Spaces appear as little diamonds, and codes look like little buttons. In Figure 11-1, for example, you see the Header A and Left Tab codes. Character and single codes look like little rectangular buttons, and paired codes (such as the two Italc codes) have pointed ends, with the points of each pair pointing at each other.

You can type, edit, and do all your normal WordPerfect activities while the Reveal Codes windows is visible. Some people like to leave it open all the time. Of course, some people consider going to the dentist to be recreational activity.

You can control the colors WordPerfect uses for the text and background of the Reveal Codes window, how much information is shown for each code, and some other arcane facets of the Reveal Codes window. Chapter 20 shows you how to customize this stuff. Watch out, though: this subject is getting into seriously nerdy activities, don't you think?

So what the heck do all those codes do? The rest of this chapter discusses the codes you usually encounter and how to get rid of the ones you no longer want.

Adjusting the size of the windows

A dividing line separates the regular window from the Reveal Codes window. Using the mouse, you can click on the line and drag it up or down.

Getting rid of the Reveal Codes window

When you are finished looking at your codes, you can make the Reveal Codes window go away. After all, it is a little distracting to see your codes leap around at the bottom of the screen. Use one of these methods to send the Reveal Codes window back into byte oblivion:

- ✔ Choose View Reveal Codes again from the menu bar.
- ✔ Press Alt+F3.
- ✔ Click on the dividing line and drag it down to the status bar.
- ✔ Click anywhere in the Reveal Codes window by using the right mouse button, and choose Hide Reveal Codes from the QuickMenu that pops up.

A note to Microsoft Word users

If you have used Microsoft Word, you may wonder whether the WordPerfect View Reveal Codes command is similar to Word's View Codes command. In a word: not really.

Microsoft Word doesn't use codes for formatting, so Word's View Codes feature doesn't show you anything about fonts, margins, page layout, and the like. Instead, Word's codes provide a way to

include text that is under the control of the Word program — today's date, for example, which Word can update automatically. Some WordPerfect codes do this too (see Chapter 25 to learn how to create a code that prints today's date), but most don't. As a result, Word's View Codes feature shows you many fewer codes — many documents contain no codes at all.

Cracking the Codes

Now that you know how to bring the secret WordPerfect formatting codes out into the light of day, what can you do with them? Unlike cockroaches (which they otherwise resemble very closely), WordPerfect codes do not scurry away when they are brought to light. In the Reveal Codes window, you can examine them, modify them, and even delete them.

If you don't want to know about codes, skip the rest of this chapter. If you run into trouble with your document and it starts acting as though it has fleas, come back here to find out what's going on.

Looking at codes

Some codes contain much more information than you might otherwise think. You might see a Header A code at the beginning of your document, for example, which indicates that you have defined a header. To see more details about this code, move your cursor directly in front of the code. Suddenly the code expands until it says Header A: Every Page, Chocolate in the Workplace. Many codes contain more information than meets the eye — move the cursor in front of it to see just what it says.

Modifying codes

To change a code, try double-clicking on it. This action tells WordPerfect that you want to do something to the code, and WordPerfect tries to guess what it is. If you used a dialog box to insert the code in the first place, WordPerfect displays the same dialog box again. If you double-click on a Para Spacing code, for example, WordPerfect pops up the Paragraph Format dialog box with the values you specified when you created the code. (This feature is rather useful.) If you change the information on the dialog box and choose OK, WordPerfect updates the code to match.

Deleting codes

The position of each code is important, and codes that are in the wrong place can be a headache. If you see a code that seems to have wandered off into the woods, you can shoot it. Move your cursor just in front of it and press Delete or move the cursor just after it and press Backspace.

When the Reveal Codes window is not displayed, WordPerfect skips over most codes when you press the Delete or Backspace keys so that you don't delete codes by accident. When the codes are revealed, however, WordPerfect figures that you can see what you are doing, and when you press Delete, it deletes.

Save your document (press Ctrl+S) before you make any changes to codes. It's easy to make a horrendous mess with this code stuff. If you have saved your document before you goof up, you can just close the messy one (press Ctrl+F4) and reopen the original (press Ctrl+O).

Now that you know how to see and dispose of WordPerfect's secret codes, let's look at the different types of codes and what they do.

Using the Open Style code

At the beginning of every document, you may notice a mysterious Open Style code. WordPerfect doesn't let you delete this code. This code tells WordPerfect that unless you insert codes to tell it otherwise, it should format the document by using the Initial Codes Style settings. What are the Initial Codes Style settings? We were wondering that ourselves. See Chapter 12 for more details; for now, just make a mental note that these settings include whatever you specify by using the Layout Document Initial Font (described in Chapter 8) and the Layout Document Initial Codes Style, which we talk more about in Chapter 12.

Using Character Codes

The most common codes in every document are carriage return (line ending) codes, including the two in this list:

- **A soft return (SRt):** A carriage return (line-ending character) that WordPerfect inserts automatically when you reach the right margin

- **A hard return (HRt):** Inserted by WordPerfect whenever you press the Enter (or Return) key to signal the end of a paragraph

This list shows some other popular character codes:

- **Left Tab:** What you get when you press the Tab key and it moves to a left tab stop (Chapter 9 discusses types of tab stops). Right Tab, Center Tab, Dec Tab, ...Left Tab, ...Right Tab, ...Center Tab, and ...Dec Tab are the other types of tab character codes that WordPerfect may insert, depending on the type of tab stop they move to.

- **Shift+Tab:** Produces a Hd Back Tab code, used mainly in hanging indents (see Chapter 9).

- **HPg:** The hard page break you produce by pressing Ctrl+Enter (or choosing Insert Page Break).

- **SRt-SPg or HRt-SPg:** When WordPerfect inserts a soft page break because a page has become full, it may be one of these codes. Don't worry about the difference.

- **Auto Hyphen EOL and TSRt:** If you use WordPerfect's automatic hyphenation feature (see Chapter 9), whenever WordPerfect decides to hyphenate a word at the right margin, it sticks in these two codes. First you see an Auto Hyphen EOL code (EOL is computerese for "end of line") and then a TSRt (temporary soft return, maybe?).

You can delete any of these codes to get rid of the characters they represent.

Hard- and soft-core codes

WordPerfect has two versions of many codes, one hard and one soft. This terminology has nothing to do with ripeness, materials used, or anything we can't mention in a G-rated book such as this one. No, it has to do with how seriously WordPerfect takes them.

WordPerfect inserts a *soft code* itself and could just as well take it right back out. WordPerfect continually shuffles the codes around. When you edit the text in the paragraph, for example, WordPerfect changes SRt codes into spaces (and vice versa) as necessary so that the margins are correct. But WordPerfect never deletes a HRt code.

Dealing with Character Formatting Codes

Chapter 8 showed you how to format the characters in your documents seven ways from Sunday. When you use character formatting, WordPerfect creates a flurry of secret codes. Most of them are paired and mark the beginning and ending of the text to be formatted. This list shows some of the character formatting codes you might see:

- **Boldface:** A pair of Bold codes enclose text in boldface.

- **Italics:** Likewise, Italc codes surround text in italics. (Can't those WordPerfect folks spell?)

- **Underlining:** Und codes appear around underlined text.

- **Font sizes:** A lone Font Size code changes the font size from its location to the end of the document or until you get to another Font Size code. A pair of Font Size codes can also enclose text that appears in a different size.

- **Fonts:** Likewise, one or a pair of Font codes changes the font (typeface).

Undoing character formatting

To undo character formatting, just blow away the formatting codes in the Reveal Codes window. For paired codes, you have to delete only one of them — when one of a pair of paired codes disappears, the other dies too (from grief, we assume).

Editing formatted text

After you have formatted your text with character formatting codes, it can be a little tricky to edit. If you have formatted a heading with boldface, for example, when you add a word to the end of the heading, it may not be boldfaced.

Why not? Because the new text was typed *after* the closing Bold code. Without using the Reveal Codes window, it is difficult to see whether your cursor is inside, or outside, a pair of formatting codes.

The leftmost entry on the status bar shows the text style and font for the text where the cursor is located. Without using the Reveal Codes window, you can tell how text you type is formatted by checking the status bar.

If you end with your formatting codes in the wrong place, you can delete them and create them again. Alternatively, you can use cut-and-paste commands (described in Chapter 6) to move the text around so that the codes are in the right places. This procedure looks weird when you do it, and it can be tricky, so be sure to save your document before trying this type of code acrobatics.

Undoing Sentence and Paragraph Formatting

In Chapter 9, you fooled around with the margins and tab stops in your document as well as some other things that affect entire paragraphs of text at a time. As you can imagine, WordPerfect inserts a secret code every time you use one of these formatting commands. This list shows some codes you might encounter:

- **Tab Set:** Contains the settings for all the tabs you can see on the ruler bar. Even if you change just one stop, the Tab Set code stores the positions of all of them. These codes belong at the beginnings of paragraphs — never in the middle of a line.

- **Hd Left Ind:** The indent character you get when you press the F7 key.

- **Hd Left/Right Ind:** The double-indent character you get when you press Ctrl+Shift+F7 key to indent from the left and right margins.

- **Hd Left Ind and Hd Back Tab:** When you create a hanging indent, WordPerfect inserts two — count 'em — two codes. First it inserts a Hd Left Ind code so that all the lines of the paragraph are indented, and then it inserts a Hd Back Tab code so that the first line of the paragraph is unindented. It's not elegant, but it works.

- **Hd Center on Marg:** Centers a line between the left and right margins.

- **Hd Flush Right:** Pushes your text to the right margin.

- **Hyph:** Indicates that you have turned on the hyphenation feature.

You may see the following codes by themselves or in pairs. If you see just one, it sets the formatting for the rest of the document or until you get to another of the same kind of code. If you see a pair of them, they set the formatting for the text enclosed by the pair. This list briefly describes the codes:

- **Lft Mar and Rgt Mar:** Set the left and right margins of your document, beginning at the position of the code; these codes belong at the beginning of a paragraph

- **The Just family of codes:** Tells WordPerfect how to justify the text between the left and right margins

- **Ln Spacing:** Sets the spacing between lines

You can delete any of these codes to remove unwanted formatting from your document. When formatting codes come in pairs, you have to delete only one of the pair and then they both disappear.

Undoing Page and Document Formatting

Most codes that affect entire pages or the entire document appear at the beginning of a document, or at least at the top of the page. That makes them a little easier to find in the Reveal Codes window. To cancel the formatting controlled by these codes, just delete the code.

This list shows the codes created by the commands described in Chapter 10:

- ✔ **Paper Sz/Typ:** Sets the paper size and paper type for the document.

- ✔ **Top Mar and Bot Mar:** Set the top and bottom margins.

- ✔ **Cntr Cr Pg:** Centers the current page between the top and bottom margins.

- ✔ **Wid/Orph:** Tells WordPerfect how to deal with widows and orphans (at least with the types of widows and orphans described in Chapter 10).

- ✔ **Condl EOP (conditional end of page):** Tells WordPerfect to keep the next few lines together (not to split them with a page break).

- ✔ **Block Pro:** Encloses text that should not be split by a page break (these codes should always come in pairs).

- ✔ **Pg Num Pos:** Tells WordPerfect where to print page numbers.

- ✔ **Header A, Header B, Footer A, and Footer B:** Define what WordPerfect prints at the top and bottom of each page. When you discontinue headers, you get codes called End Header A, End Header B, End Footer A, and End Footer B. When you suppress the printing of headers or footers on a page, WordPerfect sticks a Suppress code at the top of the page.

Finding Codes

The Reveal Codes window is not a model of readability. User-friendliness is not its middle name. (Heaven knows that it's a vast improvement over the Reveal Codes windows in earlier versions of WordPerfect, which looked like a strange form of algebra crossed with some kind of circuit diagram.)

The main difficulty in using the Reveal Codes window is finding the code you want. Because the line endings don't correspond with those in the regular window, it can be confusing to tell where you are.

Enter WordPerfect's Edit Find command, which we described in Chapter 5. In addition to using the Find Text dialog box to find text, you can use it to find codes.

You can tell WordPerfect to look for codes in two ways. Both of these methods can be useful:

  ✔ **Codes:** Tell WordPerfect the type of code to look for — a Lft Mar (left margin) code, for example. This method is useful when you want to know what the heck is going on with the margins in your document.

  ✔ **Specific codes:** Tell WordPerfect the exact code to look for (a Lft Mar code that sets the left margin to .5 inch, for example). This method is useful if you have decided to change all ½-inch margins to ¾-inch margins, so you aren't interested in any other margin settings. You can also automatically replace all ½-inch margin codes with ¾-inch margin codes — see the section "Finding specific codes," later in this chapter.

Because both these methods call for using two dialog boxes at the same time, your screen may begin to look like a Dadaist painting. Give it a try, though, if you have the courage.

Finding all codes of one type

To find all of one type of code in your document (all the Tab Set codes, for example, regardless of the tab stop positions they contain), follow these steps:

  1. **Move your cursor to the beginning of the document or to the beginning of the part of the document you want to search.**

  2. **Choose Edit Find from the menu bar.**

     You see the Find Text dialog box, as shown in Figure 11-2. Alternatively, you can press the F2 key.

     The Find Text dialog box has its own little menu bar (described in more detail in Chapter 5).

  3. **Choose Match Codes from this menu bar.**

     WordPerfect displays the Codes dialog box, as shown in Figure 11-3. The Find Codes box lists all the secret codes you can search for.

  4. **Choose the code you want to search for.**

     Choose the Tab Set code, for example.

  5. **Click on the Insert button in the Codes dialog box.**

     The code name appears in the Find box in the Find dialog box.

  6. **Click on the Close button in the Codes dialog box.**

     You have finished telling WordPerfect which code you want to look for.

  7. **Click on the Find Next button on the Find Text dialog box.**

     WordPerfect looks for the code or codes you specified and highlights the next occurrence in your document.

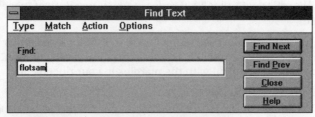

Figure 11-2:
Finding
codes
wherever
they may
lurk.

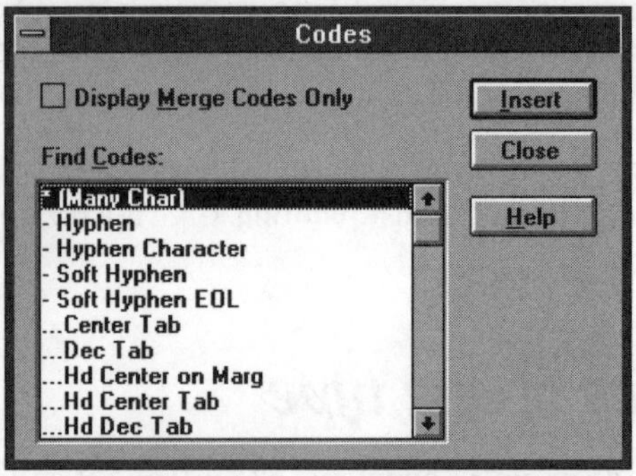

Figure 11-3:
Choosing
the code for
which to
search.

When you display the Find Text dialog box, its Find box may already contain text or codes — the last information you searched for. If it does, delete the information if you don't want to search for it again.

If WordPerfect cannot find your code, it displays a small dialog box that tells you so. Click the Close button to make this dialog box go away.

For more information about using the Find Text dialog box, see Chapter 5.

To search backward through your document, click the Find Prev button in the Find Text dialog box.

In the Find Codes list in the Codes dialog box, the first 15 codes have names that begin with punctuation, such as ...Left Tab (a tab that moves to a left tab stop with dot leaders). After these codes, the codes are listed in alphabetical order.

To find a code in the Codes dialog box whose name begins with *T*, you can click on the Find Codes listing and type **T**. The list zooms down to the Ts.

If you plan to continue looking for codes in your document, you can leave the Find Text dialog box open while you edit your document. It's faster than opening and closing it for each search, although it does clutter up your screen.

You can move the Find Text dialog box to an out-of-the-way part of your screen by clicking and dragging its title bar with your mouse.

You can also leave the Codes dialog box open if you plan to look for different codes. Just skip clicking on its Close button until you are finished with it.

You can search for a sequence of codes. WordPerfect uses the two codes Hd Left Ind and Hd Back Tab, for example, to create a hanging indent. To search for this combination of codes, in this order, choose Hd Left Ind from the Codes dialog box, choose Insert, and then choose Hd Back Tab from the list and click the Insert button again. The two codes appear in the Find box. When you choose the Find Next button in the Find Text dialog box, WordPerfect looks for the sequence of codes.

You can also search for a mixture of codes and regular characters. If you want to search for a Tab followed by an asterisk, for example, you can use the Codes dialog box to make [Tab (all)] appear in the Find box and then type an asterisk.

Finding specific codes

WordPerfect has another way to look for codes that contain additional information. A *margin code* contains extra information, for example — the size of the margin you want. On the other hand, a Bold code contains no other information. For codes that contain additional information, you can search for all codes that have a particular setting (all Font codes that set the font to Times New Roman 12 pt, for example). Follow these steps:

1. **Move your cursor to the beginning of the document or to the beginning of the part of the document you want to search.**

2. **Choose Edit Find from the menu bar.**

   WordPerfect displays the Find Text dialog box (refer to Figure 11-2). Alternatively, you can press the F2 key.

3. **Choose Type Specific Codes from the menu bar on the Find Text dialog box.**

   You see the Specific Codes dialog box, shown in Figure 11-4.

4. **In the Specific Codes dialog box, choose the type of code for which you want to search.**

   WordPerfect lists only the types of codes that contain additional information. (To search for a code that isn't on this list, use the Match Codes command, described earlier.)

5. Click the OK button in the Specific Codes dialog box.

The Specific Codes dialog box goes away and WordPerfect changes the Find Text dialog box to match the type of code you are looking for. If you choose Font, for example, as the type of code for which to search, WordPerfect transforms the Find Text dialog box into a Find Font dialog box, shown in Figure 11-5. The menu bar and buttons are unchanged, but rather than choose the text for which to search, WordPerfect lets you enter the information the code contains. The Find Font dialog box, for example, lets you enter the font name and size.

6. So go ahead and do it — enter the settings of the code for which you want to search.

Choose Times New Roman for the font name, for example, and Italics for the style.

7. Click the Find Next button to search for the next occurrence of the code.

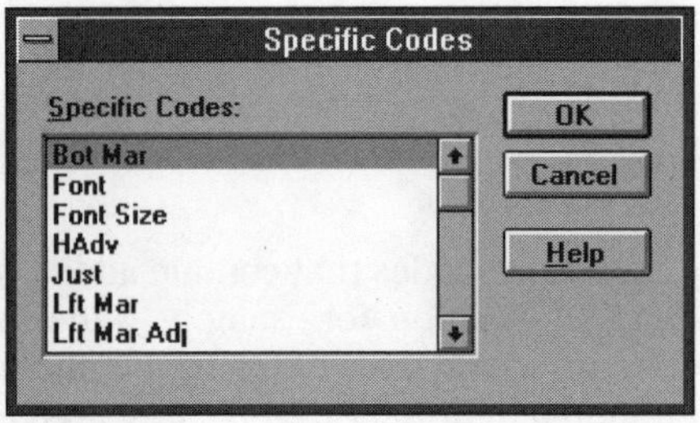

Figure 11-4:
Choosing the
type of code
for which to
search.

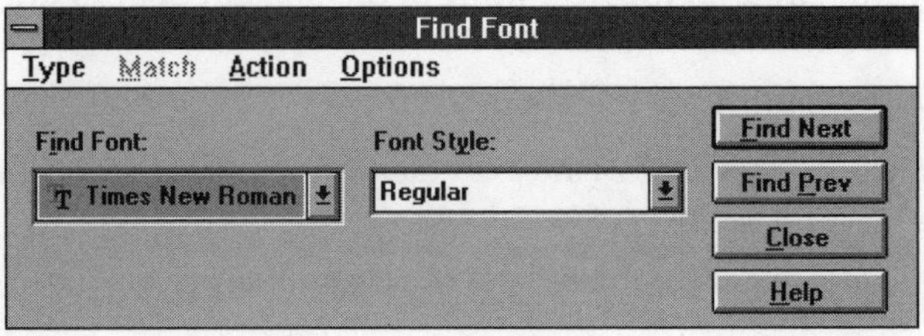

Figure 11-5:
Finding a
specific
code —
WordPerfect
waves its
magic wand
and displays
just the right
dialog box.

When you search for a specific code, you cannot search for a combination of codes and text or for a sequence of more than one code. Bummer.

If WordPerfect cannot find the code, it pops up a dialog box that tells you so. Click the Close button to make this dialog box go away. If you are sure that your code is in there somewhere, try using the Match Codes method, described in the preceding section.

Knowing what to do after you have found your code

After you have found the code you are looking for, you can delete it by pressing the Delete key. Or if it is a code that was created by using a dialog box, you can modify it by double-clicking on the code in the Reveal Codes window.

It's a good idea to use the Reveal Codes window when you are finding codes so that you can see whether WordPerfect found the one you want.

Replacing Codes Automagically

Here's a fairly common scenario: you have formatted your document very tastefully with several fonts, including the Tms Rmn font. But you find out that the Times New Roman font looks much nicer when you print. What's the best way to change all those Font codes from Tms Rmn to Times New Roman without going nuts?

Like all decent word processors, WordPerfect has a find-and-replace command, which was described in Chapter 5. It swoops through your document looking for the offending text and changing it to the proper text. The good news is that you can use it to look for and change WordPerfect's secret codes too.

The bad news is that you cannot use the find-and-replace command to replace paired codes. You might use pairs of Bold codes, for example, to make section headings in a report boldfaced and later you decide to use italics instead. If you use the find-and-replace procedures in the following section to replace all the Bold On codes (the ones at the beginning of the boldfaced heading) with Ital On codes, WordPerfect doesn't also automatically replace the corresponding Bold Off codes with Ital Off codes. Instead, you get large stretches of italics in your document and a big mess.

Probably the best way around this whole business of finding and replacing codes is to use *styles,* which enable you to standardize the codes you use for various parts of your document. Chapter 12 describes how to use styles.

Be sure to save your document before using the find-and-replace feature! You never know what might go wrong. We guarantee enormous amounts of smugness if something goes wrong and you have made a backup copy of your document first.

Replacing specific codes with other codes of the same type

Although WordPerfect's find-and-replace feature can be confusing and shouldn't be used with paired codes, it's great for replacing character codes and single codes. You can replace all the specific codes with other codes of the same type, for example, such as changing all the Font:Arial Regular codes to Font:Times New Roman Regular. Follow these steps:

1. **Move to the beginning of your document by pressing Ctrl+Home.**

   If you want to replace the codes in only part of your document, move to the beginning of that part.

2. **Choose Edit Replace from the menu bar or press Ctrl+F2.**

   WordPerfect displays the Find and Replace Text dialog box, as shown in Figure 11-6. Like the Find Text dialog box, this dialog box also has its own little menu bar (described in more detail in Chapter 5).

3. **With your cursor in the Find part of the Find and Replace Text Box, choose Type Specific Codes.**

4. **From the Specific Codes dialog box, choose the type of code you want to replace.**

   Choose Font, for example.

5. **Click the OK button to dismiss the dialog box.**

   WordPerfect transforms the Find and Replace Text dialog box in a dialog box more appropriate for the type of code you are replacing (with the Find and Replace Font dialog box, shown in Figure 11-7, for example).

   Both the Find and Replace With text boxes have been transformed into settings appropriate for the type of code with which you are working. If you are replacing Font codes, for example, WordPerfect displays settings for fonts and font styles.

6. **Choose the settings for the existing codes you want to get rid of and for the new codes you want to replace them with.**

   Choose Arial for the Find Font setting, for example, and Times New Roman for the Replace With setting.

7. **To replace the codes one by one so that you can eyeball each occurrence before making the replacement, choose the Replace button on the dialog box.**

   If you prefer to close your eyes and make all the replacements at one time, choose the Replace All button. If you are prudently replacing your codes one at a time, WordPerfect moves the cursor directly *after* the code to be replaced. To replace it, choose <u>R</u>eplace again. To skip it, choose <u>F</u>ind. To replace this code and all the rest of the codes of this type in your document, go wild and choose Replace <u>A</u>ll.

8. **When you are finished, choose <u>C</u>lose to make the Find and Replace dialog box go away.**

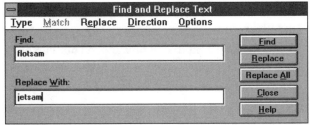

Figure 11-6: Replacing all evil secret codes with good ones.

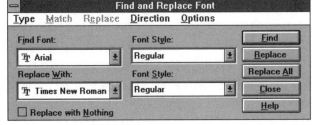

Figure 11-7: Changing all your Arial font codes to Times New Roman.

If you cannot see your codes, choose <u>V</u>iew Reveal <u>C</u>odes from the menu in the WordPerfect window to open the Reveal Codes window.

Replacing codes with other codes

So far, you have replaced WordPerfect codes with the same type of code but that contain other settings. You can also replace one type of code with another — you can replace Hd Left Ind codes (indents) with Hd Left Tab codes (regular ol' tabs), for example. The following steps show you how:

1. **Move to the beginning of your document by pressing Ctrl+Home.**

   To replace the codes in only part of your document, move to the beginning of that part.

2. **Choose <u>E</u>dit <u>R</u>eplace from the menu bar or press Ctrl+F2.**

   WordPerfect displays the Find and Replace Text dialog box (refer to Figure 11-6).

3. **With your cursor in the Find part of the Find and Replace Text Box, choose Match Codes from the dialog box's menu.**

   You see the Codes dialog box (refer to Figure 11-3).

4. **From the Codes dialog box, choose the type of code you want to replace.**

   Choose Hd Left Ind, for example.

5. **Choose Insert to stick the codes into the Find box in the Find and Replace Text dialog box.**

6. **In the Find and Replace Text dialog box, move your cursor to the Replace With text box.**

7. **In the Codes dialog box, choose the code you want to replace the old codes with.**

   Choose Hd Left Tab, for example.

8. **Choose Insert again to stick the codes into the Replace With box in the Find and Replace Text dialog box.**

   Now you have told WordPerfect what to look for and what to replace it with.

9. **Click the Close button in the Codes dialog box.**

   You're finished inserting codes and you probably want some of your screen back.

10. **Choose the Replace button in the Find and Replace Text dialog box to replace codes one at a time.**

    Or choose Replace All to go for the gold.

11. **Click the Close button when you finish replacing codes.**

    You cannot use this method to insert codes that require additional information. You cannot replace all your Bold codes with Font codes, for example, because Font codes require additional information (the name and style of the font). It's just a WordPerfect limitation. Not that we can blame them — this find-and-replace business is complicated enough as it is!

    Using this method, you can replace combinations of codes and text with other combinations of code and text.

Deleting all the codes

You can use the Find and Replace Text dialog box to get rid of all of one type of code in your document (all Font codes, for example). Use the preceding steps to tell WordPerfect which codes you want to find, but don't enter anything in the Replace With box. This action tells WordPerfect to replace these codes with nothing.

Mysterious Codes

"What the heck is the !@#$% code? And who the #$%^&* put it in my document?" This cry has been heard throughout the land since WordPerfect first shipped back in the early '80s.

If you encounter a code you have never seen and that isn't described in this chapter, stay calm. You can always delete it, after all. To find out what it is, look in the back of the *WordPerfect for Windows Reference,* that big, dense manual you received when you bought WordPerfect. One of its many appendixes contains a complete list of all the secret codes WordPerfect uses – you won't believe how many it has. This list tells you the name of the code, which you can then look up in the *Reference* or in the on-line Help (by pressing F1).

Putting codes in their place

Codes shouldn't go wandering willy-nilly around your documents. Some codes belong in certain places, and WordPerfect can help you keep them where they belong.

Most line and paragraph formatting codes (described in Chapter 9), for example, belong at the beginnings of paragraphs, never in the middle of them. Page and document formatting codes (described in Chapter 10) belong at the tops of pages, never in the middle of a page.

WordPerfect has a feature called *auto code placement.* Contrary to its name, this feature does not give WordPerfect license to go around placing codes in your documents. It just tells WordPerfect to help you place your codes in the right places: it places all line and paragraph formatting codes at the beginning of the paragraph the cursor is in, and all page and document formatting codes at the top of the current page.

In earlier versions of WordPerfect, you could turn auto code placement on or off. In WordPerfect for Windows 6.0, it is always turned on — and we can't see any reason to want to turn it off.

Chapter 12
Documents with Style

• •

• •

*W*hen Og, the popular and celebrated mammoth hunter, trimmed his body with the colorful viscera of a woolly mammoth, the "Og" style caught the popular imagination. Anyone could walk into the local haberdashery, simply request an Og, and come out with all the necessary fine points taken care of. No need to specify all the details: the woven tripe necklace, the bone in the hair, the brain-tanned bladder sporran; the word *Og* said it all. In the following year, when Og decided that the necklace should be sinew (not tripe), folks could still order an Og and be in style.

A more contemporary application of these "named styles" is text formatting. Text formatting styles take advantage of the fact that most text formatting is repetitive. In this book, for example, all the level 1 headings are the same format, as are all the level 2s, the normal text, the tips, and so on. Rather than continually respecify for each block of text all the details of typeface, point size, indentation, justification, and the rest, why not call one collection of formats Heading 1, another Heading 2, and so on? In that way, the only formatting a block of text needs is a style name. Applying a named style is a heck of a lot simpler than accurately repeating the same half-dozen formatting commands over and over again.

Another advantage is that after text is formatted by styles, any change in style definitions immediately takes effect throughout the document. An Og remains an Og — it just looks different.

What Is a Style?

A WordPerfect *style* is a combination of various types of formatting, such as fonts and indentation — the kind of stuff typically done with the Layout commands — assigned to a name. You can then apply the style by name to text in your document that you want formatted in that way.

Usually, you use a style for some simple combination of paragraph layout and font or font style, such as "centered and bold." You can also use line, page, and document formatting, however — you can use anything, in fact, that changes the appearance of your document, from margins to page breaks.

After you have used a style, any change in the definition of the style ripples through your document, changing appearances wherever you have applied that style. This capability is way cool.

When you format text by using styles, however, a bit of a conflict occurs in places where you have formatted the text directly, using Layout commands or function keys. WordPerfect resolves this conflict in favor of the directly formatted text. If you have indented a paragraph by using Layout Paragraph Format, or F7, for example, and then you apply a paragraph style that is not indented, the indentation remains. Directly applied formatting can be tricky to remove too and often requires you to delete the secret codes discussed in Chapter 11. So if you use styles, be somewhat diligent about it. As much as possible, do not revert to your old, unprincipled ways of formatting your text directly, by using the Layout commands.

Creating and Applying a Style

The style stuff lurks at the bottom of the Layout menu. If you think that you already understand styles, just launch into the Layout Styles command (or press Alt+F8). Good luck.

The rest of us can choose an easier way: do *not* launch into the Layout Styles command. Begin by formatting a bunch of text the way you want it, as an example. Then record that formatting as a style. This process is called QuickCreate. This section explains how to do it.

Subtleties in style

You don't have to understand the subtle differences among styles right now (we explain them as we go), but it helps. WordPerfect has three fundamental types of styles:

Character   Affects selected text

Paragraph   Affects an entire paragraph

Document   Affects everything from the point where the style is applied

Do not confuse the *type of style* with the *type of formatting it can do.* A *paragraph style* can contain fonts or font styles for all the text within it. A *document style* can contain fonts and paragraph layout settings for all the paragraphs that follow it.

QuickCreating a character style

Let's begin this discussion with how to create a style for formatting selected characters. Assume, for example, that you want foreign words in your document to be in bold and italic, so you want to create a style called "foreign" to format them.

These steps guide you through this process:

1. **Format some text in bold and italics, as an example for WordPerfect.**

   Preferably, format some text to which you want to apply the style, anyway. To format it in bold and italics, select it and then press Ctrl+B and Ctrl+I.

2. **With your text still selected, choose Layout Styles (or press Alt+F8) from the menu bar.**

   The Style List dialog box is displayed, as shown in Figure 12-1.

3. **Click the QuickCreate button.**

   Ignore everything else for now. The Styles Quick Create dialog box is displayed, as shown in Figure 12-2.

4. **Make up a name for your style, such as "foreign," and type it in the Style Name box, where your cursor awaits you.**

   Don't try to exceed 12 characters; WordPerfect doesn't allow it.

5. **If you want, make a reminder to yourself in the Description box that describes the style's purpose, such as "character formatting for foreign text."**

6. **In the Style Type area at the bottom of the box, click on Character.**

   This step tells WordPerfect to create a character style (see the preceding technical sidebar for the three types of styles).

7. **Click the OK button.**

   WordPerfect creates the style, but the dialog box doesn't go away.

8. **Click on either Close or Apply.**

   Use Apply if you want your example text to have this named style applied to it. If you click Close, it remains as plain, formatted text and doesn't change if the style changes. (We usually choose Apply.)

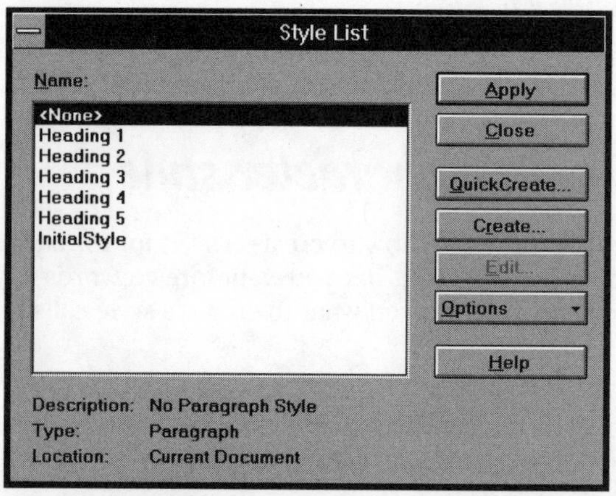

Figure 12-1:
The Style List dialog box.

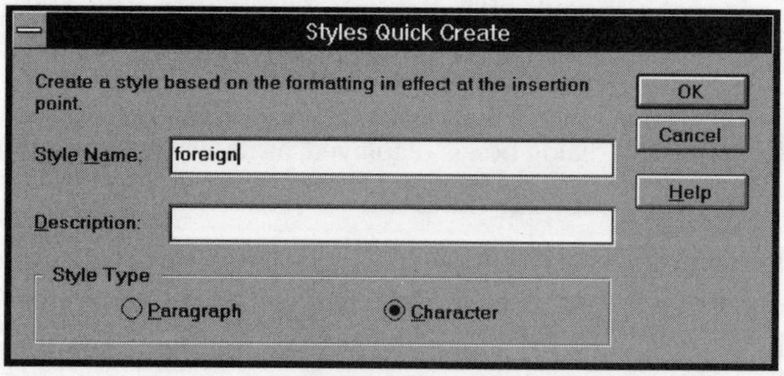

Figure 12-2:
Creating a character style called "foreign" in the Styles Quick Create dialog box.

That's it — you did it! You have created the "foreign" style, which you now can apply by name to any selected text in your document.

Applying a character style

To apply your character style, just select some text and choose Layout Styles again from the menu bar. The dialog box that was shown in Figure 12-1 reappears.

This time, the Style List contains your very own style name. Just double-click on it to apply it to your text (or click on it once and then click on the Apply button). The dialog box goes away 'cause you're finished!

QuickCreating a paragraph style

Certain types of formatting do not belong in a character type of style. Paragraphy-type things, for example — such as indentation — belong in a paragraph style. These things include stuff you normally do with the Layout Paragraph command.

But wait — the nice thing about paragraph styles is that they can *also* include both paragraph-type things and character-type formatting, such as boldface and font styles. (It doesn't work the other way. Character formatting should not include paragraph stuff.)

To create a paragraph style, you perform almost the same steps as for the character style, as shown here:

1. **Format a paragraph as an example for WordPerfect, preferably some text you want the style applied to anyway.**

   Indent it, for example, by placing the cursor before the first character and pressing F7; quadruple-click in it to select the entire paragraph and then underline it by pressing Ctrl+U.

2. **With your cursor within the formatted text, choose Layout Styles (or press Alt+F8) from the menu bar.**

   You see the Style List dialog box (refer to Figure 12-1).

3. **Click on the QuickCreate button.**

   The Styles Quick Create dialog box is displayed (refer to Figure 12-2).

4. **Make up a name for your style, such as "indent uline" and type it in the Style Name box.**

   Don't exceed 12 characters, though — WordPerfect doesn't seem to like it.

5. **If you want, make a reminder to yourself in the Description box that describes the style's purpose.**

   Use something like "indented, boldface paragraph."

6. **In the Style Type area at the bottom of the box, click on Paragraph.**

Now you have told WordPerfect to make a paragraph style.

7. **Click the OK button.**

WordPerfect creates the style.

8. **Click on either Close or Apply.**

Use Apply if you want your example paragraph to have this named style applied to it. If you click on Close, it remains as a plain, formatted paragraph and doesn't change if the style changes.

Applying a paragraph style

Applying paragraph styles is much like applying character styles. Put your cursor in the paragraph you want to style. Or for multiple paragraphs, select them. Click on Layout Styles from the menu bar. When the Style List dialog box appears, double-click on the style name to apply it to your selected paragraph.

If you have applied a paragraph style and want to change it, there's a quick alternative to choosing Layout Styles from the menu bar. With your cursor in the styled paragraph, double-click on the "status" box of the status bar at the bottom of the WordPerfect window. (It's the second box from the left, usually, which now displays the name of the current paragraph style.) This step brings up the Style List dialog box.

Creating a document style

Sometimes you want to make a style that applies beginning at a certain point and perhaps everything past it. This type of style is called a *document style,* and it is a little weird. Unlike the character and paragraph style, a document style has no predetermined point where it ends. As a result, it generally continues until another one begins.

Document styles can include not only the formatting you normally would do in the Layout Document command but also anything else from the Layout menu, including Fonts, Line, Paragraph, or Columns commands. For that matter, they can do darn near anything from the Insert, Tools, Graphics, or Table menus, including inserting page breaks, changing headers and footers, inserting dates, inserting graphics, or making quacking noises, if you go for that sort of thing and have laid out the bucks for sound.

Using a document style is a good way to set up the overall layout of a document, including the margins, the paragraph formatting for most paragraphs, and the font for most text.

You cannot make a document style by the QuickCreate method, which was described earlier for character and paragraph styles. You must use the Create method. (You can use the same method for character and paragraph formatting, but it's more work, so why bother?)

To create a document style, follow these steps:

1. **Choose L̲ayout S̲tyles from the menu bar or press Alt+F8.**

   You see the Style List dialog box.

2. **Click on Create (not QuickCreate).**

   Up pops the Styles Editor dialog box, as shown in Figure 12-3.

3. **Click on Style Name and type a descriptive name with no more than 12 characters.**

   You can also click and type a Description if you want. (You did this step for character and paragraph styles in the preceding example, except that then you were using the Styles Quick Create dialog box.)

4. **Under the word *Type* is a button. Click on it and hold down the mouse button. Choose D̲ocument (open) from the menu that pops up.**

   Certain things are "grayed out" in the dialog box so that you cannot use them. Don't worry — you don't want them.

5. **Now comes the fun part. Put in anything you want, using the Styles Editor menu bar.**

   This bar duplicates commands from the main WordPerfect menu bar. Choose L̲ayout Pa̲ragraph I̲ndent, for example, and then choose L̲ayout F̲ont and choose B̲old from the Font dialog box. These layout features now become part of your new document style. (Ignore what's going on in the Contents window of the dialog box unless you have read Chapter 11.)

6. **Click on OK when you're finished.**

   You are back in the Style List dialog box.

7. **Click on C̲lose.**

   Don't click on A̲pply unless your cursor is in the exact position at which you want this style to begin.

```
┌─────────────────────────────────────────────────────────┐
│ ─                    Styles Editor                       │
├─────────────────────────────────────────────────────────┤
│  Edit  Insert  Layout  Tools  Graphics  Table            │
│                                                          │
│  Style Name: ┌──────────────────────────────┐  ┌──────┐ │
│              └──────────────────────────────┘  │  OK  │ │
│  Description: ┌─────────────────────────────┐  └──────┘ │
│              └──────────────────────────────┘  ┌──────┐ │
│  Type:                  ⊠ Enter Key will      │Cancel│ │
│                            Chain to:           └──────┘ │
│  ┌────────────────┬─┐   ┌──────────────────┬─┐ ┌──────┐ │
│  │Paragraph(paired)│↕│   │<Same Style>      │↓│ │ Help │ │
│  └────────────────┴─┘   └──────────────────┴─┘ └──────┘ │
│  Contents                                                │
│  ┌──────────────────────────────────────────────┐       │
│  │                                                │       │
│  │                                                │       │
│  │                                                │       │
│  │                                                │       │
│  │                                                │       │
│  │                                                │       │
│  │                                                │       │
│  └──────────────────────────────────────────────┘       │
│                                                          │
│  ⊠ Reveal Codes          □ Show 'Off Codes'              │
└─────────────────────────────────────────────────────────┘
```

Figure 12-3:
The Styles
Editor dialog
box.

Applying a document style

To apply a document style, position your cursor where you want the style to begin (probably before a paragraph). If your style includes any insertions, such as page breaks, they also go here.

Revealing your secret style codes

If you have read Chapter 11 and understand the secret codes in WordPerfect, you should understand the bottom window of the Styles Edit box. It shows which codes are being encapsulated into the style, just as a Reveal Codes window does.

Moreover, you should understand why character and paragraph styles are denoted as (closed) and document styles as (open). "Closed" is another word for "paired" style codes; "Open" means "single" style codes.

When WordPerfect applies a closed style to your document (character or paragraph styles), it uses pairs of codes to bracket the affected text. These codes use only the style name, which gives you complete freedom to edit the style definition without putting a bunch of screwy codes in your text. When WordPerfect applies an open style (document style), it uses single codes — again, using only the style name. Magically, these codes can apply formats such as Bold text style, which without styles would require paired codes. Go figure.

Headings and the InitialStyle

Before you go on to changing styles, we should introduce the built-in styles, called Heading 1 through Heading 5, and InitialStyle. Unsurprisingly, Headings are styles for your headings and subheadings. Their definitions are preset for convenience because headings are what most people use styles for, most of the time. Bring up the Style List dialog box to see them. (Yes, it's still Layout Styles, or Alt+F8.)

Heading styles (Heading 1 through Heading 5) do nice things, such as make your headings all bold or italics and enter them in the Table of Contents (if you ask WordPerfect to create a table of contents). They are nicely specified styles, fortunately, because changing them often requires understanding (Ugh!) secret codes.

Apply Heading styles as you would apply any other style, as shown in these steps:

1. **Choose Layout Styles from the WordPerfect menu bar.**

   The Style List dialog box appears.

2. **Double-click on an appropriate Heading style.**

The other built-in style, InitialStyle, specifies the way your text looks when you create a new document, before you do anything to change its appearance. You don't have to apply the InitialStyle; it happens automatically at the beginning of your document. Unless you apply other styles, all the text in your document is formatted according to InitialStyle.

InitialStyle is, in fact, the central place where your choices are recorded when you use either the Layout Document Initial Font command (described in Chapter 8 and Chapter 19) or the Layout Document Initial Codes Style command (mentioned in Chapter 11).

If you want to add or change something in InitialStyle or a Heading style, check out the Styles Editor, described in the section "Changing Styles with the Styles Editor," later in this chapter.

If you want to remove something, you have to deal with secret codes (refer to Chapter 11). If you're not up to reading Chapter 11 in its entirety, you can also try a little guesswork while you are using the Styles Editor.

More Built-In Styles

WordPerfect comes with a grab bag of predefined styles you can use. They are not normally in the Style List, but you can bring them in by following these steps:

1. **Choose Layout Styles from the menu bar.**

2. **Click on the Options button.**

3. **In the Style Setup dialog box that appears, check the System Styles box.**

4. **Click on OK.**

You can then choose from a couple of dozen useful styles in the Name box. As you do with any style, you double-click on the style name to apply it to the currently selected text (for character styles) or to the place where the cursor is (for paragraph or document styles).

Changing Styles with the Styles Editor

Modifying styles requires that you learn at least something about secret codes. Fortunately, the task is worthwhile. Nothing is so satisfying as having every paragraph in your document hooked up to a style so that you can change them all at will, through the Styles Editor. We can think of one or two things more satisfying, but you can't do them with your computer.

The following steps show you how to modify a style:

1. **Choose Layout Styles or press Alt+F8.**

   WordPerfect displays the Styles List dialog box.

2. **Click on the style you want to change (Heading 1, for example).**

3. **Click on the Edit button.**

   A Styles Editor dialog box is displayed, such as the one that was shown in Figure 12-3.

Now things get dicey. To add something, such as a specific font style, use the Styles Editor dialog box's menu bar. (This procedure is the same as the one described in the section, "Creating and Applying a Style," earlier in this chapter.) Add italic style, for example, by choosing Layout Font from the Styles Editor menu bar and then clicking on Italic in the Font dialog box.

To change something, such as changing boldface to underline, you probably have to use the secret codes. Look in the Contents window at the bottom of the Styles Editor dialog box for a box with a suggestive word in it, such as Bold. Try double-clicking on it. Something should happen, such as the appearance of a Font dialog box. When it does, you can make your change. Close this dialog box, whatever it is, and you change the secret code.

To delete something in the Contents window, such as the Very Large font style, click on it and then drag it out of the Contents window and into the Real World, where scummy secret codes cannot survive.

If you make a mistake while you are modifying styles in the Style Editor, the Undo command in the Styles Editor menu bar can help you, just like the one on the main WordPerfect menu bar. Just click on Edit and then on Undo. If you accidentally delete a code, you can also use the Edit Undelete command.

Turning Styles Off and Chaining Styles

Suppose that you have applied a style and you are now merrily typing along and updating your résumé to include the phrase *Mastery of WordPerfect styles.* You finish a delightfully styled paragraph, press Enter, and — bingo! — you start another similarly styled paragraph. This automatic spawning of a similarly styled paragraph is lovely, but what if you don't *want* another similarly styled paragraph?

Or perhaps you're typing a letter to Aunt May in a character style that uses the lovely Shelley Vollante font and you want to turn it off to leave a more legible note to near-sighted Uncle George. Follow these steps:

- ✔ To turn off a paragraph style in the paragraph in which your cursor is located, choose Layout Styles from the main menu bar and then double-click in the list.

- ✔ If you have been typing along in a character style and now you want to turn it off for the following text, press the right-arrow key on your keyboard once. This step moves your cursor past the secret style-end code. When you type again, the style is no longer in effect.

Another solution is to end or change styles automatically when you create a new paragraph. How do you do this? The Highly Inquisitive Reader will have noticed in the Styles Editor a dialog box thingy labeled `Enter Key will Chain to:`. This particular thingy is what you're looking for.

This feature really asks, "What do you want to happen when you're typing along in this style and you spawn a new paragraph by pressing Enter? Do you want the new text to continue in this style, or what?"

When you click on the down-arrow key to the right of the associated box, you see that you have three possible types of answers to this nit-picking question:

- ✔ **<None>:** Means turn off the styles altogether.

- ✔ **<Same Style>:** Means "Begin a new paragraph in this same style."

- ✔ **Any of your own, homegrown styles in the Style list:** (Not the system stuff, such as Heading 1.) These styles mean "Begin a new paragraph with this style." These "chaining styles" are useful when styles normally follow each other, such as introductory text after a heading.

This feature works only for paragraph or character styles. For document styles, this dialog box thingy gets all gray and fuzzy, like a bad video copy of the closing scene in *Casablanca.* It means "I'm off duty, Mac."

For character styles, you have one more option. Click on the box next to the `Enter Key will Chain to` thingy to remove the X. This way, pressing the Enter key means "keep going in this same style." The only way this method differs from choosing `<Same Style>` is that `<Same Style>` turns off the style and then turns it on again. The difference is so subtle that you will never care unless you often deal with secret codes.

Reusing Styles

Reusing work you have already finished is always a smart idea, and styles help you reuse your formatting efforts.

You can reuse styles in one of two ways:

- ✔ Retrieve them from an existing document into a new document.

- ✔ Save them in another file.

Retrieving styles from another document is the lazy way to do it and is therefore our favorite, as shown in these steps:

1. **Choose Layout Styles from the WordPerfect menu.**

   You see the Style List dialog box.

2. **Click the Options button.**

   Now you see the Options drop-down menu.

3. **Choose Retrieve.**

4. **In the Retrieve Styles From dialog box that appears, type the filename of the document from which you want to retrieve styles.**

   Or you can click on the file-folder icon to select the file from a list (see Chapter 15 to learn how this method works).

5. **If you want just the user styles or the system styles, click on the appropriate box in the Retrieve Styles From dialog box.**

   Normally, you get both. WordPerfect asks whether you want to override the current styles.

6. **Click the OK button.**

   Click on Yes. WordPerfect asks whether you want to override the current styles.

7. **Click on Yes.**

To be Really Systematic and Organized, however, you should save your styles to a central location. This procedure lets you control styles from a single point.

In one of the two approaches, you copy your styles to a document *template* that automatically brings in styles when you create a new document. (Chapter 17 describes templates and all the wonderful things you can do with them.) The other method, in which you save your styles to a separate file, requires you to retrieve the styles manually from that file. It has the advantage, however, of letting you save all your styles — styles for memos, for example — under a name such as MEMOS.STY.

If most of what you create will use the same styles, copy your styles to the standard template, on which all documents are based. (This approach is also great for pack rats, who don't mind if every style they ever create is stored in one place.)

To copy styles to the standard template, follow these steps:

1. **Choose Layout Styles from the WordPerfect menu.**

   You see the Style List dialog box.

2. **Click on a style you want to copy.**

3. **Click the Options button in the Style List dialog box.**

   The little Options menu pops up (or down).

4. **Click on Copy in the Options menu.**

   A Styles Copy dialog box is displayed.

5. Click on <u>T</u>emplate in the Copy To area.

6. Repeat steps 1 through 5 for each style you want to copy.

Now whenever you create a new document, these styles are available.

In the other method, saving your styles to a file, you choose Save <u>A</u>s from the Options menu and type a directory and filename. (Or you can click on the file icon to use a dialog box for this procedure.) Give the file an extension which will remind you that styles are in the file, such as .STY.

To use these styles, just open your new document, choose <u>L</u>ayout <u>S</u>tyles, click the <u>O</u>ptions button, and choose <u>R</u>etrieve.

Getting Rid of Styles

After awhile, particularly if you're of the pack rat persuasion and you keep all your styles in the same place, you will want to delete a few of them. You cannot delete the built-in styles, however, just your own. These steps show you how:

1. Choose <u>L</u>ayout <u>S</u>tyles from the WordPerfect menu bar.

2. Click on a style you want to delete.

3. Click the <u>O</u>ptions button in the Style List dialog box.

   If the Delete option is grayed out, you're trying to delete a built-in style. Stop that.

4. Click on Delete in the menu that drops down.

   A dialog box is displayed that asks, in effect, whether you want to delete the style definition and take out all the codes for that style in your document (the <u>I</u>nclude Codes option) or remove the definition and leave the formatting in place (the <u>L</u>eave Codes option).

5. You decide and then choose either Include Codes or Leave Codes.

6. Click on OK when you're finished.

Part III
Things You Can Do with Documents

"PUT DOWN 'CAUSES FOOT DAMAGE.'"

In this part...

It is a little-known fact that when humans lived in the trees, they didn't have a word for *forest*. (OK, so they didn't have a word for anything else either. Be that way.) The reason was that they couldn't (everyone say it together now) "see the forest for the trees." They couldn't, that is, until they had mastered the trees, climbed the mountains, and attained the perspective that enabled them to say, "Whoa — look at them forests!"

Likewise, all who master the world of mere words and ascend the heights of word processing eventually find themselves saying, "Whoa — look at them *documents*." (Grammar hasn't progressed much over the millenia.) Accordingly, this part of the book explores the printing, dressing up, moving around, and overall whipping into shape of your documents. Head 'em up and move 'em out!

Chapter 13
On Paper at Last — Printing Stuff

• •

In This Chapter

▶ Getting the printer ready

▶ Printing the entire document

▶ Printing parts of a document

▶ Printing a document on disk

▶ Printing several documents

▶ Canceling a print job

• •

*W*e have all heard about the Paperless Office of the Future. Remember when computers were new and everyone claimed that after we all started using computers, we could stop using paper? Lo and behold, look around your office! Do you see paper? There's twice as much paper as ever before — that's how much paper you see.

Back in real life, you usually will want to print your documents, and this chapter talks about how to do it. For details about creating and printing some popular documents, including mailing labels and envelopes, see Chapter 20.

Ready to Print?

You have written and formatted your document, and it looks maahvelous. Now you're ready to see how it looks on paper. But before you can do so, you had better be sure that your printer is ready to help.

Make sure that the printer is plugged in, to both the wall and your computer. The connection to the wall provides power, and the cable to your computer provides a way for the information in your document to get from the computer into your printer.

Be sure that your computer has the appropriate ribbon, ink cartridge, or toner cartridge, depending on your printer — unless you are interested in printing your document in white on white. (See Chapter 22 to learn how to determine which type of printer you have.)

You need paper, as you may have guessed. Your printer may use individual sheets of typing paper or continuous-feed perforated paper. Whatever your printer likes to eat, make sure that your printer has paper.

You should also make sure that your printer is paying attention to what your computer has to say. Most printers can be either *on-line* or *off-line* (either listening to the computer or not listening, respectively). These printers have an on-line light that tells you whether the printer is on-line, and an on-line button you can press to switch between on-line and off-line. If your printer is off-line, it ignores any information your computer sends to it — it's like being turned off.

If your printer uses sheets of paper, you may want to print drafts of documents on the other side of used paper. We keep a stack of paper with stuff on just one side and use it for all except the final drafts of our documents.

Before WordPerfect for Windows can print anything, Windows must know all about your printer. When you (or someone) installed Windows on your computer, you should have told Windows which printer (or printers) you have. Windows shares this information with WordPerfect. If you're not sure whether Windows knows about your printer, read Chapter 22 or the book *Windows For Dummies* (IDG Books Worldwide). You use the Printers icon in the Control Panel program that comes with Windows.

Chapter 22 contains more information about printing, including what to do if printing goes wrong.

Printing the Entire Document

WordPerfect gives you a good idea of what your document will look like when it's printed. If you use page view (by choosing View Page from the menu bar or by pressing Alt+F5), you can even see where your headers and footers appear, as well as the top and bottom margins of the pages. (Chapter 10 describes page view and the other views WordPerfect provides.) But you cannot really get the total effect until you see your document on paper.

Where's the printer?

If your computer is connected to a network and you use a network printer, someone else is probably in charge of making sure that the printer is connected to all the right cables. You should still check to make sure that the printer has paper, however, because the guy in the next cubicle may have the annoying habit of printing 200-page reports without refilling the paper tray.

You may also want to talk to your network administrator to find out which type of printers you can use and how to tell Windows about it if it doesn't already know. Chapter 21 also talks about some of these things.

These steps show you how to print your document:

1. **Make sure that your printer is turned on, on-line, and ready to print.**

   Make sure that the right kind of paper is loaded — recycled paper for drafts and nice, new blank paper for final versions, letterhead, or whatever. We always keep a stack of paper near our printer with embarrassing first drafts printed on one side, ready for less embarrassing second drafts to be printed on the other side.

2. **Save your document just in case something dire happens while you are printing it.**

   Practice safe printing!

3. **Click the Print button on the power bar.**

   It's the button that looks like the front view of a boxy, white sedan. Alternatively, you can choose File Print from the menu bar or just press F5. WordPerfect displays the large and imposing Print dialog box, shown in Figure 13-1.

4. **Ignore all those interesting-looking settings and just choose the Print button.**

   WordPerfect informs you that it is preparing the document for printing. Other dialog boxes may flit across the screen as WordPerfect informs its WP Print Process program, Windows informs its Print Manager program, and the Print Manager program passes the information along to the printer. (For more information about this arcane process, if you care, see the section "Who ya gonna call?" later in this chapter.) At long last, the printer starts to hum and begins to print.

As soon as your cursor stops looking like the Sands of Time (a tiny hourglass) and returns to its normal shape, you can continue to use WordPerfect while your printer prints. You can open another document, edit the current docu-

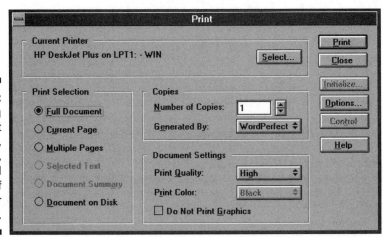

Figure 13-1:
Telling
WordPerfect
the who,
what, when,
where, and
why of
printing your
document.

TIP

Instant printing

If you press Ctrl+P, WordPerfect prints your entire document without showing you the Print dialog box. Slam! Bang! — direct to the printer. Be sure that you really want to print the whole thing before you press Ctrl+P. If you press Ctrl+P by mistake, see the section "Canceling a Print Job," near the end of this chapter.

ment, or do whatever you want. It's probably not a good idea to either close your document or exit from WordPerfect, because the chances of printing a document correctly on the first try are zero. We would bet dollars to doughnuts that you will see a large typo which was staring you in the face from the screen for the past half hour but which becomes truly visible only on paper.

If the printer doesn't print anything, don't just print it again. Your document may still be wending its way through the bowels of Windows on its way to the printer. It may have gotten stuck on its way (intestinal distress happens even to computers). Make sure that the printer is on and on-line. If nothing happens after a minute or two, see the section "Canceling a Print Job," near the end of this chapter.

If you are looking at the Print dialog box and you decide not to print the document after all, just press the Esc key or choose the Close button on the dialog box. No harm done and no paper wasted.

Before printing the final draft of a document, you may want to consider checking its spelling. See Chapter 7 for complete instructions.

Printing Part of a Document

When documents get long (like some chapters in this book), you may not want to print the whole thing. What if you have just printed a 30-page report, for example, and then you find and correct a typo on page 17? Not to worry — you can print just a single page, or any selection of text, for that matter.

Printing selected text

To print a selection of text, follow these steps:

1. **Get the printer ready (turn it on, for example).**

2. **Select the text you want to print.**

   See Chapter 6 to learn how to select text.

3. **Choose the Print button from the power bar.**

Or press F5 or choose File Print from the menu bar to display the Print dialog box (refer to Figure 13-1).

4. **Choose Selected Text for the Print Selection.**

5. **Click the Print button.**

Printing a specific page

Follow these steps to print one page:

1. **Make sure that your printer is ready to print.**

2. **Move your cursor anywhere on the page you want to print.**

3. **Choose the Print button from the power bar.**

Alternatively, you can press F5 or choose File Print from the menu bar to display the Print dialog box.

4. **Choose Current Page for the Print Selection.**

5. **Click the Print button.**

Printing a bunch of pages but not all of them

To print a few pages, do the following:

1. **Make sure that your printer is all set to print.**

2. **Make a note of the page numbers you want to print.**

It doesn't matter where the heck your cursor is.

3. **Choose the Print button from the power bar.**

Or press F5 or choose File Print from the menu bar. Just get that Print dialog box on the screen.

4. **Choose Multiple Pages for the Print Selection.**

Notice that WordPerfect, in its subtle way, adds some dots to the Print button's name. This change tips you off to the fact that when you choose it, WordPerfect plans to ask you for more information, such as which pages you want.

5. **Choose the aforementioned Print... button.**

WordPerfect displays the aptly named Multiple Pages dialog box, as shown in Figure 13-2. Ignore all except the first box (the Page(s) box) in this dialog box.

6. **In this box, type the page numbers you want to print.**

Table 13-1 shows the ways you can type the page numbers of ranges of pages.

7. Click the Print button.

WordPerfect prints the pages you specified and skips all the other pages.

Table 13-1	Print Range Page Numbers
Entry	*Meaning*
all	Print all the pages in the document
x	Print page number *x*
x,y,z	Print pages *x, y,* and *z* (separate page numbers by commas or spaces)
x-y	Print pages *x* through *y*, inclusive
x-	Print page *x* through the end of the document
-x	Starting at the beginning of the document, print through page *x*
x,y-z	Print page *x* and then pages *y* through *z.* You can include as many page ranges as you want, separated by commas or spaces.

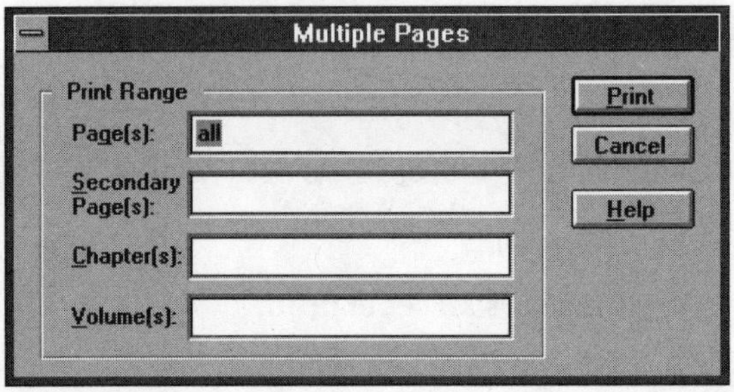

Figure 13-2:
Selecting
pages to
print.

Printing odd- or even-numbered pages

It's cool to print documents on both sides of the paper, such as in a book. This method not only makes your document look terribly official but also marks you as an Ecologically Sound Person, which is important in this day and age. If you want to print your document on both sides of the paper but your printer doesn't do it automatically, don't worry, you are not out of luck. Your Green reputation doesn't have to suffer.

Instead, you can print all the odd-numbered pages on one side of the paper, take the paper out of the printer and stick it back in, and then print all the even-numbered pages on the other side of the paper. Of course, you have to do it just right or else all the pages end up in the wrong order. The following procedure works for sheet-fed printers, such as ink-jet and laser printers:

1. Make sure that your printer is eager to print.

Also make sure that the paper you plan to use is blank on *both* sides.

2. **Choose the Print button from the power bar.**

   Or press F5 or choose File Print from the menu bar.

   You see the Print dialog box.

3. **Choose Options.**

   WordPerfect displays the Print Output Options dialog box, as shown in Figure 13-3.

4. **For the Print Odd/Even Pages option, choose Odd by clicking and holding down the left mouse button on the Both entry and sliding the highlight down to Odd.**

5. **Choose OK.**

   You leave the Print Output Options dialog box.

6. **Click the Print button as usual.**

   WordPerfect prints only the odd pages.

7. **Flip the paper over.**

   After all the odd-numbered pages have been printed, put them back in the paper tray so that WordPerfect can print on the other side of the paper. Make sure that page 1 is printed-side-down and on the top so that WordPerfect prints page 2 on its back side. (You may have to turn over each page individually, not just flop the stack over.) Also make sure that the paper is facing the right way so that page 2 isn't upside down and doesn't print on the *same* side of the paper as page 1. Because the exact orientation you need depends on your printer, you may want to experiment with a short document.

8. **Repeat steps 1 through 6. This time, select Even for the Print Odd/Even Pages option in step 4.**

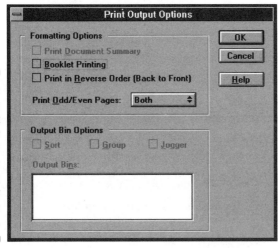

Figure 13-3:
Telling
WordPerfect
to print only
your odd
pages
(assuming
that they
aren't all a
little odd).

Printing several copies

After you have begun printing a document, you may want several copies. Hey, why not save yourself a trip to the copying machine?

To tell WordPerfect how many copies to print, follow these steps:

1. **Make sure that your printer is hot to print.**

2. **As usual, choose the Print button from the power bar.**

   Also, you can press F5 or choose File Print from the menu bar to display the Print dialog box.

3. **In the Number of Copies box, enter the number you want.**

   You can click on the little up- and down-arrow buttons to increase and decrease the numbers.

Printing a Document on Disk

What if you want to print a document that isn't open? What if you wrote, saved, and printed a magnificent letter this morning, for example, and now you want to print an extra copy to show to your mother? You can open it first, admire it on the screen for a while, and then print it, but there's a faster way, as shown in these steps:

1. **Set your printer so that it's rarin' to print.**

   It doesn't matter where your cursor is, or even which document is open.

2. **Choose the Print button from the power bar or press F5 or choose File Print from the menu bar.**

   WordPerfect displays the Print dialog box.

3. **Choose Document on Disk for the Print Selection.**

4. **Click the Print button.**

   WordPerfect displays the Document on Disk dialog box, shown in Figure 13-4.

5. **In the Filename box, enter the filename of the document you want to print.**

   If it isn't in the current directory, you must enter its full pathname. If you don't know what the heck we are talking about or if you want to know how to use that cute, little file-folder icon next to the Filename box, see Chapter 15.

6. **Choose Print from the Document on Disk dialog box.**

   WordPerfect prints the document without displaying it on-screen.

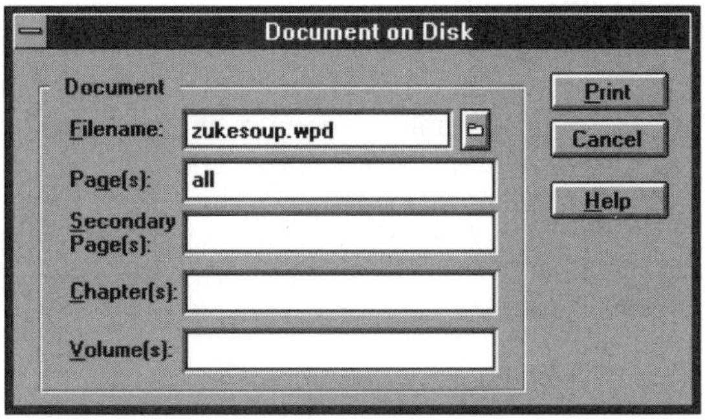

Document on Disk

Document

Filename: zukesoup.wpd

Page(s): all

Secondary
Page(s):

Chapter(s):

Volume(s):

Print

Cancel

Help

Figure 13-4:
Printing a
document
that isn't
loaded.

Following these steps is a good way to print a document you have already
printed that doesn't need additional editing.

You can print only selected pages from the document on disk, by entering page
numbers in the Page(s) box.

If the file doesn't exist or if you typed its filename wrong (it could happen to
anyone), WordPerfect displays the message that the file was not found. Choose
the OK button to get rid of the message and try again. For help in finding files,
see Chapter 15.

Make your printer do the work!

WordPerfect normally prints multiple copies by
sending the document to the printer over and
over. Many laser printers, however, can print
multiple copies of a document all by themselves.
It is a much faster process if WordPerfect can
send the contents of your document to the printer
one time and then tell it how many copies to print.
If you think that your printer is capable of this feat
of intelligence, set the Generated By option in the
Print dialog box to Printer rather than to
WordPerfect.

If you always, or even almost always, print more
than one copy of your documents, you can tell
WordPerfect to suggest 2 or any other number as
the usual number of copies to print. You can also
change the defaults (the usual suggested settings) for other items in the Print dialog box — see
Chapter 22.

Printing Several Documents

You can tell WordPerfect to print a bunch of documents, one right after the other. If you want to print ten different letters, for example, and each letter is in a separate file, it is annoying and slow to open each document, print it, and then close it. It is less annoying and slow to print each file from disk as described earlier. Instead, you can select the files you want to print and then print them all in a batch.

This method is a great way to get lots of printing done in a hurry, but it's also an effective way to waste lots of paper, so be careful when you are selecting the files to print. Follow these steps:

1. **Click the Open button from the power bar.**

   Alternatively, you can press Ctrl+O or choose File Open from the menu bar. WordPerfect displays the Open File dialog box.

   You can use any dialog box that lets you select files and that has a File Options button on it. The Open File dialog box is our favorite because if you choose OK by mistake, nothing bad happens.

2. **Choose from the file list the files you want to print.**

   If the files are listed together, click on the first filename and then Shift-click on the last one — WordPerfect highlights all the files from the first to the last. If the files aren't listed together, click on the first filename and then Ctrl-click on the other filenames — WordPerfect highlights the filenames you chose but not the intervening filenames.

3. **When you have selected the files you want to print, click the File Options button.**

   WordPerfect displays a list of things you can do with the files you have selected. We talk about most of them in Chapter 15.

4. **Choose Print from the little menu.**

   WordPerfect displays the Print File dialog box, shown in Figure 13-5, which shows the names of the files you selected.

5. **Assuming that the list of filenames looks right, click the Print button.**

   WordPerfect prints the files one after the other. The Print File dialog box disappears and leaves you looking at the Open File dialog box or whatever dialog box you opened in step 1.

6. **Choose Cancel (or press Esc) to make it go away.**

If the files you want to print are in a different directory, go directly to Chapter 15 to find out how to find them.

Information about the other things you can do to files with the File Options button is also in Chapter 15.

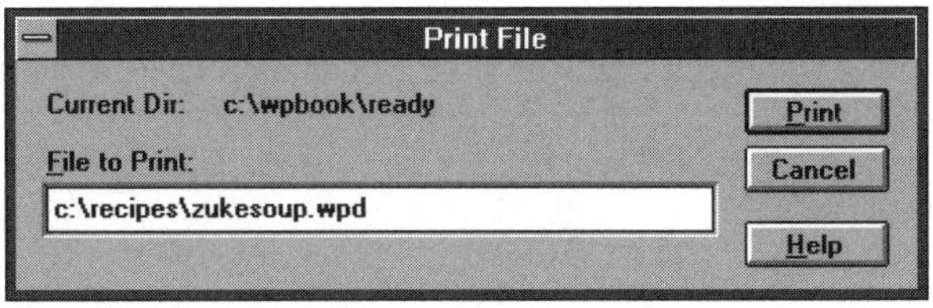

Figure 13-5:
Printing a
bunch of
files.

Print File

Current Dir: c:\wpbook\ready

File to Print:

c:\recipes\zukesoup.wpd

Print

Cancel

Help

Canceling a Print Job

So far, printing has been pretty smooth sailing. Display a dialog box or two, click the buttons, and presto — your document is on paper. Then one day, disaster strikes — you send your 150-page report to print while you are in the middle of reorganizing it. It's time to tell WordPerfect, "Stop printing! Never mind! I didn't mean it!"

The problem is that it isn't simply a matter of talking to WordPerfect. Back in the days before Windows, you were usually running one program at a time, more or less. By communicating with that program, you could control what was going on in your computer. With Windows, those days are over.

Who ya gonna call?

WordPerfect (like all Windows programs) prints by committee. Figure 13-6 shows the path your document takes on its way to your printer. WordPerfect first sends the information in your document to the *WP Print Process,* a program that comes with WordPerfect. This program formats the document to make it ready to print. The WP Print Process in turn sends your formatted document to the Print Manager, a program that comes with Windows. The Windows Print Manager hangs on to your document long enough to make sure that the printer you want to use is free and ready to print. Then it sends the document to the printer.

What a nightmare! If you want to cancel printing your document, whom do you talk to? We tell you how to tell the WP Print Process to forget about it and ditto for the Windows Print Manager.

You don't have to use the Windows Print Manager, and someone may even have turned it off. If you don't see it running on your system, don't worry.

Figure 13-6:
The tortuous
path your
document
takes to the
printer.

WordPerfect → WP Print Process → Windows Print Manager → Your printer

If your computer and printer are connected to a network rather than directly to each other, you may have an additional step. The Windows Print Manager may pass your document to the network print manager, which then sends it to the printer. Or the Windows Print Manager may be turned off so that your document goes directly from the WP Print Process to the network print manager. In either event, a talk with your network administrator may be in order, accompanied by a few chocolate-chip cookies to ensure his or her cooperation.

While a document is printing or after is has printed, one or two unfamiliar icons may appear at the bottom of your screen, outside the WordPerfect window. One is the WP Print Process icon and the other is the Print Manager icon. For more information about using the Windows Print Manager, see Chapter 22 or refer to the book *Windows For Dummies,* by Andy Rathbone (IDG Books Worldwide).

WordPerfect, stop printing!

While WordPerfect is sending your document to the WP Print Process, you can tell it to forget the whole thing, by following these steps:

1. **Choose the Print button from the power bar.**

   Or press F5 or choose File Print from the menu bar to display the Print dialog box.

2. **Choose Control.**

   WordPerfect displays the WordPerfect Print Job dialog box, shown in Figure 13-7, which shows you the status of your print job in more detail than you could possibly want.

3. **To stop the document from printing, choose Cancel Print Job.**

If WordPerfect doesn't display the WordPerfect Print Job dialog box, WordPerfect and its WP Print Process program must have finished doing their part of the work, and the ball must be in the Windows Print Manager's court. See the following section to learn how to tell Print Manager not to print.

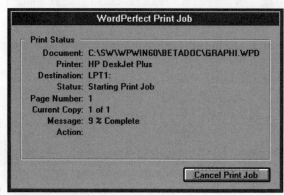

Figure 13-7:
Stop that
print job!

If you don't want to cancel the print job, no button is available to make the WordPerfect Print Job dialog box go away! (Oops.) Instead, just click in the regular WordPerfect window, and the dialog box becomes invisible.

Stop, stop, I say!

If it's too late to tell WordPerfect to stop printing, it's time to talk to the members of the Committee for Printing Your Document. To tell the WP Print Process and the Windows Print Manager to forget about printing any documents, follow these steps:

1. **Press Ctrl+Esc to display the Windows Task List.**

   It's shown in Figure 13-8.

2. **Highlight the WP Print Process.**

   You may want to scroll down the list to find it if you are running more than seven programs at a time (excessive, we think, but not our place to judge). If you don't see it, it isn't running, so skip to step 5.

3. **Choose the End Task button to tell Windows to stop running this particular program.**

   If the WP Print Process was formatting a document for printing, this step stops it cold.

4. **Press Ctrl+Esc again to see the Task List.**

   The WP Print Process should have disappeared from the list of running programs.

5. **This time, highlight the Print Manager program.**

   Line it up in your sights.

6. **Choose End Task again to cancel any printing the Print Manager might be planning to do.**

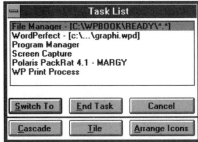

Figure 13-8:
The list of
programs
you are
running.

If you are familiar with the Windows Print Manager, rather than kill the Program Manager, you can switch to it and delete the print job for your document. You may want to refer to *Windows For Dummies* to learn how to do this. Or you can probably figure it out: choose Print Manager, select <u>S</u>witch To, highlight the print job for the document in the Print Manager, and click the <u>D</u>elete button above the print job list.

Don't worry about ending the WP Print Process and Windows Print Manager tasks. Canceling them doesn't prevent you from printing in the future — it just cancels whatever is going on right now. The next time you print a document, WordPerfect tells Windows to start them back up.

When you exit from the Windows Print Manager, you cancel not only the printing of WordPerfect documents but also any printing other programs are doing. If you just told your spreadsheet program to print something and it has not yet finished printing, for example, stopping the Print Manager may cancel the spreadsheet print job. It's not a tragedy if this happens — you just have to print whatever it was again.

Chapter 14
Juggling Documents on Your Screen

● ●

In This Chapter

▶ Working on two documents at the same time

▶ Sizing your windows

▶ Minimizing your documents

▶ Closing documents

▶ Combining documents

▶ Knowing what to do if the file already exists

▶ Using foreign files

● ●

*I*magine living in New York City in an apartment that has a powerful telescope. Using your telescope, you can look into the windows of your various neighbors. In one, you see an office worker typing away. In another, you see a warehouse. In a third, someone is washing the dishes. In the fourth — oops! — close the curtains!

In the same way, WordPerfect for Windows lets you work on more than one document at the same time. As you open each document, WordPerfect creates a *window* to display it. You can open several documents at one time and view several windows simultaneously. Hey, this is what Windows is all about!

This chapter explains this multiwindowing stuff to you. You don't even need a telescope to be able to do it. Using these techniques, you can improve your productivity by viewing and editing related documents at the same time or you can turn your WordPerfect window into a big mess, as shown in Figure 14-1. The choice is yours.

While we are on the subject of opening documents, let's talk about how to open files that *don't* contain WordPerfect documents, such as documents created by other word processors or other programs.

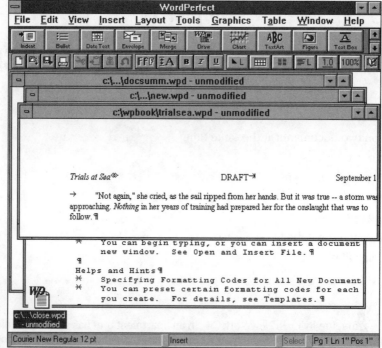

Figure 14-1:
Using
multiple
documents
can get out
of hand!

How Can You Work on Two Documents at a Time?

To work on a document, as you know, you open it by using the File Open command (or clicking the Open button on the power bar or pressing the Ctrl+O keys). WordPerfect creates a window for it that occupies the space between the power bar (if it is visible) at the top and the status bar at the bottom.

After you have opened a document, you can open *another* document. WordPerfect keeps the first document open, but covers it up with a second window that contains the second document.

Switching between open documents

How do you get back to the first open document? Aha! — the Window command on the menu bar is the solution. When you choose Window, you see a menu that contains two commands (Cascade and Tile) followed by a numbered list of the documents you have open. To switch to another open document, just choose its name from the menu.

To switch documents without using the mouse, press Alt+W to choose the Window command from the menu. Look at the menu and notice the number that precedes the name of the document you want. Press that number.

Making baby documents

When you want to begin writing something new, you need a brand-spanking new document with no text in it. No one ever told you how baby documents are made? It's about time you learned the Facts of Life.

To make a new document, choose File New from the menu bar or press Ctrl+N. WordPerfect names the new document something wild and crazy, such as Document2, and makes a window for it. You can give it a better name when you save it.

Closing the curtains

When you finish working on a document, don't leave it lying around open. Each open document slows WordPerfect down just a little. To close the window that contains a document, choose File Close from the menu bar (or press Ctrl+F4).

If the document you are closing has been changed since you last saved it, WordPerfect gives you the chance to save it before closing it so that you don't lose your work. You can choose Yes so that WordPerfect saves the document before it closes it, No so that it closes it without saving your changes, or Cancel so that WordPerfect abandons the idea of closing it.

In WordPerfect for DOS, you use the same key — the F7 key — to close a document and to exit from WordPerfect. This situation has always been confusing, and WordPerfect for Windows has two separate commands: File Close to close a document and File Exit to leave WordPerfect.

Why did the friendly folks at WordPerfect choose Ctrl+F4 to be the magic keys to close a document? Why not Ctrl+C, for example? It turns out that most Windows programs use the Ctrl+F4 key combination to close windows, so WordPerfect went along with the standard. Besides, Windows programs usually use Ctrl+C for copying text to the Clipboard, and WordPerfect does too.

Working with multiple documents

The most common use for opening multiple documents is to refer to one document while you write another — or sometimes to rip off text from one document while you write another. WordPerfect makes this technique easy: You can use all of WordPerfect's cut-and-paste commands to move or copy text from one document to another.

If you wrote a truly stellar paragraph in one letter, for example, and you want to use it in another letter, follow these steps:

1. **Open both documents.**

   Use the usual File Open command or the Open button.

2. **In the original letter, select the paragraph.**

   Quadruple-click on it if your fingers are dexterous enough.

3. **Press Ctrl+C to copy the paragraph to the Clipboard.**

   Or choose Edit Copy from the menu or use the Copy button on the power bar. Nothing seems to happen.

4. **Switch to the other document by using the Window command.**

   Or use the mouse to click on the other document, if you can see it.

5. **Move your cursor to the point where you want the paragraph to appear.**

6. **Press Ctrl+V to paste the paragraph there from the Clipboard.**

   Or you can choose Edit Paste from the menu or use the Paste button on the power bar.

After you get good at this kind of thing, it's amazing how much text you can recycle!

Maxing out

You can keep opening additional documents until nine are open. Then WordPerfect puts its foot down and prevents you from opening any more by disabling both the File Open command on the menu and the Open button on the power bar.

To open another document, you first must close one of your open documents. We have rarely found a situation in which we really had to refer to more than nine documents at the same time — maybe your brain cells have more capacity than ours do!

Windows within windows

It can be annoying to flip back and forth between two documents, copying information or just referring to what you have written. Sometimes it is more convenient to see *both* documents at the same time. Again, WordPerfect is happy to oblige.

Seeing lots of windows

You can view multiple documents on the screen in these three ways:

- ✔ Choose <u>W</u>indow <u>C</u>ascade from the menu bar. WordPerfect creates a little window for each document and stacks them up like a pack of cards, as shown in Figure 14-2.

- ✔ Choose <u>W</u>indow <u>T</u>ile from the menu bar. Again, WordPerfect puts each document in a little window. This time, however, it fills the WordPerfect window with them like a game of dominoes (see Figure 14-3).

- ✔ You may have noticed a little, gray button with an up-and-down-pointing arrow (or two black triangles) at the right end of the menu bar, just to the right of the <u>H</u>elp command. If you click this button, WordPerfect cascades or tiles your documents (using whichever command you used last).

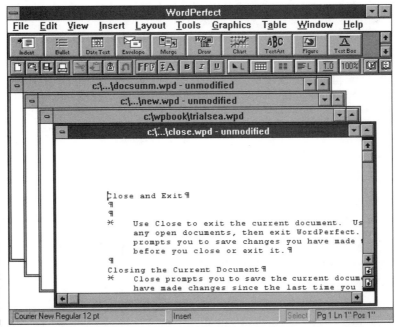

Figure 14-2: Pick a document — any document.

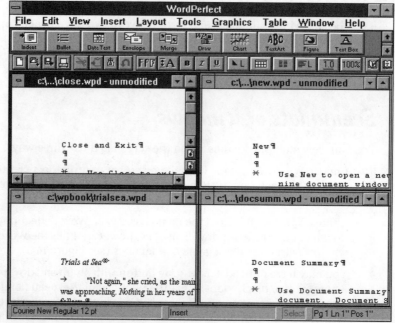

Figure 14-3:
Shuffle your
documents
and lay them
end to end.

Each document window has its own little title bar that shows the filename for the document and that has its own little scroll bars. You can move around in each document by using the same old mouse and cursor keys you read about in Chapter 3.

If you plan to look at several documents at a time, you may want to make your WordPerfect window as big as possible. To *maximize* it, click the upward-pointing triangle button in the upper right corner of the WordPerfect window. Chapter 21 describes other things you can do with the WordPerfect window.

I want that one!

When you can see multiple document windows, one of them is *active*. The active document window is the one with the highlighted title bar. It's usually on top of the other windows (no other windows obscure your view of it). The active window is the one you are editing, and your cursor is in it. Formatting commands you give affect the active window. Text you type lands in the active window.

You can switch from one window to another by clicking your mouse anywhere in the window for the document you want to use. Or you can use the <u>W</u>indow command described earlier in this chapter.

Sizing your windows

It is extremely unlikely that either cascading or tiling your documents will produce document windows that are large enough to get any work done. You probably will have to move them around a little, perhaps making the window for the main document you are working on large and the other document windows small. No problem.

Each little document window has a border, and you can move these borders around at will, as shown in these steps:

✔ If you point to the left or right border of a window, the mouse pointer turns into a little left-and-right-pointing arrow. You can click and drag the window border to the left or right to resize it vertically.

✔ When you point to the top or bottom border of a window, the mouse pointer turns into an up-and-down-pointing arrow and you can drag the window border up or down to resize it horizontally.

✔ When you point to a corner of a border, the mouse pointer turns into a diagonally-pointing arrow, and you can drag the corner around in any direction. WordPerfect adjusts the borders accordingly.

You can also move the windows around by clicking and dragging their title bars. It's similar to moving papers around on your desk except that they never get coffee stains on them. You can waste most of your work day, in fact, by moving your windows around until you get them lined up just the way you want them.

Maximizing your documents

All these windows and borders and scroll bars on your screen can become distracting. When you want to get back to work and look at just one document, you can *maximize* it so that it takes up the entire WordPerfect window again.

To maximize a document, look at the right end of its title bar. Click on the upward-pointing triangle. Poof! The other document windows are covered up by this document.

Minimizing your documents

If you click on the *downward*-pointing triangle on the title bar in a document window, it is *minimized*. That is, it gets really small and appears as an icon somewhere in the vicinity of the lower left corner of the WordPerfect window.

(Refer to Figure 14-1 to see a minimized document.) No one we know ever clicks on it on purpose, but it happens when you want to maximize your document window and you click on the wrong triangle.

Saving all your open documents

As you know, it's a good idea to save your open documents frequently. Then if all the air conditioners in the building kick in at the same time, the power dips, and your computer blips out, you don't lose your work.

If you have several documents open, you should save all of them. Many programs have a File Save All command, but WordPerfect seems to have forgotten it. Luckily, you can press the Save All key combination — just press Ctrl+Shift+S. This step saves all the documents you have edited.

Combining Documents

As you know, each WordPerfect document lives in its own cozy, little file on your disk. But sometimes you may want to break down the walls between your documents and get them together, throw a little party, or whatever.

One of your documents might contain a standard description of the product you sell — chocolate belly futures, for example. Then you create a new document in which you begin a letter to a prospective client. You realize that you want to include the product description in your letter.

Inserting one document into another one

No dirty jokes at this point, please. Let's just stick to word processing:

1. **Move your cursor to the location where you want the text from the other file to appear.**

   Move the cursor to the point in your letter, for example, where you want to wax eloquent about chocolate belly futures.

2. **Choose Insert File from the menu bar.**

   WordPerfect displays the Insert File dialog box, which looks exactly like the Open File dialog box and half a dozen dialog boxes that have to do with files.

3. **Choose the name of the file you want to insert in the current document.**

   Choose the filename for the standard product description, for example.

4. Choose Insert.

Or double-click on the filename. WordPerfect cannot quite believe what it's hearing and asks whether you want it to insert the file into the current document. Why else does it think that you chose the Insert File command, for Pete's sake?

5. Choose Yes to do the deed.

WordPerfect opens the file and sticks its contents into the current document right where your cursor is located and shoves aside any text that comes after the cursor.

Another way to include information from one document in another is to open both documents and use cut-and-paste commands to copy the information from one document to the other. The resulting combined document has the same name as the original document you opened.

You can insert more than one document in the current document. There is no limit, in fact, to the number of other documents you can stick in the current one. But watch out: don't create enormous documents unless you have to. They can become slow and unwieldy.

WordPerfect doesn't keep track of where inserted text comes from. If you want the inserted text to change with its source document, you want *linked documents*. WordPerfect can do that: you have to use the File Master Document command, which we discuss in Chapter 19.

Saving a chunk of text as a separate document

You can also do the reverse of inserting text — you can save part of the current document in a new, separate file. What if you write a letter that contains, for example, a terrific explanation of how to make vegetarian chili, your specialty? Now you want to save your recipe in its own file, as shown in these steps:

1. Select the text you want to save separately.

Chapter 6 shows you ways to select text.

2. Choose your favorite way of giving the Save command.

Give the File Save command, click the Save button on the power bar, or press Ctrl+S. WordPerfect notices that some text is selected and displays the Save dialog box, as shown in Figure 14-4.

3. To save the selected text in its own file, choose Selected Text and then choose OK.

WordPerfect shows you the usual Save As dialog box so that you can tell it the filename you want to use for the selected text. You might call the selected text VEG_CHILI.WPD, for example.

4. **Choose OK in the Save As dialog box to create the new document that contains the selected text.**

The text you selected also remains in the original document. That is, WordPerfect saves a *copy* of it in the new file.

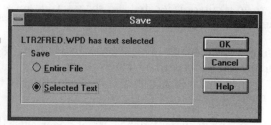

Figure 14-4:
Saving some
text in its
own file.

What If the File Already Exists?

As you work in WordPerfect, opening and saving documents, you frequently type names for new files. Because filenames are rather limited (Chapter 1 explains the rules and regulations for what you can use as a filename), it can stretch the limits of your imagination to come up with new and different, yet memorable and descriptive, names for your files in only eight letters.

The day will come when you type a name for a new file, little suspecting that you have *already* used that filename, probably for a document you have forgotten all about. According to the Rules of DOS (because DOS is the program in charge of files and disks), you cannot have two files with the same name in the same directory.

What happens? WordPerfect asks you what the heck you want to do — that's what happens. A dialog box like the one in Figure 14-5 is displayed.

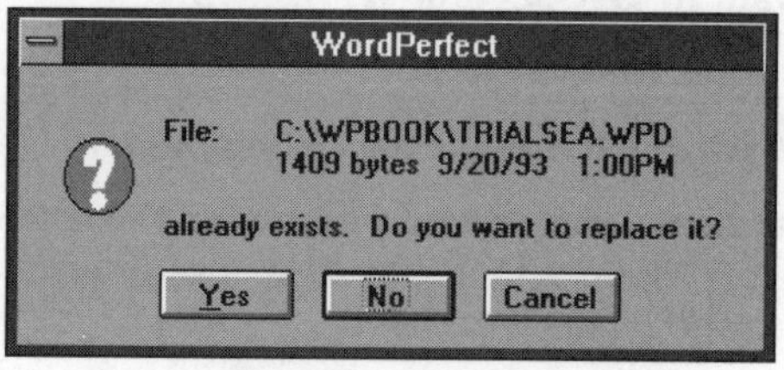

Figure 14-5:
How can
you have
two files in
the same
place at the
same time?

You have these three buttons from which to choose:

> ✔ **Yes:** Means "Blow away the existing file with this name and replace it with the one I'm saving now." Show no mercy.

> ✔ **No:** Means "Wait! I chose the wrong filename! Give me another chance to enter the right one!"

> ✔ **Cancel:** Means "Forget the whole subject of saving a document."

Using Foreign Files

I see a foreign document in your future. It is strong and handsome and exotic. You will travel over water. Oops! That's not the kind of foreign things we are talking about. A *foreign file* is one that is not stored in WordPerfect 6.0 format.

You have a number of reasons to use foreign documents:

> ✔ You receive drafts of documents on disk from someone who uses AmiPro.

> ✔ You want to give your documents on disk to someone who will edit them some more by using Microsoft Word.

> ✔ You get data files, such as lists of names and addresses, from a database program such as Microsoft Access or Paradox.

WordPerfect can both read (open) and write (save) files in other formats, including the ones in this list:

AmiPro	WordStar
DisplayWrite	Earlier versions of WordPerfect
Microsoft Word	RFT ("revisable-form text," an IBM standard)
MultiMate	RTF ("rich text format," a Windows standard)
OfficeWriter	Plain old ASCII text

Which format should I use?

If you want to read or create a file for one of the word-processing programs in the preceding list, you are in Fat City. Otherwise, see whether the other program can read or write RFT, RTF, or ASCII text files. If so, you should be able to communicate with WordPerfect.

ASCII text files are known also as *DOS text files*. These files contain nothing but regular old letters, numbers, spaces, and other punctuation — no formatting. They are called ASCII text files because they contain character codes defined by the *A*merican *S*tandard *C*ode for *I*nformation *I*nterchange — ASCII.

ASCII no questions, I'll tell you no lies

You can use WordPerfect to edit ASCII files. You might someday be called on, for example, to edit one of the special text files that tell DOS and Windows how to work, such as your AUTOEXEC.BAT, CONFIG.SYS, or WIN.INI files.

When you edit an ASCII file, you must be sure to save it again as an ASCII file, not as a WordPerfect document. Follow the directions in the next section for opening the text file in WordPerfect. Then edit it, but don't use any formatting or insert any special characters. Finally, save it as an ASCII text file by following the steps later in this chapter.

For most ASCII-editing purposes, it is easier to use the Notepad program that comes with Windows. It's in your Accessories program group. Double-click on it to run it, use the File Open command to open a text file, do your editing, use the File Save command to save it, and choose File Exit to leave.

Creating a foreign file

Making a file in a format other than a regular old WordPerfect document is also called *exporting* a file. To export a WordPerfect document, follow these steps:

1. **First save the file in WordPerfect format.**

   In case you want to do more editing later, you can open this file and export it again.

2. **Choose File Save As from the menu bar or press F3.**

   You see the dialog box shown in Figure 14-6. The Format setting usually says WordPerfect 6.0 (*.wpd, *.wpt, *.doc, *.wp). This message is WordPerfect's way of saying that it plans to save the document in the usual WordPerfect 6.0 format and suggesting some commonly used file extensions.

3. **Click on the Format setting box and choose the format you want to use.**

   For many programs, such as Microsoft Word, several formats are listed. Use the scroll bar to see more formats. If you are not sure which one to use, choose the most up-to-date one.

4. **In the Filename box, type a name and extension (a period followed by as many as three letters) for the new file.**

   Don't type the .WPD extension that is used for WordPerfect files. It's a good idea to use the file extension that is appropriate for the type of file you are creating (DOC for Microsoft Word documents, for example, or SAM for AmiPro documents.) Look at the Format setting to see the extension WordPerfect suggests. (We suggest reserving the extension WPD for WordPerfect files only.)

5. **Choose OK.**

WordPerfect flashes a little message that conversion is in progress while it saves the file.

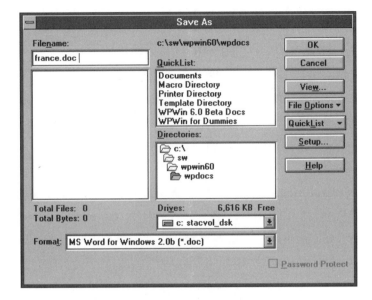

Figure 14-6:
Sending your WordPerfect document overseas.

Now you have created a foreign file right on your own disk.

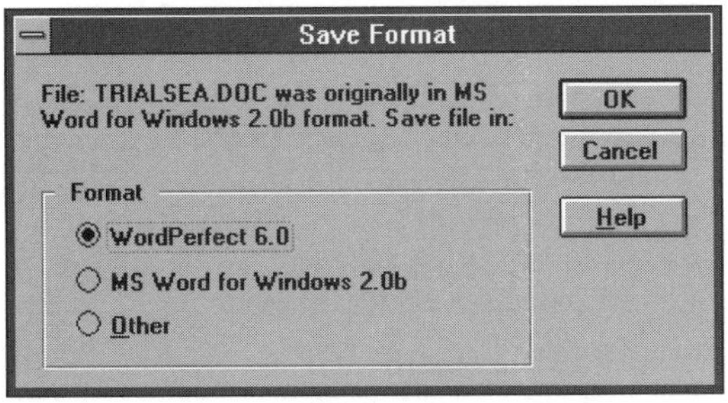

Figure 14-7:
And how would you like your document saved, Monsieur?

Reading a foreign file

Reading files in other formats, also called *importing* documents, is pretty easy. Just use the same File Open command you use to open a regular WordPerfect document as shown in these steps:

The name doesn't match the face

Here's one confusing thing: After you have saved a file in a foreign format, WordPerfect changes the document name in the title bar to the name of the foreign file. If you save the file again by using File Save, Ctrl+S, or the Save button on the power bar, WordPerfect wonders which format you have in mind and displays the Save Format dialog box, shown in Figure 14-7.

WordPerfect suggests that you save the file in regular WordPerfect 6.0 format, in the format you last used, or in some other format. If you want to use the format you used last time, just tell it what you want. But if you want to save it in WordPerfect format now, you have a problem. We suggest that you just Cancel out of this dialog box and use the File Save As command instead.

The reason is that if you choose WordPerfect 6.0 format, WordPerfect does indeed save the docu-

ment as a WordPerfect file. Unfortunately, it still uses the filename you typed when you exported the document. Suppose that you saved an important marketing report as CHOCOLAT.WPD in WordPerfect format and then saved it as CHOCOLAT.SAM in AmiPro format. Now the filename that appears in the title bar is CHOCOLAT.SAM. You press Ctrl+S to save the document again, the Save Format dialog box is displayed, and you choose WordPerfect 6.0 format. Now WordPerfect saves the report in a file named CHOCOLAT.SAM in WordPerfect format.

It's confusing if a file has the wrong type of extension for its contents, and you (and WordPerfect) can get bollixed up this way. Watch out! You are better off using the File Save As command (or pressing F3), which lets you specify both the format and the filename.

1. **Choose File Open from the menu (or click the Open button from the power bar or press Ctrl+O).**

   You see the usual Open File dialog box.

2. **Choose the filename from the list or type it in the Filename box.**

3. **Choose OK.**

   Doesn't all this seem strangely familiar? These steps are the same ones you follow for opening a WordPerfect document!

   Aha! WordPerfect notices that something is amiss when it tries to open the file. It flashes the Convert File Format dialog box, as shown in Figure 14-8. It even takes a stab at guessing the format of the file.

4. **For the Convert File Format From setting, choose the format of the file.**

5. **Choose OK.**

   WordPerfect displays its message that a conversion is in progress and opens (imports) the file.

6. **Save the file as a WordPerfect document by choosing File Save As from the menu (or pressing F3).**

Enter a filename that ends with the WordPerfect extension WPD and choose WordPerfect 6.0 as the format.

7. Choose OK to save it.

Figure 14-8:
Hey — this isn't a WordPerfect document! What is it?

If you don't see your foreign file listed in the Open File dialog box, WordPerfect may deliberately be showing only its own WordPerfect format files. For the List Files of Type setting, choose All Files (*.*).

Word processors versus food processors

Although WordPerfect does a great job of importing and exporting files in many other formats, it isn't perfect. Not that this is WordPerfect's fault — the problem is that different word processors have different capabilities and do things in different ways. Sometimes files that have been imported or exported look as though they have been put by mistake in a food processor for a few seconds.

When you are using a foreign file, take a look around it before blithely editing or printing it. The formatting may be fouled up. Fonts may change mysteriously. You may find extra line-ending characters (carriage returns) where they don't belong. Some cleanup may be in order.

RTF: The Esperanto of file formats

If you must regularly use or provide foreign files but they don't translate well, see whether your foreign buddy can export and import as RTF, or Rich Text Format. RTF is a format designed especially for document exchange; it's sort of a universal language, such as Esperanto. Not everybody speaks it (like Esperanto), but many word processors do, including WordPerfect and Microsoft Word on both the Macintosh and the PC. RTF keeps most of your formatting intact as long as both computers have similar fonts. It is particularly useful if you have to transmit documents by modem, even between the Mac and the PC. It's an ASCII text file, not a binary one like other document files, and it's easier for the communications software to handle.

The 5th Wave
By Rich Tennant

"I WISH SOMEONE WOULD EXPLAIN TO PROFESSOR JONES THAT YOU DON'T NEED A WHIP AND A LEATHER JACKET TO FIND A LOST FILE."

Chapter 15
Juggling Files on Your Disk

● ●

In This Chapter

▶ Naming files

▶ Using directories

▶ Recognizing different kinds of files

▶ Copying, renaming, deleting, and moving files

▶ Finding a file with a Forgotten Name

● ●

Sorry, old-timers, gone are the days of keeping your documents on a nice, thin 5¼-inch disk, which you could conveniently stuff in a file folder. Oh, you can still do it that way, all right. It's just that the New and Improved Way of Doing Things is designed to keep everything on one, big, humongous hard disk that is bolted into your computer, where you cannot (without risking a hernia) grab it and run out if the house catches fire. (Maybe this is the reason that laptops are so popular.)

Anyway, this is now the way things are, so you might as well enjoy its benefits. Not that the situation is all bad: With everything on one disk, you're not continually shuffling floppies, writing labels for them, putting your coffee cup on them, or losing them. It's also easier to copy stuff from an old document to make a new one when everything is on one big disk. And thanks to WordPerfect's QuickFinder, you no longer have to remember whether your treatise on hermaphroditic mealworms is called HERMMEAL, MEALWORM, or WORMSEX.

Doing all this great stuff — doing darn near anything on the PC, in fact — requires a working knowledge of files and directories: what files are called, where they hang out, and how to reproduce them, change their names, find them, move them, or just kill them off. If you're already conversant with these topics, just read the section "Finding a File with a Forgotten Name," later in this chapter. Skim the rest of the chapter to learn how you can do these things without the File Manager and then move along.

A File By Any Other Name

Giving names to your files is not much fun on the PC, no matter which program you're using. For perfectly ridiculous historical reasons that have to do with DOS, you cannot give a file a name that is longer than eight characters (made up mostly of letters and numbers). You cannot use spaces, most punctuation, or anything else that might allow you to create a useful name.

This list shows the boring, detailed rules of file-naming on a PC:

✔ In DOS and Windows, files have two parts to their "name:" the really, truly, up-to-eight-characters *name* part that, in WordPerfect, you must supply, and the up-to-three-characters *extension* part that WordPerfect takes care of more or less automatically. When both parts are shown, the extension is separated from the filename by a period, as in the file called FILENAME.EXT.

✔ You cannot use more than eight characters in the filename; use fewer if you want.

✔ Uppercase and lowercase characters are identical, which is probably a good thing. Imagine trying to remember whether your document was MealWorm, MEALworm, or MeAlWOrm. In this book, we use capital letters for filenames, but you can type them by using either upper- or lowercase letters. Neither we nor Windows cares.

✔ You can use only letters, numbers, and certain standard typewriter characters in the filename. You can (if you are demented) use any of the following characters:

` ~ ! @ # $ % ^ & ( ) - { }

This line is not considered cartoon-language cursing. It represents the row on typical keyboards that has most of the Shift+number-key characters. Notice that * and + are among the unacceptable characters. It's hard to remember all these funny characters, so you probably shouldn't use any of them except perhaps the underscore (_) symbol, which substitutes well for a space.

✔ No spaces are allowed.

The following examples of filenames (just the real name part, not the extension) are OK:

LETTER

SMITH (but it's no different than "smith")

READ

But these filenames aren't OK:

JAN MEMO (you cannot use a space)

$/&@\(-! (this one has some funny characters you cannot use)

LETTERTOMOM (too long)

Using Directories

The price of having everything on a single hard disk is that it must be organized or you can never find anything. To accomplish this organization, your hard disk is organized like a file cabinet. Within it are "file folders" called *directories* or *subdirectories.* It also has directories within directories (like folders within folders). Each directory has a name that follows the same rules as a filename (no more than eight characters, for example).

This organization helps you live with the eight-character filename rule. Without it, every file on your entire hard disk would have to have a different name. With it, you can have a file called MEALWORM, about mealworm reproduction, in the SEX directory, and another file, also named MEALWORM but about mealworm digestion, in the EATING directory (not to be confused with the RECIPES directory).

To help keep mealworms out of your recipes, in fact, you might want to keep these directories separate by putting them in their own directories, such as BIOLOGY and PERSONAL. This arrangement leads to a kind of hierarchy, as shown in Figure 15-1. In the figure, folders represent directories, and the folder labeled C:\ represents your hard disk.

Even though we're talking about directories on the hard disk, called C:, everything we're discussing applies also to floppy disks (those little 3½-inch disks that are more crunchy than floppy), called A: or B:. You can certainly keep documents on these disks if you want and use directories too. WordPerfect runs somewhat more slowly, though, when you use these floppy disks.

Figure 15-1:
A hierarchy
of directories.

Pathnames

The directory structure that is shown in Figure 15-1 raises a question: when you want to talk to the computer about these files, how do you distinguish between files with the same name (the MEALWORM file in the SEX directory versus the one in the EATING directory)? One solution is pathnames, which tell your software how to navigate the hierarchy to get to the right place. They consist of the disk (written as A:, B:, C:, or D:, with C: usually representing the hard disk) and the directories, separated by a backslash (\).

A pathname to the SEX folder (directory) looks like this:

```
C:\BIOLOGY\SEX
```

A pathname to the EATING folder looks like this:

```
C:\BIOLOGY\EATING
```

If you want to be precise in telling your computer about a file, you can use the pathname with the filename and its extension. The pathname looks something like this line:

```
C:\BIOLOGY\EATING\MEALWORM.WPD
```

WordPerfect automatically puts the .WPD extension on your document files.

You don't normally have to type things with a pathname because WordPerfect keeps track of the directory separately from the filename. Moreover, WordPerfect generally knows the correct file extension from the context, so you don't have to type it. Most of the time, all you have to type is the filename. If you want to include the path, it doesn't hurt.

Even though you don't have to type pathnames, you often see them in WordPerfect. They tell you where WordPerfect is getting or putting files, in case you care. The most obvious example is the name of the file you're working on, shown in the title bar (the top line of the WordPerfect window).

WordPerfect creates some directories on your hard disk when it's installed. The one you will care about the most is the WPDOCS directory because that's where your documents go unless you say otherwise.

WPDOCS is sometimes called the *default document directory.* It's a folder within a folder, in that it's within another directory called something similar to WPWIN60 (unless you or your guru have set things up otherwise). You probably will not want to put all your documents here, but that's OK. It's easy to specify a different directory when you go to save your document. You can also change your default document directory (see the section "Expressing Your Preferences," in Chapter 20 for more information about changing the default document directory).

You can create your own set of folders by using WordPerfect. Use them to organize your documents and other WordPerfect files. Just as with your paper files, the organization is up to you. Generally, you put these folders within the WPDOCS folder.

WordPerfect gives you a simpler way to deal with all these folders within folders: the *QuickList,* as it's called, is described later in this chapter.

Creating a directory

A WordPerfect feature that's nice for novices is the capability to perform file and directory management without leaving the program. You can manage things from any of several different file-related commands, such as File Open or Insert File — they all work in the same way. Using the File Save As command as an example, these steps show you how to create or remove a directory:

1. **Choose File Save As from the menu.**

   Alternatively, you can press F3 or click on the Save As icon on the power bar, usually third from the left. The Save As dialog box appears, as shown in Figure 15-2.

2. **In the Directories list, click once on the directory in which you want your new directory to be located.**

   The box labeled Directories shows where WordPerfect will put your directory unless you tell it otherwise. If you haven't done anything with directories yet, this list displays the default document directory.

   You interpret the directory list in this way: the top folder is the disk, probably C:\ (your hard disk). Indented underneath that is a directory on your disk. Indented underneath that is another directory within that directory, and so on. Your file goes in the file folder that's open and shaded.

   To create a directory that isn't within any other directory, click on the top folder in the stack, the one named C:\ (or some letter other than C). You can also use the QuickList here, if it's turned on (the QuickList is discussed later in this chapter).

3. **Click on the File Options button in the dialog box.**

   A drop-down menu appears.

4. **Click on the Create Directory selection in the drop-down menu.**

   A Create Directory dialog box appears.

5. **Type a directory name in the New Directory box.**

   Press the Enter key or click on the Create button when you finish. Despite the inviting length of the box, remember to keep the name to eight characters or fewer, with no spaces or weird punctuation.

   WordPerfect creates the new directory, and it appears in the directory list.

Removing a directory

To remove a directory, first make sure that you don't want the files in it and that none of the files in it is open (currently being used). Then follow these steps:

1. **Choose File Save As from the menu.**

   You see the Save As dialog box. It's not that you want to save anything: you want to see your list of directories and use the File Options button.

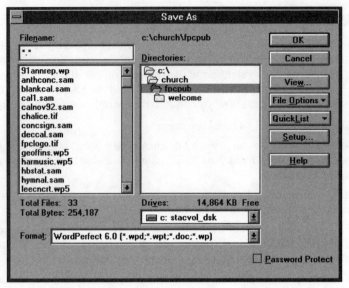

Figure 15-2:
Specifying a
directory.

2. **In the Directories panel, click once on the directory you want to delete.**

   You can also use the QuickList, if it is on. See the following section, about the QuickList, for more information.

3. **Click the File Options button in the dialog box.**

   A drop-down menu appears.

4. **Click on the Remove Directory selection in the drop-down menu.**

   A Remove Directory dialog box appears.

5. **If the name of the directory shown in the Directory to Remove box is correct, click the Remove button.**

   If any files are in the directory, a WARNING! box tells you so. It asks whether you want it to remove the directory anyway. If you click on Yes, WordPerfect removes the directory and deletes the files in it. If you click on No, nothing happens and you return to the Remove Directory dialog box. *You cannot delete a directory if any of the files in it is in use.*

Make sure that no files you want are in a directory you are removing. If you tell WordPerfect to remove a directory and its files, you have virtually no way to Undo it, apart from calling your friendly local PC guru immediately.

If you are comfortable with pathnames, you can use them anywhere you are prompted for a filename or pathname. If you provide a full path — that is, all the way up to the C:\ directory — it overrides any currently selected directory. If you do not specify a full path, WordPerfect prefixes it with the directory selected in the dialog box. Typing C:\PERSONAL\LETTERS\HIMOM.WPD where a filename is requested, for example, specifies precisely that file regardless of any path shown in the dialog box.

Using the QuickList (a much easier way to talk about directories)

Let's face it — this stuff about hierarchical directories within directories is a drag. Wouldn't it be nicer to just call your C:\WPDOCS\CONTRACT directory something like Current Contracts?

This scenario is exactly what a great feature called QuickList provides. By letting you give descriptions to directories, it eliminates all the hierarchical stuff. It also lets you use more than eight characters to describe directories.

The following example descriptions are already set up in the QuickList by WordPerfect:

Description	*Directory*
Documents	C:\WPWIN60\WPDOCS
Graphic directory	C:\WPWIN60\GRAPHICS
Template directory	C:\WPWIN60\TEMPLATE

You can also use QuickList descriptions for documents or other files, not just directories. Suppose that you have a document with telephone numbers you have to read or change often. Rather than specify its name and directory over and over (such as C:\WPWIN60\WPDOCS\PERSONAL\PHONE.WPD), you can give it a QuickList description, such as Phone Numbers.

You can use or set up the QuickList from any file-saving or file-opening command, such as File Open or Insert File — they all work in the same way. After you set it up, you can use it from any file-saving or file-opening command. Using the File Save As command as an example, let's see how to use and set up the QuickList.

To "turn on" the QuickList feature, follow these steps:

1. **Choose File Save As from the menu bar.**

   Alternatively, you can press F3 or click on the Save As power bar icon, usually third from the left. The Save As dialog box appears (refer to Figure 15-2).

2. **Click the QuickList button in the dialog box.**

3. **Choose Show QuickList or Show Both in the drop-down menu that appears.**

   Show Both is probably the better choice because it enables you to work with either standard directory names or the QuickList descriptions.

The QuickList appears in the Save As dialog box. It also appears in any other file-saving or file-opening dialog box from now on. Now you can use the names in the QuickList rather than directory names or filenames.

At the moment, however, the QuickList shows only the standard WordPerfect descriptions. These steps show how to add descriptions for your own directories or files:

1. **Click the QuickList button in the dialog box.**

   A little menu appears.

2. **Choose Add Item from the drop-down menu.**

   The Add QuickList Item dialog box appears.

3. **Type the name of your directory in the Directory/Filename box.**

4. **Enter a description.**

   Click on the Description box. Delete the name WordPerfect enters and type the QuickList description you prefer to use.

5. **Click the OK button.**

You can change your description or the directory your description represents. Click once on your description in the QuickList. Then click the QuickList button and choose Edit Item. The Edit QuickList Item dialog box works like the Add QuickList Item box we just described.

You can just as easily change the definition of standard QuickList descriptions, such as Documents. This directory is normally C:\WPWIN60\WPDOCS. You can make it anything you want by using Edit Item in the QuickList menu.

You can also delete a QuickList description. Click once on your description in the QuickList. Then click the QuickList button and choose Delete Item.

After the QuickList is turned on, you can use items in the QuickList panel rather than folders in the Directories panel, in any file-related dialog box in which the QuickList appears. If the QuickList description refers to a file, just double-click on the description to specify that file to whatever dialog box you're using.

Saving a document to a new directory

Let's assume that you have some directories (other than WPDOCS) in which you want to save your documents. To start, make sure that you know where these directories are on your hard disk. Are they within some other directories? If so, which ones? Of course, if you have used the QuickList to set up descriptions for these directories, you don't have to worry about directories within directories. Just use the descriptions in the QuickList area of the Save As dialog box.

Follow these steps when you're ready to save your document:

1. **Choose File Save As from the menu bar.**

   Or press F3 or click on the Save As power bar icon, usually third from the left. The Save As dialog box appears (refer to Figure 15-2).

   The list labeled Directories on the right side in the dialog box shows where WordPerfect will save your file unless you tell it otherwise. If you haven't done anything with directories yet, this list displays the default document directory.

   You interpret the list in this way: The top folder is the disk, probably C:\ (your hard disk). Indented underneath that is a directory on your disk. Indented underneath that is another directory within that directory, and so on. Your file goes in the file folder that's open and shaded.

   You can also use the QuickList rather than the Directories list if the QuickList is on. See the preceding section, about the QuickList, for more information.

2. **If your file will go on the hard disk (C:\), skip to step 4.**

3. **If you want to save your file on a floppy disk, click in the window labeled Drives and choose drive A: or B: from the menu that drops down.**

   Make sure that your floppy disk is in the drive and that the drive door is closed.

4. **Double-click on the top folder in the Directories window.**

   This step "opens" the top folder. The window now shows all the top-level folders on the disk. Folders within these folders are not shown, though. You have to open (double-click) on a folder to see the folders within it.

   Again, you may use the QuickList rather than the Directories list, if the directory you want has a description here.

5. **Double-click on the folder you want.**

   If you want a folder within a folder, keep "opening" down the hierarchy until you have opened the one you want. (For those who savvy path terminology, the path appears in a line above the Directories list.)

6. **Type a filename.**

   Find the box labeled Filename in the top left corner of the dialog box. Type a filename there and press the Enter key or click on OK. Your file is saved in the folder you selected.

Kinds of Files

WordPerfect can and does use many different files. Some are its own, WordPerfecty kind of files. Others are of the import-export variety, such as spreadsheets, databases, graphics, and documents from other word processors. You have to be slightly aware of their differences to avoid confusion when, for example, a graphics file and a document file have the same name and are stored in the same directory.

For now, let's focus on three principal groups: documents, graphics, and templates.

You can usually tell a WordPerfect document file when you see it listed (as in a dialog box). It always has a three-letter WPD extension appended to the name and separated by a period (HIMOM.WPD, for example), unless you deliberately gave the document a different extension when you created it (not a good idea). Documents from other word processors use other extensions.

Graphics files also generally have distinctive two- or three-letter extensions, but hundreds of variants exist. Some of the common ones are WPG for WordPerfect Graphics, BMP for Windows Bitmap, plus DIB, WMF, TIF, PCX, EPS, PGL, and more. They are used in the Graphics Figure command and elsewhere.

Template files are patterns for creating a new document. They typically store styles and standard text for a given type of document, such as a purchase order. WordPerfect supplies many templates, and you can create your own (see Chapter 17). They always have a .WPT extension and are used principally in the File Template command, which lets you create a new file based on a template.

Most of the time, WordPerfect knows just which kind of file you want from the type of command you're giving and displays only the right sort of file. But, considering all the settings you can fool with, it's only a matter of time before you do something to make WordPerfect throw up its hands and leave you to sort things out from the extensions.

Copying, Renaming, Deleting, and Moving Files

Just as it does for directories, WordPerfect provides a way to manage files without ever leaving the program: the File Options button.

The File Options button is in the dialog boxes for File Open, Insert File, File Save, and other file-related commands. You can use this button in any of the dialog boxes to copy, rename, delete, and move files.

Telling WordPerfect which file you're talking about

Whether you are going to copy, rename, delete, or move a file, the first step is to identify on which file you will operate. We use the File Save As command as an example, but remember that you can copy, rename, delete, or move a file from nearly any file-related command.

To tell WordPerfect which file you are going to copy, rename, delete, or move, follow these steps:

1. Choose File Save As from the menu bar.

Or press F3, etc. You see the Save As dialog box.

2. Double-click on the directory in which your file is located.

Look in the list below the label Directories. If you don't see the directory you want, double-click on the top folder (C:\) to open it. This step displays all the first-level directories, but not all the directories within those. To see folders within folders, you have to double-click on each folder in turn and return to the C:\ folder every time.

You can use the QuickList rather than the Directories list, if the directory you want has a description here. See the preceding section, about the QuickList.

3. Click once on the filename.

In the list of filenames on the left side of the dialog box, click once on the file you want to highlight.

To prepare to copy, delete, or move a group of files, hold down the Ctrl button and click once on each file. This step highlights each one. Click and drag the highlight to select a contiguously listed group of files.

Now you have selected the file or files on which to operate, and you are ready for action. Read on in the following four sections, which tell you how to copy, move, rename, and delete a file.

Copying a file

Begin by following the steps in the beginning of this section, "Telling WordPerfect which file you're talking about."

Then, with the file dialog box open, follow these steps:

1. Click the File Options button in the Save As dialog box.

A drop-down menu appears.

2. Click on the Copy selection in the drop-down menu.

The Copy Files dialog box appears.

3. **Fill out the To box.**

Your selected files are listed in the From box. WordPerfect also foolishly fills in the To box with exactly the same text. You have to replace this text. If you understand paths, you can type a destination path or edit the one that's there. (Click anywhere within the box to place the cursor, press either the Delete or Backspace key to edit, and type the path.) Skip to step 5.

If, on the other hand, paths are Greek to you (and you're not Greek), click on the microscopic button to the right of the To box with a subatomic file folder icon in it. This steps wins you a Select Directory dialog box.

4. **Double-click on your destination directory in the Directories box.**

Look in the list below the Directories label. (If you don't see the directory you want, double-click on the top folder (C:\) to open it. This step displays all the first-level directories, but not all the directories within those. To see folders within folders, you have to double-click on each folder in turn and return to the top-level folder every time.)

5. **Click on the OK button in the Directories box or press Enter.**

6. **Click on the Copy button in the Copy File dialog box or press Enter.**

WordPerfect makes a copy of the file in the directory you chose. The original file is unaffected.

Moving a file

Pardon us if we get a little brief here. Moving a file is so much like copying a file that we don't want to put you to sleep by repeating everything.

Just refer to the section "Copying a file," earlier in this chapter. Replace the word *copy* with the word *move.* Do the same stuff. The difference? The original file is deleted.

Renaming a file

Renaming a file is just like copying a file except that you type a new filename rather than a new directory in the To box.

Begin by following the steps in the beginning of the section "Telling WordPerfect which file you're talking about." Then, with the file dialog box open, follow these steps:

1. **Click the File Options button in the dialog box.**

A drop-down menu appears.

2. **Click on the Rename selection in the drop-down menu.**

The appropriate dialog box appears.

3. Fill out the To box.

Your selected file is listed in the From box. WordPerfect also foolishly fills in the To box with exactly the same text.

4. Press the Delete key.

You have to replace this text with a new filename. Delete it and then enter a new filename. Alternatively, you can edit the filename in the To box to change it to the new filename.

5. Type a new filename (with an extension).

Don't type a pathname (as in the From box); the file automatically remains in the same directory.

6. Press Enter or click on the Rename button when you finish.

Deleting a File

Begin by following the steps in the beginning of the section "Telling WordPerfect which file you're talking about." With a file dialog box open and your file selected, follow these steps:

1. Click the File Options button in the Save As dialog box.

A drop-down menu appears.

2. Click on the Delete selection in the drop-down menu.

A Delete File dialog box appears.

3. Check to make sure that you're deleting the right file, listed in the File to Delete box.

4. Click the Delete button.

Poof! Your file goes away unless it's open in WordPerfect, someone else on your network is using it, or it's in some way protected. In any of these circumstances, see your guru (and bring Milano Mint cookies).

Making Backups

While we are talking about copying files, we should point out that you should make backup copies of your documents regularly. Just think how you might feel if you arrive at your office tomorrow and find that your computer — and all the files stored on its hard disk — have been destroyed by a freak ceiling cave-in or have been stolen by masked men? Not too good, right?

Because you probably have lots and lots of important files on your hard disk, including files created by using programs other than WordPerfect, it is a good idea to talk to a computer guru about a system for making daily backup copies of all your important files, either on floppy disks or backup tapes.

In the meantime, take the precaution of copying your most prized WordPerfect documents to a floppy disk every day or so. You will feel smug when you delete one by accident and know that you have a backup copy!

To back up the files, follow these steps:

1. **Choose File Save As from the menu bar.**

   You see the Save As dialog box.

2. **Double-click on the directory in which your files are located.**

   If you're using the QuickList, double-click on the name of the directory you want, such as Documents.

   Look in the list below the Directories label. If you don't see the directory (folder), double-click on the C:\ directory at the top. Now you can see all the top-level directories. If you still don't see your directory, you must double-click on them one at a time to open them and find your directory.

3. **Select the filenames to copy.**

   A list of filenames is on the left side of the dialog box. While you hold down the Ctrl key, either click once on each file you want or drag the highlight down to select a block of files.

4. **Click the File Options button in the dialog box.**

   A drop-down menu appears.

5. **Click on the Copy selection in the drop-down menu.**

   The appropriate dialog box appears.

6. **Fill out the To box.**

   Your selected files are listed in the From box. WordPerfect also foolishly fills in the To box with exactly the same text. You have to replace this text with the drive designation for your floppy disk (type **A:** or **B:**). Make sure that you have a formatted floppy disk in that drive and that it's not write-protected. You can use the same disk repeatedly until it fills up.

7. **To save time, click on the box labeled `Don't replace files with the same size, date, and time`.**

8. **Click the Copy button.**

   Your files are copied to the disk. Be sure to label the disk and store it in a safe place, where no freak ceiling cave-in can destroy it.

Finding a File with a Forgotten Name

Boy, is WordPerfect ever glad that you want to know how to find your files. It has invested heavily in creating the Star Wars of file finding; the Saint Bernard of lost and stranded files; the veritable "Rescue 911" of technology-assisted document search and rescue. It's called QuickFinder, and it's on the Find menu in the main menu bar. It lets you find files that have certain text in them. If you want to find a letter to Ms. Tannenwald, for example, but you cannot remember the name of the file, you just have to type **Tannenwald** in the right place.

QuickFinder then sounds the alarm; dispatches armies, navies, and air forces to execute your humble request; and comes marching back, proudly carrying in its teeth any and all files that have any hint of the word *Tannenwald* appearing within them! This feature works for phrases and various word combinations too.

Before we go any farther, let's see how to perform a simple single-word search. Follow these steps:

1. **Choose File QuickFinder from the main menu bar.**

   The QuickFinder dialog box appears, as shown in Figure 15-3.

   You generally search a group or directory of files, not every file on a disk.

2. **If the group of files you want to search is not the default document directory, select a new directory.**

   Click on the tiny button with the file-folder icon to the right of the File Pattern box. A Select Directory dialog box is displayed. Choose the directory, as described in steps 2 through 5 in the section, "Saving a document to a new directory," earlier in this chapter. Click on OK.

3. **Back in the QuickFinder dialog box, click in the Search For box.**

   Type a word you want to search for in the files (such as *Tannenwald*, in our example).

4. **Click the Find button.**

   QuickFinder uses a Searching dialog box to announce that it is searching and lets you watch. Click on Stop if you think that you recognize the filename you want as it flashes by. Ultimately (unless you Cancel), the Search Results List box is displayed, as shown in Figure 15-4.

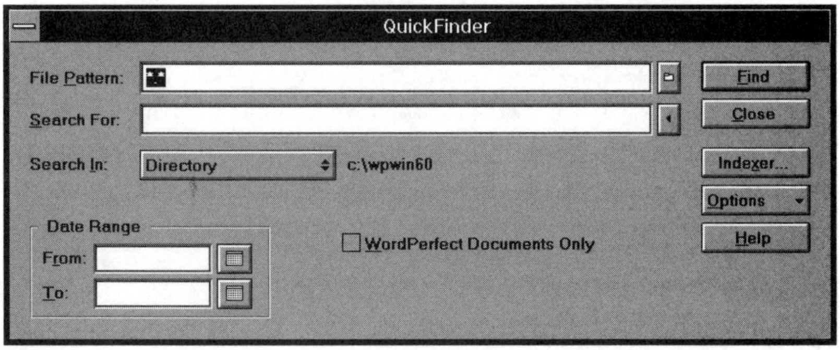

Figure 15-3:
The
QuickFinder
dialog box.
Does this
look official,
or what?

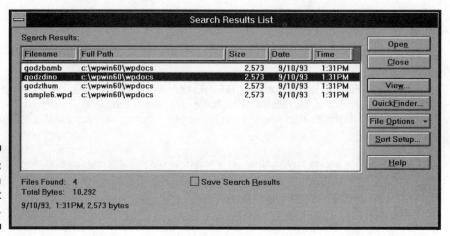

Figure 15-4:
The Search
Results List
dialog box.

Technically, now you're finished. QuickFinder has found all the files that have your word in them. You can just click the Close button and go about your business, but there are some useful things you can do while you're here:

✔ Peek at the file contents to see which document is the one you want: use the View capability of QuickFinder. Click on any file in the Search Results List and then click on View. The file is displayed in the Viewer window (see Figure 15-5). It displays a draft-like view, with every incident of the search word highlighted.

To check out another file, leave the Viewer up and click on another filename in the Search Results List. When you're finished, double-click on the minus sign in the upper left corner to make the Viewer go away.

✔ Open any of the documents that are listed. Just click on the file you want in the Results list and then click the Open button.

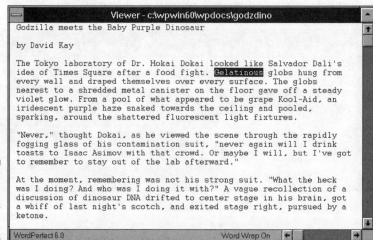

Figure 15-5:
The
QuickFinder
Viewer.

✔ Sort the file list in different ways. Click on Sort Setup and a new dialog box pops up. Click and hold down the button next to the By label. Drag the highlight and release it to sort by file extension, size, date, document "summary" data (such as the descriptive name and type), or path. You can also sort in a different order by clicking on the Order button and choosing ascending or descending order.

✔ Copy, move, rename, or delete files. Use the File Options button, as discussed in earlier sections of this chapter.

✔ Do some more QuickFinding. Just click the button labeled QuickFinder to go back to the QuickFinder dialog box.

Searching other disks and multiple directories

To search a drive other than C:, click and hold on the box labeled Search In in the QuickFinder dialog box (refer to Figure 15-3). While you hold down the mouse button, drag the highlight to the word *Disk* and release it.

A disk drive selection box appears just to the right of the Search In box. Click once on the down-arrow button next to it to see a drive-selection menu.

You can also search multiple directories if they all are under a common higher-level directory (such as EATING and SEX, which are under the BIOLOGY directory in our earlier example). Click and hold the Search In button and choose Subtree from the menu. Now all directories under the one in the File Pattern box are searched.

Another way to specify which directories and files QuickFinder should search is to create an index. This procedure is more complicated than most people need or want.

Searching for files by using more than one word

Sometimes a single word is not enough to specify the file you want. As a real-estate lawyer, you may have dozens of letters to Ms. Tannenwald but only one that discusses her forest property. Likewise, you probably have dozens of letters to other clients with forest property, but only one to Ms. Tannenwald. Neither *forest* nor *Tannenwald* alone is sufficient to find the correct file. You want the file that mentions both words.

To specify this sort of thing, you have to put special characters, called *operators,* between the words in your search line. In the following example, you type this search phrase:

Tannenwald & forest

where the **&** character means *and,* as in "Find me a document that has both *Tannenwald* and *forest.*" Some other useful operators that can be used in this position are shown in this list:

(the vertical bar symbol)	Means *or,* as in "Find a document that has either word A or word B." The vertical bar can be darn near anywhere on your keyboard. Look around — it may be over the backslash symbol.
Space (the space character, not the word *space*)	Means the same thing as the "or" symbol, unless you tell QuickFinder that you're giving it a phrase (see the following section, "Searching for phrases").
! (the exclamation point)	Means *not,* as in "Find a document that has word A but not word B."

If you're really fussy, you can even specify such things as how close the two (or more) words can appear, which parts of the document to search, and whether QuickFinder pays attention to upper- and lowercase. This procedure requires you to type fancy "switch" codes that begin with a slash mark (/) and that must *precede* your search text. Rather than remember these codes, you can click on the innocuous-looking yet powerful button to the right of the Search For label in the QuickFinder dialog box. It has a left-pointing triangle in it (refer to Figure 15-3). Here, under Closeness of Words, for example, you can tell QuickFinder to look for documents in which the words appear within the same Page, Paragraph, Sentence, or Within (some number of) Words — whatever makes sense to you. When you click on the appropriate selection, the code is typed in the Search For line for you, wherever your cursor is.

Searching for phrases

A final instance in which a single word may not be enough is when you're looking for phrases. You cannot just type a phrase in the Search For box. QuickFinder interprets it as a list of individual words and finds files that have any of those words. (A space means the same as an "or" symbol in the normal mode of operation.)

To tell QuickFinder that you are typing a phrase, put it in quotation marks (the regular double marks). Click on Find and away you go.

Chapter 16
Dressing Your Document for Success

· ·

In This Chapter

▶ Columns

▶ Borders

▶ Graphics

▶ Text boxes

▶ Tables

· ·

*T*he cool thing about today's word processors is that you can dress up a document in ways that only a designer, typesetter, or printer could do a few years ago. The trouble is, now that people (your boss, for example) know that normal people can do this kind of thing, they begin to expect it.

The other less-than-cool thing about today's word processors is that, in giving you all this wonderful stuff, "they" have gone absolutely overboard. WordPerfect, for all practical purposes, performs not only word processing but also drawing, charting, spreadsheet-like calculating, and elements of typesetting!

The problem for the average shmoe is getting around all the fancy stuff to do the basic stuff. That's what you will learn about here. We don't give you a course in spreadsheets or computer art — we just help you get started in creating basic columns, tables, graphics, and stuff.

With these caveats said, welcome to the exciting world of Doing Nifty Things to Your Documents.

Working with Columns

Columns are great for newsletters, newspapers, magazines, scripts, lists, and certain charts or tables. With newspaper and magazine documents, even if you don't print the document yourself, you can use columns and the correct character and paragraph formatting to determine approximately how long your article will be when it's printed.

WordPerfect can lay out columns in the following four styles (when was the last time we said that there was only *one* way to do something in WordPerfect?):

- **Newspaper:** Fills one column to the end of the page before beginning another column. Use this option for newsletters and long, incoherent, raving letters to the editor.

- **Balanced newspaper:** Continuously shuffles your text to make sure that all columns are of more or less equal length. Use this style (which has nothing to do with a balanced editorial policy) when a document alternately uses a single column and multiple columns, such as when you have a long, multicolumn list in the middle of a regular document. You can also use it for ending the last page of a multicolumn newsletter before the end of the physical page.

- **Parallel:** Creates rows across your columns, and creates "cells" of text in a manner similar to a table. When you use this style, you create a row one cell at a time, by inserting a hard column break when you want to begin writing the next cell to the right. This style is useful for scripts and contracts.

- **Parallel with Block Protect:** Similar to Parallel but makes sure that automatic page breaks don't mess things up if your rows must continue on the next page.

If all these styles sound confusing, take heart. The WordPerfect Columns dialog box shows you neat pictures of what sort of columns are used for each option.

Creating columns

To turn on columns in your document, follow these steps:

1. **Place your cursor where you want columns to begin.**

   If you want your entire document to appear in two newspaper columns, for example, except for the title at the top, move your cursor to the first line after the title.

2. **Choose Layout Columns from the menu.**

   You can also use the power bar to turn on columns. Click and hold on the icon that looks like two newspaper columns. Drag your cursor to select the number of columns you want. Or drag it all the way down to Define to display the dialog box shown in Figure 16-1 (and skip to step 4).

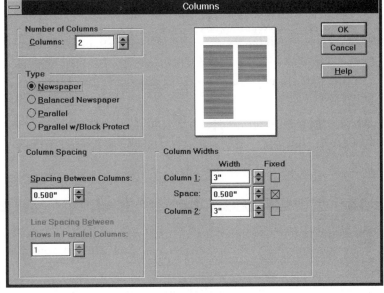

Figure 16-1:
Getting, like,
totally
columnar
with the
Columns
dialog box.

3. Click on Define from the Columns menu.

The Columns dialog box is displayed, as shown in Figure 16-1,

4. Choose the number of columns you want.

In the upper left corner, under Number of Columns, WordPerfect suggests two columns (unless you are working with text that is already in columns, and then it shows you the current setting). Change this number by typing a number or by clicking on the up-and-down arrows next to the Columns box.

5. Choose the type of columns you want.

In the area labeled Type, click on one of the types (Newspaper, for example) described earlier.

6. Adjust the column widths or spacing, if you want.

In the area labeled Column Widths, WordPerfect suggests nice, even column widths with a half-inch space between them. It also lets column widths vary if you change the page margins, but it keeps the spacing "fixed."

To fix (or unfix) any column or space dimension so that it doesn't vary, click in the box in the Fixed column to the right of the Width setting.

To change widths, click in the Width box and edit the value by typing and deleting or click on the adjoining up-and-down (increment and decrement) arrows. Use the " symbol for inches or **mm** or **cm** for metric values.

You can also adjust the intercolumn spacing in the Column Spacing area. (Why you can do this in two places, we can't imagine. If the two don't agree, the winner seems to be the last one you set.)

If you have made your columns look sort of like a table, by using Parallel or Parallel with Block Protect, you may also choose the number of blank lines WordPerfect leaves between rows. Click on the up-and-down arrows in the small box with the long name (Line Spacing Between Rows in Parallel Columns) in the lower left corner.

7. **Click on OK or press Enter when you finish (like we had to tell you that, right?).**

To turn off columns at some point in your document, place your cursor where you want things to go back to normal. Then choose Layout Columns Off from the main WordPerfect menu bar.

Bad breaks and what to do about them

There are good breaks and there are bad breaks — column breaks, that is. When your columns don't break where you want them to, you can regain some control by inserting "hard" column breaks.

To insert a hard column break, follow these steps:

1. **Place your cursor in front of the line where you want a column to begin.**

2. **Choose Layout Columns Column Break.**

Column breaks don't always do what you think they will do. It depends on which type of columns you have: newspaper, balanced newspaper, or one of the parallel styles. The following list shows the types of columns in the column-break story:

✔ **Newspaper:** Column breaks begin a new column in the way you think that they should.

✔ **Balanced newspaper:** A column break begins a whole new block of balanced columns; it's almost like turning columns off and then on again. This style probably isn't what you had in mind if you're trying to fix the way WordPerfect has balanced your columns. So rather than use a column break to change the balance, try putting in blank lines where you want a column to end. (Press Shift+Enter for a blank line.) It's tacky, but it works.

✔ **Parallels:** A column break moves you *across your current row* to the next column. It doesn't put you at the *top* of a new column, as you might expect. When you insert a column break at the end of the row, you're back in the left column, in a new row.

Putting selected text in columns

Sometimes you may want to put a block of text in columns. You might put a long list of words, such as a packing list, into several columns to save space, for example.

Begin by highlighting the block of text you want columnated. (Columnarized? Columnified?) Then give the Layout Columns Define command. In the Columns dialog box, choose the style you want.

The Balanced Newspaper style probably works best unless you want to control where the columns break, in which case you use the Newspaper style. Click on OK.

Using highlighted text in this way is equivalent to turning columns "on" before the block and "off" after it.

Column breaks are invisible no matter what you do, unless you use the Reveal Codes window (see Chapter 11), and who wants to do that? So if you want to delete hard column breaks, have faith that they are located just before the first character in a column (or just before the current "cell" in a Parallel-type column). To delete hard column breaks, place your cursor before the first character in the column and press the Backspace key. (Don't try to delete soft column breaks — the ones WordPerfect puts in. Because they're soft, they just squish up and slither to safety.)

Don't try to navigate between columns by pressing the navigation keys — you will drive yourself nuts. Use the mouse.

Working with Borders and Backgrounds

For some reason, nothing looks as neat as text in a box. At least, that's what the folks at WordPerfect must believe because their border features are yet another case of overkill for most of us common folks. WordPerfect lets you choose from among a dizzying array of tasteful (and not-so-tasteful) borders. You can "fill" the background of your document with subtle, interesting, or downright bizarre patterns.

Basic borders

To put a snazzy border around a single paragraph or multicolumn area, first select the area. Unless you select (highlight) text or specifically instruct WordPerfect otherwise when you apply a border to one page, paragraph, or column, you apply the border or fill (background) to all subsequent pages, paragraphs, or columns.

Choose the Layout *whatever* Border/Fill command (substitute Page, Paragraph, or Columns for *whatever*) from the menu. A dialog box like the one shown in Figure 16-2 is displayed.

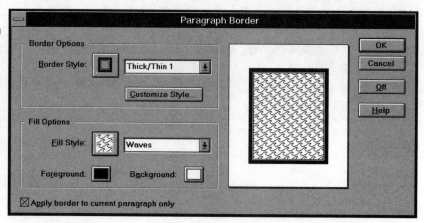

Figure 16-2:
The Paragraph Border dialog box, which is just like the Page and Columns Border boxes.

Most of what you can do in this dialog box is just fun stuff that has fewer practical applications than propeller beanies on space suits. To do it, though, click the button next to the Border Style label (the one that, unless you already have a border, says "No border") and choose a border from the crazy-quilt panel that appears. The most useful borders are the boring ones in the first two rows. You can choose styles by name rather than by picture, by clicking in the box next to Border Style rather than clicking the button. **Remember:** If you use a border that is too elaborate, your text will look like an obituary.

If you *really* want to make your text illegible but snazzy, click the button labeled Fill Style and choose a groovy, psychedelic background, like waves. You can even choose colors! It doesn't matter which colors you choose because — of course — you don't have a color printer. But, man, does it look cool on the screen. It looks grody on the printer, though.

You can do some nit-picky things with borders. If you're really a frustrated picture-framer at heart, choose a border with the Border Style button and then press the Customize Style button. You can change the appearance of the top, bottom, and side borders; the spacing; and even the existence of borders. Check out the Line Style and Line Styles buttons and go from there.

Some miscellaneous thoughts about borders

"But I'm not an artist!" you cry nervously. "What am I going to do with all these borders and backgrounds, other than make my documents totally illegible?" This section lists some things you might want to do.

Limit your borders to the paragraph, page, column, or whatever area your cursor is in: In the Border/Fill dialog box, put a check in the box in the lower left corner that says, `Apply border to current` *`whatever`* `only`. Checking this box is an alternative to selecting an area of text before you give the Border/Fill command.

Put lines between columns: Highlight your columns. Choose Layout Columns Border/Fill. Click on the text box next to Border Style (the one that says `<none>` at the moment) and choose Column Between. Select Column All instead if you want borders also.

Turn off borders: Place your cursor where you want the borders to stop. In whichever border dialog box you're using (Paragraph, Page, or Columns), click the Off button in the upper right corner.

Don't use borders at all: Use a horizontal or vertical line. For a 6½ inch-long horizontal line, press Enter to make a new paragraph, place your cursor there, and then choose Graphics Horizontal Line from the menu bar. For a nine-inch vertical line down the left side of your text, choose Graphics Vertical Line. To make a custom line, you're on your own; use the Graphics Custom Line command.

Working with Graphics

Michaelangelo probably had fewer tools for doing the Sistine Chapel than WordPerfect has for doing graphics. For art's sake, it's probably a good thing, or else the descendants of Michaelangelo would still be figuring out how many degrees to rotate whom and what color palette to use.

Let's ask the Assumption Fairy (the patron spirit of mathematicians) to grant us three Simplifying Assumptions about what you might want to do. Assume that the things you want to do are limited to the ones in this list:

- ✔ Insert a picture, diagram, or chart that someone has created for you or that came with WordPerfect.
- ✔ Create a simple picture or chart.
- ✔ Size or position a graphics image, and possibly put a border around one.

Inserting existing graphics

Suppose that you already have a graphical file somewhere in your computer or on a floppy disk. This assumption is a pretty safe one to make because WordPerfect gives you a bunch of graphical files. If you or your guru completed the standard installation procedure, they're in your PC.

The simplest way to insert graphics is shown in these steps:

1. **Put the graphics file on a disk in your PC (or on your network).**

   The file can be either on a floppy disk or copied in a directory on your hard disk. The best hard disk directory for it is usually C:\WPWIN60\GRAPHICS. If you don't know how to copy the file, weasel out of it by subtly implying to the person who made the file that it's his or her responsibility. If that doesn't work, dig out the ol' cookie package and go get your PC guru.

2. **Click on the location in the text where you want the picture to be placed.**

   It probably won't end up there, but at least you tried. Things seem to work best if you place the cursor immediately before a paragraph begins.

3. **Choose Graphics Figure from the menu.**

   The Insert Image dialog box appears, as shown in Figure 16-3. By default, it shows you graphics files in the default graphics directory, which is usually C:\WPWIN60\GRAPHICS. If your file isn't there (because it's on a floppy disk, for example), see Chapter 15 for information about how to use the dialog box to tell WordPerfect where a file is located.

   WordPerfect shows you (also by default) only files in WordPerfect's own graphics format – files with an extension of WPG. Alas, your file is probably not in that format. To see other types of files, click on the box labeled List Files of Type at the bottom of the dialog box and click on All Files (*.*). Or if you know which format your file is in (such as *.TIF, for Tagged Image Format), click on that format.

4. **Double-click on the name of the graphics file you want.**

   If you're just experimenting with graphics, try one of the files WordPerfect provides, such as COYOTE.WPG.

   Several things have happened on your screen, as shown in Figure 16-4.

   • Miracle of miracles — the image has been inserted! It has a frame around it with little, black squares. The squares are part of a sizing tool, but hold that thought for a minute. We'll come back to it.

   • An arrow with four heads is in your picture. This positioning tool is your mouse pointer for the moment. Hold that thought too.

   • Holy smokes — another menu bar appears, under the power bar and up near the top of the screen! It's the graphics box menu bar, also called a "feature bar" by WordPerfect. Yeesh. Who wants another menu bar? Definitely hold this thought for a while.

If everything looks perfect — the image is the right size and in the right place (ha!) — you can just click anywhere outside the image to continue with your writing. The funny frame goes away and your mouse pointer goes back to normal.

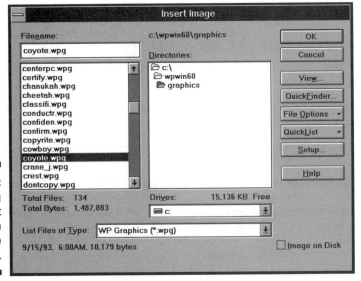

Figure 16-3:
Telling
WordPerfect
which
graphics file
to use.

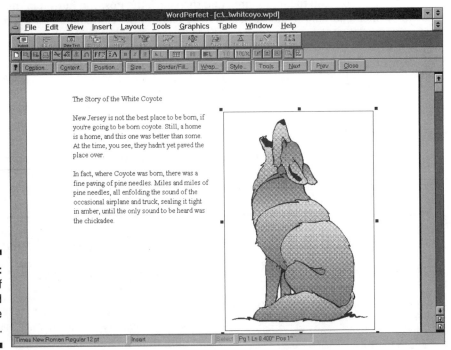

Figure 16-4:
The call of
the wild
graphics file
is answered.

Positioning an image

The first trick is to put your image where you want it:

1. **Move your mouse pointer into the image area.**

   It may be there already.

2. **If the pointer is not a four-headed arrow, click once (do *not* double-click — see the following sidebar).**

   Now your image should look like Figure 16-4 — except, of course, that you probably aren't using a coyote.

3. **Click and drag the image to where you want it.**

Text more or less flows around the image, more or less satisfactorily. When you're finished, click in the text area again.

If you're fussy, you can position the image more precisely by using the Position button in the graphics box menu bar (the "feature bar"). Click on your image and choose Graphics Edit Box or Shift+F11 to make it appear if it's not visible. Click once in the image area and then click the Position button in the edit box menu bar. In the dialog box, choose Place in the Horizontal and Vertical areas and type the dimensions.

If you don't like the graphics box menu bar (feature bar), click Close on the bar to make it go away.

Sizing an image

Perhaps you want Mr. Coyote to be shorter. If you were a roadrunner with your own cartoon series, you would drop a rock on his head. WordPerfect is less picturesque about it, but it is nonetheless effective — and more versatile.

Uh-oh, Toto, we're not in Kansas anymore — again.

If you click on a graphics image to select it and you suddenly get an hourglass icon, a bunch of disk noises, and your picture displayed in a big box titled `WP Draw - [file-so-and-so in WordPerfect]`, do not panic. You simply clicked twice where you should have clicked only once (or at least WordPerfect thought that you did). Double-click on the big minus sign in the upper left corner of *this window* (not the WordPerfect window) to make things go away.

WordPerfect has decided that, because you double-clicked on the picture, you must want to edit it by using the WP Draw program. If you want to edit a picture, this is just the way to do it , of course (see the section "Creating your own graphics," later in this chapter).

The following steps show you how to "scale" your image (change its size and shape):

1. **Move the mouse pointer into the image area and click once to change it to a four-headed arrow.**

   Now WordPerfect knows that you want to scale the image.

2. **Position this new mouse pointer over one of the tiny squares around the image frame.**

   You know that you have it right when the pointer changes to a two-headed arrow. The tiny squares around the image are "handles" with which you can drag the sides or corners of the image to make it larger or smaller.

3. **Click and drag in either of the two directions indicated by the arrow.**

   The edges of the image move with your mouse pointer.

4. **Release the mouse button when things look good.**

If you use the handles on the top, bottom, or sides of the image, you distort its proportions. To keep the proportions correct, use only the corner handles. Keep in mind that the proportions you see on your screen aren't exactly the ones you see when you print. Print your document to check it.

You can also size the image to exact dimensions by using the Size button in the feature bar. Click once in the image and then click the <u>S</u>ize button. Choose <u>S</u>et in the Width and Height areas of the next dialog box that appears and type the dimensions.

Graphics borders

To fool with borders around your graphics (including charts and text boxes, you use basically the same overkill border system described earlier in this chapter, in the section "Working with Borders and Backgrounds." The only difference is that the command you use to fool with borders and backgrounds is harder to find. It's in the graphics box menu bar (or feature bar).

How to see where you're going

To make it easier to see where you're positioning an image, turn on the Zoom feature before you begin step 1 in the preceding steps. Click outside the image area, somewhere in the text. Click the button labeled 100% in the power bar and choose Full Page from its menu. (You can do the same thing with the <u>V</u>iew <u>Z</u>oom command.) Now begin with step 1.

When you're finished positioning and sizing the image, click in the text somewhere. Use the same power bar button (or menu selection), which now reads something like 52%, to reset the zoom to 100%.

The following steps show you how to put a border around your graphics image, chart, or text box:

1. **Click somewhere in your picture.**

   This click selects the image.

2. **If the graphics box menu bar (feature bar) is not already on, press Shift+F11.**

   Or choose Graphics Edit Box from the main menu bar.

3. **Click on the Border/Fill button in the feature bar.**

   You see a dialog box that shows your options.

4. **Specify what you want.**

   See the section "Working with Borders and Backgrounds," earlier in this chapter, for details.

Captions

It's virtually impossible to use regular document text to put a caption where you want it, such as under a picture. You have to use the special caption feature, as shown in these steps:

1. **Click within the graphics image you want to caption.**

   The image is selected.

2. **Click the right mouse button.**

   WordPerfect displays a QuickMenu.

3. **Choose Create Caption from the QuickMenu that appears.**

   WordPerfect suggests a caption.

4. **Press the Backspace key.**

   This step deletes WordPerfect's suggested caption of Figure 1 or whatever.

5. **Type your caption.**

   You can use any of the usual Layout commands or formatting buttons, such as bold or different type sizes.

You don't have to do anything special when you're finished. Just click somewhere else in the document.

You can use this same procedure to edit the caption. When a caption already exists, the QuickMenu mentioned in step 3 displays Edit Caption rather than Create Caption.

Creating your own graphics

For creating and modifying graphics, WordPerfect has a drawing program called WordPerfect Draw (or WP Draw, by its friends).

So you're not Norman Rockwell — with WP Draw you can still create your own, home-style graphics and have them look, well, OK. Hey, at least you can't color outside the lines here.

You can fire up WP Draw in a number of ways. If you're editing an existing image that is already in your document, just double-click on it. If you're creating a new graphic from scratch, click on the WP Draw button in the button bar, or choose Graphics Draw from the main menu bar.

WP Draw pops up and looks like Figure 16-5.

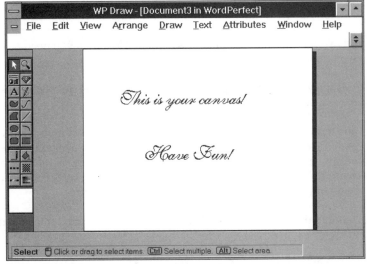

Figure 16-5:
Let's get
graphical —
WordPerfect
Draw!

The center of the screen is your "canvas."

That bunch of oddly shaped stuff down the left side is your very own set of drawing tools for drawing odd shapes. You can figure out on your own how to use them; they're kind of fun to play with. If you move your mouse cursor over them, WP Draw describes in the title bar at the top of the window what they do.

The menu bar across the top does many things, but the most important commands and their most important functions are shown in this list:

✔ **File:** The Exit command takes you back to your document. The Insert File command lets you bring in other graphics files and draw on top of them.

- ✔ **Edit:** The Undo command undoes things. Duplicate duplicates selected objects. Delete (or the Delete key) deletes selected objects. Edit Points lets you change a shape by dragging points that define its perimeter.

- ✔ **View:** Gives you drawing aids, such as grid lines and a ruler. Snap to grid means that your shapes are determined in part by the gridlines. Zooming the drawing area is a good feature to use if your drawing gets big.

- ✔ **Arrange:** Is useful mostly for putting a selected object behind another object (Back) or in front of another object (Front). It's also useful for flipping objects left to right or upside-down.

- ✔ **Draw:** An alternative to the tool icons down the left side. Chart lets you put a chart in your drawing by using chart mode (see the following section, "Using graphs and charts").

- ✔ **Text:** Controls the way text looks in your drawing. You put text in your drawing by using the icon with a big A on it.

- ✔ **Attributes:** Lets you change colors, use dotted or dashed lines, and determine (through Fill) whether your shapes are filled in.

The remainder of this section tells you the basic things you need to know to use these commands to draw amazing pictures.

Everything you create is a graphic "object" that can be deleted, moved, duplicated, or otherwise changed independently from the rest of your drawing.

To do anything to an object, you must select it. To select it, first click on the arrow icon in the upper left corner of the tool area. Then click on the object. A frame appears, with handles around the edges, for sizing and positioning. Sizing rules are the same as in the section, "Sizing an image," earlier in this chapter. To move an object, click anywhere inside the frame and drag.

You should draw so that you fill the "canvas" area. Expand things and move them around, if necessary.

Objects can overlap, with one apparently "in front of" another. You can change this look by selecting one object and using the Arrange command.

To delete an object, select it and press the Delete key on your keyboard.

Closed shapes are filled in by default and in a default color. To change this fill or make it go away, select an object and use the Attributes Fill command. Or select the object and then click and hold on the icon with the spilling paint can. Choose Fill or No Fill from the menu.

Colors are translated into shades of gray when you print unless you are fortunate enough to have a color printer. If you don't like the way things look when they're printed, try fooling with the File Adjust Image command to change brightness, contrast, or "warmth." Save a tree when you're doing this: reuse paper from earlier attempts by printing on the clean side unless your printer manual forbids it. Put it upside down in your printer.

To use a tool, select it and then follow the mouse instructions at the bottom of the window.

If you insert an image from a separate file, you probably cannot change things within it because it is all one object. You can draw on top of it.

To leave WP Draw, choose File Exit from the menu bar or double-click on the big minus sign in the upper left corner. The Exit command appears as Exit and Return to followed by your document name. Talk about wordy!) Answer the query box that follows, which asks whether you want your work saved in your document: answer Yes unless you don't want to save your graphics work.

After you are back in WordPerfect, to edit your drawing again, double-click on it.

Using graphs and charts

Using the graph/chart tool, WordPerfect can create a variety of data charts, including pie, bar, line, and other forms. No, that's not quite correct. Fill a gymnasium with economists. Give them all colored pens and rulers. Lock the doors and come back in ten years. WordPerfect can do more graphing than these guys can. (If you had fed them, they might have a fighting chance, of course, but why pass up such an opportunity?)

To create a chart in your document, you begin by clicking on the chart icon in the button bar (or choosing Graphics Chart from the main menu bar). A WP Draw window appears, although it doesn't look or act much like WP Draw. It looks like Figure 16-6, with a sample chart displayed.

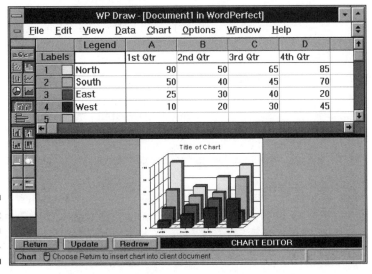

Figure 16-6:
WP Draw in chart mode.

Notice that the top of your screen contains a spreadsheet. In the white area, you can put data for graphing or charting. Words and numbers are there now as an example. This spreadsheet is linked to the sample graph beneath it. See where the Labels (top row) are placed; notice how colors are used; observe how the words in the Legend column (the column on the left) appear in the Legend box in the graph.

Down the left side are buttons for changing your chart type (to choose line or pie charting, for example) and style (such as 3-D versus 2-D or stacked-bar versus side-by-side bars). If you move your mouse pointer across these buttons without clicking, WP Draw describes what they do in the title bar (the top line in the WP Draw window).

The menu bar across the top can do lots of stuff, but its most useful functions are shown in this list:

- ✓ **Edit:** Cuts and pastes data
- ✓ **Data:** Changes the way numbers are displayed (Format)
- ✓ **Chart:** An alternative to the buttons down the left side for choosing types and styles of chart
- ✓ **Options:** A way to change the details or style of your chart, such as whether gridlines are shown

To make the sample chart into *your* chart, follow these steps:

1. **If you want another type of chart, use either the buttons down the left or the Chart command on the menu.**

    If you want excitement in your life, you can also choose from screaming-color graphical representations of these variants by clicking on the Gallery button on the Chart menu. Enjoy the riotous color of the Chart Gallery. Double-click on the one you want, such as Bar Chart. Enjoy the equally colorful Style variants that are displayed. Double-click on a nice one (BAR01, for example).

2. **Delete the sample data.**

    Click on the cell in the upper left corner of the white spreadsheet area; hold down the mouse button and drag to extend the highlight to the lower right corner of the data. Release the button and press the Delete key on your keyboard. In the Clear dialog box that appears, click on OK (or press Enter). You can also delete individual cell values by clicking on them and pressing the Delete key.

3. **Click on individual cells and type your own data, legends, and labels.**

4. **To put your own title on the chart, choose Options and then Titles.**

    Type a title in the Titles dialog box that appears and then press Enter.

5. **Press Ctrl+F3 to redraw the chart by using your data.**

    Or click the Redraw button in the bottom left corner.

6. **When the chart is the way you want it, click the Return button in the lower left corner of the window.**

   In the query box that appears, click on <u>Y</u>es to answer the question about saving changes to your document.

If you want to change your chart after you have returned to the document, just double-click on it.

Working with Text Boxes

Suppose that you're reading a serious article, from *People* magazine, for example, about a celebrity ("Tom Hanks — Does He Really Hanker After Meg?"). In the corner of the page, bordered in fuschia, are two columns of text about some frivolous, annoying peripheral subject, such as "Tom Hanks and Cher: Separated at Birth?" Guess what? You too can make annoying sidebars such as this one in your document, by using text boxes.

To create a text box, follow these steps:

1. **Click in your document where you want the text box to appear.**

   It won't appear there, but it will be close.

2. **Click the Text Box button on the button bar.**

   Or, under <u>G</u>raphics in the main WordPerfect menu bar, choose <u>T</u>ext.

   Another one of those frame gizmos appears, this time with thick bars at the top and bottom and no real frame connecting the "handles" (the little, black squares).

   You also get another one of those feature bars, such as the one you get with graphics. A blinking cursor in the box invites you to type text.

3. **Type the text you want boxed.**

   You can format this text by using the <u>L</u>ayout commands, just as you would format any other text. You can even put text in columns. Don't try to use the Layout commands to change the border of the text box, though. All you get is boxes within boxes.

4. **To change the border or background, use the <u>B</u>order/Fill button in the feature bar. Follow the instructions in the sections "Graphics borders" and "Working with Borders and Backgrounds," earlier in this chapter.**

   Or leave it alone.

5. **To position or size the text box, follow the instructions in the sections "Positioning an image" and "Sizing an image," earlier in this chapter.**

6. **When you're finished, just click anywhere outside the text box.**

To edit your boxed text afterward, double-click on it.

To make the text box feature bar go away, click on <u>C</u>lose. To bring it back, click first on your boxed text and then select <u>G</u>raphics <u>E</u>dit Box from the main WordPerfect menu bar.

Working with Tables

When it comes to tables in WordPerfect, guess what? Yup — overkill again. WordPerfect is a word processor that swallowed a spreadsheet program. It can do such tasks as automatically compute sums of columns and rows. It can, in fact, automatically compute the standard deviation of the arc tangent of the logarithm of the net present value of your mortgage, over multiple random variations of the interest rate.

Fortunately, for those of us who would just as soon leave spreadsheets to the accounting department, WordPerfect also does ordinary tables. It even makes them easy to create.

Making tables with Table <u>Q</u>uick Create

The fastest way to create a table is by using the Table Quick Create button on the button bar:

1. **Click on the Table Quick Create icon and hold down the mouse button.**

   The Table Quick Create icon is the button on the button bar that looks like a tiny calendar. As you hold down the mouse button, a grid titled "No Table" appears right on top of the icon. You can use this little grid to tell WordPerfect how big to make your table.

2. **While you hold down the mouse button, drag the mouse cursor down and to the right on the grid to highlight the number of rows and columns you want.**

   The number of `columns x rows` appears above the grid (5 x 2 for a table with five columns and two rows, for example).

3. **Release the mouse button.**

   Your table is ready. Would Madame please follow me? Walk this way, please.

To fill your table with goodies, simply click in a cell and type. You can use text, numbers, and even graphics! And you can format your text in the usual way, by using the <u>L</u>ayout commands.

Adding or deleting rows and columns

To make tables larger or smaller (that is, to increase or decrease the number of rows), you have to use the Tables commands on the main menu bar.

This list shows you how to add one or more rows or columns to your table:

1. **Click in any row or column that will adjoin your new row or column.**

   Click anywhere in the bottom row, for example, to add a new row to the bottom of your table.

2. **Choose Table Insert from the main menu bar.**

   An Insert Columns/Rows dialog box appears.

3. **In the Insert area of the dialog box, click on Columns for columns or Rows for rows.**

   If you want more than one new row or column, type the number in the box next to Columns or Rows, or increment the number with the adjoining up-and-down arrows.

4. **In the Placement area of the dialog box, click on Before if you want the row to go above (or the column to go to the left) of the cell you selected in step 1. Otherwise, click on After.**

   In the example of adding a row to the bottom of your table, you click on After.

To delete a row or column from your table, follow these steps:

1. **Click anywhere in the row or column to be deleted.**

   For multiple rows or columns, click and drag to highlight them.

2. **Choose Table Delete from the menu bar.**

   A Delete dialog box appears.

3. **In the Delete section, click on Columns or Rows.**

4. **Click on the OK button.**

To delete the entire table, begin by clicking and dragging a highlight across all the cells. Then if you press the Delete key on your keyboard, a Delete Table dialog box appears. You can either delete the Entire Table or (and this is kind of nice) delete just the Table Contents and leaving the table framework behind. Other weird options are available too. Ignore them.

To delete the contents of a bunch of cells, click and drag a highlight across them and press the Delete key. No dialog box appears; the contents are simply erased.

Changing the width and other appearances of a table

Changing individual column widths is simple. Click on the vertical line that divides the columns and drag it. The mouse pointer turns into a little, horizontal arrow gizmo, to tell you that you are moving a column divider. When you release the mouse button, the column divider moves over so that the column on one side of the line gets wider and the other one gets narrower.

If you hold down the Shift key (with your third hand) while you move the column divider, only the column to the left of the divider gets wider or narrower as you move the divider. The column to the *right* of the divider line stays the same size. All the columns to the right of the divider line just *move* rather than get resized.

Changing the width of a more than one row or column or changing the entire table is not hard, but it requires that you use a slightly intimidating dialog box. You change other appearances also in this dialog box, such as left-right justification and alignment of numbers, column margins, table left-right justification on a page, and even text style variations by column or row.

Take a deep breath and follow these steps:

1. **Click in the cell, row, or column or anywhere in the table you want to change.**

2. **Choose Table Format from the main menu bar (or press Ctrl+F12).**

   The Format dialog box appears.

   The selections across the top let you choose whether to format an individual cell, a row, a column, or the entire table.

3. **To change the entire table, click on Table.**

   To change just the currently selected cell, column, or row, click instead on Cell, Column, or Row. The dialog box changes its appearance with each of these selections, but not too much (except when you select Rows, which gives you fewer things to fool with in the dialog box).

4. **To change the column width, change the value in the Column Width area (the box marked Width).**

   Click in the box and type a new number or click on the increment-decrement arrows. (Notice that you probably cannot increase the width now because the table is set up to fill the width of the page.) If you "fix" a width by checking the Fixed Width box, it cannot be changed by changes in page margins or other columns, if you're formatting an individual column's width.

   • To change left-right justification within a cell, click and hold the button next to the label Justification. Choose a justification from the menu. The option for aligning decimals is nice for numbers, especially money, because it aligns columns of numbers along their decimal points.

- You can set a text style here, such as bold or italics. When you do, it cannot be turned off with the Layout Text command or the power buttons, although you can add styles in those ways.

5. Click on OK or press the Enter key when you're finished.

Dealing with incredibly complex spreadsheet-like tables

Spreadsheet-like tables don't have to be incredibly complex, but they can certainly get that way. Tables become like spreadsheet programs when they begin to calculate values automatically. Let's see how this process happens in WordPerfect: we will focus on a simple example of summing rows and columns. For more complicated stuff, go get a spreadsheet program!

First, however, this list explains some basics for creating a spreadsheet-like table:

✔ Every cell in a table has a reference name that describes its row and column position. Rows use single letters, beginning with *A* in the top row. Columns use numbers, beginning with 1 in the left column. The top left cell therefore is A1, and so on. Users of Lotus 1-2-3 and other spreadsheets should feel right at home.

✔ The calculations are based on formulas entered in a special, invisible way, in the cell in which you want the answer to appear. To add cells A1 and B1 and put the answer in C1, for example, the formula A1+B1 must be invisibly stuffed in cell C1. We talk more about this subject in a minute.

Look at the simple expense report shown in Figure 16-7. It has sums of rows and columns and even a little multiplication to calculate mileage allowance from miles.

It's pretty hard to tell that formulas, not numbers, are entered in the bottom row and right column and in the Mileage column. The only way to tell, in fact, is to turn on the formula bar (refer to Figure 16-8).

To enter or see formulas, choose Table Formula Bar from the main menu. (Click on its Close button to make it go away.)

The white box on the left side of the bar shows you which table WordPerfect thinks you're in (such as A, B, or C, which WordPerfect uses to keep track of tables) and in which cell your cursor is located. In Figure 16-8, it's Table A, cell B7, where the Miles column is totaled.

The other white box shows you the formula in this cell, SUM(B2:B6). The colon symbol means "through," so this formula means "Sum up cells B2 through B6." (Does this look like a spreadsheet formula, or what?)

To create this formula, you could have either clicked in the box and typed it or pressed the Sum button. If you type it, click on the adjoining check-mark button to test it and insert it in the cell.

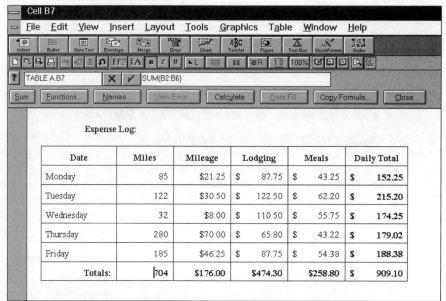

Figure 16-7:
Automatic
calculations
in tables.

The Sum button is kind of magic. It inserts a formula for the sum of cells either above or to the left of the cell in which you're putting the formula. It's not excessively bright (kind of a "dim-sum"), so sometimes it guesses wrong about what you want.

Try it. If the Sum button guesses wrong, you can always edit the formula in the formula box and press the check-mark button (incidentally, values must be in the cells to be summed in order for this to work). So put the values in first and then use the Sum button.

To get your numbers to look as pretty as ours do in Figure 16-7, with dollar signs and stuff, use the Table Number Type command. You can format an individual cell or a column or the entire table. WordPerfect has "types" for fixed decimal point numbers, scientific, currency, accounting, and others.

To perform multiplication and other simple math, such as computing mileage allowance from miles by multiplying by 0.25, you can use these symbols in your formulas:

- ✔ * (Multiply)
- ✔ / (Divide)
- ✔ + (Plus)
- ✔ - (Minus)

Other formulas are available by using the Functions button in the formula bar, but — hey — go get a spreadsheet program. This stuff is pretty heady for a mere word-processing program to be doing.

Chapter 17
Using Templates

Confess — you have been plagiarizing, haven't you? Plagiarizing yourself, that is.

Nearly everyone who writes much, especially for business, ends up stealing from documents that have already been written to make new ones. Who wants to go to all the hassle of laying out a business letter to fit properly on the letterhead, for example, every time she writes a new letter? No, thanks! So what do you do? You probably begin with an older letter, change the name and address, and delete the text. The problem is trying to keep the formatting, text, and graphics you want to keep and still replace other text.

Templates are an attempt to solve this problem in a better way. They're one of those ideas, like frozen pie crusts, that can be a real convenience — but mostly only as long as somebody else makes them. If you have to make them yourself, be sure that you make a large amount of pie, or else it's not worth the effort.

What Are Templates?

Templates are prototypes for certain types of documents. They're similar to blank forms you fill in. They may not even contain text, though. They may contain just a collection of the particular fonts and layout styles you want to use in a particular type of document.

You might want a template for letters that specifies, for example, 10-point Times Roman. A template for new product announcements might use 14-point Helvetica for titles and 12-point type for other text. A template for a newsletter, however, might also contain title text, a logo graphic, and three-column formatting, in addition to specifying the fonts.

The big secret about templates is that, for ordinary, everyday use, they're really not much different from documents. They do get special treatment in WordPerfect; for example, they get called "templates" and have special filenames and their own directory, which makes them feel special and important. They also must be used differently from ordinary documents. For people who want or need to make automatic, macro-driven, standard documents for other people to use, templates have some nice features.

For most practical purposes, though, you cannot do much more with a template than you can do by creating an ordinary document as a prototype, reusing it (opening it and changing the text) every time you want to write a similar document, and being careful to use Save As to save your new documents with new names. If the template stuff is too weird for you, just use this method.

Using Templates

You're probably not aware of it, but you use a template every time you create a new document. This *standard template* determines the layout styles when you create the document.

It's not that there's much in the standard template — at least, not much as it comes out of the box from WordPerfect (you can change it, though). Most of what the standard template contains is the initial paragraph, character, and page formatting that WordPerfect uses for your documents unless you tell it otherwise with the Layout commands Initial Font and Initial Codes. It's good to know about the standard template if you find that you're having to change the layout every time you create a new document.

To use any template other than the standard one, you have to use a special File command: File Template. Don't get confused — you're not going to open the template — you're going to open an ordinary, new document that looks and acts just like the template. Follow these steps:

1. Choose File Template from the menu bar.

A Templates dialog box appears, as shown in Figure 17-1. Template filenames are listed on the left. Single-click on one to see a description in the Description box at the bottom.

Where do templates live?

The directory (both WordPerfect's and your own) that is usually used for templates is C:\WPWIN60\TEMPLATE. You can change this directory by using the File Preferences File command (see Chapter 20).

2. Double-click on the template name you want (in the scrollable list on the left).

If you're not sure which template you want, you can peek at them while the Templates dialog box is displayed. Click once on a template name to highlight it and then click on the View button. A special View window appears and displays the template. To peek at another template without putting away the viewer, just click once on its name. To put away the viewer, double-click on the minus sign in the Viewer title bar.

As shown in Figure 17-1, many templates other than Standard usually are listed in the Templates dialog box. These templates came with WordPerfect; read the following section before you try to use them.

Templates That Come with WordPerfect

WordPerfect supplies a bunch of templates that, like supermarket frozen-pie crusts, can be conveniently filled in with anything you want as you use them.

These templates, shown in the following list, include fairly useful stuff:

Newsletters	Signs
Invoices	Résumés
Mileage records	Reports
Memo forms	Title pages
Packing lists	Daily planners
Press releases	Legal forms
Overhead-projection transparencies (slides)	

These templates also serve as examples of the clever things you can do in WordPerfect. Just keep in mind that professional templatologists made these templates, so don't get carried away trying to do this stuff. It takes a long time to get some of the tricks they use to work correctly.

WordPerfect calls its templates ExpressDocs, and it even gives you a cute, little, separate booklet that shows them all. If your copy of WordPerfect was installed in the normal way, you have all these ExpressDocs, and they're listed when you use the File Template command. (If your PC was a little short on disk space, you or the person who installed WordPerfect may have omitted them.)

The remainder of this section describes the strange and wondrous things that happen when you use one of these templates.

Whenever you use an ExpressDoc, an *Autofill macro* begins working. A macro is a sort of program that runs in WordPerfect. The Autofill macro's job is to prompt you for certain information that is filled in automatically. It's a little slow, so it displays an Autofill Macro box to amuse you while you wait.

The first time you use an ExpressDoc, Autofill announces that it's about to let you personalize your templates. When you see this announcement, click on OK (not that you have much choice). Fill out the Personal Information dialog box that appears next and click on OK there. This information lets WordPerfect fill in such things as return addresses, which don't change very often.

Autofill may also give you one of a variety of other dialog boxes, depending on which template you choose. These boxes request information that is filled in for just this particular instance of template use. The newsletter templates, for example, request an issue number (for the issue of the newsletter) and a date. These dialog boxes typically also have a button that lets you change the personal-information data.

If you cancel out of any of the Autofill stuff (or press the Esc key), you have to do Autofill's job of filling in information yourself. There's usually no trick to this; just highlight (select) the stuff in brackets ([ ] or < >) and type new text. If you have trouble deleting or changing something, it may be "locked" in a table (see the following Tip Sidebar).

The button bar may change. The designer of the template has the option to change this bar to suit the nature of the template. If a table has spreadsheet-like calculations, for example, there might be a Calc Doc button that updates the calculations.

"I can't edit the danged text!"

There's a good reason you cannot edit some of the text ExpressDocs creates. To prevent edits in certain areas, the clever people who made these templates put the text in a cell in a table and "locked" it. To determine whether that's your problem, move your mouse pointer over the text. If *cell addresses* (such as Cell A1) appear at the top of the window, your text is in a table and may be locked.

To unlock the text, first you must put your cursor inside the table. Move the mouse pointer slowly to the left of the uncooperative text. At some point, the mouse pointer changes from an I-bar shape to a horizontal arrow. As soon as it does, click the (left) mouse button.

Now click the right mouse button and choose Format from the QuickMenu. This step displays the Format dialog box for tables. Click on Table at the top. At the bottom of the dialog box, click on the box labeled Disable Cell Locks so that it shows an X. Click the OK button and wait. You should now be able to edit the text.

Creating Templates

One way to create a template is to begin with a document. Suppose that you want to make a template for business letters that will go on your preprinted corporate letterhead. You have to position the text so that it doesn't overprint the logo and has the correct margins, for example.

Go ahead and write a document in the normal way (starting with File New). Fool with the layout until you get it right. (Chapter 19 has some tips on how to lay out various documents.) Press Ctrl+Shift+F3 to display the paragraph marks if they're not visible. Use View Page so that you can see exactly what you're doing. Set up the margins. If you want, set up styles for each different type of paragraph or character layout (see Chapter 12 for information about styles).

It's not magic

The document you get when you use a template is not a special document, even though it may look really cool. It's an ordinary WordPerfect document made up of text, tables, borders, and the like. It looks cool only because an official Very Clever Person created the template.

You can change the document, add stuff to it, delete stuff, and so on. But remember that you're changing just the document, not the template. To change the template, see the last section in this chapter, "Editing or Deleting Templates."

This list shows a few tips for creating a template from a document:

✔ When you finish making the document, replace with little notes any text that you don't want to appear every time — perhaps in brackets, such as [Addressee's Name] and [Addressee's Company]. In ExpressDocs, these sorts of bracketed notes are filled in automatically; it doesn't happen in your templates unless you create your templates by editing an ExpressDoc (see the following section).

✔ So that you don't change the font when you replace text with notes, don't delete the existing text; just highlight the text and start typing replacement text over it.

✔ Leave permanent items: your name under the signature area and the *Dear* in the salutation of a business letter template, for example.

Finally, use the File Save As command to save the document as a template. Make sure that you save it in the template directory, not in the document directory. In the Directories dialog box, double-click on the WPWIN60 directory so that other directories appear. Among them is the TEMPLATE directory; double-click on it. Now click in the Filename box and type a name with an extension of WPT (for *WordPerfect template*).

If you're using the QuickList approach to saving and retrieving files, as described in Chapter 15, you can skip all the clicking-on-directories stuff when you use the File Save As command: just click on Template Directory in the QuickList. You still have to click in the Filename box and type a name with an extension of WPT, however.

Editing or Deleting Templates

Unlike the composition of frozen-pie crust from the supermarket, the composition of your templates (and of ExpressDocs), can be changed.

To change a template, you have to open it first. Not surprisingly, you use the File Template command, as shown in these steps:

1. **Choose File Template from the menu bar.**

   The dialog box shown in Figure 17-1 is displayed.

2. **In the Filename panel in the dialog box, click once on the template you want to edit.**

   Check the description of the template in the box at the bottom of the dialog box. If you're still not sure which one is the template you want, click on the View button in the Open File dialog box to produce a Viewer. Then click once on any template filename to view it. To close the Viewer, double-click on the minus sign in its title bar.

3. Click on the Options button. Choose Edit Template from the drop-down menu.

Notice also the Delete Template option and the Create Template option. Delete Template does what you think it does: it deletes the highlighted template. Create Template is just another way to begin making your own template. After you have chosen Create Template, the process is identical to the one described in the preceding section of this chapter. The only difference is that when you're finished making the template, you don't have to tell WordPerfect to save your document as a template; it already knows. Just use File Save to save your template when you use this method.

Now you're editing the template. It's just like editing a document, unless you try to use the advanced features, such as macros and objects.

Anything you change, including styles and any text you add, appears in *new* documents you create by using this template. Documents you have *previously* created by using this template, however, are not affected by these changes.

If you're editing an ExpressDoc and you run into trouble editing some text, it may be because the text is "locked" in a table. See the preceding Tip, titled "I can't edit the danged text!"

Notice the new bar of buttons (oh, goodie). For the most part, these buttons enable you to do vastly complicated things we don't even want to think about.

The few things in the new bar that may be useful to you are shown in this list:

- ✔ The Description button lets you enter or edit descriptive text that appears in the Templates dialog box (refer to Figure 17-1) . Use this button to make notes to yourself about the template, such as "Use this template for interoffice memos."

- ✔ The Initial Style button lets you set up the default layout and fonts for the document — in other words, the layout and fonts it uses (except where text has been explicitly formatted otherwise). For more information about this subject, see the section "Formatting the Entire Document," in Chapter 8.

- ✔ The Exit Template button does just that: exits from the template. WordPerfect asks whether you want to save changes to your file. Answer Yes unless you have just been practicing your template skills and don't want to keep your work (or you have really messed up the template and don't want to save the changes).

If you want to create a template that gets filled in automatically by the Autofill macro, the easiest way is to use an existing ExpressDoc that fills in the sort of information you want, such as [Addressee's Name]. Edit the template, retain the bracketed text as placeholders for the information to be filled in, and save the template under a new name. Text that is bracketed like <this> is replaced with the personal data you entered during customization. Square-bracketed information like [this] is requested by the Autofill macro whenever the template is used.

Chapter 18
Creating Your Own Junk Mail

. . . .

In This Chapter

▶ Generating tons of letters fast

▶ Creating a data file

▶ Creating a form file

▶ Merging your files

▶ Printing your data file

▶ Printing envelopes

. . . .

Don't you just *love* getting junk mail? Doesn't it warm your heart to know that some direct-mail marketing executive thinks enough of your buying (or donating) power to send you a cleverly personalized letter? Yes, JOHN, we know that you and the entire SMITH household really enjoy getting heaps of junk mail.

So it's natural that you might want to create junk mail. Why not share the joy? You should be thrilled to hear that WordPerfect can help you out. Not that creating personalized letters is a piece of cake in WordPerfect, but it's no worse than root canals.

How Does the Junk-Mail Feature Work?

To create personalized junk mail, you need two documents: a data file and a form file.

The *data file* contains the names and addresses of your victims, which you must enter in a special format. WordPerfect helps you do this by creating a dialog box for your data file that lets you just fill in the blanks. In addition to names and addresses, your data file can also contain other information about each person, such as the amount they owe you, the name of their firstborn son, or any other information you might want to include in a form letter. The data file is in effect a mini-database. Each piece of information is called a *field*. All the information about one person is called a *record*.

The *form file* contains the form letter. In place of a name or address, the form file contains *merge codes* that tell WordPerfect to use information from the data file.

When you "perform the merge," you tell WordPerfect to create one copy of the form file for each person in the data file. You can either send this combined file directly to the printer or store it as a new, third document.

So far, so good. Let's step through the procedure for creating a data file and a form file and then see how to merge them. It's not that bad, really — although we do suggest that you either learn to meditate or get a Valium prescription before beginning.

WordPerfect's merge feature is cool, but it's not worth using unless you want to send a bunch of letters. For two or three letters, or even four or five, it's not worth the effort. Instead, type one letter and print it and then edit the address and print it again, and so on.

Creating a Data File

When you choose Tools Merge from the menu bar, WordPerfect displays the dialog box shown in Figure 18-1. You can also press Shift+F9 or choose the Merge button on the button bar to see this dialog box.

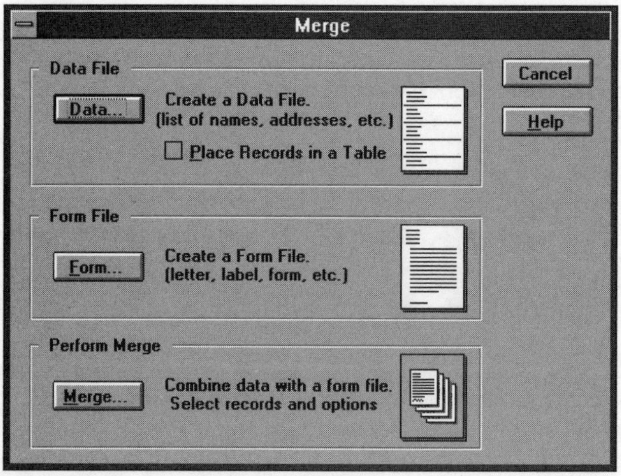

Figure 18-1:
The Merge
dialog box
serves as
Mission
Control for
creating
personalized
junk mail.

> **Merge**
>
> **Data File**
> [Data...] Create a Data File.
> (list of names, addresses, etc.)
> ☐ Place Records in a Table
>
> **Form File**
> [Form...] Create a Form File.
> (letter, label, form, etc.)
>
> **Perform Merge**
> [Merge...] Combine data with a form file.
> Select records and options
>
> [Cancel]
> [Help]

As you may have guessed, you choose the Data button to create the data file. A little box just below the Data button determines which of two formats your data file will be in:

Ugly: Shows each piece of information in the data file on a separate line, with lots of weird-looking WordPerfect merge codes in various colors.

Tasteful: Arranges the data file information in a table, with one row of the table for each record and one column of the table for each field.

We show you pictures of these two formats a little later in this chapter. You should use whichever format you prefer, of course, but if you use the ugly method, you're nuts.

Follow these steps to make a data file:

1. **Choose Tools Merge from the menu bar.**

   You see the Merge dialog box (refer to Figure 18-1).

2. **If you want to create a tasteful (not ugly) data file, click on Place Records in a Table box so that an X appears in it.**

   Suit yourself!

3. **Choose the Data button.**

   WordPerfect wants to know which document you want to use as the data file and displays the Create Merge File dialog box. You have two choices: Use File in Active Window or New Document Window.

4. **Choose New Document Window and then choose OK.**

   You might as well begin with a nice, fresh document. WordPerfect makes a new document (named something like Document3) and displays the Create Data File dialog box, shown in Figure 18-2.

   Now is your opportunity to decide which pieces of information (the fields) you want to store about each person (the record). Naturally, you need Name, Address, City, State, and ZIP. You might want to have separate fields for First Name and Last Name so that your letter can begin "Dear Joe" and mention "The Bloggs family" later. You can also create fields for other facts the letter will include. A letter to members of a church asking them to make donations can mention the amount each family donated last year.

   If you run a day-care center, for example, and you want to send form letters to families with children planning to attend, the fields might be First Name (of the kid's parent), Last Name, Child's Name, Address, City, State, ZIP, and Start Date.

5. **Enter the names of the fields.**

   For each field, type the name in the Name a Field box. When you choose Add (or press Alt+A), the field name appears in the Field Name List.

6. **Choose OK when you finish naming fields.**

WordPerfect does three things to prepare the data file for your use. First, it sticks information about your fields at the beginning of the document. If you chose the ugly method, you see special merge codes, which are visible even though you aren't using the Reveal Codes window. You can see FIELDNAMES and ENDRECORD codes at the top of the document window. If you chose the tasteful method, you see a table with one column for each field.

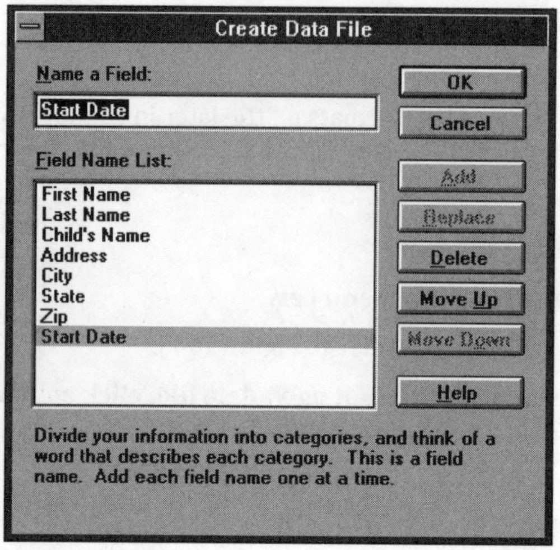

Figure 18-2: Which pieces of intrusive personal information do you want to include in your form letters?

Second, obscuring your view of the document is a fill-in-the-blanks data-entry screen. (That's ComputerSpeak for a dialog box with blanks for each field you created.) Figure 18-3 shows the Quick Data Entry dialog box that WordPerfect created for our hypothetical day-care center.

Third, WordPerfect displays another row of buttons — in this case, the merge bar. (Sounds like a swinging singles joint, doesn't it?)

Now your data file is ready to use.

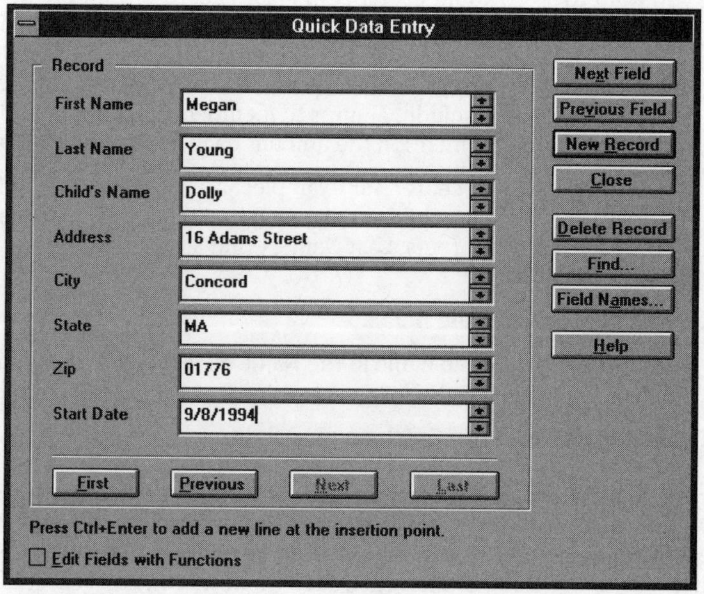

Figure 18-3: To mail a form letter to someone, just fill in the blanks.

Entering the addresses of your victims

Before you can pester someone with form letters, you must type the address. These steps show you how:

1. **If the data file isn't already open, open it.**

   If you just created the data file, it's still open.

2. **If the Quick Data Entry dialog box isn't visible, display it.**

   Choose the Quick Entry button from the merge bar, the row of buttons just above the top of your document.

3. **Fill in a value for each field, to create one record.**

   That is, fill in all the facts about one person. Press the Tab key to move down a field (or press Enter or choose Next Field) and Shift+Tab to move up.

4. **Choose New Record to start the next record (the next person).**

   When you get to the last field in a record, pressing Enter chooses this button for you.

5. **When you finish entering all the facts (field data) about all the people (record data), choose Close.**

   WordPerfect asks whether you want to save the changes to disk. Unless you have been typing names just to see your fingers move, the answer is Yes. WordPerfect then displays the Save As dialog box so that you can enter the filename. (Oddly, WordPerfect displays it every time you add records rather than assume that you probably want to continue to use the same filename as before. Go figure.)

6. **Enter a filename and choose OK.**

   If you are updating an existing data file, WordPerfect becomes alarmed and warns you that a file already has that name. Of course, it does! It's the file you are updating! When WordPerfect asks whether you want to replace it, choose Yes.

   When you enter information in a data file, be sure to enter it as you want it to appear in your letters.

Ugly data files

If you chose the ugly method, you now can see the fields, each on a separate line. Between one record and the next is an ENDRECORD merge code and a page break. At the end of each field is the word ENDFIELD (another merge code). Figure 18-4 shows a record or two in ugly format.

To see more than one record at a time, choose View Draft so that page breaks appear as a double horizontal line. Otherwise, with only one record per page, most of what you see is blank.

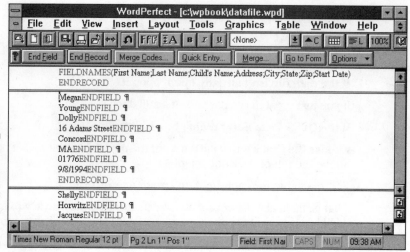

Figure 18-4:
Records in a
data file,
with lots of
ugly merge
codes.

If you don't like your screen to be cluttered with these long merge codes, you
can display them as little blobs. Choose Options from the merge bar (the button
on the right). The menu that appears probably has a check mark in front of the
Display Codes command which indicates that right now WordPerfect displays
the names of merge codes in your document. If you choose Display as Markers,
the code names are replaced by little, red diamonds — much more tasteful. If
you choose Hide Codes, they disappear, but this idea is usually a bad one — in
case you edit the records in the document, you should be able to check that the
ENDFIELD codes remain at the end of each field.

Tasteful data files

If you chose the tasteful method, you see a table like the one in Figure 18-5. For
more information about using tables, see Chapter 16.

Making corrections

Later, you have to fix up the addresses you have entered or delete the names of
people who have threatened to sue. You can edit the data file as though it were
a normal document, but you have to be careful not to mess up the ENDFIELD
and ENDRECORD merge codes. A better way is to use the Quick Data Entry
dialog box to make all your corrections. First display the Quick Data Entry
dialog box by choosing the Quick Entry button from the merge bar.

While you are using the Quick Data Entry dialog box, you can use these buttons
and keys:

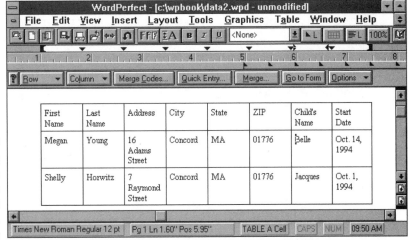

Figure 18-5:
Records in a
data file in a
nice, neat
table.

✔ To find a record, choose the Find button. You see the same old Find Text dialog box (see Chapter 5 if you don't recognize it). It doesn't matter which field your cursor is in when you do this — you can look for the information in any field.

✔ To move from record to record, choose the First, Last, Next, and Previous buttons.

✔ To delete the record in the dialog box, choose the Delete Record button. But watch out — WordPerfect doesn't ask for any confirmation before blowing the person away. Click with care!

✔ To add more records, choose New Record.

✔ To update the information in a record, find the record, move your cursor to the field you want to correct, and edit it.

When you are finished using the Quick Data Entry dialog box, choose Close. WordPerfect asks whether you want to save your work. Choose Yes. Choose the filename (probably the same filename it has had all along) and reassure WordPerfect that you do in fact want to replace the previous version with the corrected version. Sheesh!

When you close the Quick Data Entry dialog box, the additions and corrections also appear in the document.

Creating a Form File

After you have created a list of recipients for your form letter, you can type the letter. The document that contains the form letter is called the *form file*.

A form file is a regular old WordPerfect document. But in place of the name and address at the top of the letter, you enter funky-looking merge codes, as shown in these steps:

1. **Choose Tools Merge from the menu bar and then choose the Form button.**

   WordPerfect wants to know whether you want to create a new document to contain the form letter or whether you want to use the document on the screen.

2. **Choose New Document Window and then choose OK.**

   If you have already typed the letter and it is the current document, choose Use File in Active Window instead.

   Either way, WordPerfect asks which data file will provide the data for this form letter, by using the dialog box shown in Figure 18-6.

3. **Enter the name of your data file and then choose OK.**

   You can also click on the little file-folder button at the right end of the box, which lets you choose the filename. If you haven't created the data file yet, choose None.

   WordPerfect opens a new document and displays the merge bar just above it. When you are editing a form file, the merge bar contains different buttons than when you are working on a data file.

4. **Type any information that you want to appear before the date and name of the addressee.**

   Type the text for your letterhead, for example, if you print on blank paper. For a normal letter, the next thing you want to see is today's date.

5. **Choose Date from the merge bar.**

   WordPerfect inserts a colorful DATE code in your document. When you merge this form file with a data file, today's date appears here.

   Press Enter to start a new line. Press Enter again to leave a space before the name and address.

6. **Choose Insert Field from the merge bar.**

   WordPerfect displays the Insert Field Name or Number dialog box, shown in Figure 18-7. The dialog box lists all the fields you defined in the data file associated with this form letter.

7. **Choose the first field from the data file to appear in the form letter and then choose Insert.**

   Choose the First Name field, for example. WordPerfect sticks in FIELD(First Name) in a variety of colors. You're looking at a

WordPerfect merge code, which displays each person's first name when you print the form letters. The dialog box is still visible, which is nice because you have to use it a few more times.

8. Type a space (to appear between the First Name and Last Name fields), select Last Name from the dialog box, and choose Insert again.

Now codes for the First Name and Last Name fields appear in the form letter.

9. Press Enter to start a new line.

Continue in this vein by inserting codes and typing spaces, pressing Enter, or doing whatever between the codes, until you have laid out the entire address. Check out Figure 18-8 for an example.

10. Type your letter.

You can use all the usual formatting, fonts, and margins you use in a normal letter. You can even include merge fields in the body of the letter — JOHN, for that personalized touch.

11. Save the document.

Choose File Save As, as usual.

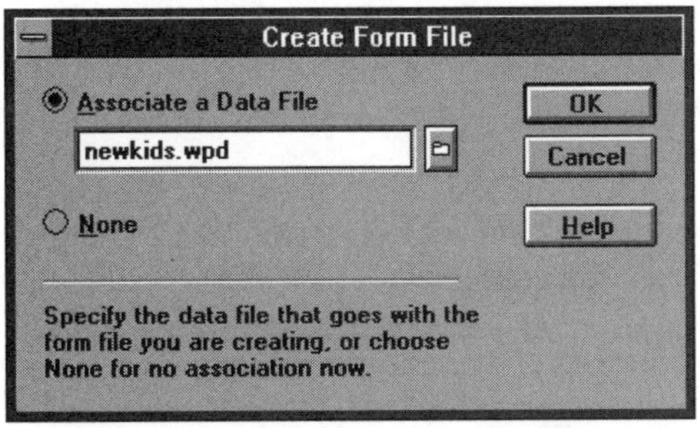

Figure 18-6:
Which document contains the names and addresses for this form letter?

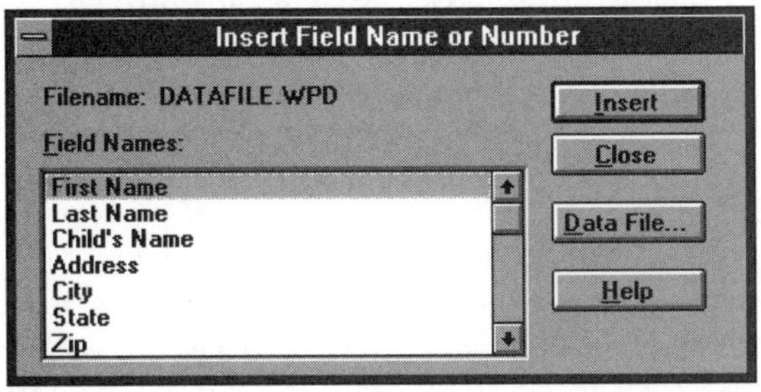

```
┌─────────────────────────────────────────────┐
│ ═          Create Form File                  │
├─────────────────────────────────────────────┤
│ ⦿ Associate a Data File          ┌────────┐ │
│   ┌──────────────────────┐ ┌─┐   │   OK   │ │
│   │ newkids.wpd          │ │▼│   └────────┘ │
│   └──────────────────────┘ └─┘   ┌────────┐ │
│                                   │ Cancel │ │
│ ○ None                            └────────┘ │
│                                   ┌────────┐ │
│                                   │  Help  │ │
│ ─────────────────────────────    └────────┘ │
│ Specify the data file that goes with the     │
│ form file you are creating, or choose        │
│ None for no association now.                 │
└─────────────────────────────────────────────┘
```

Figure 18-7:
Which piece of information from the data file do you want to use?

```
┌─────────────────────────────────────────────┐
│ ═       Insert Field Name or Number          │
├─────────────────────────────────────────────┤
│ Filename: DATAFILE.WPD          ┌──────────┐ │
│                                 │  Insert  │ │
│ Field Names:                    └──────────┘ │
│ ┌──────────────────────┐ ▲      ┌──────────┐ │
│ │ First Name           │ │      │  Close   │ │
│ │ Last Name            │ │      └──────────┘ │
│ │ Child's Name         │ │      ┌──────────┐ │
│ │ Address              │ │      │Data File…│ │
│ │ City                 │ │      └──────────┘ │
│ │ State                │ │      ┌──────────┐ │
│ │ Zip                  │ ▼      │  Help    │ │
│ └──────────────────────┘        └──────────┘ │
└─────────────────────────────────────────────┘
```

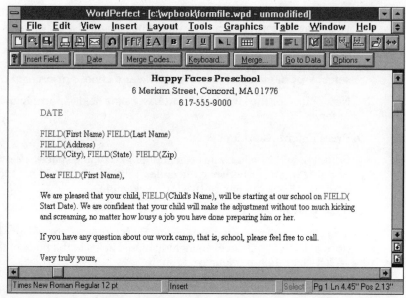

Figure 18-8:
Creating a
form file.

You can create several form files for one data file. If your data file contains a list of people who owe you money, for example, you can make one form file that contains a polite letter requesting payment. A second form file can contain a letter using firmer language, and a third form file can contain the letter telling your pal Vinnie whose legs to break.

You can make a form file that prints envelopes for the letters. See the section "Printing Envelopes," later in this chapter.

What if you choose the wrong data file for this form letter? Or what if you create a new data file and want to use an existing form file? No problem! To associate a different data file with your form file, choose Insert Field to display the Insert Field Name or Number dialog box. Choose the Data File button, specify the filename, and choose OK.

Merging Your Files

After you have a data file and a form file, you're ready to merge. We know, folks, that this explanation is taking a while, but if you have a large number of letters to send, it's worth it. Here we go! Call the post office and tell them to stand back before you follow these steps:

1. Choose Tools Merge from the menu bar and then choose the Merge button.

WordPerfect displays the Perform Merge dialog box, shown in Figure 18-9.

2. Enter the filename of the form file.

Click on the little button at the right end of the box and choose Select File. WordPerfect lets you select the filename and inserts the complete pathname of the form file (C:\LETTERS\THREAT1.WPD, for example).

As soon as you enter the name of the form file, WordPerfect enters the name of the associated data file.

3. Tell WordPerfect where to put the resulting form letters.

Click on the little button at the right end of the Output File box. We recommend the following choices:

<New Document>: Our favorite. WordPerfect makes a new document and sticks all the copies of your form letter in it for you to review before printing them.

<Printer>: Print the form letters without reviewing them. This choice is the "go for the gold" approach. You can waste a great deal of paper this way if you have a typo in your form file.

4. Choose OK.

WordPerfect makes one copy of your form file for each record in your data file and puts the results where you told it to put them. Figure 18-10 shows a letter to our hypothetical day-care center.

5. If your merged letters are in a new document, print the document.

You can look through the letters first, to make sure that they look appropriately personal. You can even make changes to them so that they really are personalized: "P.S. As you requested, we have added bars on the windows of our classrooms so that little Frederika will be sure to stick around."

After you have printed your form letters, you can either save the document that contains them or close it without saving it. After all, you can always create the letters again by repeating these merge steps.

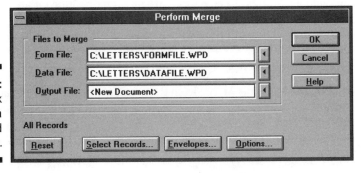

Figure 18-9:
Making junk
mail from a
data file and
a form file.

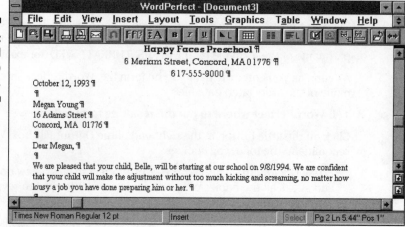

Figure 18-10:
Junk mail
ready to
print.

Printing Your Data File

If you want to print an address list of the people to whom you sent letters, you can just print the data file. If your data file is in ugly format, it looks fairly stupid with all those merge codes in there. If your data file is in tasteful table format, it looks rather nice.

To hide the merge codes in ugly format, choose Options from the merge bar and then choose Hide Codes.

Printing Envelopes

After you have printed your personalized junk mail, you may just want to shove the letters into window envelopes. To complete the personalized look, however, individually addressed envelopes are much more appropriate.

We talk about envelopes in more detail in Chapter 19, but for now, these steps show you how to print envelopes by using addresses from your data file.

1. Create a new form file.

That is, choose Tools Merge from the menu (or press Shift+F9) and choose the Form button. Choose New Document Window as the place for this new form file to live and then choose OK.

2. Tell WordPerfect which data file contains the addresses you want to print.

When you see the Associate a Data File box, enter the name of your data file and choose OK. WordPerfect makes a new document, complete with merge bar at the top.

3. Choose Layout Envelope from the menu bar.

WordPerfect displays the Envelope dialog box, shown in Figure 18-11.

4. In the Return Addresses box, type the return address that you want to appear on each envelope.

There's a catch: at the end of each line of the address, *don't* press Enter. If you press Enter, WordPerfect thinks that you are done with the whole Envelope dialog box. Instead, press Ctrl+Enter to start a new line. Tricky!

5. In the Mailing Addresses box, enter the merge codes to print addresses by using data in your data file.

Choose the Field button at the bottom of the dialog box to display the list of fields in your data file. Select the first field from the data file to appear on the envelope and then choose Insert. Choose the First Name field, for example. WordPerfect inserts FIELD(First Name).

Type a space (to appear between the First Name and Last Name fields) and then choose Field again, select Last Name, and choose Insert again.

Press Ctrl+Enter to start a new line.

Continue inserting codes and typing spaces, pressing Ctrl+Enter, or doing whatever between the codes, until you have laid out the entire address, as shown in Figure 18-11.

6. Choose Append to Doc so that WordPerfect stores the codes which make up this envelope format in your form file document.

The Envelope dialog box goes away and the envelope format appears in your document, complete with ugly merge codes.

7. Save your document.

Call it something like MERGEENV.WPD.

8. Print the envelopes.

Follow the directions in the section "Merging Your Files," earlier in this chapter. For the form file, use the document you just created.

• For more information about envelopes, see Chapter 19.

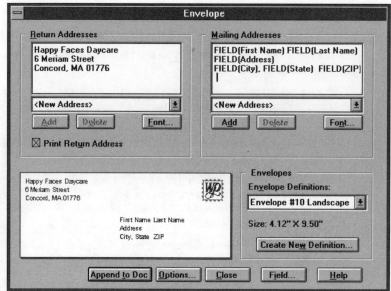

Figure 18-11:
Creating
envelopes
for your junk
mail.

Chapter 19
Recipes for Popular Documents

. . . .

In This Chapter

▶ Letters

▶ Memos

▶ Faxes

▶ Envelopes

▶ Mailing labels

▶ Booklets

▶ Books and other big documents

. . . .

*T*here's no point in reinventing the wheel. For years, the Great Minds of Word Processing have been contemplating the best ways to create many popular types of documents, such as the ones listed here. This chapter has recipes for whipping up crowd-pleasing documents in several standard styles.

If you frequently create documents in a standard format, you should think about creating a WordPerfect template that contains all the formatting (see Chapter 17).

Letters

Every office has its own office style for letters, and we wouldn't presume to tell you how your letters should look. This section, however, has some letter-writing tips.

Skipping space for the letterhead on stationery

If you are printing on stationery, you have to leave a bunch of space at the top of the letter so that your text doesn't type right on top of the letterhead. Get out a ruler and measure how far down you want your letter to start (that is, where you want the first piece of text to appear, which is usually the date).

For one-page letters, you can just set the top margin of the document to the amount of space to skip at the top of the paper. If your letter continues on the next page, however, you have a huge top margin on the second page too.

Another approach is to press Enter repeatedly until the cursor gets to the correct position for the letter to begin.

The most advanced approach to this problem is to use WordPerfect's Advance feature. With your cursor at the top of the page, choose Layout Typesetting Advance from the menu bar (don't ask us what advancing down the page has to do with typesetting). WordPerfect displays the Advance dialog box. For the Vertical Position setting, choose From Top of Page and fill in the Vertical Distance box with the number of inches (or centimeters) you want to move down the page. When you choose OK, WordPerfect inserts an Advance code (VAdv, actually) that moves down to the position you want.

Printing your own letterhead

If you are too cheap (as we are) to buy stationery, you can print your own as part of the letter. Using WordPerfect's many fonts, lines, boxes, and other effects, you can make a pretty snazzy letterhead. It can even include graphics. When you have created a letterhead you like, save it as a template (see Chapter 17) so that all your letters can include it automatically.

Dating your letter

Be sure to make WordPerfect enter today's date rather than type it yourself — press Ctrl+D.

Numbering the pages

For multiple-page letters, it is imperative that you number the pages. Use the page-numbering, headers, or footers feature described in Chapter 9. Be sure to tell WordPerfect *not* to number the first page.

Memos

Everything we said about letters goes for memos too. If you don't use pre-printed memo paper, check out WordPerfect ExpressDocs (ready-to-use templates, described in Chapter 17). They include five awesome memo formats, named, amazingly enough, MEMO1, MEMO2, MEMO3, MEMO4, and MEMO5).

Faxes

If you have a boring, old-fashioned fax machine into which you feed boring, old-fashioned pieces of paper, we don't have much to suggest. You might want to look at the five WordPerfect ExpressDocs templates for faxes (as described in Chapter 17). They look very trendy and designerish.

If your computer has a fax modem, however, you may be able to send faxes directly from WordPerfect without printing the fax on paper at all. Direct digital communication from your machine to theirs. Very advanced.

What do you need?

For this process to work, you need the following items:

✔ **A fax modem:** A gizmo that connects your computer to a phone line and pretends to be a fax machine. The fax modem can live inside your computer or it can be a small box that sits next to it.

✔ **A fax program:** The software that makes the fax modem do its thing. Be sure to get a fax program that works with Windows — the key phrase to look for is "installs as a Windows printer driver." In English, this phrase means that the fax program pretends to be a printer so that when you want to fax a WordPerfect document, you just tell WordPerfect to "print" the document on the fax modem. Unbeknownst to WordPerfect, the document, far from being printed on paper, wings its way telephonically as a fax.

✔ **A phone line:** For your fax modem to talk on.

✔ **A computer guru:** To set all this up. Be sure to have not just one or two cookies but a whole bag of Mint Milanos up your sleeve.

Just the fax, ma'am

After your computer has been rendered fax-capable with this list of equipment, all you have to do to send a fax directly from WordPerfect is follow these steps:

1. **Create a document that contains your fax.**

   The WordPerfect document must contain everything you want in the fax. You cannot print the fax on your letterhead, for example — the document must contain your name and return address. Consider using one of WordPerfect's snazzy-looking ExpressDocs templates (see Chapter 17).

   Because the document is actually "printed" by your fax program, some fonts may not work. Your fax program cannot use fonts that exist only in WordPerfect. You may need to experiment, by sending a fax or two to a friend, to see whether the fonts you use look right in faxes.

2. Save the document.

You can never be too careful.

3. Choose File Select Printer from the menu.

WordPerfect displays the Select Printer dialog box, which contains a list of the printers (and things that pretend to be printers) that WordPerfect knows about. Your fax program should be listed — if it's not, your computer guru didn't do the job right.

4. Select your fax program from the Printers list and choose Select.

The dialog box goes away. WordPerfect reformats the document a little bit because it thinks that you have just changed the printer on which the document will appear.

5. Choose File Print from the menu (or choose the Print button from the power bar or press F5).

WordPerfect displays the usual Print dialog box. The Current Printer setting should show your fax program, not your usual printer.

6. Choose Print.

At this point, WordPerfect thinks that it prints the document: it sends all the information about the document to what it thinks is a printer. It sends it to your fax program, in fact, which stores it until it is ready to send the fax.

7. Use your fax program's dialog boxes to enter the fax number to which the fax should be sent.

Each fax program performs this procedure differently. Most offer a dizzying array of options, including cover sheets and annotations and sending the fax to an entire list of people — you name it. Enter the fax number to which you want to send the fax and look for a button called something like Send.

Your fax program should tell you when the fax has been sent, whether it has trouble getting through, and the hair and eye color of the person who receives it (just kidding). Our program displays a cute, little picture of a fax machine with the paper rolling into it.

8. After the fax is sent, select your regular printer again.

Repeat steps 3 and 4 but select your printer. Otherwise, the next time you try to print a memo, it may get faxed!

Signing your faxes

To include your signature on a fax, you need your signature in digital form, in a graphics file. Using a draw program (such as WP Draw, described in Chapter 16, or Windows Paintbrush) you can attempt to write your signature. It may look more like your second-grader's signature, however.

Alternatively, you can find someone with a scanner (you better have some more cookies on hand!)

and ask to scan your signature, which converts it into a graphics file. Bring along your signature written in black ink on a clean, white piece of paper.

Either way, you end up with a file you can include in your document by using the Graphics Figure command (described in Chapter 16).

Envelopes

After you have written the world's most clear and cogent letter, you need an envelope to put it in. (We have stooped to using window envelopes because we are too lazy to print envelopes, but we suspect that you haven't fallen that far.) If your printer cannot accept envelopes (but most printers can), skip this section.

The folks at WordPerfect created a command that formats a document (or one page of a document) as an envelope. Wow. We are talking about convenience. Word processing takes a major step forward.

Printing the address on the envelope

To print an address on an envelope (we are talking about regular number 10 envelopes here), follow these steps:

1. **If you have already written the letter to go in the envelope, open the document that contains the letter.**

   If not, no big deal.

2. **Choose Layout Envelope from the menu.**

   Or click on the Envelope button on the button bar, if you see it there.

   WordPerfect displays the Envelope dialog box, shown in Figure 19-1. If the current document contains a letter in a fairly normal format, WordPerfect — get this — *finds* the name and address at the top of the letter and displays it in the Mailing Addresses box. This capability is really cool; you don't have to type the address again!

3. **Enter your address in the Return Addresses box.**

   If you have used this dialog box before, WordPerfect remembers the address you entered the last time. A nice touch.

4. **To print the envelope now, choose Print Envelope.**

   Depending on how your printer works, you may be prompted (by a cute, little dialog box) to insert an envelope.

5. **To print an envelope as part of your document, choose Append to Doc.**

   WordPerfect adds the envelope as a separate page at the end of your document, along with all the formatting you need to make it print correctly. This feature is great when the current document is the letter that goes inside the envelope. Whenever you print the letter, you print an envelope too.

Figure 19-1:
Creating an envelope. You don't even have to type the address!

Tips for printing envelopes

When you choose the Layout Envelope command, WordPerfect may demand that you create an "envelope definition." This is bad news because it means that WordPerfect isn't already familiar with printing envelopes on your type of printer. You have to tell it the length and width of your envelopes, the margins — the works. You may want to get some help for this task.

On most laser printers, you insert envelopes face up with the right end of the envelope entering the printer first. You may have to do mechanical things to your printer too; check the manual, under "envelopes." For printers with platens, like most impact printers, stick in the envelope upside down with the front facing away from you so that it is right side up facing toward you after it has come up under the platen. Most ink-jet printers have special envelope-feeding buttons — check your printer manual. Refer to Chapter 13 to learn how to tell which kind of printer you have.

Depending on your printer, WordPerfect may know how to print more than one size of envelope. In the Envelope dialog box, check out the Envelope Definitions setting. If you click on it, you may find that several sizes and shapes are available.

Mailing Labels

Zillions of kinds of labels exist, including sheets of mailing labels, continuous rolls of mailing labels, disk labels — you name it. These steps show you how to print addresses on them: luckily, WordPerfect can handle an amazing variety of formats.

Printing addresses on mailing labels

These steps show you how to print addresses on mailing labels:

1. **Begin with a new, blank document.**

2. **Tell WordPerfect which kind of labels you are using.**

   In technical jargon, you are providing a *label definition.* Choose Layout Labels to display the Labels dialog box, shown in Figure 19-2.

   WordPerfect already knows about an amazing variety of labels, including most of the ones manufactured by the Avery company. Most label definitions listed under Labels in the dialog box are identified only by their Avery part number. This number is pretty useful because most label manufacturers now include the equivalent Avery number on their packages. Choose the type of labels you have.

Printing bar codes

If you want to make the U.S. Postal Service happy (and who wouldn't?), you can print a USPS POSTNET bar code. It will impress your friends too. Just select Options in the Envelope dialog box, choose Include USPS POSTNET Bar Code, and then choose OK in the Envelope Options dialog box. Now a POSTNET Bar Code box ap-

pears in the Envelope dialog box, just below the mailing address. Type the U.S. ZIP code here. When you print the envelope, a tasteful row of little, vertical lines appears above the address. Some machine at the post office must know what they mean.

In case you're not sure which kind you have, WordPerfect displays a little diagram of the labels you have selected. Avery 5160 Address labels come in sheets, for example, with three across and ten rows per page. The Label Details part of the dialog box describes the size and shape of the sheets and individual labels you have chosen.

3. Choose Select.

The dialog box goes away and your document now looks truly weird. An area the size of a label stays white (or whatever background color you use for WordPerfect documents — see Chapter 20), and the rest of the page is draped in shadow, as shown in Figure 19-3.

4. Type the addresses.

Or type whatever it is you want printed on the labels. WordPerfect lets you enter only as much information as fits on a label. To move to the next label, press Ctrl+Enter. After you have entered a bunch of labels, you can use Alt+PgUp and Alt+PgDn to move from label to label. (If you cannot remember these arcane key combinations, just use your mouse!)

5. Save the document.

6. Print 'em!

Put the labels in your printer. For sheet-fed printers, be sure to insert them so that you print on the front, not on the back.

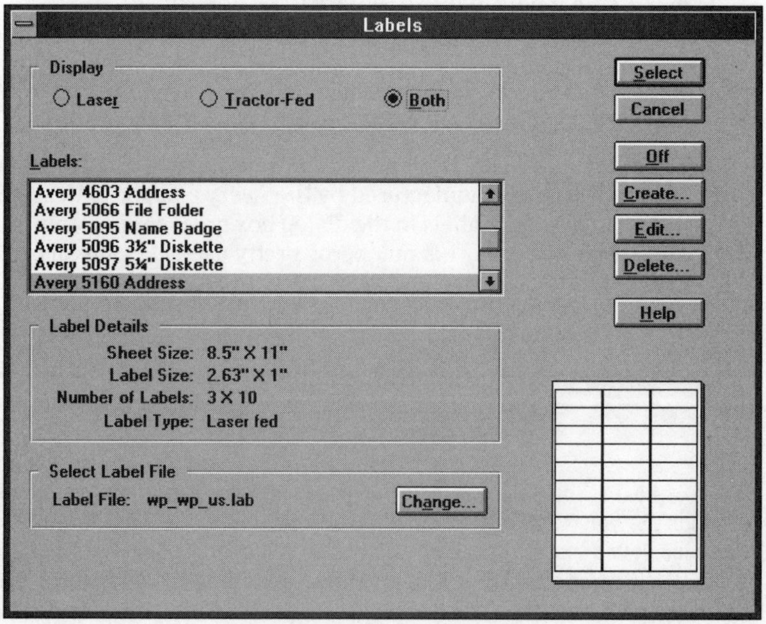

Figure 19-2:
Sheets, rolls,
or stacks of
labels.

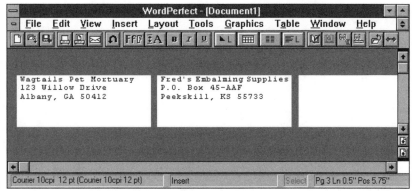

Selecting which addresses to print

You don't have to print an entire page of labels at a time. To print selected labels, you can refer to them by number. WordPerfect thinks of each label as its own minipage — on the status bar, in fact, the "Pg" number is the number of the label.

When you know which labels you want to print, choose File Print and then choose Multiple Pages. When you choose Print, WordPerfect lets you enter the print range. In the Page(s) box, enter the number or numbers of the label or labels you want. Enter **3** to print the third label, for example; **5-12** to print a range of labels; **2,14,23** for several labels; or **15-** for all the rest of the labels beginning at label 15.

Tips for printing labels

You can use all the usual formatting for labels — choose a nice font, make the ZIP code boldface, or whatever.

WordPerfect's list of label definitions is awfully long. To make it shorter, choose Laser or Tractor-Fed in the Display section of the dialog box. WordPerfect lists only that type of labels. Then choose Print again.

If you have used WordPerfect's merge feature to enter a list of addresses for creating junk mail (refer to Chapter 18), you can print these same addresses on mailing labels. Create a new form file (the merge term for the document that contains the form letter) and use the Layout Labels command to format it for labels. In the first mailing label, enter merge codes for the parts of the address. Then use the Tools Merge command to print the labels.

If you are using a type of label that WordPerfect doesn't already know about, you can define your own label definitions. Choose Create from the Labels dialog box and tell it all about the size and arrangement of your labels.

Booklets

A very common typing job is a pain in the neck with most word processors: a little booklet that consists of regular sheets of paper folded in half, like the one shown in Figure 19-4.

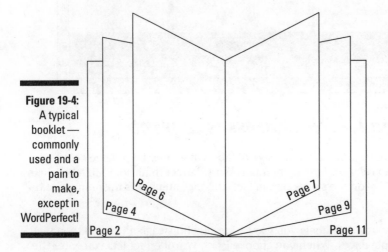

Figure 19-4:
A typical
booklet —
commonly
used and a
pain to
make,
except in
WordPerfect!

Page 6

Page 7

Page 4

Page 9

Page 2

Page 11

But wait! WordPerfect has a special booklet feature for making just this kind of document. This feature is a really cool one that makes us want to take back all the snide things we have said about WordPerfect. (Almost all of them, anyway.)

Creating a booklet document

These steps show you how to make a 5½-by-8½-inch booklet that consists of folded sheets:

1. **Type the text for your booklet.**

   Do all the character and line formatting you plan to use, including fonts, boldface, and centering. Set up page numbering, headers, and footers as you want them.

2. **Save your document.**

   Whatever else happens, it would be a pain to have to type the text again!

   The next step is to tell WordPerfect to print sideways (landscape orientation) on the paper, with two "pages" of your booklet printed on each sheet of paper.

3. Choose Layout Page Paper Size from the menu bar.

Be sure that your cursor is at the beginning of the document when you do this step so that the formatting affects the entire document. (Press Ctrl+Home to get to the tippy-top.) WordPerfect displays the Paper Size dialog box.

4. From the Paper Definitions list, choose Letter (Landscape), which is regular-size paper that prints sideways, and then choose Select.

Europeans should choose A4 Landscape.

5. Choose Layout Page Subdivide Page from the menu bar.

WordPerfect displays the Subdivide Page dialog box, shown in Figure 19-5.

6. Enter 2 for the Number of Columns and then choose OK.

Your text moves around big-time. Subdividing a page into columns works like regular columns (described in Chapter 16), except that WordPerfect knows that you want to consider the columns as separate pages. Way cool!

If you don't see your text in two columns, choose View Page from the menu.

7. Set your margins.

If you didn't set them before, you probably will want to set them now. Then look through and see how your text looks in these small pages. You may want to move your graphics, lines, boxes, and headings around a little.

8. Create a front cover, if you want one.

At the beginning of the document, enter the title or other material to appear on the cover. Press Ctrl+Enter to insert a page break between the cover text and the next page. You can center the cover text up and down on the page by using the Layout Page Center command.

Now your document looks like a booklet, with two pages per sheet of paper.

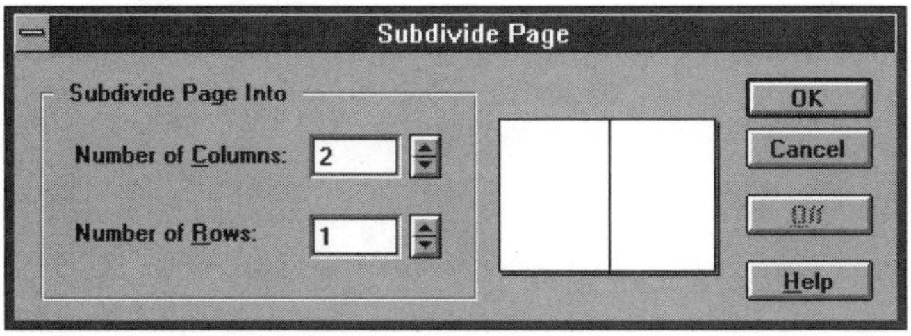

Figure 19-5:
How many booklet pages print on each piece of paper?

Subdivide Page

Subdivide Page Into

Number of Columns: 2

Number of Rows: 1

OK
Cancel
Off
Help

Printing your booklet — the magic part

Now comes the really tricky part — telling WordPerfect to shuffle the order of the pages so that they are in the right order when you fold your booklet in half. Luckily, WordPerfect does almost all the work! Just follow these steps:

1. **If your printer can print on both sides of the page (*duplex*), tell WordPerfect to print the booklet that way.**

   Choose Layout Page Binding and choose From Short Edge for the Duplexing setting. (If that doesn't work, try From Long Edge.)

2. **Choose File Print from the menu bar (or press F5 or choose the Print button on the power bar).**

   When you are ready to print, that is.

3. **In the Print dialog box, choose Options, choose Booklet Printing, and then choose OK.**

   This step tells WordPerfect to switch the order of the pages so that when the sheets of paper are folded, the booklet "pages" are in order.

4. **Back in the Print dialog box, choose Print.**

   WordPerfect thinks about it for a long time. A long, long time. After all, it is reshuffling the entire document. Many minutes later, your printer fires up and spews out the booklet.

Tips for creating booklets

If your printer doesn't print duplex and you use a WordPerfect (rather than Windows) printer driver, WordPerfect prints half the pages and then prompts you to reinsert the pages so that it can print the remaining pages on the back. This procedure can get a little confusing because you must be sure to insert the right page, the right way around, at the right time. We think that it's simpler to print everything on one side of blank sheets of paper and then photocopy them. After all, you probably want more than one copy anyway.

As usual, to insert a page break and move you to the top of the next page, you press Ctrl+Enter. When you have subdivided your pages, you move to the next booklet "page," not to the next sheet of paper. To move to the next or previous booklet "page," press Alt+PgUp or Alt+PgDn.

Reports and Other Big Documents

These days, people use word-processing programs for much more than writing letters. You may want to use WordPerfect to typeset a book, for example. It's not as stupid an idea as it sounds: WordPerfect can handle large documents, including creating tables of contents and indexes.

The secret is not to store the entire book (or report or whatever) in one, big document. Instead, break it up into chapters or sections, one per document. Then make a *master document* to connect them all together.

What's a master document? We're so glad that you asked. It's a WordPerfect document which contains secret codes that link it to other documents. These other documents are called *subdocuments*. When you are writing a book (to pick a wild, hypothetical example), each subdocument might contain one chapter. The master document contains a secret code for each chapter document, in addition to introductory text, the table of contents, and the index.

To go about creating a really big document, such as a book or long report, first you create the subdocuments. Then create the master document. Finally, set up the table of contents and the index. Don't worry, we step you through it.

Creating the master document and subdocuments

To create the master document and its subdocuments, get the text of the book organized first, as shown in these steps:

1. **Create a document for each chapter.**

   Because you want all the chapters to be formatted in the same way, consider making a template that contains the formatting (see Chapter 17). Don't worry about page numbering, headers, or footers in the subdocuments — they are controlled by the master document. Give the documents names such as CHAP1.WPD and CHAP2.WPD.

   Type the text in each chapter document or copy it from existing documents.

2. **Create the master document.**

   Make a new document and type the title page and other front matter. Skip the table of contents for now (we get to it in the following section). If the introduction, preface or whatever are short, you can include them here. If they are long, store each one in its own document, like chapters. Save the document with a name such as BOOK.WPD or REPORT.WPD.

3. **For each chapter, create a secret code in the master document.**

   Move your cursor to the spot in the master document where you want the chapter to appear. If you want the chapter to begin on a new page, insert a page break by pressing Ctrl+Enter. Then choose File Master Document Subdocument from the menu bar. In the Include Subdocument dialog box, choose the filename of the chapter and choose Include.

Not much happens at this point. If you are in page view, you see a little subdocument icon in the left margin of your master document. If you are in draft view, you see `Subdoc: C:\CHOCBOOK\CHAP1.WPD` or whatever the filename of the subdocument is (it looks something like Figure 19-6). Personally, we prefer to work in draft view so that we can see the filenames of our chapters all the time.

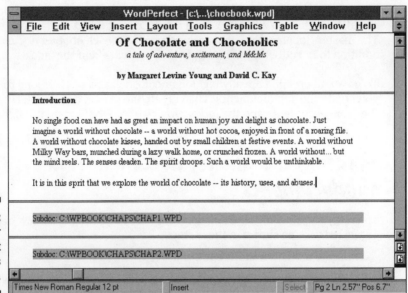

Figure 19-6:
The master document and its subdocs.

> In page view, to find out which document the little subdocument icon refers to, click on it.

> A faster way to give the File Master Document Subdocument command is to use a QuickMenu. With your mouse pointer in the left margin of the document (where it appears as an arrow), click the *right* mouse button. Choose Subdocument from the QuickMenu.

Expanding the master document

WordPerfect can display (and store) a master document in one of two ways: expanded or condensed. When a master document is expanded, WordPerfect retrieves the text of each subdocument and sticks it right where it belongs in the master document. When a master document is condensed — you guessed it — the text of each subdocument is stored back in its separate file and you see just subdocument icons.

To expand a master document, choose File Master Document Expand Master. WordPerfect displays the Expand Master Document dialog box (shown in Figure 19-7), which lists all your subdocuments. To expand them all, just choose OK. To skip expanding one, click on its little box so that no X appears in it.

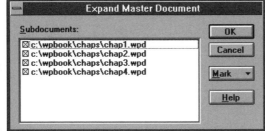

Figure 19-7:
Expand, oh
master!

When you expand a master document, you still see the little subdocument icons. You see twice as many, in fact — one appears at the beginning and at the end of each subdocument, as shown in Figure 19-8.

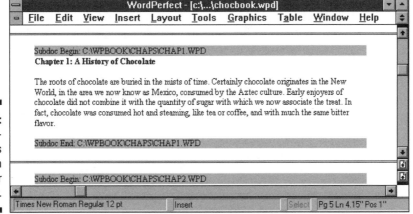

Figure 19-8:
Your sub-
documents
appear in
the master
document.

When you are working on a master document, don't open any of its subdocuments in other windows. Early versions of WordPerfect for Windows get upset when you save a master document if any of its subdocuments are also open.

Saving a master document

When you save a master document, WordPerfect wants to know two things about each of its subdocuments:

Do you want to *save* the text of the subdocument back in the subdocument's file?

Do you want to *condense* the subdocument so that only its icon appears in the master document?

You answer both of these pithy questions in the Condense/Save Subdocuments dialog box. When you want to save your master document, follow these steps:

1. **Choose File Save or press Ctrl+S or choose the Save button on the power bar.**

   If you haven't expanded your master document or if you have condensed it (see step 2), WordPerfect just saves the document with no comment. If your master document is expanded, however, WordPerfect asks, `Docu-` `ment is expanded. Condense?"`

2. **Choose No to save the document as is.**

   WordPerfect saves the master document with the text of all the expanded subdocuments too. It *doesn't* save the text of the subdocuments back to the separate subdocument files. If you have edited the text of your chapters in the master document, therefore, your edits are not saved in CHAP1.WPD, CHAP2.WPD, and so on — only in BOOK.WPD.

   Or **choose Yes to save each subdocument back in its own separate file.**

   WordPerfect displays the Condense/Save Subdocuments dialog box, shown in Figure 19-9. Each subdocument is listed twice — once for choosing whether to condense it (remove the text from the master document) and once for choosing whether to save it (save the text back in its own separate file). We always leave all the boxes checked. Go for the gold, we say.

   When you choose OK, WordPerfect saves and condenses as you indicated.

You can also condense a master document by choosing File Master Document Condense Master from the menu.

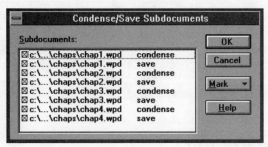

Figure 19-9: Saving your book: do you want to save each chapter back in its own file?

Editing a master document

After you have the master document set up, what do you do when you want to edit a chapter of your book? What if you get new information about early uses of chocolate among the Aztec nobility, for example, and you want to include it in Chapter 1?

You have these two choices:

- ✔ **Edit the chapter file:** In this case, make sure that your master document is condensed, to ensure that the text of your chapter is stored in the subdocument file, not in the master document. Make your changes and save the chapter file. The next time you open and expand the master document, the updated chapter appears.

- ✔ **Edit the master document:** In this case, make sure that your chapter file is closed. Open the master document and expand the subdocuments (or at least the one you want to edit). Make your changes and save the master file.

This process can get rather confusing when you try to remember where the text of your chapters is *really* stored. We recommend that you always do your editing in the same way and always store your master document in the same way (either expanded or condensed).

Creating a table of contents

"What good is a table without contents?" we always say (when we're sitting down to dinner). WordPerfect can automatically generate a table of contents for your book (or any document) by using the headings in the file. Sort of. These steps show you how:

1. **Open your master document and expand it.**

   You want to be able to see all your lovely chapters so that you can decide which ones should appear in your table of contents.

2. **Choose the Tools Table of Contents command from the menu bar.**

   More lovely buttons appear, mostly named Mark (see Figure 19-10). This is — what else? — the table of contents bar.

3. **Mark the lines of text (headings) you want in the table of contents.**

   Your table of contents can have several levels (chapters and sections within chapters, for example). To mark each heading, select it and click on the appropriate Mark button. Mark each chapter title using Mark 1, for example.

   When you do this step, nothing seems to happen. WordPerfect inserts secret codes at the beginning and end of each selected heading (the Mrk Txt ToC code, if you were wondering).

4. Make a new page where you want the table of contents to appear.

For most books, you want the table of contents to be on a page by itself right after the title and copyright pages. Press Ctrl+Enter to insert a page break.

5. Beginning with the first page of the master document, tell WordPerfect to number the pages with small roman numerals.

Most books number the front matter (including the table of contents) with roman numerals and then start the page numbers over again at 1 at the beginning of the introduction or first chapter. You can do that too — won't your document look just like a real book?

Move your cursor to the beginning of the master document and choose Layout Page Numbering. Set the Position to Alternating Top or Alternative Bottom so that the numbers appear on the right side of lefthand pages and on the left side of righthand pages. Then choose Options and set the Page setting to Lowercase Roman. Choose OK to save this option, and choose OK again to finish page numbering.

You may want to suppress page numbers on the title pages and some other front-matter pages — use the Layout Page Suppress command.

6. Go to the first page of the introduction or Chapter 1 and reset it to page number 1.

With your cursor at the top of the page you want to be page 1, choose Layout Page Numbering. Choose Value, set the New Page Number to 1, and click on OK. Then choose Options, set the Page setting to Numbers, and choose OK. Choose OK again to finish page numbering.

Now WordPerfect knows which page numbers should appear on every page. You are ready to make the table of contents (and not a moment too soon!).

7. Move your cursor to the location where you want the table of contents to appear and choose the Define button on the Table of Contents bar.

In the Define Table of Contents dialog box (see Figure 19-11), tell WordPerfect the number of levels and which style to use for each level (whether to include page numbers and dot leaders). When you choose OK, WordPerfect inserts an (invisible) code and the text `Table of Contents will generate here`. Don't worry, WordPerfect does better than that in a minute.

8. Click on the Generate button and choose OK on its dialog box.

The Generate button is at the right end of the table of contents bar — you may have to make your WordPerfect window wider to see it. Some messages flash by and then — poof! A table of contents!

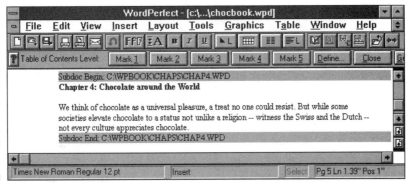

Figure 19-10:
Marking the headings you want to appear in your table of contents.

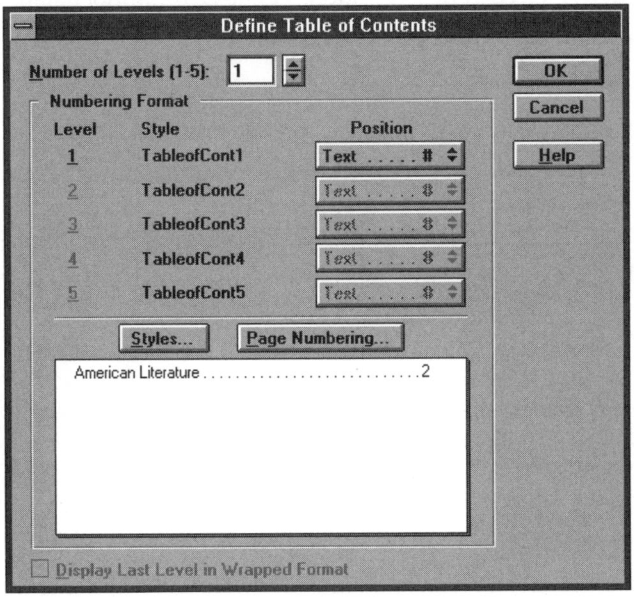

Figure 19-11:
What contents do you want in your table?

No big deal, you may say. It would have been faster to copy the chapter titles by hand. But here's the nice thing: if you update your book and make chapters shorter or longer, when you choose the Generate button again, WordPerfect updates the table of contents and corrects the headings and page numbers.

When you finish fooling with the table of contents, you can choose the Close button on the Table of Contents bar. To get the bar back, you can always use the Tools Table of Contents command.

Creating an index

Making an index is similar to making a table of contents. You mark stuff in the text of the book, define the format of the index so that WordPerfect creates a secret index code, and then generate away. The difference is that the index always looks terrible the first time you generate it — you find typos and inconsistencies galore. Don't despair — just correct the entries in the text and keep generating it until it looks right.

Inserting the index codes

Follow these steps to add the secret index codes to your document:

1. **Open your master document and expand it.**

2. **Choose the Tools Index command from the menu bar.**

   You see yet another bar, the index bar, as shown in Figure 19-12.

3. **For each place in the text for which you want an index entry, create a secret index code.**

   If the term to be indexed appears in the text, select it and click in the Heading box on the index bar. The text appears in the box and you can edit it if necessary. To make this text an index entry, choose the Mark button.

   The term you want in the index may not appear in the text. For the sentence *The roots of chocolate are buried in the mists of time,* for example, you might want the index entry to be History. Just click your mouse where you want the entry to refer, click in the Heading box, type the index entry, and choose the Mark button.

4. **Make a new page at the end of your master document for the index.**

   At the end of the document, press Ctrl+Enter to insert a page break. Type a title for the index too.

5. **With your cursor on the new last page of your master document, choose the Define button on the Table of Contents bar.**

   You see the Define Index dialog box, as shown in Figure 19-13. We usually leave all the settings and options alone — it makes a perfectly nice-looking index just as it is. When you choose OK, WordPerfect inserts a secret index code and the text `Index will generate here.`

6. **Click on the Generate button and choose OK in its dialog box.**

   Away it goes!

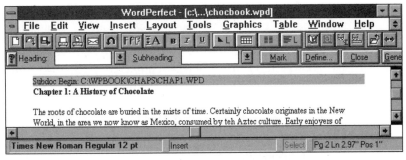

Figure 19-12:
Using the
index bar to
decide
which terms
to index.

Figure 19-13:
How do you
want your
index to
look?

Tips for making a good index

Be consistent in your index entries. For example, we usually capitalize all entries (except subheadings). We use plurals of all nouns and gerunds of all verbs ("Cakes, making" and "Making cakes").

When you see typos in the index, don't correct them in the index. If you do, the next time you click on Generate, the changes are blown away. Instead, you must laboriously find the index codes in the text and fix them. Use Reveal Codes view (described in Chapter 11) so that you can see the index codes. You can also use the Edit Find command to find them. When you move your cursor directly before the index code in Reveal Codes view, they look like this:

```
Index: Milky Way bars.
```

You cannot edit the text of the index code. Instead, delete it by pressing the Delete key and make a new index entry. What a pain! It's enough to make you think about chucking the whole thing and hiring a professional indexer.

To make index entries with subentries, enter text in both the Heading and Subheading boxes on the index bar before choosing the Mark button.

Making a good index is trickier than you think. You must include all the terms a reader is likely to look up, including synonyms you might never use yourself. Refer to a good book on the subject, such as *The Chicago Manual of Style* (University of Chicago Press).

Part IV
Help Me, Rhonda!

"THE PHONE COMPANY BLAMES THE MANUFACTURER, WHO SAYS IT'S THE SOFTWARE COMPANY'S FAULT, WHO BLAMES IT ON OUR MOON BEING IN VENUS WITH SCORPIO RISING."

In this part...

*I*s all going well with your word-processing experience? No? You've run into a snag? Well, you've come to the right place.

This part of the book solves a number of thorny problems, including dealing with Windows itself (which is sometimes unavoidable) and talking sense into your printer. You also learn how to make WordPerfect's behavior more socially acceptable. If you run into bug trouble, run (do not walk) to Chapter 23 for solutions to the most common WordPerfect problems.

Chapter 20

Improving WordPerfect's Behavior

. . . .

In This Chapter

▶ Seeing information about your documents

▶ Setting the font you usually use

▶ Zooming around in your documents

▶ Expressing your preferences

▶ Controlling your zooms

▶ Changing the way WordPerfect looks

▶ Controlling the ruler bar, button bar, power bar, and status bar

▶ Determining where WordPerfect stores your files

▶ Assigning different meanings to keys (Yikes!)

. . . .

*Y*ou know how software can be — badly behaved, saving files in the wrong directories, displaying incomprehensible things on your screen, and being generally rude. It's time for some lessons in deportment. You can teach WordPerfect to behave more like a gentleman (or a lady).

It's pretty nifty that WordPerfect lets you customize so much about the way it works. In this chapter, you find out how to display longer names for your documents, how to zoom in on the text of your document in close-up, how to control which buttons appear on the power bar and button bar, how to control where WordPerfect stores things (in which directories on your disk), and other preferences.

If you are happy with WordPerfect just the way it is, you can skip this chapter. On the other hand, if you are really, really happy with WordPerfect, you may want to see a shrink. Leaving WordPerfect's behavior alone is not such a bad idea. One advantage of this approach is that your WordPerfect will work just like everyone else's (unless they have customized *their* copy), so it is easier to get help from your WordPerfect-savvy friends.

Seeing Information About Your Documents

DOS is really the pits — the way it limits your document filenames to eight letters (plus the WPD extension) is positively inhumane. After a few months have passed, who can remember what was in documents with names like LTR2 or BUD_RPT6 or EGGPLANT?

Luckily, WordPerfect lets you enter a longer name for each document. You can also ask it to display these longer names in the Open File dialog box and in other dialog boxes that show lists of filenames. This section explains how to outwit DOS.

Entering better names for your documents

The place you can enter a descriptive name for your document is in the Document Summary dialog box. To see this dialog box, choose File Document Summary from the menu bar.

Along with the descriptive name, you can enter all kinds of other information. The spaces for all these facts, in fact, don't fit in the dialog box and you can use the little scroll bar to slide down to see the rest.

The information you enter in the document summary is stored along with your document. You can view or edit it any time.

What if you don't want to enter something in the Description Type box in the document summary? (What if you don't even have the faintest idea what a Descriptive Type might be? We don't.) What if you want to keep track of the document's version number instead? Wow — WordPerfect lets *you* choose which blanks appear on the Document Summary dialog box. To change the facts included in all summaries you create, choose the Configure button in the Document Summary dialog box. WordPerfect pops up the Document Summary Configuration dialog box and lets you choose from a long list of possible facts about a document, including Authorization, Checked By, Document Number, Project, Status, and Version Number. Does this sound official, or what?

Seeing your descriptive names

If you faithfully enter a descriptive name in the document summary for each document you create, you can use them to identify your documents rather than use DOS's painfully short filenames. Way cool!

These steps show how to see the descriptive names of your documents when you open or save a file:

1. Get the Open File dialog box up on the screen.

Choose File Open from the menu or press Ctrl+O or choose the Open button from the power bar.

2. Choose the Setup button.

WordPerfect displays the Open/Save As Setup dialog box, shown in Figure 20-1. The choices you make here control the way WordPerfect displays files in both the Open and Save As dialog boxes.

3. Use the Show setting to choose the information you want to display about each file.

It starts out by saying Filename Only, but by clicking on it, you can choose the following:

- Filename, Size, Date, Time
- Descriptive Name, Filename
- Custom Columns

Forget about Custom Columns unless you are a glutton for punishment. Instead, try the Descriptive Name, Filename setting. When you choose it, WordPerfect adds some settings at the bottom of the dialog box — just leave them alone.

4. Choose the way you want the filenames sorted.

WordPerfect usually displays the list of documents alphabetically by filename, but you can choose to sort them by their descriptive names, dates, sizes, or extensions.

If you choose to sort them by date or size (not that we have ever met anyone who has), you might also want to sort them in descending order, from newest to oldest or from largest to smallest.

5. Choose the OK button (or press Enter).

If you just switched to displaying descriptive names, WordPerfect may ask you for permission to create a new directory in which to store some extra files it uses to do this. What the heck — choose Yes.

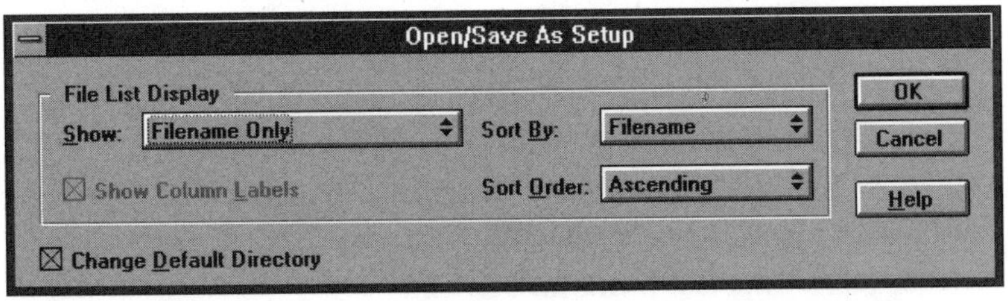

Figure 20-1:
What information do you want to display about your files?

Now the Open and Save As dialog boxes display both the descriptive name and the regular old filename.

You will find that you forgot to enter descriptive names for lots of your documents — if you are compulsive, open each one and enter a descriptive name now.

WordPerfect occasionally flashes a message that it is scanning document summary information when it is getting ready to show you a list of descriptive names and filenames. Hey, whatever makes it happy.

As you may have noticed, when you choose File from the menu bar, at the bottom of the File pull-down menu you see the names of the last four documents you opened. Normally this list displays filenames, but if you enter descriptive names, you see them instead. WordPerfect also uses the descriptive name in the title bar at the top of the WordPerfect window. How nice!

Setting Your Favorite Font

Have you ever gotten annoyed at WordPerfect for always suggesting the same font whenever you create a new document? We have. Enough with the Times New Roman already — we are in the mood for Arial!

Solutions to this problem are shown in this list:

✔ **Use templates:** Templates let you predefine all the styles you use for the kinds of documents you usually create. You can make one template for letters, one for memos, and one for faxes, each with the proper fonts selected.

✔ **Tell WordPerfect the name of your favorite font:** WordPerfect then uses this font for all new documents unless you select another one.

For instructions about using the first approach, see Chapter 17, which is all about templates. These steps show you how to use the second approach:

1. **Choose Layout Document Initial Font from the menu bar.**

   WordPerfect, ever ready to pop open another dialog box, displays the Document Initial Font dialog box.

2. **Choose your favorite font, size, and style.**

   Show some restraint here — no one can read your polished prose if you print it in Shelley Volante.

3. **Choose Set as Printer Initial Font.**

   Make sure that an X is in the little box by this setting, at the bottom of the dialog box. Otherwise, this step only sets the font for the current document.

4. Choose OK (or press Enter).

You have just told WordPerfect to use your favorite font whenever you create a new document to be printed on the selected printer. Unless you use several different printers, you are all set.

If you use several printers, use the File Select Printer command to see the Select Printer dialog box. Select a printer. Then follow the preceding steps to set your favorite font for this printer. Repeat them for each printer you use. See Chapter 22 for more information about choosing printers.

See Chapter 8 to learn how to change fonts within a document.

Zooming Around in Your Documents

Maybe we're just getting old. Or the light bulb in the desk lamp might be getting dim. Or it might be our monitor — its phosphors are probably running down or something. Anyway, when we edit documents in 10-point type, we used to press our noses to the screen to read the teeny-tiny letters WordPerfect uses. After a few visits to the chiropractor, something had to be done.

Then we found WordPerfect's new Zoom feature. You can blow up the text on your screen as much as you want, without changing its size on the printed page. These steps show you how:

1. Choose View Zoom from the menu bar.

WordPerfect displays the Zoom dialog box.

2. Choose one of the percentages shown in the dialog box.

The larger the percentage, the bigger the text looks on the screen (as though you were sticking your face closer to it). If you don't like any of the options WordPerfect offers, choose Other and enter the percentage you want (we like 120%).

3. Choose OK.

In addition to numerical percentages, the Zoom dialog box contains these three other options:

✔ **Margin Width:** Blows up the text until it fills the window from side to side, with the left margin up against the left edge of the window and the right margin against the right edge. This option automatically zooms the document to the maximum percentage that lets you see the full width of your text.

✔ **Page Width:** Blows up the page until it fills the window from side to side, including the left and right margins. The left edge of the paper is just inside the left edge of the window, and the right edge is just inside the right edge. You see a little, black space between the edge of the paper and the edge of the window. This option always gives you a smaller zoom percentage than Margin Width.

✔ **Full Page:** Blows up the page until it fills the window from top to bottom. The top edge of the paper is against the top edge of the window, and the bottom edge of the paper is against the bottom edge of the window. If you use normal paper in its normal orientation so that the paper is taller than it is wide, it produces a rather small, not to say unreadable, image, but it lets you get the overall effect of the page.

If you use zooming to increase the size of the text on your screen and you *still* cannot read it, save your document (or documents) and then get a clean, damp handkerchief and wipe all the dust off the front of your monitor. Something about the way computer screens work creates static electricity that attracts dust from all over your house. There! Isn't that better?

You cannot use zooming when you are in two-page view (see Chapter 10). No one we know uses two-page view, so who cares?

One problem with using a large zoom percentage is that most documents get so wide that you cannot see an entire line of text. It is annoying to have to scroll left and right to read each line of the document. Here's an alternative: at the beginning of your document, switch to a large font size, maybe 12 or 14 points. WordPerfect reformats the document (at least, up to the next font size code) by using larger characters and wraps the text to fit within the margins. Now you can read it just fine. On the other hand, when you print it, the text is enormous. To fix it, delete the font-size code you just added (see Chapter 11 to learn how to use the Reveal Codes window to delete a formatting code).

Expressing Your Preferences

The process of teaching WordPerfect how to behave is generally simple: you tell WordPerfect your preferences and it whips into line. Wouldn't it be nice if everyone worked this way (especially your teenager)?

You tell WordPerfect what you want by using the File Preferences command, which displays the Preferences dialog box, shown in Figure 20-2. Instead of the dull, boring boxes and buttons you see on most dialog boxes, this one has nifty little icons for the different types of preferences you can express, as shown in this list:

✔ **Display:** What WordPerfect displays on the screen, including what the ruler bar includes, how the Reveal Codes windows looks, and whether you want to see symbols where your spaces, tabs, and returns are. We describe these settings in detail later.

✔ **Environment:** Miscellaneous stuff that didn't fit in any of the other types of preferences.

✔ **File:** Where WordPerfect stores your documents, templates, macros, and other files, and whether you want it to keep backups of your files. This stuff is described later in this chapter.

✔ **Summary:** How document summaries work and when you want to see them (if ever).

✔ **Button Bar:** Which buttons you want to include; whether you want to see words, pictures, or both on the buttons; and where the button bar should appear. WordPerfect comes with a bunch of predefined button bars or you can make your own. (We discuss this subject later in this chapter.)

✔ **Power Bar:** Which buttons you want to include on the power bar, and which fonts and font sizes should appear when you use the Font and Font Size buttons (also described later in this chapter).

✔ **Status Bar:** Which information to display, in addition to the font and general appearance you prefer. (Read on for more information.)

✔ **Keyboard:** What you want each key on the keyboard to do. (This subject is mentioned later in this chapter, although we refuse to go into detail.)

✔ **Menu Bar:** Which commands you want to appear on each menu on the menu bar, believe it or not.

✔ **Writing Tools:** Which writing tools you want to be able to use (Speller, Thesaurus, or Grammatik).

✔ **Print:** How many copies and what print quality to use in printing documents.

✔ **Import:** How graphics files, ASCII delimited-text files, WordPerfect 4.2, DCA, and DisplayWrite documents are imported.

Figure 20-2:
Wow! A dialog box with lots of little pictures!

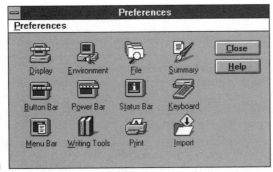

Yikes! This list presents an unbelievable number of things to think about. The scary part is that you can control how all these things work. Does this give you a feeling of power? It gives us a feeling of stark terror: think of all the things we might break!

To use the Preference dialog box to express your preferences, double-click on the icon of your choice. It displays one or more dialog boxes. When you dismiss them, you return to the Preference dialog box one more time. When you finish fooling with WordPerfect's innards, click the Close button from the Preference dialog box or press the Esc key.

The rest of this chapter explains how to change some of the settings in the Preference dialog boxes and why you would want to. Don't worry — you can always change them back!

It's a bad idea to change too many things at the same time. When you're fooling around with preferences, make one or two changes and then close all the dialog boxes. Look around in WordPerfect to see what you have done.

Many of the preferences dialog boxes contain a Default button, which undoes all your changes and returns the settings to the way they are set when you first install WordPerfect. If things get completely bollixed up, use this button to return to ground zero. But watch out — clicking on Default wipes out *all* your changes to the settings in the dialog box.

Changing the Way WordPerfect Looks

As you have noticed, WordPerfect displays a zillion gizmos on the screen. These steps show some things you may want to change, with instructions for changing them. All these settings appear in the Display Preferences dialog box, which you get by following these steps:

1. **Choose File Preferences from the WordPerfect menu bar.**

2. **Double-click on the Display icon.**

    You see the Display Preferences dialog box.

What's confusing about this dialog box (and many of the other preferences dialog boxes, for that matter) is that, depending on which option you choose in the top part of the dialog box, the rest of the dialog box changes. Figure 20-6 shows the way the dialog box looks when it first appears and the Document option is selected. If you choose Show ¶, View/Zoom, Reveal Codes, Ruler Bar, or Merge, the rest of the dialog box changes to show settings which pertain to that subject.

A quicker way to see the Display Preferences dialog box is to click on the scroll bar with your *right* mouse button. Then choose Preferences from the QuickMenu.

Zooming

We always end up zooming in our documents a little because the usual 100% display is a tad too small for us to read comfortably. How annoying to have to do this every time we open a document! Instead, you can tell WordPerfect once and for all what zoom percentage you want to use. While you are at it, you can tell WordPerfect which view you usually want to see: draft, page, or (Ugh!) two page.

Follow these steps to tell WordPerfect how you want to zoom:

1. **Choose File Preferences from the menu bar.**

2. **Double-click on the Display icon.**

   WordPerfect shows you the Display Preferences dialog box.

3. **Click on the View/Zoom option at the top of the dialog box.**

   WordPerfect reshuffles the information in the dialog box to show two groups of settings: Default View and Default Zoom.

4. **Choose the Default View (Draft, Page, or Two Page).**

5. **Choose the Default Zoom.**

   You see the same options listed earlier in this chapter.

6. **Click on OK and then the Close button to escape from the world of dialog boxes.**

When you close the Preferences dialog box, WordPerfect changes the zoom of the current window to the one you just chose; whenever you open a document or create a new one, it also uses this zoom percentage. On the other hand, you can still change the zoom for individual documents as necessary.

The button bar

Button, button, who's got the button? You do — that is, you can control which buttons you have. WordPerfect comes with 12 predefined button bars — 12 sets of buttons the folks at WordPerfect think would be useful for different sorts of documents. The Generate button bar, for example, contains buttons for tasks you do with large documents, including generating tables of contents and indexes. The Font button bar contains buttons for selecting many different text styles.

The following two sets of steps show you how to choose which button bar you see:

1. **Choose File Preferences from the menu bar.**

2. **Double-click on the Button Bar icon.**

   You see the Button Bar Preferences dialog box.

3. **Choose one of the predefined button bars.**

4. **Choose §elect to select this button bar.**

   You leave the dialog box, too.

5. **Choose Çlose to leave the Preferences dialog box.**

These steps show you a faster way:

1. **Use the *right* mouse button to click on any button on the button bar.**

   WordPerfect displays a list of defined button bars. The one you see now has a check mark by its name.

2. **Choose one by clicking on it.**

   Poof! A new set of buttons appears.

   The button bar that appears when you first install WordPerfect and the one we have shown in the figures in this book is called simply "WordPerfect."

 If you plan to fool around with your preferences, as described in this chapter, you can display the Preferences button bar, with one button for each icon in the Preferences dialog box. If you use templates (described in Chapter 17), you can tell WordPerfect which button bar to use whenever you open a document by using that template. You then can display buttons that are appropriate for the type of document you are creating.

 You can define your own button bars by using buttons to choose any WordPerfect command, run any macro (a prerecorded series of keystrokes, which is a subject we don't get into in this book), run another program (this seriously cool Windows-type stuff), or type something from the keyboard. Use the Çreate and £dit buttons on the Button Bar Preferences dialog box.

The power bar

Unlike the button bar, WordPerfect comes with only one predefined power bar. You cannot switch between different power bars. As you can do with the button bar, however, you can change the buttons that are on power bar. These steps show you how to see the Power Bar Preferences dialog box:

1. **Choose £ile Pr£ferences from the menu bar.**

   You see the now-infamous Preferences dialog box.

2. **Double-click on the P̲ower Bar icon.**

   The Power Bar Preferences dialog box is displayed. To make changes to the power bar, you use both this dialog box and the power bar. The Ï̲tems list in the dialog box shows all the possible buttons that can appear on the power bar. Those that appear have Xs in their little boxes.

These steps show a quicker way to see the power bar:

1. **Click on any button on the power bar with the *right* mouse button.**

   WordPerfect displays a QuickMenu that lists commands related to the power bar.

2. **Choose Preferences from the QuickMenu.**

After you see the dialog box, you can use some of the methods in this list to customize your power bar:

✔ **To add a new button to the power bar:** Find it on the Items list in the Power Bar Preferences dialog box. It's a long list, in alphabetical order. To find something fast, type the first letter of the command. WordPerfect scrolls down to the first command that begins with that letter.

   When you find the command you want, click on it to put a little X in its box. It immediately appears as the rightmost button on the power bar. Now you can move it where you want it.

✔ **To remove a button from the power bar:** Click the button on the power bar and drag it off the power bar. It falls off the bar and hits the floor with a splat (metaphorically speaking).

✔ **To move a button to a new location on the power bar:** Drag it by using your mouse.

✔ **To add a little space between two buttons (called a *separator*):** Click on the picture in the Separator section of the dialog box and then drag it to the spot on the power bar where you want it. Separators don't mean a thing to WordPerfect, but they make your power bar easier to use by letting you separate your buttons into groups. For clarity, you can insert as many separators as you want, including using more than one separator between buttons.

Choose your power buttons with care

If you find that you never use a button on the power bar, get it out of there! There's no point in staring something useless in the face every day while it takes up valuable screen real estate. We never use the Cut, Copy, or Paste buttons, for example — it's faster to press Ctrl+X, Ctrl+C, and Ctrl+V. So we dragged those puppies off to oblivion.

On the other hand, if you find yourself using the same command a million times a day, add a button for it to the power bar. We like to add these buttons, for example:

✔ File Close

✔ File Exit

✔ Layout Styles Combobox (it displays the list of styles you have defined so that you can quickly choose a style to apply; see Chapter 12 for information about using styles)

✔ View Ruler Bar

✔ View Show ¶

When you finish fooling with the power bar, choose OK from the Power Bar Preferences dialog box.

The ruler bar

If you like to see the ruler bar on your screen, you can tell WordPerfect to display it more often, by following these steps:

1. **Choose File Preferences from the menu bar.**

2. **Double-click on the Display icon.**

    WordPerfect shows you the Display Preferences dialog box.

3. **Click on the Ruler Bar option at the top of the dialog box.**

    WordPerfect reshuffles the information in the dialog box to show settings for the ruler bar.

4. **Click on Show Ruler Bar on New and Current Document.**

    Make sure that an X appears in its box.

5. **Click the OK button and then the Close button in the Preferences dialog box.**

The status bar

Status is important in our society. The status bar lets you keep track of your status. You can find out whether you are a lowly Courier or one of the Prestige Elite.

When you first install WordPerfect, it displays the following information on the status bar:

- ✔ Font and font size
- ✔ Insert versus typeover mode (see Chapter 4)
- ✔ Whether text is selected
- ✔ Your cursor location on the page, both horizontally and vertically

Lots of other pieces of information would be useful to see, however, such as whether your Caps Lock key has gotten pressed accidentally or what time it is.

To choose what you want to see on the status bar, display the Status Bar Preferences dialog box, as shown in these steps:

1. **Choose File Preferences from the menu bar.**

2. **Double-click on the Status Bar icon.**

    WordPerfect shows you the Status Bar Preferences dialog box.

Alternatively, you can follow these steps instead:

1. **Click on the status bar with the *right* mouse button.**

   WordPerfect displays a small QuickMenu with commands pertaining to the status bar.

2. **Choose Preferences from the QuickMenu.**

   Either way, the Status Bar Preferences dialog box is displayed.

Fooling around with the status bar works just like changing your power bar, described earlier in this chapter. You can add items, remove them, or switch them around. In addition, you can change the size of an item on the status bar by using the mouse to drag its left or right edge.

When you are finished, choose OK in the Status Bar Preferences dialog box and then the Close button in the Preferences dialog box, if it's in your way.

This list shows the items we like to keep track of on the status bar:

- ✔ Font
- ✔ Combined Position (horizontal, vertical, and page number)
- ✔ General Status (usually shows insert or typeover: you can make this item much smaller than WordPerfect suggests)
- ✔ Caps Lock State (in case it's On by mistake)
- ✔ Num Lock State (ditto)
- ✔ Time (12 Hour)

Many of the items on the status bar do things if you double-click on them. Try it!

Displaying spaces, tabs, indents, and returns

It can be useful to see exactly which characters are in your text. After all, spaces, tabs, and indent characters all leave blank spaces in your text, but they behave very differently. If you want to be nosy about this stuff, you can ask WordPerfect to display little gizmos where your spaces, tabs, indents, and returns appear.

To see the characters in your text, follow these steps:

1. **Choose File Preferences from the WordPerfect menu bar.**

2. **Double-click on the Display icon.**

   WordPerfect shows the Display Preferences dialog box.

3. **Choose Show ¶.**

   WordPerfect displays settings about this topic.

4. **If you want to see gizmos for these characters all the time, choose Sho<u>w</u> Symbols on New and Current Document.**

   You can always turn the symbols off if you get sick of them, by choosing <u>V</u>iew <u>S</u>how ¶ from the menu bar.

5. **Remove the Xs from items for which you don't want to see symbols.**

   To remove an X, click on the setting in the Symbols to Display list. It gets ridiculous, for example, if you display a special symbol for each and every space in your document! We turn this one off.

6. **Choose the OK button and then the <u>C</u>lose button in the Preferences dialog box.**

   Your document is suddenly littered with little arrows, paragraph marks, and other gizmos. (If you didn't select Sho<u>w</u> Symbols on New and Current Document in step 4, you must choose <u>V</u>iew <u>S</u>how ¶ from the menu bar to get the effect.)

Alternatively, you can use the Reveal Codes window to see all your codes, not just the spaces, tabs, indents, and returns. See Chapter 11 for details.

Changing your colors

Normally, WordPerfect displays your documents in a realistic but eye-tiring black-on-white color scheme. You may be glad to hear that you can change this. Especially if you have a laptop with a monochrome or LCD display, this procedure is a way to make your WordPerfect window much more readable.

Changing screen colors requires talking to Windows. If you want to change the colors used in the document, not just on the menus, dialog boxes, or title bar, you have to change one WordPerfect setting too. Follow these steps:

1. **If you don't want to change the colors of the document text, skip to step 5.**

2. **Choose <u>F</u>ile Pr<u>e</u>ferences from the menu and then double-click on the <u>D</u>isplay icon.**

   WordPerfect displays the Display Preferences dialog box.

3. **In the Show section of the dialog box, choose <u>W</u>indow System Colors.**

   This step tells WordPerfect to use the colors that Windows suggests for the document text rather than always use black on white. Make sure that an X appears in the box for this setting.

4. **Click the OK button and then the <u>C</u>lose button to exit from all the dialog boxes.**

   The next step is to tell Windows which colors you want.

5. **Switch to the Windows Program Manager.**

   You can do this in a number of ways (Chapter 21 lists all of them). Press Ctrl+Esc to see the Windows Task List dialog box and then double-click on the Program Manager.

6. **In the Program Manager, find the Control Panel icon (it's in the Control program group) and double-click on it.**

7. **Double-click on the Color icon (the one with the crayons).**

   You see the Color dialog box. At the top of the dialog box is a list of Color Schemes, which are predefined sets of colors that some color-blind person at Microsoft thought looked good.

8. **Choose a color scheme by clicking on the arrow at the right end of the Color Scheme box and choosing one from the list.**

   To show you what the color scheme looks like, the middle of the dialog box shows two miniature windows with a miniature menu bar and menu. The part labeled Window Text corresponds to the document text part of the WordPerfect window.

   Look at the color schemes to see which one you dislike the least. For a truly hideous selection of colors, try Fluorescent (it's good to know that Microsoft has a sense of humor). Ocean, Rugby, and The Blues aren't too bad.

   You can make your own Windows color schemes too. We don't get into that here: choose Color Palette and fool around with it. If the situation and the screen get ugly, you can always click on Cancel.

9. **Choose OK to leave the Colors dialog box.**

   Poof! Your screen colors change! If you hate them, go back to step 7.

10. **Choose Settings Exit from the Control Panel menu.**

    It goes away.

11. **Switch back to WordPerfect by pressing Alt+Tab.**

    Or you can use the Ctrl+Esc trick from step 5.

You can spend all day getting your screen colors just right (and many people have). The key consideration is how your eyes feel at the end of the day.

Where Does WordPerfect Put Your Files?

You have a hard disk, and heaven knows how many files are on it. Through the miracle of subdirectories (described in Chapter 15), you don't have to look at all of them whenever you decide to pop open a document. The vast majority of files on your disk are probably program files, which you would just as soon never see.

Telling WordPerfect about directories and backups

To tell WordPerfect where you want to store your documents in general (you can always choose different directories for some documents), as well as when to make automatic backups of your documents, follow these steps:

1. **Choose File Preferences from the menu and then double-click on the File icon.**

   WordPerfect displays the File Preferences dialog box. The Documents/ Backup option is selected, so the dialog box shows the settings that have to do with documents.

2. **To indicate where you want your documents to go, enter a directory name in the Default directory box.**

   This name must be a complete pathname from the root directory of a disk drive, including the drive letter (such as C:). You can enter C:\DOCS or C:\LETTERS or C:\WPDOCS\MEMOS, for example. You can use the little button with the file folder on it to find the directory you want.

3. **To tell WordPerfect that you want all new documents to be given the filename extension WPD, choose the Use Default Extension on Open and Save setting.**

   WordPerfect suggests the extension WPD and we do too. You can change it, though.

4. **To make a backup copy of your open documents at regular intervals, select the Timed Document Backup every setting.**

   This step tells WordPerfect to save copies of all your open documents every so often. If the power goes out or you kick the computer's plug out of the outlet, this option is a godsend. See the section "Getting back your timed backups," later in this chapter, to learn how to get these files back if you need them.

   If you choose this setting, enter a number of minutes in the box between "every" and "minutes." This number specifies how often WordPerfect makes the backups.

5. **To prevent accidentally replacing good files with bad ones, choose the Original Document Backup setting.**

   If this setting is selected, every time you save a document, WordPerfect renames, rather than deletes, the old version. It renames these backup documents by using the filename extension BAK.

   If you mess up a document irretrievably and then you compound your error by saving it, it prevents WordPerfect from deleting the previous version of the document. You can close the document without saving it and then open the BAK version of the document.

6. **If you use the QuickList, choose Update QuickList with Changes.**

   See Chapter 15 to learn what the QuickList is and how handy it can be if you store your documents in more than one directory.

7. **If you use templates, choose Templates at the top of the dialog box.**

   You can change the directory in which WordPerfect looks for your templates (it's the Templates Default Directory setting). See Chapter 17 for a description of using templates.

8. **Ditto if you use graphics or macros: choose Graphics or Macros to change their default directories.**

   You are probably better off leaving these alone, though. Why mess with success?

9. **Click the OK button and then the Close button to get rid of all these dialog boxes.**

   WordPerfect puts your changes into effect (invisibly).

Getting back your timed backups

If WordPerfect (or Windows or something else) crashes and you use timed backups as described in the previous section, listen up. The next time you run WordPerfect, it notifies you if timed backup files are lying around. If you had opened a number of documents, there may be a number of them.

WordPerfect displays a Timed Backup dialog box with the message that a Document1 backup file exists. Unfortunately, WordPerfect doesn't remember the name of the file that this is a copy of, so it calls it Document1.

You have these three choices:

✔ **Rename:** WordPerfect stores the backup files in an out-of-the-way place (usually in your \WINDOWS directory) with an out-of-the-way name (such as WP{WP}.BK1). If you are pretty sure that you want the backup file, you can rename it and save it in the directory where you want it.

✔ **Open:** Open the backup file in WordPerfect. Then you can look at it to determine whether you want it or whether it is an incomplete version of a document you saved before the crash. If you want to save the file, use File Save or File Save As to save it with the name you want in the directory you want. *If you don't want it, just use File Close.*

✔ **Delete:** You're sure that you don't want the backup file. It's hard to imagine why you would want to choose this option — why not open the backup file just to be sure?

If you choose to open the file or if you rename it and then open it, take a look to see whether it is the latest version of the document or whether you did some additional work on it after it was saved. Timed backups are usually made every ten minutes, so you might have done nine minutes of editing since the backup was saved. You have to do that editing again.

If more than one document was open when WordPerfect bit the dust, WordPerfect goes on to tell you that a Document2 backup file exists. Repeat ad nauseam.

Assigning Different Meanings to Keys

WordPerfect has been around for a long time. (The first versions of WordPerfect weren't even for PCs!) As the world of software settled on certain standards for what all the keys on the keyboard should mean, the folks at WordPerfect were in a quandary. Older versions of WordPerfect had always used the F3 key to display on-line help, for example, and WordPerfect users the world over were used to it. Now the world of software agrees that F1, not F3, was the key to use. What to do?

The answer: wimp out and try to please everyone. WordPerfect gives you the opportunity to tell it which set of keyboard meanings you want to use: the old-fashioned WordPerfect meanings (WPDOS) or the newfangled standard meanings (WPWin). These sets of meanings are stored as *keyboard definitions*.

Keyboard definitions don't affect most of the keys on the keyboard. The Q key on your keyboard types a *Q* on your screen regardless of whichever keyboard definition you use. But the keyboard definition controls the meanings of the function keys and what keys do when you hold down Ctrl and Alt.

As we mentioned in the introduction to this book, all the instructions in this book assume that you are a modern, 20th century kind of person and that you are using the newfangled standard meanings of the keys (the WPWin keyboard definitions). The following steps show how you can check this out:

1. **Choose File Preferences from the menu and then double-click on the Keyboard icon.**

   WordPerfect displays the Keyboard Preferences dialog box. Three keyboards are listed: the Equation Editor Keyboard (forget about this one), WPDOS Compatible (the old-fashioned one), and WPWin 6.0 Keyboard (our hero). The one that is highlighted is the one you are using.

2. **Click the Close button in both open dialog boxes.**

   Get the heck out of this dialog box before you change anything!

Most people use the WPWin 6.0 keyboard because it makes the keys use the Windows-standard meanings, such as F1 for help, Ctrl+C for copy, and Ctrl+V to paste.

This list shows some reasons to use the old-fashioned WPDOS-compatible keyboard:

- ✔ You have upgraded from an older version of WordPerfect and don't want to learn any new habits. (Who does?)

- ✔ You work in an office with lots of people who use the old-fashioned WPDOS keyboard and you want to be able to swap WordPerfect techniques with them.

- ✔ You love pain.

Chapter 21
Fun with Windows

*I*t seems like an idiotic thing to point out, but while you are running WordPerfect for Windows you are also running Windows. You know already that this statement is true, but it occurred to us that there might be some things you want to use Windows to do — WordPerfect just doesn't do everything.

WordPerfect does lots of things that other word-processing programs drop the ball on. Most other programs don't provide ways, for example, for you to delete, rename, or copy your files. Instead, you must use the dreaded Windows File Manager. WordPerfect thoughtfully lets you do these things, however, by using the Open File or Save As dialog box (see Chapter 15).

This chapter describes tasks you can do with Windows, such as switching to other programs, changing the size and shape of the WordPerfect window, or running WordPerfect automatically.

If you are not technically inclined, feel free to skip this chapter. Nothing here is absolutely necessary for your word-processing well-being. On the other hand, if you just love the stuff in this chapter and you want to know more Windows tricks, consider buying its companion book, *Windows For Dummies*, by Andy Rathbone (IDG Books Worldwide), which is full of this kind of stuff.

Switching to Other Windows Programs

Windows has several big selling points: the cute little pictures (icons) you get to see, use of the mouse, and lots of different typefaces shown on-screen. Another big advantage is its capability to run several programs at the same time.

At this very minute, for example, we are running WordPerfect, the Windows File Manager, a program for sending and receiving faxes, and a screen-capture program (for making the pictures of WordPerfect dialog boxes that litter this book). Windows can keep track of all these different activities going on in its brain and on its screen. (Sometimes we have trouble, though.)

Windows has one reasonable and three ultra-unmemorable ways to switch from one Windows program to another, as shown in this list:

- ✔ **Click on a visible window:** If you can see part of a program on-screen, use your mouse to click on it. The program's window immediately "comes to the front" so that you can see the entire window.

- ✔ **Press Alt+Esc:** Windows switches to another program. Every time you press this key combination, Windows switches again. By pressing it enough times, you cycle through all the programs you are running and get back to the program you started with.

- ✔ **Press Alt+Tab:** This combination works like Alt+Esc, except that you keep holding down the Alt key and pressing Tab until you get to the program you want. Rather than switch to the programs one at a time, it displays the titles of the programs. It's supposed to be a little faster than the Alt+Esc method.

- ✔ **Press Ctrl+Esc:** This combination displays the Windows Task List, shown in Figure 21-1. To switch to one of the programs that is listed, just double-click on its name. If you have trouble double-clicking, just select the program and click on the Switch To button.

Figure 21-1: Which programs are you running, anyway?

```
┌─────────────────────────────────────┐
│ ▬            Task List               │
├─────────────────────────────────────┤
│ WordPerfect - [c:\wpbook\trialsea.wpd - unmo│
│ Program Manager                      │
│ Screen Capture                       │
│ Polaris PackRat 4.1 - MARGY          │
│ File Manager                         │
│ WinFax PRO                           │
│                                      │
│                                      │
│  ┌─────────┐ ┌─────────┐ ┌─────────┐ │
│  │Switch To│ │End Task │ │ Cancel  │ │
│  └─────────┘ └─────────┘ └─────────┘ │
│  ┌─────────┐ ┌─────────┐ ┌─────────┐ │
│  │ Cascade │ │  Tile   │ │Arrange Icons│
│  └─────────┘ └─────────┘ └─────────┘ │
└─────────────────────────────────────┘
```

We can never remember which of these totally forgettable key combinations does what, so we usually use Ctrl+Esc to see the Task List and then forget about the other two keyboard methods.

You can tell which program is selected, because its title bar is highlighted.

The Program Manager is always running: it is the master control program for Windows. When you exit from the Program Manager, you exit from Windows too and from any Windows programs you are running. Don't try closing Program Manager, therefore, unless you are ready to leave Windows (such as at the end of the day when you are getting ready to turn off your PC).

The WordPerfect Window Revisited

In Chapter 1, you learned about all the parts of the WordPerfect window. It can be one of these three sizes:

✔ Itty-bitty — that is, an icon (also called *minimized*). The WordPerfect icon is a little picture of a fountain-pen nib, with WPWin and the name of the current document, if one is open.

✔ Huge — it takes up the entire screen (also called *maximized*).

✔ Somewhere in between (also called "*in a window*").

This section describes some things you can do with WordPerfect, depending on how big it is on your screen.

What you can do when WordPerfect is minimized

When WordPerfect is minimized, it appears as a little icon at the bottom of your screen somewhere. You can switch to it by using any of the methods described earlier in this chapter. When you switch to it, it grows to a more useful size (either maximized or in a window, whichever size it was when you minimized it). Another way to switch to it is to double-click on the icon. Or you can click on the icon once and then choose <u>R</u>estore from the little menu that appears.

When WordPerfect is minimized, you can exit from WordPerfect. Click once on the icon and choose <u>C</u>lose from the little menu that appears. If you have been editing documents and haven't saved them, don't panic — WordPerfect asks whether you want to save each one and cleans things up properly before closing down. You can also maximize WordPerfect. Click once on the icon and choose Ma<u>x</u>imize from the menu that appears.

You can move the icon around on the screen by dragging it. This process is always fun, if pointless.

What you can do when WordPerfect is maximized

When WordPerfect is maximized, it takes up the entire screen. You cannot see any other programs, but you have lots of space to see your documents. You can minimize WordPerfect by clicking on the Minimize button. It has a downward-pointing triangle and sits in the upper right corner of the screen, at the right end of the title bar.

You can put WordPerfect into a window by clicking on the Resize button, just to the right of the Minimize button. This button has both upward- and downward-pointing triangles.

You can switch to other programs by using any of the keyboard methods described earlier in this chapter. (The mouse method doesn't work because you cannot see any other programs to click on them.)

What you can do when WordPerfect is in a window

This section describes some of the things you can do when WordPerfect is running in a window.

You can minimize WordPerfect by clicking on the Minimize button, with the downward-pointing triangle at the right end of the title bar. You can maximize WordPerfect by clicking on the Maximize button, the upward-pointing triangle button next to the Minimize button.

Switch to other programs by using any of the methods described earlier in this chapter.

Change the size of the WordPerfect window by using the thin borders around the window. Click and drag any of the sides or corners of the border to make the window bigger or smaller. You can move the window around on the screen by clicking and dragging the title bar.

We usually run WordPerfect in a window. We make the window the full height of the screen so that we can see as many lines of our documents as possible. We make the window just wide enough to show the full width of the document, from the left to right margin. This technique leaves some blank screen to the side of the WordPerfect window, in which we can see part of our Program Manager window plus the icons of some minimized programs at the bottom of the screen, as shown in Figure 21-2.

Having Fun with the WordPerfect Program Icon

When you first fire up your PC, you run Windows and see the Program Manager. Then you click on the WordPerfect program icon to get WordPerfect started. (We explained all this in Chapter 1.) There are several places in which the WordPerfect program icon may be lurking. Let's talk about where icons live and things you can do with them.

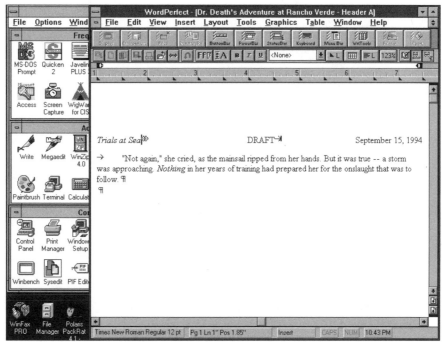

Figure 21-2:
Our favorite
screen
layout.

The Program Manager window can be minimized so that it appears as an icon. (The last few sections described things you can do when a program appears as an icon.) If you don't see a big Program Manager window, look for a little icon of a tiny window titled Program Manager. Double-click on it to bring it back to life.

Icons and icons

You may see the now-familiar fountain-pen-nib WordPerfect in two different forms, with two different purposes, as shown in this list:

- ✔ The Windows *program item* you double-click on to get WordPerfect started. This WordPerfect icon is in the Windows Program Manager. When you (or whoever) installed WordPerfect, it created this icon, which stays in the Program Manager indefinitely.

- ✔ The *minimized program*, which can appear anywhere on the screen (usually at the bottom). When you minimize WordPerfect while it is running, you create this icon. It lasts only until you restore it to a larger size. Earlier, this chapter listed things you can do to a minimized WordPerfect icon.

To tell the difference between these two icons, click on them once. The program item icon does absolutely nothing when you click on it once. The minimized program icon displays a little menu (listing such commands as Restore, Move, Size, Minimize, and Maximize). Click somewhere else to make this menu go away.

The good news is that you can't get fouled up by clicking on the wrong WordPerfect icon. If you are already running WordPerfect and you double-click on the WordPerfect *program* icon rather than on the WordPerfect *minimized* icon (horrors!), WordPerfect guesses what you mean. Rather than run a second copy of WordPerfect (which would be completely pointless), it switches you to your WordPerfect window, which is already in progress.

Group therapy

In the Windows Program Manager, your WordPerfect icon may be hiding in a program group. A *program group* is, not surprisingly, a group of programs, and the Windows Program Manager uses them to organize all its little icons. You probably have program groups named Control, Accessories, and WPWin 6.0, in addition to groups you or someone else made (our Program Manager looks like Figure 21-3).

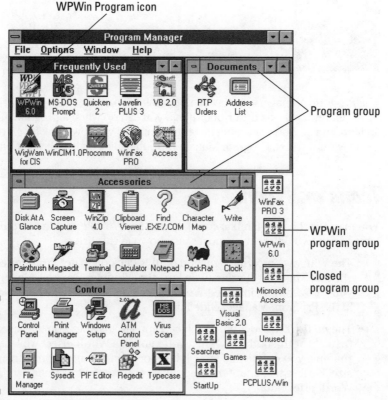

Figure 21-3: Program groups in the Program Manager.

When program groups are closed, they appear as little rectangular icons with six little, colored blobs in them. When they're open, they are windows that contain icons you can click on. To open a program group, double-click on it. To close one, click on its Minimize button.

Getting your icons organized

If you don't like the program group an icon is in, you can move or copy the icon. We don't like, for example, to have to look at all those WordPerfect utilities we never use, such as WPWin Installation and Kickoff (which is described in Chapter 26). Instead, we make a program group named Frequently Used to contain the icons we use frequently. Then we can copy icons into our new program group and close most or all of the other program groups. It really reduces on-screen clutter.

Making your own program group

To create a new program group in Program Manager, follow these steps:

1. **Switch to Program Manager.**

   Use one of the methods described at the beginning of this chapter.

2. **Choose File New from the Program Manager menu.**

   You see the New Program Object dialog box. (Sounds terribly official, doesn't it?)

3. **Choose Program Group from the dialog box.**

   You want to create a group of programs, not a program icon.

4. **Click on OK.**

5. **Enter the name for the new program group in the Description box.**

   You can use a computerese-type name, such as Applications, or a more homey-sounding name, such as Karen's Favorite Programs. (This type of name makes the other people in your office wonder who Karen is.)

6. **Click the OK button again.**

   You see a nice, new, empty program group. You can resize it by moving its edges and move it by dragging its title bar.

Putting program icons in your program group

To copy an icon into your new program group, hold down the Ctrl key while you drag the icon from one program group to another. To copy the WPWin icon — the one that runs WordPerfect, which is what we're supposed to be talking about here — from the WPWin program group into your new one, for example, highlight the WPWin icon, hold down the Ctrl key, and drag the icon into your new program group (hold down the mouse button while you move the mouse pointer to the new program group). Now you have identical icons in two program groups. You can click on either one to run WordPerfect.

We have copied our WPWin into our Frequently Used program group, and we leave our WordPerfect program group closed.

Starting WordPerfect automagically

One program group has a special meaning to the Windows Program Manager. When you start up Windows, this program group (called Startup) automatically runs all the programs in this group. This method is a super easy and super cool way to run WordPerfect whenever you start Windows. These steps show you how:

1. **Make a program group named Startup.**

   Follow the instructions in the section "Making your own program group," earlier in this chapter.

2. **Copy the WPWin program icon into this group.**

   Hold down the Ctrl key while you drag the WPWin program icon from the WPWin program group into the Startup program group.

3. **Copy any other programs in there too.**

   We always like to have the Windows File Manager running, for example, so we have copied its program icon from the Control program group into the Startup program group. Ditto for our fax software so that our computer is ready to receive a fax any time.

4. **Decide whether you want any of these programs to be minimized automatically.**

   You can tell Windows to run the program and then to minimize it so that it doesn't clutter up your screen. We like File Manager and our fax software to be minimized, for example, so that they're ready for us to use at a moment's notice but don't take up space on the screen.

   To tell Windows to minimize the programs when it starts them up, highlight the program icon in the Startup program group and press Alt+Enter. When you see the Program Item Properties dialog box, select the Run Minimized box (so that it contains an X). Then choose OK.

5. **Close the Startup program group.**

   There's no reason to look at the Startup program group all day long. It runs those programs all by itself whenever you start up Windows, so click on its Minimize button to turn it into a little icon.

Chapter 22
Solving Printing Problems

· ·

In This Chapter

▶ Looking at types of printers

▶ Fixing jams

▶ The care and feeding of your printer

▶ Selecting which printer to use

▶ Setting up a new printer

▶ Printing on a network

· ·

*A*fter enduring the technical complexities of formatting your document, you would think that getting it on paper would be easy. In Chapter 13, we talked about how to print an entire document or just parts of it, as well as how to cancel printing if something goes wrong. But if you have a problem with printing, you may have to learn about how to fix it, such as unjamming the printer or using a different printer. We talk about these topics in this chapter.

Goldilocks and the Three Printers

You probably don't care that there are three basic kinds of printers, but if something goes wrong, you may want to know. The three types of printers use different types of paper and ribbons (or the modern-day equivalent of ribbons), and you handle paper jams differently. Just in case, here's the low-down. The three general types of printers you may find attached to your computer or network are impact, ink-jet, and laser.

Impact printers

The oldest (and slowest) kind of printer is the impact printer, which works by pressing an inked ribbon against the paper, like a typewriter. In fact, some early impact printers looked exactly like typewriters without keyboards. (You could even get a kit to convert your typewriter to a computer printer!) Most typewriter-like impact printers use a flat, plastic wheel called a daisywheel to form the letters. These printers are called *daisywheel printers*.

More modern impact printers are *dot-matrix printers*, which use a matrix (or grid) of tiny pins to press the ribbon against the page. By sticking out different sets of pins, the printer can form different letters.

Impact printers (such as dot-matrix printers) have the advantage that they are relatively cheap, they can print duplicate copies using carbon paper, and they use continuous-feed perforated paper and forms. Their disadvantages include slowness and noisiness (they usually sound like mosquitoes on steroids). Most of them cannot print on individual sheets of typewriter paper, unless you feed each sheet by hand or install a clunky sheet feeder that jams all the time. Daisywheel printers cannot print graphics, special characters, or any font other than the one on their daisywheel. Dot-matrix printers can print graphics and different fonts, but the quality of their printing is not so hot.

Ink-jet printers

A better alternative is the ink-jet printer, which squirts itty-bitty drops of ink at the page. Ink drops are quiet, and so are ink-jet printers. By using very small drops and precise positioning, ink-jet printers produce a fairly nice print quality and can print graphics and different fonts. Their advantages include the use of typewriter paper and being fairly cheap. Their disadvantages are that they are relatively slow (although they're faster than impact printers) and the ink can smear.

Laser printers

The top of the line, printer-wise, is the laser printer. Laser printers work like photocopiers except that instead of duplicating a paper original, they draw a picture or text on the copier drum. Laser printers are usually more expensive than are the other types of printers, and they are usually large (bigger than your computer), but they produce high-quality output quickly. Laser printers use sheets of paper, not continuous perforated stock, and they can print different fonts and graphics.

Fixing Jams

In this age of advanced data processing, what the world needs is better paper processing. Rather than print nicely, our printer frequently crumples up its paper and smears ink all over it like a recalcitrant two-year-old. If the weather is a little humid, the paper curls and doesn't feed properly. If the air is dry and crisp, static electricity builds up and sheets stick together. And just when the paper is moving along fine, it's time to print on checks, or mailing labels, or envelopes.

Enough grousing. Into every word processing life a little rain — or in this case, ink — must fall.

When your printer mashes up its paper like a baker kneading bread, the first thing to do is to tell WordPerfect to stop printing. The sooner you can stop the printer from smearing any more ink around, the better. Refer to Chapter 13 to learn how to cancel a print job.

If you use a laser printer or print using a network printer, you may not have to tell WordPerfect to stop printing. After the paper in a laser print jams, it stops by itself. Most laser printers and networks are even smart enough to reprint the page that jammed before continuing to print the rest of the document.

Stop that printer!

After you have told WordPerfect to stop printing, the printer may struggle along for a while longer. Most printers contain an *internal buffer*, which is a temporary storage place for it to store the next page or so to be printed. Even after you tell your computer (or the network) to stop printing your document, the printer may continue for a page or so and print the information in its buffer.

There is no easy way to prevent printing the information in the printer's internal buffer. Here's what not to do: don't turn the printer off and on. With laser printers, this technique may let loose a bunch of black, smeary toner dust that gets all over your hands and on the next 1,000 pages the printer prints. Instead, follow these steps:

1. **Push the printer's Stop or Off-Line button.**

   The printer's On-Line light should go out. You have told the printer to stop printing, as soon as it feels like it.

2. **Wait for the paper to stop moving.**

   Aha! It heard you.

3. **Turn the printer off.**

   Wait about ten seconds, to make sure that the printer's internal buffer forgets everything.

4. **Unjam the printer.**

   The following section discusses this highly technical topic.

5. **Turn the printer back on.**

   It should have forgotten about printing your document.

6. **If the printer isn't on-line, press its on-line button.**

Clean up your mess!

If you have an impact printer, the paper is probably wrapped around the platen ten times at this point. While the printer is turned off, rewind the platen knob to eject all that paper.

If you are printing on sticky labels, *don't* rewind the platen to get them out. If you do, they might stick themselves to your printing right under the platen and then you will have a devil of a time getting them out. Instead, pull gently on the labels to bring them out the front and move them forward so that the labels don't touch the platen.

If you have an ink-jet printer, flip the top open and take out the paper. It's a piece of cake (but don't get any cake in the printer).

If you have a laser printer, pop open the lid and pull out all the shreds of paper inside. Be careful — some of the parts are hot. Then slam the lid shut.

The Care and Feeding of Your Printer

Depending on which kind of printer you have, it likes different kinds of supplies to eat. No matter which kind of printer you have, it is a good idea to blow the dust out of it from time to time.

Impact printers

Impact printers use ribbons. Always be sure to have an extra ribbon on hand because the one you are using will suddenly break or run out of ink on the final draft of your report.

You can get almost any kind of paper these days as continuous feed, including continuous-feed labels, letterhead, invoices, and even envelopes. If you are looking for supplies, we recommend The Drawing Board, in Dallas, Texas (800-527-9530). You can also get continuous-feed paper with perforations so fine that after the sheets of paper have been separated, you cannot tell that they were perforated. This type of paper is sometimes called *micro-perf*.

Amaze your friends with your prodigious vocabulary. What's the name for the strip of paper that runs down the side of continuous-feed paper — the strip with the little holes in it? Answer: *perfory*.

Ink-jet printers

Ink-jet printers use little ink cartridges. The early cartridges contained ink that was water-soluble, so you could wash your document right off the paper. An interesting recycling idea, but not too hot for business correspondence. Newer cartridges have corrected this problem, and you can even get them in different ink colors. Color ink-jet printers, of course, take special multicolor cartridges.

You can buy little bottles of ink with which you recharge your ink-jet cartridges, but we haven't had terrific luck with them.

You can use regular photocopying paper in ink-jet printers. The tiny drops of ink shot out by an ink-jet printer look different on different types of paper because of differing absorbencies (sounds like a paper-towel commercial, doesn't it?). If you are unhappy with the print quality of your ink-jet, try a different kind of paper.

Laser printers

Laser printers, like small photocopying machines, use *toner cartridges* to provide the black. Toner cartridges contain, not surprisingly, *toner*, which is a fine, black dust you can get all over your clothes if you don't treat your laser printer with respect.

Your laser printer tells you that its cartridge is running out of toner by flashing a light on its panel, displaying a message, or changing an indicator on the side of the printer from green (full) to yellow (low) to red (empty).

To change the toner cartridge, pop open the lid of the printer, remove the cartridge (some slide sideways), and insert the new one. Look on the cartridge box for additional instructions: many require you to pull a tab to release the packet of toner into the cartridge. Most also suggest that you use a little Q-tip to clean the printer's *corona wire*. This idea is a good one because it lets your printer make clearer copies. While the printer is open, you may want to clean out the dust and cat hair too.

You can generally extend the life of an empty toner cartridge by taking it from the printer, dancing vigorously (not too vigorously) with it to shake the toner around, and putting it back in the printer.

Rather than buy new toner cartridges all the time, you can have your cartridges refilled with toner dust. Look in the back of your PC magazines to find services that refill cartridges. Each cartridge can be refilled only once, however, and sometimes the print quality is not as good as the original's.

Selecting Which Printer to Use

Enough about hardware — let's get back to software issues. If you have more than one printer attached to your computer (or to the network to which your computer is attached), for example, how do you tell WordPerfect which one to use when printing?

WordPerfect gets its information about printers primarily from Windows. When you install Windows, you tell it which printer or printers you have and it creates a *printer driver* for each one. A printer driver contains information about how this particular printer works, including which fonts it can print and how to tell it to use fancy type styles.

Just to confuse matters, WordPerfect also provides printer drivers. We don't really understand why because Windows printer drivers have always worked fine for us.

To see a list of the printer drivers installed on your computer, both Windows' and WordPerfect's, and to select which one to use, follow these steps:

1. **Choose File Select Printer from the menu bar.**

   WordPerfect displays the Select Printer dialog box. The Windows printer drivers have little waving flags to the left of their names. A WordPerfect printer driver has a script *WP* next to its name.

   The selected printer is highlighted on the list, and its name appears at the top of the dialog box.

2. **To use a different printer, select its driver and click on the Select button.**

   WordPerfect switches to the printer driver you selected, and the dialog box disappears.

The list of printer drivers may include drivers that aren't for real printers. The Generic Text/Only printer driver shown in Figure 22-1, for example, is used for saving text in a text file rather than printing it on a printer. The WINFAX printer driver is used for sending a document as a fax by using the WinFax Pro program, from Delrina Software (Chapter 19 explains how to format and print faxes).

It's absolutely necessary to tell WordPerfect the correct printer to use. Every printer has its own weird and bizarre codes to tell it which fonts to use and when to print things in boldface or italics, not to mention how to print lines, boxes, and pictures.

Setting Up a New Printer

But what if you get a new printer and it's not listed on the Select Printers dialog box? Yikes — it's time to install a printer driver. This procedure is fairly techy, and you may want to call for help from your local computer wizard at this point.

Still with us? After you physically install the printer, the next thing to do is to decide between installing the Windows printer driver and the WordPerfect printer driver. We recommend installing the Windows printer driver first because you need it if you want to print anything from the other programs you use. Then if you're unhappy with the way the Windows printer driver works, you can consider installing the WordPerfect printer driver.

Ready to install your new printer? Here goes!

Operating the printer out of the box

First set up the printer — unwrap it, remove all the little tabs and doohickeys that protected it during shipping, clear a space on your desk, and peruse the printer manual.

Turn off the computer before you connect the printer cable to the computer. Most printers (*parallel printers*) connect to the printer port on the back of your computer. Some printers (*serial printers*) connect to the communications port instead. Refer to your printer manual or get some help with this part. Laser printers are especially likely to be serial printers.

Telling Windows about your new printer

Next tell Windows about your printer so that WordPerfect and any other programs you use can print on it. To install the Windows printer driver, you use the Printers program that comes with Windows. WordPerfect is happy to help you run this program, if you prefer.

To install a new Windows printer driver, you need your Windows program disks, which is the large stack of disks that you (or someone) used to install Windows in the first place. The good news is that you don't have to use them all: Windows knows which disk contains the driver you want.

To run the Printers program directly from Windows, follow these steps:

1. **In the Windows Program Manager, in the Control program group, double-click on the Control Panel icon.**

   The Control Panel window opens.

2. In the Control Panel window, double-click on the Printers icon.

You see the Printers dialog box, shown in Figure 22-1.

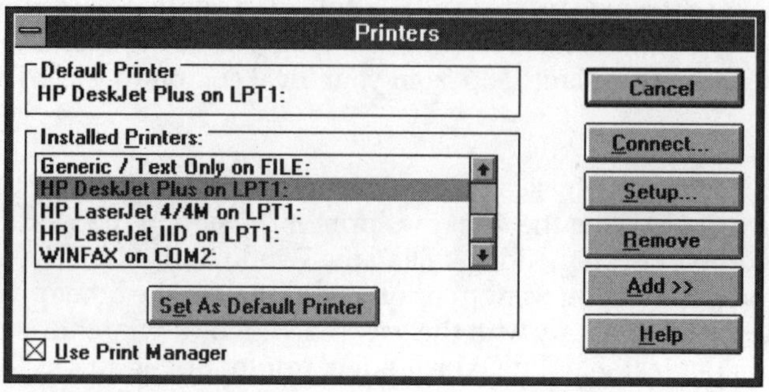

Figure 22-1:
Installing a
new
Windows
printer
driver.

Printers

Default Printer
HP DeskJet Plus on LPT1:

Installed Printers:
Generic / Text Only on FILE:
HP DeskJet Plus on LPT1:
HP LaserJet 4/4M on LPT1:
HP LaserJet IID on LPT1:
WINFAX on COM2:

Set As Default Printer

☒ Use Print Manager

Cancel
Connect...
Setup...
Remove
Add >>
Help

3. To install the driver, follow the next set of instructions.

4. Close the Printers dialog box by choosing the Close button.

5. Close the Control Panel window by choosing Settings Exit from its menu bar.

To run the Printers program from WordPerfect, follow these steps:

1. In WordPerfect, choose File Select printer from the menu bar.

WordPerfect displays the Select Printer dialog box.

2. Choose Add Printer.

WordPerfect displays a tiny menu with two choices: WordPerfect and Windows.

3. Choose Windows.

WordPerfect displays the Printers dialog box (refer to Figure 22-1).

4. Follow the next set of instructions to install the driver.

5. Close the Printers dialog box by choosing the Close button. You return to the Select Printers dialog box.

Whichever way you get there, you use the Printers dialog box to install the Windows printer driver for your new printer, as shown in these steps:

1. Choose Add from the Printers dialog box.

The dialog box expands to show a list of Windows printer drivers that are available.

2. Find your printer on the list and highlight it.

3. Choose Install from the dialog box.

Windows displays the Install Driver dialog box. Unless you have installed this printer before, the printer driver is probably not on your hard disk.

Instead, it is on one of the zillions of Windows program disks you used when you (or someone) installed Windows.

4. **Windows tells you which Windows program to put in your disk drive. Do so, and choose OK.**

5. **Windows copies the printer driver from the disk to your hard disk.**

   Voilà! It appears on the list of Installed Printers in the Printers dialog box.

6. **If this printer is the one you plan to use for most of your printing, make it the *default printer*.**

   Highlight it on the list of installed printers and choose Set as Default Printer.

7. **Choose Close to bid the Printers program a fond farewell.**

Now the new Windows printer driver appears on the list of printers in WordPerfect's Select Printer dialog box too. Follow the instructions given earlier in this chapter to select it.

If your printer is a new type, the printer driver may not be on the list of Windows printer drivers. Instead, a disk containing the Windows printer driver may come with the printer. If so, in step 2 in the preceding series of steps, choose Install Unlisted or Updated Printer. Windows asks you to put the disk in the drive.

If your new printer is not connected to the LPT1: port of your computer, you have to tell Windows. If you don't know which port your print is attached to, you had better get some help. The ports your printer might use are LPT1:, LPT2:, COM1:, and COM2:. The LPT ports are for parallel printers, and the COM ports are for serial printers.

Knowing what to do if your Windows printer driver doesn't work

If you are not happy with the way WordPerfect's documents look when you print them on your new printer, you can try installing the WordPerfect printer driver. Maybe it will do a better job. Then again, maybe not.

To install a WordPerfect printer driver, follow these steps:

1. **In WordPerfect, choose File Select printer from the menu bar.**

   WordPerfect displays the Select Printer dialog box (refer to Figure 22-1).

2. **Choose Add Printer.**

   WordPerfect displays a tiny menu with two choices: WordPerfect and Windows.

3. **Choose WordPerfect.**

You see the Add Printer dialog box. The Printers area of the dialog box shows two options: Additional Printers (*.all) and Printer Files (*.prs). When the Printer Files option is selected, you see a list of the printer drivers that are installed. When you select the Additional Printers option, you see some other printer drivers that WordPerfect stuck on your hard disk.

4. Select the Additional Printers option and look in the list of printer drivers to see whether the one for your new printer is listed.

Probably not — if not, see the following set of steps. If it is, click in the little box to its left so that an X appears in it and choose OK.

WordPerfect displays the Create Printer dialog box and suggests a filename for the printer driver. Who cares what WordPerfect wants to call its printer driver?

5. Choose OK.

Lights flash and disk drives whir while WordPerfect does whatever it does to install the new printer driver. You return safely to the Select Printer dialog box, which now lists your new printer among its drivers.

6. Highlight the printer driver you want to use and click the Select button.

Now you have installed both the WordPerfect and Windows printer drivers for your new printer. You can use the Select Printers dialog box to switch between them to see which one works better.

If the Additional Printers option doesn't reveal your printer (from step 4 in the preceding set of steps), you have to run the WordPerfect Installation program to install it, as shown in these steps:

1. Exit from WordPerfect.

The installation program refuses to run if any WordPerfect programs are open.

2. In the Windows Program Manager, find the WPWin 6.0 program group. If it's an icon, double-click on it.

3. Double-click on the WPWin 6.0 Installation icon.

You see the Installation Type dialog box, which you may recognize if you installed WordPerfect yourself. Don't worry — you don't have to install the whole thing all over again.

4. Choose Options.

You see the Additional Installation Options dialog box.

5. Choose Printers.

You see the Select Printer Directory dialog box, shown in Figure 22-2.

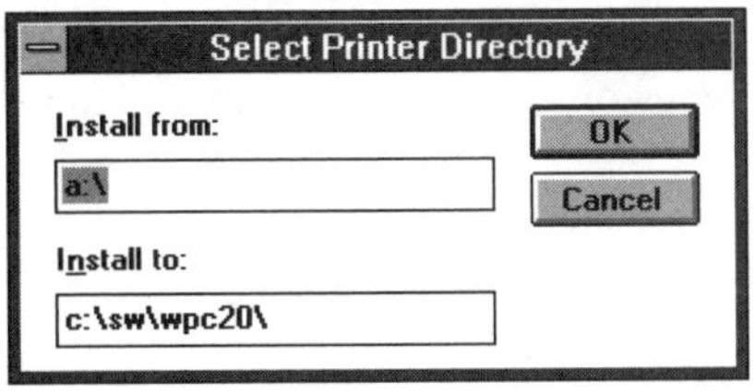

Figure 22-2:
Telling
WordPerfect
where to put
new printer
drivers.

Select Printer Directory

Install from:

`a:\`

OK

Cancel

Install to:

`c:\sw\wpc20\`

6. **Put the WordPerfect for Windows Install 1 disk in your disk drive.**

   Insert the disk even though the program may not tell you to do so. It wants to read this disk in a minute.

7. **Make sure that the disk drive letter is correct.**

   Leave the Install To directory alone because WordPerfect probably knows where it wants to put these things.

8. **Choose OK.**

   WordPerfect displays the WordPerfect Printer Drivers dialog box.

9. **Choose the printer you have just installed.**

   This list is a long one; you can find a printer fast by pressing the first letter of its name.

10. **Choose Select.**

    The name of the printer appears in the Printers to Be Installed list. You can choose several printer drivers, if you want. In fact, now that you have gone to the trouble of running this installation program, you might as well install any printer driver you might conceivably need — such as drivers for any other printers in your office, printers you might borrow from friends, or any printer you have been longing to buy.

11. **When you have chosen the printers, click the OK button to install the WordPerfect printer drivers.**

    WordPerfect may prompt you to insert various disks in the disk driver. Follow its instructions to the letter.

12. **You return to the Additional Installation Options dialog box. Choose Close.**

13. **When the Installation Type dialog box appears, choose Exit.**

Thank heavens, it's over. Put away your WordPerfect program disks and run WordPerfect. It may display a Please Wait message while it claims to be building PRS files or updating fonts or whatever printer-related activities it has to do to welcome this new printer. Your new printer driver should appear on the Select Printers dialog box now so that you can use it.

The folks at WordPerfect are diligent about writing drivers for new printers. If you cannot find a driver for you printer, give them a call. They have a raft load of phone numbers for different types of support — you should have received a list of them with your program.

Printing on a Network

If you work in an office that has a computer network, the printer you use may not be in your own office. It may not be anywhere near your office. You may be able to quit going to the health club, in fact, because you get such a workout running up and down the stairs to the printer three floors above you to get your documents.

If you don't know where your network printer is, you may have to ask people in nearby cubicles or stand quietly in the center of the office and listen for the sound of printing (whirring and clicking, if it is a laser printer). If all else fails, ask someone.

After you find the printer, you probably want to find the document you printed. If you are lucky, no one else has printed anything recently and the paper in the printer is all yours. More likely, lots of people have printed things and a pile of paper waits for you on top of the printer.

Correct network etiquette requires that you sort through the pages and be careful to keep them in order. Pull out the documents that are yours without shuffling the pages or dropping the whole mess on the floor. If you cannot find your document, maybe someone else decided to drop it off at your office on her way to lunch. Or else someone decided that your document looked interesting and sneaked off with it.

Networks usually have their own print-management programs. You may want to ask your network administrator to show you how to cancel a print job after it is in the hands of the network, how to see the *queue* (the waiting line) of documents waiting to be printed, and which other printers on the network you can use.

Chapter 23

Don't Panic! Read This Chapter!

*W*ith this trusty book by your side, of course, nothing should go wrong while you are using WordPerfect. The IRS should never audit your tax returns, of course, and your toast should never burn. So much for living in a perfect world. This chapter describes some things that just might, once in a while, perhaps, happen to you or to someone you know.

Where's WordPerfect? (Part 1)

Hmm. I know it was here yesterday. Where is that WPWin icon?

Chapter 21 describes the places where your cute little WordPerfect fountain-pen-nib icon might have wandered off. In the Program Manager, check in all your program groups. If you copied your WPWin program icon to another program group (as described in Chapter 21), look for the icon in your WPWin program group.

The jerky know-it-all in the cubicle down the hall may have deleted your WPWin icon from the Program Manager. Don't panic — you may have another one lying around; if not, you can make a new one. Follow these steps:

1. Switch to the Windows Program Manager.

See Chapter 21 if you don't know what we are talking about.

2. Select the program group you want the WordPerfect icon to be in.

We like our WPWin icon to be in our Frequently Used program group. (We made this group ourselves; you probably don't have a group named this way. See Chapter 21 to learn how to make your own program groups.) You can also put it in the WPWin 6.0 group. To select a group, click on its title bar.

3. Choose File New from the menu.

Program Manager displays the New Program Object dialog box. (Wow! You are making a new program object! It's something to tell the family when you get home.) You have two options: Program Group and Program Item. Program Item is selected.

4. Choose OK.

You see the Program Item Properties dialog box, shown in Figure 23-1.

5. For the Description, enter WPWin.

You can enter whatever name you want to see on the screen just under the little fountain-pen nib. Keep it short — *Dumb Docs* or *Edit Ho!,* for example.

6. For the Command List, enter this line:

```
c:\wpwin60\wpwin.exe /PI=c:\windows\
```

Entering this line assumes that your WordPerfect program is installed in a directory named C:\WPWIN60. If it is not, substitute the name of the WordPerfect program directory.

Type this line exactly as it appears here. The first part (C:\WPWIN60\WPWIN.EXE) has no spaces and uses only backslashes, with no regular slashes. That's a zero after the six, not the letter *O*. Then there's a space. The second part (/PI=C:\WINDOWS\) also contains no spaces and uses a confusing mixture of regular slashes and backslashes. Check your typing three — yes, three — times.

7. For the Working Directory, enter the name of the WordPerfect program directory.

This directory is usually C:\WPWIN60.

8. Choose OK.

A new WPWin icon appears in the program group you selected! Double-click on it to make sure that it runs WordPerfect.

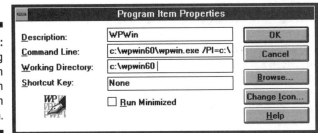

Figure 23-1:
Creating
your own
WPWin
program
icon.

If you ever want to change the program icon (if you want to change the Description, for example), click on the icon once and press Alt+Enter. You see the Program Item Properties dialog box again.

If you always run WordPerfect when you use your computer, you may want to tell Windows to run it automatically when Windows starts up. See the section "Starting WordPerfect automagically" in Chapter 21.

Where's WordPerfect? (Part 2)

Another way for you to lose WordPerfect is for it to vanish before your very eyes. You are working away and click on something, probably something in the upper right corner of the WordPerfect window. Blammo! Without even so much as a puff of smoke, the entire WordPerfect window disappears and takes your documents with it.

What probably has happened is that you clicked on the Minimize button, the tiny button in the upper right corner of the WordPerfect window. This button has a downward-pointing arrow on it. Pressing this button freeze-dries WordPerfect into an icon, which probably appears in the vicinity of the lower left corner of your screen.

If you see the WordPerfect icon, double-click on it to bring it back to life. Is it still breathing? Pulse steady? Whew!

If you don't see the WordPerfect icon, press Ctrl+Esc to see the Windows Task List. One of the tasks should be WordPerfect. Double-click on it — it's back!

Another possibility is that you exited from WordPerfect by mistake. It is difficult to choose File Exit from the menu bar by mistake, but what if you have added an Exit button to your power bar? (We did.) You can easily choose it while intending to italicize some text. Alternatively, you might have pressed Alt+F4, which also exits from WordPerfect.

Where's My Document? (Part 1)

Uh-oh. You want to open that important report so that you can do some more work on it, but there's no sign of it on your disk. Looks like it ran off with that cute, little memo you wrote yesterday. Call in the bloodhounds.

But first, try looking around. You probably saved it with a different name or in a different directory. Try the things in this list:

✔ Use the File Open command and look in the directory in which you thought you left it. Oh, yeah, you probably already tried this trick.

✔ While you are in the Open File dialog box, look in some other directories you use.

✔ Consider the possibility that you used the wrong name when you saved the document. You never know when a brain spasm might strike.

✔ Use the QuickFinder program that comes with WordPerfect. This feature can look in all the files on your hard disk and search for some text that you know is in your document. See the section "Finding a File with a Forgotten Name," in Chapter 15, for directions.

Where's My Document? (Part 2)

Here's another twist on losing a document: you open the document and work on it diligently. You click on something (you're not sure what) and Zip! — your document vanishes.

You may have minimized your document accidentally. As part of its capability to edit multiple documents at the same time, WordPerfect lets you temporarily shrink your document to the size of a postage stamp while you work on other documents. It's hard to imagine a good use for this feature, but there it is — you minimize a document by clicking on the *document's* Minimize button, which is in the upper right corner of the document's window. (Chapter 14 discusses how to see multiple documents in multiple document windows, and other confusing topics.)

To find your lost document, choose Window from the WordPerfect menu bar. After the Cascade and Tile commands, you see a list of the documents that are open. With luck, yours is one of them. Choose it, and voilà! It's back.

Where Am I?

You click on something and find yourself in the unexplored reaches of your document. Where are you and how do you get back to where you were?

Luckily, WordPerfect has a "go back to where I was a minute ago" command. It's in the Go To dialog box. Follow these steps to go back to where you were:

1. **Press Ctrl+G.**

    You see the Go To dialog box, described in Chapter 2.

2. **Click on Last Position in the Position list.**

    This location is the "where I was a minute ago" place.

3. **Choose OK.**

    WordPerfect zips your cursor back to where it was just before the last search or Go To command.

If this technique doesn't work, try searching for a word or phrase that appears near where you were editing. Use the Edit Find command (or press F2) to see the Find Text dialog box. (Chapter 5 describes searching in detail.)

The Entire Document Is Boldface!

Or it's in italics or in a weird font. WordPerfect's character-formatting commands can sometimes get out of hand. The usual way to format some text (as explained in Chapter 8) is to select the text first and then do the formatting. This method tells WordPerfect to insert a secret code to start the special formatting at the beginning of the selected text and to insert another code at the end of the selected text to turn off the formatting.

If your codes get bollixed up, your carefully chosen formatting can be applied to your entire document rather than to just a small selection of text.

Use the Reveal Codes window (press Alt+F3) to check for the code or codes that turn on the formatting. (Chapter 11 explains how to use the Reveal Codes window.) When you find the offending code, delete it. Then try your formatting again.

The Screen Looks Weird!

The WordPerfect screen usually looks weird, so it's nothing to worry about. If the screen looks even weirder than normal, this list shows some things you can try:

✔ Choose View Page or View Draft from the menu. Maybe WordPerfect has switched into the alternate reality of outline view.

✔ Choose View Zoom and select a reasonable zoom size. (Chapter 20 describes zooming, for you zoom freaks.)

- ✔ Use the Reveal Codes window (press Alt+F3) to check for bizarre codes that may have arrived from outer space (see Chapter 11). If you see a code you don't like the looks of, delete it. It's a good idea to save your document under a different name first.

- ✔ Close your document and open it again. Maybe it feels better.

- ✔ Exit from WordPerfect and run it again. This step may exorcise the cooties that inhabited it.

- ✔ Exit from Windows and run it again. This step is necessary only when the situation has become serious.

- ✔ Exit from Windows, turn off your PC, and go out for a walk. Who knows? Maybe your eyeballs have flipped out and need a rest.

- ✔ Sell your computer and go into another line of work, such as flower arranging.

My Document Isn't Printing!

You click on the cute, little Print button on the power bar or use some other method to tell WordPerfect that you want it to arrange some ink tastefully on some paper. Is this such an unreasonable thing to ask?

In the World of Windows, arranging ink certainly can be complicated. Chapter 13 describes the Committee for Printing Your Document, the group of programs that get involved as soon as you give that print command.

Here's the key thing: if the printer doesn't print anything, don't just try printing again. Your document may still be en route to the printer. If you issue another print command, you probably will end up with two copies. Instead, figure out where your document got stuck.

This list shows some things to try when your document won't print:

- ✔ Make sure that the printer is on and on-line. For information about taking the shreds of jammed paper out of your printer (and even *finding* your printer), see Chapter 22.

- ✔ Tell WordPerfect to cancel printing the document so that you can start over. Display the WordPerfect Print Job dialog box by pressing F5 and then choosing the Control button. (See the section "WordPerfect, stop printing!" at the end of Chapter 13.)

- ✔ If the situation is out of WordPerfect's hands, it's time to speak firmly to the WP Print Process and the Windows Print Manager. Press Ctrl+Esc to see the Windows Task List and then locate these two errant programs and end them. (See the section "Stop, stop, I say!" at the end of Chapter 13.)

✔ If you use a network, the problem undoubtedly can be blamed on it. Ask other computer users in your office whether they can print with the printer you want to use. You may have to talk to your network administrator — ask such questions as "How can I tell whether my print job is in the queue?" and "Can you make sure that my system is attached to the right printer?" Who knows — the joke memo you just finished writing may be printing on the fancy printer in the executive suite!

✔ It is worth checking into silly, pedestrian problems such as the printer cable falling out the back of either the printer or the computer. If it has detached itself, you should shut down WordPerfect, Windows, the computer, and the printer before reconnecting the cable. Electricity is your friend, but you might as well play it safe.

Yikes! I Didn't Mean to Delete That!

The finger is quicker than the brain, especially when it is heading straight for a key that deletes something. In WordPerfect, like all powerful word processors, it is horrifyingly easy to blow away hours or weeks of work.

✔ If you have just deleted some text, you can bring it right back by pressing Ctrl+Shift+Z. This step, in fact, displays the Undelete dialog box, which lets you bring back any of the last three things you deleted. (Choosing Edit Undelete works too.)

✔ If you just deleted a picture or some other fancy-pants item in your document, pressing Ctrl+Shift+Z can undelete it too.

✔ If you just deleted a code, try pressing Ctrl+Z to undo the change (or choose Edit Undo from the menu).

If you just deleted an entire document by using the File Options button in the Open or Save As dialog box, you have a more serious problem. This list shows some approaches to take when you have deleted something accidentally:

✔ If you told WordPerfect to keep the previous versions of your documents, you can retrieve the previous version and make all the changes since it was saved. It's tedious but better than typing everything again. Chapter 20 tells you how to tell WordPerfect to keep backups. Backups of your documents have the same name as the documents, but they use the filename extension BAK.

✔ If you told WordPerfect to make timed backups of documents you are editing and you were just editing the document you deleted, the timed backup may still be around. Choose File Open from the menu and go to your Windows program directory (usually C:\WINDOWS). Chapter 15 explains how to move to a different directory. Look for a file named WP_WP_.BK1. Open it immediately. If it is the file you want, save it in another directory and use another name. If it is not, try WP_WP_.BK2 and so on.

- ✔ If you use DOS 6, you can use its undelete feature. Don't do *anything* else on your computer — most especially, don't save any files. Run — do not walk — to your nearest DOS expert to find out how to undelete a file. Bring Mystic Mint chocolate cookies, refrigerated, and a cold glass of milk.

- ✔ In the worst case, dredge around in your wastepaper basket and find the last version of the document you printed. It is a tremendous waste of time to type the document all over again, although we usually find that in the process we improve it considerably. (Maybe we should have deleted all the files that contain the chapters of this book!)

They Can't Open My Document!

You create a marvelous document and copy it to a disk to give to your co-worker, Fred. Fred also uses WordPerfect, so you figure that he should be able to open the file right up and edit it. (Not that it needs any editing, of course — your prose is too pristine and luminescent to be improved.)

Rather than oohs and aahs, you hear the gnashing and grinding of teeth emanating from Fred's office. "This WordPerfect document is no good," he reports. No good? That document is Pulitzer prize material, you think. It turns out that Fred never even got to lay his eyes on your finest prose to date — his version of WordPerfect refused to open your document.

Here's an ugly truth about WordPerfect: every version of WordPerfect stores documents in its own, slightly idiosyncratic format. Luckily, newer versions of WordPerfect can *always* read the formats of earlier versions. Beginning with version 6.0, WordPerfect for DOS and WordPerfect for Windows use the same format.

You can run into a problem if you give one of your WordPerfect documents to someone who uses an older, inferior version of WordPerfect, such as WordPerfect 5.1 or 5.2. To avoid problems, you can save your document in a format that one of these older programs can read.

To save your document in an older format, choose File Save As from the menu. Type a new filename so that you don't replace the version you have already saved in regular WPWin 6.0 format. In the Format box, choose WordPerfect 4.2, WordPerfect 5.0, or WordPerfect 5.1/5.2. Then choose OK.

Then give this new document in a moldy, old WordPerfect format to your friend Fred and see what else he can find to complain about!

WordPerfect's Not Listening to Me!

You try choosing a command from a menu. Nothing happens. You try choosing a button from the power bar or button bar. Nothing. You press the right mouse button — no QuickMenu. Hmm. WordPerfect must be deliberately and maliciously ignoring you. Maybe it's taking its afternoon siesta.

If you cannot get WordPerfect's attention, your first inclination may be to pound on the keyboard, shout at it, or slap it around. For technical reasons too complex to explain here, we recommend the shouting approach (assuming that you are responsible for paying for a broken keyboard and that you are not interested in breaking your hand on the side of the monitor).

After you get your frustrations out, follow these steps:

✔ Try talking to Windows. Press Ctrl+Esc to see the Windows Task List. If it doesn't appear, Windows is incommunicado. If it does appear, try switching to another program and then switching back to WordPerfect. If you can switch to any other program, exit from that program. Maybe it and WordPerfect are having an argument.

✔ If nothing else works, wait about five minutes. Maybe some part of your computer system is so busy doing something that it hasn't had a chance to respond to you. You never know.

If talking to Windows doesn't help, even after five minutes, it's time for serious violence. Time to bash some bits! Unfortunately, this technique blows away WordPerfect and the documents you have opened. With luck, you have saved your documents recently or you use timed backups (see Chapter 20).

Follow these steps when WordPerfect is out to lunch:

1. **Hold down the Ctrl and Alt keys and then press the Delete key.**

   This infamous Three-Finger Salute kills programs in their tracks. It should just kill WordPerfect, but in some cases it kills everything, including Windows.

   The screen should jiggle and your Windows display should be replaced with a screen full of instructions.

2. **Follow the instructions Windows displays.**

   Windows tells you if a program ("application") isn't responding, and tells you how to kill it. You lose your most recent edits in WordPerfect. In addition, you may lose your most recent work in any other programs you are running.

3. **Restart Windows.**

If you have killed WordPerfect and returned to Windows, it's a good idea to exit from Windows and restart it. From the Program Manager menu, choose File Exit and then choose OK. When you see the DOS prompt (something like C:> or C:\WINDOWS>), type **WIN** and press Enter. Windows starts back up.

A Document1 Backup file exists?

If WordPerfect crashes or another program crashes and takes WordPerfect with it, or if you turn off your computer while WordPerfect is running, or if lightning strikes your house and causes a temporary blackout, WordPerfect doesn't get a chance to do the housekeeping chores it usually does when you exit. One of these chores is deleting the timed backup files it creates (assuming that you use timed backups — see Chapter 20).

The next time you run WordPerfect, you get the bizarre message that a Document1 Backup file exists. This message means that WordPerfect has discovered the timed backup copy of one of your documents — probably one of the documents you were editing when WordPerfect went west.

These timed backup files can be a godsend if you did a lot of editing and had not saved your document before disaster struck. See the section "Getting back your timed backups," in Chapter 20, to learn how to use these timed backup files to recover from these types of disasters.

Part V
The Part of Tens

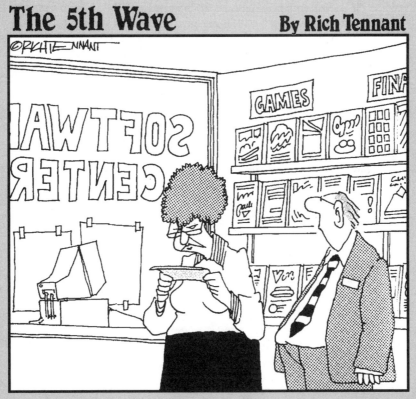

"YOU KNOW THAT GUY WHO BOUGHT ALL THAT SOFTWARE? HIS CHECK HAS A WARRANTY THAT SAYS IT'S TENDERED AS IS AND HAS NO FITNESS FOR ANY PARTICULAR PURPOSE INCLUDING, BUT NOT LIMITED TO, CASHING."

In this part...

Y ou would think that humanity would have gotten beyond its fascination with tens by now. Yes, it is an utterly amazing fact that we have ten fingers and ten toes. Big deal. If you count on your fingers in base 2, you can count to 1023, but do you see "1,023 Ways To Please Your Spouse" in *Reader's Digest*? No.

So, because we seem to be stuck with ten, here's the Part of Tens. This part provides more-or-less useful facts that are so small they might get lost if they didn't have a place of their own. Some of the "tens," like "Ten (or So) Awesome Tricks" and "Ten Features We Don't Use but You Might" easily could have been "1,023 Ways . . . " but our environmental sensitivities don't allow us to waste that many trees. So take off your mittens and count along with us as we explore the fascinating world of WordPerfect trivia.

Chapter 24
The Ten Not-to-Be-Broken Rules of WordPerfect

* * *

In This Chapter

▶ Tell WordPerfect what you have in mind

▶ Do not use extra spaces or tabs

▶ Do not keep pressing Enter to begin a new page

▶ Do not number your pages manually

▶ Save early and often

▶ Save before using the Edit Replace command

▶ Back up your work

▶ Do not turn off your PC until you exit from Windows

▶ Turn on your printer before printing documents

▶ Always keep printer supplies on hand

* * *

*O*K, you unbelievers. You don't have to follow the rules explained in this chapter, but don't blame us if lightning strikes you (or, more likely, strikes somewhere near your office and the power goes out, destroying your valuable documents)!

1: Tell WordPerfect What You Have in Mind

Tell WordPerfect what you have in mind for your document. If you want multiple columns, use WordPerfect's Columns feature. If you want wide margins, tell WordPerfect to widen them by using the Layout Margins command. Don't think that it would be easier to skip all that and just use extra Enters, spaces, or tabs to put the text where you want it. This method always means extra work in the long run, when you go to edit your text later.

WordPerfect's word-wrap feature, for example, enables it to begin a new line whenever it sees you getting perilously close to the right margin. In WordPerfect's mind (such as it is), a bunch of text ending with an Enter is a paragraph, so type your paragraphs like that and let WordPerfect do the rest of the work. Don't press Enter until you get to the end of a paragraph (see Chapter 1).

2: Do Not Use Extra Spaces or Tabs

In high school, your typing teacher taught you to type two spaces after each period. Other than that, you should never type more than one space consecutively (with rare exceptions). If you want to move across the line and leave some white space, use tabs (see Chapter 9 to learn how to set tab stops and use different types of tabs).

In the world of typesetting, with proportionally spaced fonts, it is considered good form to type only *one* space after each period. Somehow, after the text is typeset, it looks fine. But we can understand if your ingrained two-space habits are too hard to break.

Incidentally, if you are using tabs to make something that looks like a table, adjust the tab stops so that there is one for each column. This technique enables you to press Tab just once between each entry (see Chapter 9). Better yet, use WordPerfect's table feature (see Chapter 16) — remember the first commandment.

3: Do Not Keep Pressing Enter to Begin a New Page

When you decide to begin a new page, tell WordPerfect so in no uncertain terms — press Ctrl+Enter. Don't pussyfoot around the issue by pressing Enter repeatedly until you fill the current page with blank lines. This technique is yet another example of the first commandment in action — if you want a page break, say so. (Chapter 10 explains why the Ctrl+Enter method works best.)

4: Do Not Number Your Pages Manually

WordPerfect can number your pages for you and place the page numbers at the left, center, or right of either the top or bottom of the page. What more could you ask? So don't type page numbers yourself: they become a mess if you edit your document and the page breaks move around. Chapter 10 tells you how to number your pages and print over information in headers and footers.

5: Save Early and Often

Be prepared for disaster! Every time you squirm around in your chair, scratch your foot, or take a sip of coffee, press Ctrl+S to save your document. 'Nuff said. Yes, a timed document backup helps (see Chapter 20), but are you really willing to lose your last ten minutes or so of work?

6: Save Before Using the Edit Replace Command

WordPerfect's find-and-replace feature (described in Chapter 5) has awesome power, either to make lots of wonderful updates throughout your document or to trash it big-time. What if you mean to replace *Smith* with *Smythe,* for example, but you type a space by mistake in the F̲ind box just before choosing Replace A̲ll? Poof — all the spaces in your document are replaced by *Smythe.* Your important letter has just been transformed into performance art.

Just in case, save your document before you use the Edit Replace command (also known as Ctrl+F2).

7: Back Up Your Work

Saving is good, but saving your documents on your hard disk doesn't help if your hard disk dies. We don't mean to sound alarmist here, but it can happen. Talk to someone in your office about setting up a backup system for you, by using either disks or backup tapes. At least you can use the File Options button in the Open File dialog box to copy your important documents to disks occasionally (see Chapter 15).

8: Do Not Turn Off Your PC Until You Exit from Windows

Oops — you're running late! Time to go! Don't just turn off your computer. If you turn it off while Windows is still running, you can cause problems. Either leave the computer on (just turn off its screen) or exit from the Windows Program Manager before you turn off your computer. You know when you have exited from Windows when you see a DOS prompt (such as C:\WINDOWS>).

9: Turn On the Printer Before Printing Documents

If your document refuses to print and you see strange error boxes on the screen, the first thing to check is whether your printer is on, the on-line light is on, and paper is in the tray. If that doesn't fix things, see Chapter 13 and Chapter 22.

10: Always Keep Printer Supplies on Hand

Oooh — how does the printer *know* when you are about to print the final draft of something big? But it does, and that is the moment when your ribbon goes dry, your ink cartridge runs empty, or your toner cartridge ejects its last hiccup of toner. Rats!

Be sure to have extra printing supplies on hand so that you can foil the printer when these things happen.

Chapter 25
Ten (or So) Awesome Tricks

In This Chapter

▶ Cutting, copying, and pasting with other programs

▶ Dragging and dropping text

▶ Returning to where you were

▶ Using QuickMarks and bookmarks

▶ Reopening an earlier document

▶ Inserting the date

▶ Using international symbols and other cool codes

▶ Using unbreakable hyphens and spaces

▶ Inserting bullets

▶ Converting tabs to tables

▶ Inserting other files

▶ Linking spreadsheets and databases

*W*ordPerfect has more awesome tricks than trained seals in Alaska. But personal taste varies when it comes to "awesome," so we have picked out a dozen tricks that one person may find fabulously useful and another may find completely stupid.

Cutting, Copying, and Pasting with Other Programs

Part of the overall coolitude of Windows programs is that most of them use the same cut-and-paste feature, the Clipboard. You can copy stuff from spreadsheets to word processors, from databases to "personal information managers," and from graphics programs to page-layout applications.

In WordPerfect, you can generally cut (or copy) and paste from Windows spreadsheets, databases, and graphics programs, and from other Windows word processors or text editors.

To cut and paste something from *anything* to *anything else,* follow these steps:

1. **Run both programs.**

   This step isn't absolutely necessary, but it makes life easier. They both must be Windows programs.

2. **In the *anything* program, select the text, graphics, or spreadsheet region you want to copy.**

   In most programs, you can use the mouse to select text.

3. **Copy the selected text to the Windows Clipboard.**

   In most programs, you press Ctrl+C; in others, check the Edit selection on the menu for a Copy command.

4. **In the *anything else* program, click in or select the area where you want to paste.**

5. **Paste a copy of the contents of the Clipboard.**

   In most programs, you press Ctrl+V; in others, check the Edit selection on the menu for a Paste command.

   You can paste as many copies as you want.

If stuff doesn't copy as nicely as you want, placate yourself by reflecting on the amazing fact that it can be done at all, considering how different the programs can be.

Dragging and Dropping Text

The fastest way to move text is just to highlight it, click on it, and drag it somewhere else.

Returning to Where You Were

If you're moving around a great deal between two places in your document, it's nice to be able to switch easily. To go back to where you were, use the Edit Go To command (or press Ctrl+G). Double-click on Last Position in the Go To dialog box. (That grumbling noise you hear is from old WordPerfect users. No, it's not as convenient as before, but it's still useful.)

Going Back to That Old Same Place

If you want to keep returning to one important place in your document, try using a QuickMark. Click in that important place and press Ctrl+Shift+Q. Now you can go back there any time by pressing Ctrl+Q.

If you're dancing around several places in your document, you might try using bookmarks. Highlight a word or phrase unique to that place, such as *little grass shack* (this phrase serves as a name). Choose Insert Bookmark and then Create from the Bookmark dialog box. Click on OK in the Create Bookmark dialog box to accept the highlighted text as a name.

To go back to your "little grass shack," press Ctrl+G for the Go To dialog box, click on the name in the Bookmark box, and then click on OK. You can have several bookmarks in a document.

Reopening an Earlier Document

WordPerfect keeps track of the last four documents you worked on. To reopen them, click on File and then click on any of the four documents listed at the bottom of the drop-down menu.

Inserting the Date

WordPerfect gives you two — count 'em — two ways to put today's date in your document. Choose one of these methods:

- ✔ Insert today's date as though you had typed it. Press Ctrl+D, use the Insert Date Date Text command, or click on the Date Text button in the button bar.
- ✔ Insert a secret "date code" that changes to the current date every time you open the document. Press Ctrl+Shift+D or use the Insert Date {Date Code} command.

An Insert Date Date Format command lets you choose any format, from European to American to Martian. This command also lets you insert the time, with or without the date.

Both these methods are also found in the Insert Date command, which has a Date Format command also. This command lets you choose any format from European to American to Martian.

Use the Insert Date Date Format command if you want the time, with or without the date.

Inserting Cool Characters

Use the Insert Character command (press Ctrl+W, for "weird characters") to insert anything from a trademark symbol to Passover greetings in Hebrew. This command is also home to those convenient, little characters (such as the cent symbol and standard fractions) that were on your $150 typewriter but are annoyingly absent on your $150 computer keyboard.

When you click the button under Character Set and hold down the mouse button, you have your choice of characters: multinational (such as accented vowels), phonetic (such as in the dictionary), box-drawing (guaranteed weirdness), typographic symbols (a mish-mash of stuff, such as trademark symbols and fractions), iconic symbols (happy faces and pointing hands), math and scientific (inequalities and the aangstrom symbol), and such languages as Cyrillic, Japanese, Greek, Hebrew, and Arabic. Drag the highlight to the selection you want and release the mouse button.

You can insert only one character at a time. Click on it in the Characters box and then on the Insert button.

The neat thing about the WordPerfect Characters dialog box is that you can leave it lying around on the screen, ready to provide strange-looking characters at a moment's notice, while you type. You don't have to close the dialog box before you can continue typing your document. Just select a character from the Characters box and click on Insert whenever you want to use a strange character.

When you finish inserting funky characters in your text, click the Close button to make the WordPerfect Characters dialog box go away.

After you have inserted a strange character in your text, you can copy it to other places just as you would copy normal text — copy it to the Clipboard by pressing Ctrl+C and paste it from the Clipboard by pressing Ctrl+V (see Chapter 6 if this is new news to you).

Using Unbreakable Hyphens and Spaces

Normally, when you insert a hyphen, WordPerfect takes that as a license to break the line there, if necessary. This breaking capability is inconvenient for compound terms, such as *Figure 1-17* or phone numbers, such as 555-1212. For these types of things, you should insert unbreakable (*hard*) hyphens by pressing Ctrl+-. Likewise, you can also insert hard spaces, which prevent a line break between two words, by pressing Ctrl+spacebar.

Chasing Speeding Bullets

To "bulletize" a bunch of paragraphs, just select them and click on the Bullet button in the button bar. (You can also use the Insert Bullets & Numbers command.)

In the Bullets & Numbers dialog box, double-click on any bullet symbol or numbering scheme. You can even start the numbers from a particular value, by using the Starting Value box.

Converting Tabs to Tables

Sometimes you wish that you could create a table the old-fashioned way: by using plain, old text with tabs in it rather than by using the Table Create command and filling in the cells. This capability is also valuable when you're importing unformatted text from some other program, so WordPerfect doesn't know that the text is supposed to be a table.

WordPerfect helps you create a real WordPerfect table from tabular text. Each row of the table-to-be must be a line that ends with a *hard return* (the HRt secret code; see Chapter 11). To insert a hard return at the end of a line, place your cursor there and press the Enter key. Within each line, separate your columns by pressing the Tab key. (Hard returns are displayed as paragraph marks; press Ctrl+Shift+F3 to display paragraph and tab marks if they're not already visible.)

Highlight the entire table-to-be so that the highlight forms a nice, neat rectangle. When you press F12 (which is the same as Table Create), a Convert Table dialog box appears. Click on Tabular Column and then on the OK button. Zap! You're tableized. The last column is probably a little too large. To reduce its width, move your mouse pointer over the right edge of the column until it changes form; then click and drag this edge to the left until the column is the width you want.

Inserting Other Files

WordPerfect is nothing if not accommodating, including the fact that it lets you insert other document files into your document. This feature is similar in its results to the Windows cut-and-paste feature; rather than copy a piece of another file, however, you copy the entire file.

Use the Insert File command to choose any file. WordPerfect displays a Convert File Format dialog box. Choose the filename and press the Insert button. WordPerfect asks whether you are sure, sure, sure that you want to insert the file in your current document.

If WordPerfect can recognize the kind of file it is, such as Microsoft Word for Windows, it suggests the file type in the Convert File Format From dialog box. If you know that the suggestion is wrong, you can view WordPerfect's conversion repertoire by clicking on the Convert File Format From box; choose the correct one. Click the OK button when you're ready to go, and watch the lovely Conversion in Progress display pulsate.

If all goes well, the file is converted to text that is at least remotely similar to the original. You may have to fool with the Layout commands to get it to look right, though.

Linking Spreadsheets and Databases

When you're making a report that includes spreadsheet or database data, the data often changes even after you have finished writing it. To keep your report up-to-date, you can *link* to the spreadsheet or database file rather than insert it. Choose Insert Spreadsheet/Database and then Create Data Link. In the dialog box, specify the Data Type (spreadsheet, for example), how you want it to appear (Link As), and the Filename.

Chapter 26

Ten Features We Don't Use but You Might

. . . .

. . . .

*I*n WordPerfect, as in any software package today, there are a few features most people will never use. Like maybe a couple hundred of them. They're not bad features; it's just that if you happen to use them, you're in a Definite Minority. So that we don't leave you In A Pickle as well, we figured that we would at least tell you what the commands are for these features, and a little bit about how they work.

Comments

The folks at WordPerfect must have felt bad for little, orphan features such as Comments and made up for it by making them cute as a bug. Comments are a type of annotation to your document but not part of the final document. They serve as a communication mechanism between you and someone else who is working on the same document, such as your editor.

To insert a comment, click on the text you want to annotate. Move your mouse pointer into the left margin, click the right mouse button, and choose Comment from the QuickMenu. Type your comment and click on Close when you're finished. A little cartoon voice-balloon appears in the left margin. Click on it to view it. Double-click to edit it. Delete its secret code, Comment, to delete it (see Chapter 11).

Cross References

Miss Manners undoubtedly would disapprove of providing references if they're going to be cross, but that's today's society for you. We're talking about references that say such things as "See page 7 for the herring cobbler recipe," where, after editing, your herring cobbler could end up on page 8 or darn near anywhere.

The solution here is to not type the page number. Instead, use the Tools Cross-Reference command to mark the recipe text with a secret name, such as "herring cobbler," and likewise link the words "see page" to the same name. When you choose this command, you get a bunch of buttons (what — again?). Type the secret name in the Target box and click on the Mark Reference button, the herring cobbler recipe, and then the Mark Target button. Click on Generate and watch the fun. Regenerate it if you edit later.

Line Numbering

For all you lawyers out there writing contracts with numbered paragraphs, the Layout Line Numbering command numbers every paragraph. Enough said. You're smart, highly paid professionals — you figure it out.

Hypertext

At last, word-processing scientists have found a way to create document features that cannot even be put on paper. Despite its name, hypertext is not a product of excessive caffeine. Hey, wait! Maybe it is! (Sorry, Ted Nelson.) Hypertext is sort of similar to the way Help works, and now you can make your documents work like that. Click on a button or on a green-highlighted word or phrase and Phwap! — you're in another part of the document, such as a footnote or maybe even another document. The Tools Hypertext command sets this stuff up by using bookmarks.

Kickoff

Sorry, Super Bowl fans, Kickoff isn't a football feature. Like football, however, it's totally unrelated to word processing! Kickoff is a separate program that comes with WordPerfect; its icon (which features a football) is in the WPWin program group in the Windows Program Manager. Kickoff automatically launches (starts) any program, including WordPerfect, at a particular time or at particular intervals. You can automatically launch your Windows appointment book (such as Calendar), for example, at 9 a.m. and noon every Monday through Friday. Or you can launch Solitaire or Minesweeper at 5:01 p.m. every afternoon.

Hyperwhat?

This information isn't that technical — it's just arcane. Don't worry that we're going to tell you to do something uncomfortable.

Everyone in the computer biz talks about hypertext. Every program has a hypertext help system. The *New York Times* has even reviewed hypertext novels. So where did hypertext come from? It turns out that it was the brainchild of one guy, a rather wild and wacky guy named Theodor H. Nelson. Beginning in the 1950s, he was thinking of wonderful ways for computers to make informa-

tion available to everyone, and he was around when word processing was first invented. ("Use a $1 million computer to do what!?")

Hypertext is part of a much bigger, not to say grandiose, plan: Xanadu. Xanadu is designed to be a worldwide network of libraries, with all their books on-line. All books are written, updated, and read interactively as hypertext (it's hard to describe). Read Ted's books — *Computer Lib* and *Literary Machines*, among others — for the full description.

Equations

You scientists, mathematicians, and engineers out there already know that you're in a definite minority. Yet WordPerfect doesn't forget you. It does nice mathematical equations, with Greek symbols and all that. You can do them in-line with the text or in a separate area. Check out the <u>E</u>quation or <u>G</u>raphics Styles selection in the <u>G</u>raphics menu.

Outlines

You wouldn't think that you would need special features for writing an outline. You're right. But WordPerfect gives you special outline features anyway, in the <u>T</u>ools <u>O</u>utline command. You get automated numbering, tab settings, and a feature bar with buttons to change the levels and "hide" levels of detail you don't want to see at the moment.

Macros

Macros are a feature for people who enjoy spending endless hours trying to get the computer to correctly perform a series of keystrokes when you press some Alt/Shift/Ctrl+key combination. Macros work like this: suppose that you decide that you want to insert a herring icon before every paragraph that has the word *herring* in it. A macro is a way to record all the steps you would need to take in WordPerfect and play them back with a single keystroke. To record or play a macro, choose <u>T</u>ools <u>M</u>acro from the menu bar.

TextArt

As our friend Art says, "Expose yourself to Art." Here's your chance to make swoopy, loopy headings and other artsy typography. Buckets o' fun for posters and presentations. Click on the TextArt button in the button bar (or Graphics TextArt).

Footnotes and Endnotes

Footnotes and endnotes are among the more useful features you won't use, but we just couldn't resist putting footnotes and endnotes at the end of this chapter. You use footnotes when you have annotations at the bottom of each page; you use endnotes when all the annotations appear at the end (such as references). WordPerfect automatically positions, orders, and numbers them, although you can fool with them.

To add a footnote or endnote, click at the end of a word or sentence and then use Insert Footnote (or Endnote) Create. Wait and then type your note in the space that is already numbered at the bottom of the screen. Click on the Close button in the special feature bar that has appeared. Use Insert Footnote Edit to change the text of a footnote.

"IT'S A MEMO FROM SOFTWARE DOCUMENTATION. IT'S EITHER AN EXPLANATION OF HOW THE NEW SATELLITE COMMUNICATIONS NETWORK FUNCTIONS, OR DIRECTIONS FOR REPLACING BATTERIES IN THE SMOKE DETECTORS."

Appendix
Installing WordPerfect for Windows

. . . .

In This Chapter

▶ Types of installation

▶ Standard installation: the easy way

▶ Custom installation: the tricky way

▶ Minimum installation: the last resort way

▶ Additional features

. . . .

*F*or excitement, software installation is right up there with watching your laundry go around in a Laundromat drier. It used to be exciting in the same way that dental surgery is exciting, but software vendors (such as WordPerfect) have become more clever. Now at least the process is relatively painless and you have a chance to do it successfully yourself.

If your PC is on a network, don't try to do the installation yourself; go browbeat your network administrator.

Right out of the Box — Installing WordPerfect the First Time

Here you are with a lovely, new box of software — pristine packaging and shiny, shrink-wrapped manuals — the whole works. (We wonder how many psychiatrists they employ to do that shrink-wrapping stuff.)

The first question that must be answered is, "Will WordPerfect work at all on my PC?" To use WordPerfect, your PC must have a "386 or higher processor" and Windows 3.1. At the very, very, least, it must have 4 megabytes (4 MB) of memory and 14 megabytes (14 MB) of available disk space. You probably won't be happy without at least twice that much RAM and disk space. For the best operation, you should have 8 MB of RAM or more and 40 MB of available disk space.

How do you know whether your PC measures up? Figuring out your "processor" or measuring RAM on your PC can be tricky; instead, check your PC purchase invoice or ask someone who was involved in purchasing the PC.

To measure disk space, power up your PC. Don't run Windows yet. If Windows has run itself automatically and is now on your screen, double-click on the minus sign in the upper left corner of the Program Manager window and then press the Enter key to exit from Windows. You're now in DOS. Type the magic word (**CHKDSK**) and wait. Look for the line that ends with "bytes available on disk." The number that precedes that number, divided by about a million, is the number of megabytes of disk space that are available on your disk. If this process is too complicated, don't worry about doing it. Things will work out.

Starting the installation program

Fire up your PC and start Windows. (Type **WIN** if you're in DOS.)

Find the WordPerfect disk labeled "Install 1" and put it in disk drive A or B.

Find the Program Manager window on your screen. (If you cannot find it, press Ctrl+Esc and double-click on Program Manager in the Task List window that appears. Refer to Chapter 1 if "double-click" is gibberish to you.)

Click on File in the Program Manager menu bar and then on Run in the menu that drops down.

A Run dialog box appears. If the Install 1 disk is in drive A, type **A:INSTALL** in the Command Line area; if it's in B:, type **B:INSTALL**. Press the Enter key or click on OK.

Wait. Eventually a Registration Information box appears. Type your name in the box; press the Enter key when you're finished and type the number from your registration card. Press the Enter key.

An Installation Type dialog box should appear, as shown in Figure A-1.

Deciding which type of installation to perform

Now it's decision time. You must choose from one of three basic types of installation. Your first consideration is how much disk space you have. The second is how much space you want to consume with features you may not care about.

If you have no idea how much disk space you have, choose the standard installation. See the following section, "Standard installation — the easy way."

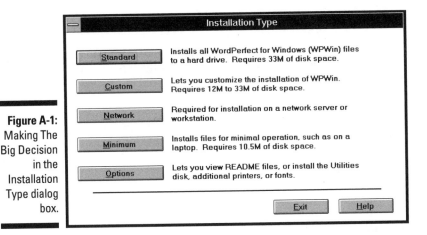

Figure A-1:
Making The
Big Decision
in the
Installation
Type dialog
box.

If you know that you have 33 MB or more of space available on your disk, your decision can be very easy: choose the standard installation. This choice installs everything. If you have the space but aren't sure that you want to use it all up, see the section "Custom installation — the tricky way."

If you have between 14 MB and 33 MB, see either the section "Custom installation — the tricky way" or "Minimum installation — the last-resort way."

Standard installation — the easy way

To install everything (or try to), choose standard installation from the Installation Type dialog box. Click on the Standard button. A Select Drive dialog box asks on which (hard) drive you want to install your disks; most people choose drive C, which is what the installation program suggests. Click on OK.

If you don't have enough disk space, the program lets you know. Try Custom installation instead.

An Install Files dialog box then appears, as shown in Figure A-2.

Fun and amusing facts about WordPerfect are displayed on your screen.

Figure A-2:
Now you're
cooking!
The Install
Files dialog
box.

Install Files		
WordPerfect Program		Cancel
Copying:	wpwp60us.dll	
To:	c:\wpwin60\ ...	
This Disk:	45%	
All Disks:	5%	

Custom installation — the tricky way

To be fussy about which features you're going to install or if you don't have the space to install everything, choose the custom installation. Click on the Custom button in the Installation Type dialog box. The Custom Installation Options dialog box appears, as shown in Figure A-3.

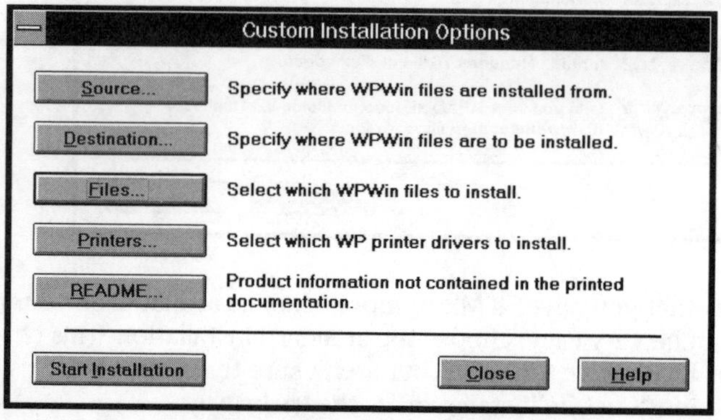

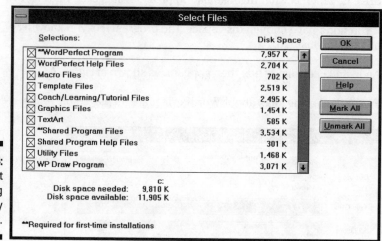

Figure A-3:
Choose Files
from the
Custom
Installation
Options
dialog box.

Unless you want to get fussy about which directories are used for installation, ignore the Source and Destination buttons. Likewise, ignore the Printers button; it installs WordPerfect's printer drivers, which most people don't really need because Windows comes with its own drivers. If you really want to know the most up-to-the-minute information about WordPerfect, click on the README button and follow the directions. Otherwise, ignore that button too.

Click on the Files button. The Select Files dialog box appears, as shown in Figure A-4.

Figure A-4:
The Select
Files dialog
box for picky
people.

The way this dialog box works, anything that has an X next to it will be installed; your job is to get rid of Xs next to features you don't want. The amount of memory a feature requires (in _kilobytes:_ 1,000 K = 1 M) is shown on the same line. Anything you _must_ install is marked with a double asterisk (**). Scroll down the list by clicking on the down arrow on the slider next to the Selections panel.

To turn off an X, click on it. (Click on it again to turn it back on, if you change your mind.) As you do, WordPerfect computes the amount of disk space you need at the bottom of the dialog box and shows how much disk space you have available. Deselect features by clicking on them until the line that says Disk space needed shows less space than the message Disk space available.

Good choices for elimination are shown in this list:

- ✔ Macro
- ✔ Template
- ✔ Coach/Learning/Tutorial
- ✔ Graphics
- ✔ Utility
- ✔ TextArt
- ✔ Utility
- ✔ WP Draw Program
- ✔ QuickFinder File Indexer
- ✔ Grammatik Grammar Checker
- ✔ Speller
- ✔ WordPerfect Help (if you absolutely must)

When you're finished, click on the OK button. The Custom Installation Options box reappears. The WordPerfect installation program is ready to install the features you selected. When you click on the Start installation button, the Install Files dialog box reappears (refer to Figure A-2).

Minimum installation — the last-resort way

If you're really short on disk space, try a minimum installation. Click on the Minimum button in the Installation Type dialog box. The installation program puts up a box that notifies you of all the goodies you're going to miss by choosing this bare-bones option. Click on Yes to proceed.

A Select Drive dialog box asks on which (hard) drive you want to install files; most people choose drive C:, and that's what the installation program suggests. Click on OK.

The Install Files dialog box appears (refer to Figure A-2).

Installing Additional Features

Things change. All is flux. Tempis fugit. And in the general flux of things, you may someday say to yourself, "Fugit! I wish that I had installed that feature." If you find, after reading our glowing description of WordPerfect's Coach feature, that the files for it are not on your PC's disk, for example, you may want to install them.

If you did the standard installation, this problem is not likely to occur; you already installed darn near everything there is to install. (Remember reading an entire issue of *National Geographic* while you did the installation?) Only if you originally did a custom or minimum installation are you likely to need to add a feature later.

To add a feature, run the Install program. But first, if WordPerfect (or any of the WordPerfect subprograms, such as WP Draw) is running, you must exit from it, or "close" it. Double-click on the big minus sign in the upper left corner. If any documents are in use, WordPerfect asks whether you want your work saved.

You can start the installation program either as you did originally, from the Install 1 disk (see the section "Starting the Installation Program"), or from your hard disk. To do the latter, follow these steps:

1. Press Ctrl+Esc and double-click on Program Manager in the Task List window that appears.

2. Locate the WordPerfect program group in the Program Manager, labeled something like WPWin 6.0.

3. Find an icon that depicts a PC and is labeled WPWin 6.0 Installation. Double-click on this icon.

   The Installation Type dialog box appears (refer to Figure A-1).

Your choices now are to perform an Options or Custom installation.

The Options installation: printer drivers, fonts, and README

We can think of only three likely reasons you would want to use the Options installation:

✔ The printer you want to use doesn't have a printer driver under Windows, but WordPerfect has one.

✔ You previously performed a custom installation and didn't load WordPerfect's TrueType fonts, and now you want to.

✔ During installation, you forgot to read the README file, with the latest information on WordPerfect, and now you want to.

To perform any of these tasks, choose Options from the Installation Type dialog box and follow the directions.

Installing new features with a custom installation

You most likely are interested in something other than adding a printer driver, installing fonts, or reading the README file, so you will want to choose Custom installation in the Installation Type dialog box.

Click on the Custom button. The Custom Installation Options box appears (refer to Figure A-3).

Click on the Files button. The Select Files box appears (refer to Figure A-4).

Click on the Unmark All button to remove the X from every selection shown in the Selections panel.

Click on the selection for the feature you want to install, such as Coach/Learning/Tutorial Files. An X appears to the left of the feature you select. If you don't see the feature you want, scroll down the list by clicking on the down arrow on the slider bar next to the Selections panel. You may select more than one, if you want.

Click on the OK button. The Custom Installation Options box reappears.

The WordPerfect installation program is now ready to install the features you selected. If, for peculiar reasons of your own, you don't want to install WordPerfect files in the customary directories, click on the Destination button and change the directory that is specified for the feature you're trying to install. If you're this advanced, you don't need us, so we won't bother to explain it in detail.

Click on the Start Installation button in the Custom Installation Options dialog box.

The installation program displays the Install Files box (refer to Figure A-2). If you immediately see a New Diskette Needed dialog box that overlays the one in the figure, type the designation of the disk drive you will use, such as **A:** or **B:**, for inserting the disks that come in the WordPerfect box. Insert the disk requested by the New Diskette Needed box, probably Install 1, into the disk drive you specified, and click on the OK button.

The Installation Process

The Install Files box displays the progress of the installation on its bar charts (refer to Figure A-2). To let you know how fast things are going, it displays two bar charts: one for the current disk and one for the entire installation process. By seeing how fast the current disk bar moves, you can guess whether to go out for coffee or for lunch while the installation proceeds.

Don't take too long, though: a New Diskette Needed box appears regularly during installation and requests a new disk. Insert the disks as requested and click on OK or press the Enter key after you insert each one. When all files have been installed, an Initialization box appears briefly and goes away.

A Set Up Program Manager Group dialog box may appear, suggesting that you put "the program icons" in a particular "Program Group," probably WPWin 6.0. Just press the Enter key to continue.

Ever diligent to ensure that you have read everything, the installation program probably will display a README Files dialog box, and ask whether you want to peruse the latest info about WordPerfect. Click on Yes or No as you see fit.

Finally, a self-congratulatory Installation Complete dialog box pops up. Acknowledge the brilliant success of the WordPerfect installation program by clicking on OK.

Index

● **E** ●

• *P* •

IDG BOOKS WORLDWIDE REGISTRATION CARD

Title of this book: WordPerfect For Windows For Dummies

My overall rating of this book: ❑ Very good [1] ❑ Good [2] ❑ Satisfactory [3] ❑ Fair [4] ❑ Poor [5]

How I first heard about this book:

❑ Found in bookstore; name: [6] _____ ❑ Book review: [7]

❑ Advertisement: [8] _____ ❑ Catalog: [9]

❑ Word of mouth; heard about book from friend, co-worker, etc.: [10] ❑ Other: [11]

What I liked most about this book:

_____

_____

What I would change, add, delete, etc., in future editions of this book:

_____

_____

Other comments:

_____

Number of computer books I purchase in a year: ❑ 1 [12] ❑ 2-5 [13] ❑ 6-10 [14] ❑ More than 10 [15]

I would characterize my computer skills as: ❑ Beginner [16] ❑ Intermediate [17] ❑ Advanced [18] ❑ Professional [19]

I use ❑ DOS [20] ❑ Windows [21] ❑ OS/2 [22] ❑ Unix [23] ❑ Macintosh [24] ❑ Other: [25] _____
(please specify)

I would be interested in new books on the following subjects:
(please check all that apply, and use the spaces provided to identify specific software)

❑ Word processing: [26] ❑ Spreadsheets: [27]

❑ Data bases: [28] ❑ Desktop publishing: [29]

❑ File Utilities: [30] ❑ Money management: [31]

❑ Networking: [32] ❑ Programming languages: [33]

❑ Other: [34]

I use a PC at (please check all that apply): ❑ home [35] ❑ work [36] ❑ school [37] ❑ other: [38] _____

The disks I prefer to use are ❑ 5.25 [39] ❑ 3.5 [40] ❑ other: [41] _____

I have a CD ROM: ❑ yes [42] ❑ no [43]

I plan to buy or upgrade computer hardware this year: ❑ yes [44] ❑ no [45]

I plan to buy or upgrade computer software this year: ❑ yes [46] ❑ no [47]

Name: _____ Business title: [48] _____ Type of Business: [49] _____

Address (❑ home [50] ❑ work [51] /Company name: _____)

Street/Suite# _____

City [52] /State [53] /Zipcode [54]: _____ Country [55] _____

❑ **I liked this book!** You may quote me by name in future
IDG Books Worldwide promotional materials.

My daytime phone number is _____

IDG BOOKS

THE WORLD OF
COMPUTER
KNOWLEDGE